SHIPPING FREIGHT BY WATER IN BRITAIN AND IRELAND

Calculating Economic Cost and Environmental Opportunities

Dirty British coaster with a salt-caked stack butting
through the Channel in the mad March days with a
cargo of Tyne coal, road-rail, pig–lead, firewood, iron-
ware and cheap tin trays.
From the poem, *"Cargoes"*, John Masefield, Poet and Sailor,
(1902).

Short Sea Shipping has proved to be a transport success story
with healthy growth rates and we must ensure that continues.
The new plan unveiled today will help provide real alternatives
to road congestion through more efficient and more
economical use of other transport modes.
The Late Loyola de Palacio, Vice President Transport and Energy,
European Commission(10.4.0).
Painting by permission of Rev Clifford Strong. Photograph by
permission of Terry Hammond

SHIPPING FREIGHT BY WATER IN BRITAIN AND IRELAND

Calculating Economic Cost
and Environmental Opportunities

Merv Rowlinson

With a Foreword by
David Hilling

The Edwin Mellen Press
Lewiston•Queenston•Lampeter

Library of Congress Cataloging-in-Publication Data

Rowlinson, Mervyn.
    Shipping freight by water in Britain and Ireland : calculating economic cost and
environmental opportunities / Mervyn Rowlinson ; with a foreword by David Hilling.
    p. cm.
    Includes bibliographical references and index.
    ISBN-13: 978-0-7734-4850-6
    ISBN-10: 0-7734-4850-0
    1. Shipping--Great Britain. 2. Shipping--Ireland. 3. Freight and freightage--Great
Britain. 4. Freight and freightage--Ireland. I. Title.
    HE823.R75 2008
    387.5'440941--dc22
                                                                2008048008

A CIP catalog record for this book is available from the British Library.

Front Cover: Arklow Shipping Vessels pass in the Manchester Ship Canal.
Painting permission by Jack Leggett; photographed (and permission) by Ian Leggett.

        The Edwin Mellen Press   The Edwin Mellen Press
              Box 450   Box 67
        Lewiston, New York   Queenston, Ontario
        USA 14092-0450   CANADA L0S 1L0

                     The Edwin Mellen Press, Ltd.
                     Lampeter, Ceredigion, Wales
                     UNITED KINGDOM SA48 8LT

                Printed in the United States of America

Dedicated to my Dad, Clifford, who devoted
a big part of his life to the highway

TABLE OF CONTENTS

LIST OF TABLES

LIST OF FIGURES

iv

LIST OF PLATES

Plate 1: Sea-Rail Integration. Coal Traffic, Manchester Ship Canal. *Photo Permission by: Captain Keith Rowlinson, Carmet Towage.*
Plate 2: The Marine Motorway? Grimaldi Line's European RoRo Service. The 4300 car capacity, *Grand Benelux* discharges Ford Transits, Port of Flushing. *Photo Permission by: Grimaldi Line.*Plate 3: A Coaster? The 127,535dwt, North Sea Shuttle Tanker, *Stena Alexita* (Norwegian Flag), arrives in Southampton Water (Esso Fawley). *Photo Permission by: Russ Wilmott.*
Plate 4: A Regular Trader on the UK Coast, the 2004 dwt, Singapore Flag, LPG Tanker, *Sigas Lydia* arrives at Esso Fawley. *Photo Permission by: Mike Hammond.*
Plate 5: Scapa Flow Ship-To-Ship Transfer Russian Oil to 300,000dwt, VLCC, *Iran Delvar. Photo Permission by: Dr. Alfred Baird, Napier University.*
Plate 6: Lapthorn Shipping's 1300dwt, *Hoo Maple*, demonstrates Self-Discharge flexibility in London Docklands. *Photo Permission by: Richard Buffey, Buffey & Buffey.*
Plate 7: Union Transport and Lapthorn Dry Cargo Vessels serve the East Anglian Agricultural Trade, Sutton Bridge, Cambridgeshire. *Photo Permission by: Author.*
Plate 8: The Blue Highway! Alderney Shipping's, 1020 dwt, *Mungo,* Departs the Environmentally Sensitive Poole Harbour. *Photo Permission by Grant Ausden.*
Plate 9: Lafarge Aggregates 500dwt Motor Barge, *Battlestone,* reaches the Castleford Terminal, 142km up-stream from the Trent-side Quarry at Besthorpe. *Photo Permission by Roger Dodman, Lafarge Aggregates.*
Plate 10: Union Transport's Low Air-Draft Vessel, *Union Sun,* moves up the River Medway. *Photo Permission by: Richard Gough, Union Transport.*
Plate 11: K.D. Marine (UK) 965dwt Vessel, *Gina D,* awaits Grain Discharge in the heart of Manchester Docklands. *Photo Permission by: Author.*
Plate 12: Thames Lineage - Representing a Long Family Line of Watermen aboard Cory Environmental's Tug, *Merit. Photo Permission by: Karim Yoshida.*
Plate 13: Urban Highway - Cory Environmental's Barge Train Replaces >100 Heavy Lorry Round-Trip Journeys in Central London. *Photo Permission by: Author.*
Plate 14: Cory Environmental's Barge Train Slides Under Tower Bridge *Photo Permission by: Ozlem Kir.*
Plate 15: Aggregate Movements on the River Severn. The 180dwt Barge, *Perch. Photo Permission by: David Hilling.*
Plate 16: The 500 dwt Petroleum Barge, *Rix Eagle,* in the Aire & Calder Navigation, Ferrybridge Yorkshire. *Photo Permission by: Fred Andrews.*

ACKNOWLEDGEMENTS

Many thanks to the many shipping and transport specialists who assisted my research. In particular, I am most grateful to: Dr. David Hilling MBE, Greenwich Maritime Academy. Also, Professor Patrick Alderton, Visiting Professor, London Metropolitan University. Mr. Alan McClelland, Maritime Researcher, Liverpool Nautical Research Society. Mr. John Hoar, Principal Lecturer in Maritime Studies, Southampton Solent University.

Also big thanks to:
Dr. Ademun-Odeke, Professor in Maritime Law, National University of Ireland, Galway.
Mr. Rory Addison, Transport Advisor , NZ Government, Wellington.
Mr. Fred Andrews, Inland Shipping Expert, Leeds.
Professor John Armstrong, Business School, Thames Valley University.
Captain Neil Caborn, Lighterage Manager, Cory Environmental, Charlton.
Mr. Jon Challacombe, Senior Lecturer Maritime Studies, University of Plymouth.
John Cobb ex M.D. Fishers, Barrow.
Ms.Cassandra Crisp, ex Operations Manager, Crescent Tankships, Southampton.
Mr. Sebastien Courtrade, Development Manager, IMDO, Dublin.
David Cross, ex Operations Director, CMA-CGM Line, London.
Mr. Keith Dawson, MD, KD. Marine (UK), Runcorn.
Captain Ian Dobson, m/v *Battlestone*, Lafarge Aggregates, East Midlands.
Mr. Roger Dodman, Production Manager, Lafarge Aggregates, East Midlands.
Mr. Phil Dunham. MD, KD. Marine (UK), Runcorn.
Ms. Anna Elliason, Logistics Manager, Brostrum Tankers, Gothenburg.
Mr. Michael Everard CBE, Chairman, F.T.Everard & Sons Ltd, Greenhithe, Kent.
Captain Alan Feast, Deputy Harbour Master, Eastham Locks, Mersey Ports.
Dr. Roy Fenton, Maritime Historian, Wimbledon.
Captain Ken Garrett, Maritime Writer, East Malling, Kent.
Ms. Marcy George-Kokkinaki, Hyperion Shipbrokers, Piraeus.
Dr. David Glen, Reader in Transport & Trade, London Metropolitan University.
Mr. Norman Hardaker, Shipping Correspondent, The Bideford Buzz.
Captain Paul Haysom, Executive, UK Marine Pilots' Association, Lowestoft.
Mr. Max Heinimann , C/E Union Transport, Bromley, Kent.
David Hutson, ex Iberian Feeder Services Manager, NYK, London.
Captain Reg Kelso, Southampton Master Mariners Association, Southampton.
Mr. Peter Johnson, Director, Cory Environmental, London.
Mr. David Lapthorn, ex M.D Lapthorn, Hoo Creek, Kent.
Mr. Brendan Martin, Tanker Analyst, Gibsons, London.

Mr. Michael Magnus, Shipping Operations Director, Foster Yeoman, Frome, Somerset.
Mr. James McConachie, Charterer, Carisbrooke Shipping, Cowes.
Dr. Tom McNamara, Office Manager, CMA-CGM, Southampton.
Mr. Tobias Metten, Information Director, Port of Duisburg.
Captain Paul Haysom, Executive, UK Maritime Pilots' Association, Lowestoft.
Captain Heather Mitchell, Director, River-Sea Trading, Weston Point.
John Healy, ex Port Director, Port of Boston.
Captain Chris Payton, Master, *Bergefrost*. Bergeson Worldwide Gas ASA.
Mr. Martin Pettinger, Shipbroker, Sussex.
Captain Keith Rowlinson, Carmet Towage, Eastham.
Captain Robert Smitton, Senior Lecturer, Liverpool John Moores University.
Derek Smith, Business Development Manager, Southampton Container Terminals.
Mr. James Stewart, Chief Executive, Poole Harbour Commissioners.
Dr. Mehdi Shamszadeh, C/E. 3A Marine, London.
Bill Stoker, Freight Services Manager, Harwich International Port.
Mr. Paul Storey, Corporate Affairs Director, Hutchinson-Whampoa, Felixstowe.
Mr. Sandy Struthers, M.D. J.& A. Gardner &Company Limited, Glasgow.
Mr. Pat Sweeney, Maritime Correspondent, Dublin.
Captain Viv Thomas, Weaver Pilot, Runcorn.
Mr. Bill Wearmouth, Feeder Operations Manager, Clydeport, Glasgow.
Mr. Paul Whyte, Terminal Manager, Clydeport, Glasgow.
Mr. John Wright (ex Manager, Adsteam Towage, Southampton), Solent Blue Line, Southampton.

Additionally I am most grateful to a number of proof-readers, information gatherers, IT specialists, photographers and bibliographers. In particular, Mr. Richard Ashman, Senior Librarian, Southampton City Libraries, who spent much of his summer holiday reading the draft. Big thanks to Jacky for her help with the indexing task. Thanks also to,

Ms. Mieko Abe Shipping & Transport Student, London Metropolitan University,
Mr. Murat Aktas, Shipping & Transport Student , London Metropolitan University,
Mr. John Ellis, Maritime Historian, Andover, Minneapolis.
Mr. Jeff Fanning, Marine Information Association, Southampton.
Mr. Enzo Di Carmine Shipping & Transport Student, London Metropolitan University.
Ms. Dawn Kinnersley, Business Librarian, London Metropolitan University.

ix

Mr. Alan McClelland, Maritime Researcher. Liverpool Nautical Research Society.
Dr. Reza Mirmiran, Senior Lecturer in Logistics, London Metropolitan University
Mr. Anil Onur, Shipping & Transport Student, London Metropolitan University.
Mr. Panos Patsadas, Shipping & Transport Student, London Metropolitan University.
Ms. Marianne Williams, Maritime Solicitor, London.
Mr. Russ Wilmott, IT Specialist, Southampton for an excellent job on map illustrations.
The Library Staff in Lending, Reference and Maritime Archives, Southampton City Libraries.

Finally, I would also like to thank the following for their word processing expertise:

Mrs Madeline Dunwoody, Departmental Secretary and Ms. Jenny Franke, Placement Student from Dresden, both at London Metropolitan University. Ms. Hyun-Jeong Moon, Shipping Student, London Metropolitan University.

AUTHOR'S NOTE

A number of significant and surprising changes have occurred during the writing of this book. In this period the environmental debate has intensified. The term "carbon footprint" has made a rapid and forceful entry into the post-2000 national interest lexicon. Biofuels have become highly topical. The Green Highway has evolved significantly in this period. Three specific areas of change have been identified – transport policy, ownership and organisation, and market image.

In the world of transport policy, shortsea shipping has increasingly been championed as a sustainable alternative to the intensifying problems of road transport. In the UK, the shortsea shipping bureau, Sea and Water, has become increasingly active in promotion and the UK Tonnage Tax has continued to attract ships to the registry. Likewise, the Irish Marine Development Office (IMDO) has promoted shortsea European linkages and the Irish Tonnage Tax has global appeal for the Republic's flag. The Scottish Parliament has shown particular interest in sustainable alternatives to road haulage. Shipping's green integrity has continued to be questioned. This includes increased attention to exhaust emissions from shipping. The 2006-2007 imposition of the Sulphur Emission Control Areas (SECA) in the Baltic-North Sea English Channel regions can be seen as an EU response to air pollution from shipping. The foundering of the large British flag container ship, *MSC Napoli* in January 2007 induced intense media attention. The decision to tow the stricken vessel into Lyme Bay was critically scrutinised. However, the text-book, environmentally damage limiting, salvage and rescue marine operation was testament to vastly improved coastal custodianship – tangible evidence of enhanced maritime policy and a positive signpost towards a sustainable Green Highway. The honorary award of the MBE to Dr. David Hilling in 2003 is further evidence of political commitment to domestic shipping.

In the world of shipping ownership and organisation, a number of unforeseen and unpredicted circumstances have occurred. The sell-off of P&O's shipping and port's empire has radically altered the composition of British shipping and raised questions over long term commitment by the investment community. However, the return of BP to directly owned Red Ensign shipping has proved some compensation. In the small ships sector, two family companies identified (here) as champions of the Green Highway have surprisingly withdrawn from shipping. The sale of the Lapthorn dry cargo fleet and Everard's tanker fleet has also changed the composition of British shortsea shipping. Despite the shock of the withdrawal of two of the Green Highway's most active proponents, it is reassuring that their considerable fleets have passed into the safe-hands of reputable owners.

By 2007 it was evident that a process of capital concentration was occurring in the shortsea sector and also in port ownership. The emergence of the Iceland conglomerate, Samskip, into European shortsea operations has considerable implications, certainly strengthening the finances of the concentrated industry. Evidence of a vibrant Green Highway was provided by the successful emergence of the new entrants, including Europe Lines serving the Drogheda route in autumn 2006. The consolidation of three ports – Clyde, Mersey and Manchester into the Peel Ports has provided a template for shipping-port integration and has proved a revival boost for the Manchester Ship Canal. The introduction of a container barge service on the canal in October 2007 was clear evidence of the desire of Peel Ports, as well as the supermarket giant, Tesco, to promote the water alternative.

Changes in the way shipping is perceived are reflected in literature. A once neglected sub-sector is now attaining a higher profile. As shippers and shipping lines seek to promote a greener image more attention is given to sustainable transport strategy. Increasingly evident in the post-2000 period has been a re-working of the image and performance of shipping.

In short summary, the Green Highway has already progressed, as well as evolved, in the first seven years of the new Millennium. The omens in the political, organisational and academic worlds can be seen as auspicious for further development. The Green Highway is now well positioned for delivering the goods!

Dr. Merv Rowlinson

ABBREVIATIONS

ABP	Associated British Ports
ACOPS	Advisory Committee on Protection of the Sea.
AFRAMAX	Average Freight Rate Assessment. Tanker size 80-120,000dwt
ALH	Average Length of Haul
BACAT	Barge Aboard Catamaran Ship
BW	British Waterways
CHIRPS	Confidential Human Factors Incident Reporting
CPP	Clean Petroleum Products
CPRE	Campaign to Protect Rural England
DEFRA	Department of Environment, Food & Rural Affairs
DETR	Department of Transport, Environment & the Regions
DfT	Department for Transport (UK Government)
DWT	Dead Weight Tonnes
DP	Dubai Ports
ECMT,	European Conference of Ministers of Transport
ESN	European Shortsea Network
EWSR	English Welsh & Scottish Railway Company
FEU	Forty Foot Equivalent Unit (Container
FFG	Freight Facility Grant (UK)
FMCG	Fast Moving Consumer Goods
FOC	Flag of Convenience
GT	Gross Tonnage
HGV	Heavy Goods Vehicle
JIT	Just-in-Time
Km	Kilometre
Kn	Knot
IBIA	International Bunker Industry Association
ICS	Institute of Chartered Shipbrokers
ICS	International Chamber of Shipping
ILO	UN International Labour Organisation
IMCA	International Marine Contractors Association.
IMDO	Irish Maritime Development Office
IMO	International Maritime Organisation (UN)
ISM	International Safety Management (IMO Code)
ITF	International Transport Workers Federation
ITOPF	International Tanker Owners' Pollution Federation Ltd.
LASH	Lighter Aboard Ship
LNG	Liquefied Natural Gas
LoLo	Lift on, Lift off
LPG	Liquefied Petroleum Gas

MARPOL	International Convention for the Prevention of Pollution from Ships, 1973
MAIB	Marine Accident Investigation Branch
MCA	Maritime & Coastguard Agency
MEHRA	Marine Environmental High Risk Areas in the UK
MSC	Manchester Ship Canal.
NDLS	National Dock Labour Scheme
NIS	Norwegian International Registry
NM	Nautical Mile
NOx	Nitrogen Oxides
NUMAST	National Union of Marine, Aviation and Shipping Transport Officers (now Nautilus UK)
OMBO	One Man Bridge Operation
OOCL	Orient Overseas Container Line Ltd
PLA	Port of London Authority
PSC	Port State Control
RINA	Royal Institution of Naval Architects
RMT	National Union of Rail & Maritime Transport Workers
RoRo	Roll on-Roll off.
RNLI	Royal National Lifeboat Institution
SECA	Sulphur Emission Control Area
SOLAS	IMO, International Convention for the Safety of Life at Sea,1974
SORADO	Safety Officials and Reporting of Accidents and Dangerous Occurrences Regulations,1982
SOSREP	Secretary of State's Representative (salvage)
STCW	IMO, Standards of Training, Certification and Watchkeeping,1978
SOx	Sulphur Oxides
TEU	Twenty Foot Equivalent Unit (Container)
TKM	Tonne x Kilometre
TPD	Vessel Fuel Consumption Tonnes per Day
TSS	Traffic Separation Scheme
UKOOA	United Kingdom Offshore Operators Association
VLCC	Very Large Crude Carrier
VOC	Volatile Organic Compounds

FOREWORD

For an enthusiastic Sea Scout Bristol's City Docks in the late 1940s was paradise. The Red Duster and flags of Denmark, Finland, Holland, Norway and Sweden were always to be seen and continental lines such as Bratt, Lauritzen and Dutch Steamship lined up at the quays with ships of Bristol Steam Navigation, Coast Lines, General Steam and William Sloane.

In addition were frequent 'spot market' callers, mainly in bulk trades. There were links with 14 other Bristol Channel ports, 23 other British ports, twice weekly liner services to Liverpool, Glasgow and Belfast, weekly services to Dublin, London, Penzance and Waterford and connections with 55 continental ports. There was a daily service to Lydney, Sharpness, Gloucester and the Midlands operated by the Severn Carrying Company and Scandinavian wood pulp was barged inland to Bristol's paper mills.

While Britain's imperial and global trading interests placed an emphasis on deep-sea routes there can be no doubting the huge significance of waterborne freight at the domestic level. Bristol was just one node in a high density water transport network with multiple access points yet only 20 years later cargo handling had ceased at the City Docks and was fast disappearing from many other ports. It is not therefore unreasonable to think of a revolution in maritime transport with a switch from labour intensive, low productivity, dispersed, fragmented operations to capital intensive, higher productivity technology which gained from geographical and organisational concentration. The changes in shipping were associated with changing industrial structures, a changing energy base, growing significance of road transport and a general shift of emphasis from local and national to continental and global considerations in the organisation and control of industry and transport. Dr Rowlinson's book examines these factors and is a timely contribution to the current debate about transport options. The great density of in-text referencing reflects the range of his own research but also the extensive nature of the literature now available. Why more one might ask? Simply, much of the published work is unlikely to reach and influence the political and planning decision makers and the public that will be affected. Rowlinson provides a valuable distillation filling a gap in the literature which reflects a widespread ignorance and neglect of shipping – the possible alternative to road transport is invariably seen as the railway and rarely is shipping brought into the frame. How many of our parliamentarians appreciate that about one million tonnes of freight in barges pass Westminster every year – but try putting that on the roads around Parliament Square! Are the generators of freight aware of the capabilities of shipping and the manner in which it is already effectively integrated into a number of specific supply chains? Is the investment community aware of the opportunities that exist for shipping in coastal and short-sea trades?

Rowlinson's central argument is that Britain and Ireland need to rediscover their water freight routes and it is this which provides the book with its timely relevance. There is no shortage of evidence that shipping is the most environmentally friendly of the modes and provides us with a Green Highway in contrast to road transport which has come overwhelmingly to dominate domestic freight movement but is profligate with finite resources (fuel, aggregates, land), subject to growing congestion and consequent delays and costs to other users and a main contributor to local and global pollution. Fullest consideration must be given to maximum use of other modes. On many rail routes there is little spare capacity and freight has to compete with high speed passenger services. Rail maintenance and upgrading of existing or provision of additional capacity is at great expense. In contrast, except at the approaches to ports, the coastal waterways are 'natural' and not greatly demanding of maintenance. On inland waterways maintenance at a standard suitable for freight movement may incur greater cost but these are likely to be a fraction of those for road and rail transport. This does raise a question of finance and a strong case can be made for bringing the now disadvantageous funding regime for inland waterway transport closer into line with that for roads and railways. British Waterways, the controlling body for a number of the freight-carrying waterways, generates some revenue from tolls and property but also receives a grant from the Department of Environment, Food and Rural Affairs rather than the Department for Transport which would seem to be wholly more appropriate. A late 2006 reduction in the DEFRA grant was a factor in redundancy for the British Waterways freight management team and a likely cut back in the engineering needed to encourage freight movement. Both historically and today there is a functional interdependence of deep-sea, short-sea, coastal and inland shipping each being a part of Rowlinson's Green Highway. These interface with road and rail transport and there is great scope for the development of a wide range of rational supply chains in which the modes are seen to be complementary rather than competitive.

It is perhaps surprising that an island nation that has been, indeed still is, so dependent of waterborne freight should have been so slow in the modern period in adopting the strategies that would have ensured the maximum use of this mode. Fortunately there are signs of change. Many large firms are seeking 'green' transport solutions, reducing carbon footprints is emphasised, government rhetoric is far more positive and the creation in 2003, well after all our neighbours, of a government sponsored, industry led water freight promotion group, Sea & Water, was a great step forward. Sea & Water is actively engaged in coordinating the activities of the parties concerned that greater use is made of waterborne freight and is a necessary focus for data collection and the dissemination of information and publicity regarding waterborne freight.

Dr Rowlinson's book is not a plea for a return to the shipping patterns of the past because he articulates very effectively the changes in shipping, ports and economic activity that make this both undesirable and impossible. What he does is present a balanced and realistic case for greater attention to, and use of, water transport and the adoption of more positive and proactive approaches which will capitalise on the mode's 'green' characteristics. There is considerable scope for waterborne freight to play a more substantial role in supply chain logistics and environmental concerns make it essential that this is brought about. This book will help.

Dr David Hilling MBE
Greenwich Maritime Institute
European River-Sea Transport Union

CHAPTER 1
Introduction

This study sets out to identify, discuss and critically analyse the role and potential of shipping in the domestic and European freight trades of Britain and Ireland. In particular, this includes shipping's capacity for making increased contribution towards solving the transport problems facing both countries, given the context of European integration, sustainable mobility and an expanding European Community. Within this ambit, the role of shipping in helping to reduce pressure on the congested road systems, thus serving the cause of sustainable European economic integration and growth, is specifically considered.

The challenge facing shipping is whether it can produce alternative transport choices to the freight mover, in a competitive, efficient and environmentally sustainable manner. In other words, can the "Green Highway" of shipping on British and Irish shortsea, coastal and inland waterway routes be considered as a sustainable, alternative, transport mode in the early decades of the Millennium? Can shipping ever return to anything like the significant market shares of traffics it once enjoyed? The emphasis will be on both the domestic traffics of British and Irish regions and the continental European freight flows to the two islands. The use of the term "Green Highway" denotes the inherent environmental advantages possessed by shipping, as well as the obvious green ocean metaphor. The "Green Highway" term is used throughout this study as a generic descriptor of the three distinct sectors of British and Irish shipping: inland shipping, coastal shipping and shortsea shipping. Inland shipping is via rivers and canals, such as the River

2

Figure 1: Comparative Exhaust Emission, Road Haulage & Shipping

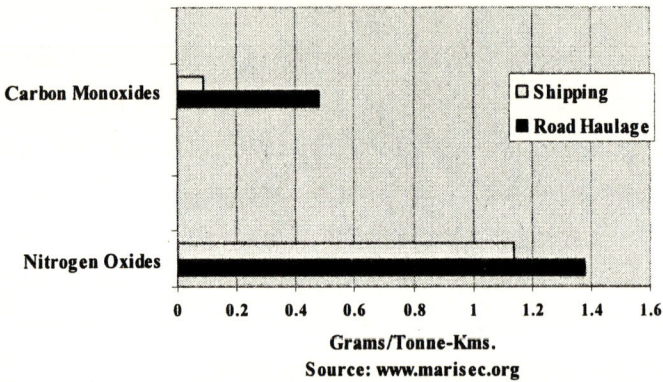

Carbon Monoxides

☐ Shipping
■ Road Haulage

Nitrogen Oxides

0   0.2   0.4   0.6   0.8   1   1.2   1.4   1.6

Grams/Tonne-Kms.
Source: www.marisec.org

Figure 2: Comparative Fuel Consumption by Transport Modes.

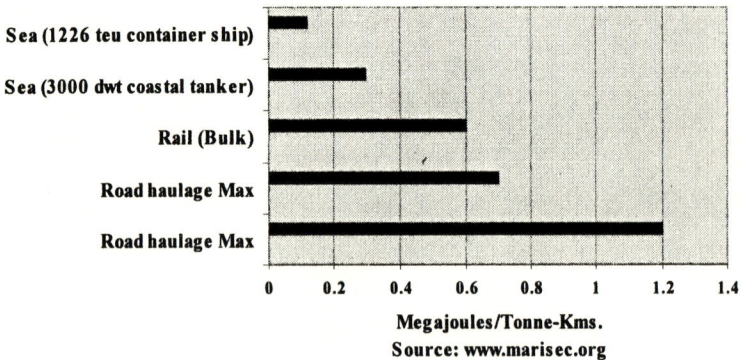

Sea (1226 teu container ship)

Sea (3000 dwt coastal tanker)

Rail (Bulk)

Road haulage Max

Road haulage Max

0   0.2   0.4   0.6   0.8   1   1.2   1.4

Megajoules/Tonne-Kms.
Source: www.marisec.org

Severn or the Gloucester and Sharpness Canal. Coastal shipping is defined by domestic traffics moving around the coastline. For instance, oil product movements between Cork and Galway or grain traffics between Kings Lynn and Port Ellen. An example of shortsea shipping trade is container flows between two countries, such as Rotterdam to Grangemouth or to Tilbury or Drogheda. Figure 1 demonstrates the lower exhaust gas emissions from shipping *vis-à-vis* road haulage. Figure 2 identifies the significantly lower fuel consumption of shipping compared to the road and rail modes. It can be accepted that shipping's fuel consumption per tonne-kilometre (tkm) is consistently more than 50% lower than the best case road situation. This makes shipping a contender for the role of championing sustainable transport,

1.1   Outlining the Problem

It is evident that, given its history, the island and ex-Empire trading status of Britain places great emphasis on the deepsea routes. Britain's traditional trading role has been focused on the long distance trade lanes – North Atlantic, Africa, Asia, Oceania. The shift in trading emphasis to the short distance (shortsea) European freight flows brought about by increased European integration has also been primarily shipping based. For Ireland, European integration has brought more trade with continental Europe and less economic dependence on Britain. Despite the re-focusing on shortsea ferry European trades, the intensive pattern of shipping activity disguises the low utilisation of shipping within the coastal context. For example, freight movement between Swansea and Cork is naturally accepted as sea transport, but for onward traffics between say Cork and Belfast, road haulage becomes the usual choice, not shipping. Even more surprising is the fact that such congested island nations with long maritime traditions should ignore their relatively unhindered coastal sea routes and inland waterway systems. Overlooking the opportunities that the economic geography of the two islands provide for increased use of shipping is bad enough; disregarding the considerable domestic labour supplies of maritime expertise – seafarers, designers, technicians, commercial practitioners - is a waste of national talents!

In May 1992, *Lloyd's List* provided insight into the state of coastal shipping, "A special report on the UK maritime industries: A wet roadway awaiting to be used,"[1] in which one leading authority in the industry bemoaned the low profile of the shipping industry which possessed significant potential for the alleviation of traffic congestion: "the trouble with coastal shipping is nobody knows it's there."[2] By 2005, *Lloyd's List* , was proclaiming,

> Water freight is indeed an idea whose time has come, or perhaps come again, bearing in mind the extraordinary trade that there was around our coasts before we sold our souls to road haulage.[3]

Similar concerns were beginning to be registered around the world by the early Millennium. Even in the USA, the need to revive coastal shipping was becoming apparent by 2002 when US Government Marine Administration official W.G. Schubert, asserted, "it was when, not if" that the USA increased its shipping alternatives.[4] This reflects the need to switch from the over-reliance on road transportation in the world's premier energy user.

Whilst there has been growth in deepsea trades and in the intensive ferry shuttle routes between both islands and Europe; there has been a decline in the market share of freight moving around the respective coastlines *vis-à-vis* land transportation. If the problem is one of shipping's poor and dated perception then this study sets out to provide a challenge to this view. However, the intention is not to provide an uncritical view of shipping's prospects; if the Green Highway is to fulfil its economic and environmental potential it must achieve high quality standards of operation. The feasibility of this aim will be assessed within the context of a highly competitive market.

Part of the shipping sector's problem lies in its low public profile, with common knowledge of its role being obscured by the myths and legends of the maritime glories (and disasters) of the past. Only when a serious maritime

5

accident occurs on the coastline does shipping attain a high, albeit unwanted, level of media exposure. Tanker oil spill disasters such as the *Erika* (1999) and the *Prestige* (2002) attained global front page notoriety. The media attention to oil spills, particularly in environmentally sensitive areas of the developed world has created an impression of a reckless "rust bucket" shipping industry. The environmental disaster following the sinking of the *Erika* along the French coastline was reported by the headline: "300,000 Seabirds dead. Only now can Europe count the cost of Sea of Filth."[5] The break up of the *Prestige* off the Spanish coast focused attention on the state of the world's ageing tanker fleet and its off-shore management. *The Independent* article, "A saga of single hulls, double standards and too many flags of convenience,"[6] directed criticism at a globally fragmented, substandard industry that was more interested in cost cutting than maintaining safe and environmentally acceptable standards of operation.

The North Sea wreck of the large automobile carrier, *Tricolor* in December 2002 provoked widespread interest in the press. Attention, however, was given to the $45m loss of luxury car exports; the amazing seafaring skills of the Captain and 23 crew in evacuating a rapidly sinking ship in the middle of the night and in freezing waters, achieved much less attention. The BBC news headline, "£30m cargo lost as ship sinks," illustrates the portrayal of maritime disaster in monetary rather than humanistic terms.[7]

The need for improved public perception of the role and opportunities for merchant shipping is integral to the success of the Green Highway. It is important that freight generators are aware of the extent and capabilities of shipping. The dated perception deserves challenging; examples of shipping's successful integration in specific supply chains requires highlighting. The profile of the Green Highway needs to be raised if new customers are to be encouraged to sample the alternative to road haulage logistics. Similarly, it is vital that the investment community is relieved of the perception that shipping is not a dated sunset industry and that considerable opportunities exist within the European trades. The long years of decline have also had a negative effect on the perception of shipping as a professional career choice. In August 2005, a School Inspector, with an insight into the Merchant Navy, expressed disappointment with careers advisors in schools. From her own experience in ten years of schools inspection not once had Merchant Navy careers information been available for pupils![8]

The UK maritime community was somewhat shocked in 2000 to learn that the British public, as represented by the popular TV quiz, "Who wants to be a Millionaire," had difficulties in distinguishing between the flags of the Royal Navy and Merchant Navy.[9] Further evidence of the lack of popular insight into the role of merchant shipping was provided at Portsmouth's UK Festival of the Sea in 2001. In recognition of the important role of the Merchant Navy, the dry cargo coastal vessel, *Hoo Falcon,* was displayed and opened up to the public. The vessel's owner, David Lapthorn, along with the master, were somewhat bemused by the confused questions they fielded from the public. A sample of the questions were:

1. Is it a swimming pool?
2. Why is this ship not grey?
3. What does it do in the [Royal] Navy?
4. Is it a tanker?
5. Where do you keep it when not on display?
6. What's the point? [10]

Where positive public perception of shipping exists it tends to be shaped by large, high profile, passenger ships such as the new *Queen Mary 2,* the *Queen Elizabeth 2,* the *Oriana* and *Aurora.* The vital role of shipping in the coastal, shortsea and inland trades is rather neglected. This study sets to help rectify this shortcoming by identifying the extent and scope of shipping in trades around the coasts, rivers and canals of Britain and Ireland. It is intended that this will serve the cause of assessing shipping's role and potential. Therefore the rationale for this study is drawn from four relevant perspectives:

> (1) the imminent transport gridlock situation in Britain and Ireland demands a serious reconsideration of the shipping alternative;
> (2) in recent history, Britain and Ireland have both neglected and undervalued shipping in the national agenda, particularly in contrast to continental European trading partners;
> (3) shipping can achieve greater participation in the British and Irish transport networks;
> (4) shipping can make a much larger contribution to the environmental objective of Sustainable Mobility in Britain and Ireland.

The transport concerns of the new Millennium are shaped very much by road grid lock and all its associated negative impacts – accidents, pollution, road surface damage, road building and replacement costs, declining transport productivity, rising transport costs. The life style choices of a road oriented economy spawns the problem of ever increasing car journeys and road freight tkm. The demands on land use generated by road oriented consumer expectations makes transport planning one of the most intractable of policy areas.[11] In the British Isles, the problem of limited land resource is becoming critical, particularly in the areas of high economic concentration. The grid-lock scenario is also accompanied by the global warming issue. Concerns over exhaust gas emissions from transport are becoming elevated in the European political agenda. Increasingly sustainable transport alternatives are being sought. This ranks the water transport option highly in the debate on transport.

The extent of the road traffic growth problem and the shipping alternative has even reached the land-rich USA. In 2002-3, the US State Marine Administration (Marad) actively considered the support of shortsea shipping. With one 15 barge tugboat-tow capable of taking 870 trucks off US roads, shipping was recognised as a much more sustainable alternative to trucks.[12]

Around the world it is becoming apparent that shipping can make significant and positive contribution to the congestion problem. By its ability to reduce tkm volumes of road haulage activity, shipping can make a significant contribution to environmental strategy in Britain and Ireland. This means fewer truck journeys, less congestion, reduced carbon-fuel emissions and improved fuel efficiency. One 1000 tonne barge trading between Liverpool and Manchester (discussed more fully in Chapter 7) has the ability to replace 370,000tkm of loaded trucks per week!

The surge in the "Celtic Tiger" Irish economy in recent years has brought transport problems in the "hot spots" of growth, particularly Greater Dublin and the Cork region. The Irish solution appears to be an emulation of the British approach of the last four decades – bigger and faster roads! New Millennium debate has identified serious flaws in the prevailing road building/widening strategy. The Campaign to Protect Rural England (CPRE) has been critical of the environmental and economic efficacy of new road and road improvement projects. Particular emphasis in the 2006 CPRE report, *Beyond Transport Infrastructure: Lessons for the Future from Recent Road Projects,*[13] has been placed on the acceleration of traffic growth following such new road schemes as the Newbury bypass The shipping alternative is only now beginning to be taken seriously as an option to limit the excesses of the road problem. The Green Highway, therefore, offers a more environmentally sustainable, less crowded route around the British Isles and Ireland.

Although there has been a significant growth in European shortsea shipping tonne-kilometre activity this has been outstripped by road haulage: between 1990 and 1999 shortsea shipping grew by 30%, an annual average of 2.9%; in the same period road haulage grew by 41%, an annual average of 3.9%.[14] Italian maritime economists, Musso and Marchese have appraised the nature of shortsea growth. Scrutinising prevalent shortsea shipping strategies that focused on retaining and/or developing captive markets, rather than new markets, Musso and Marchese have identified lost opportunity. Implicit in this criticism is the need for shipping to competitively attack markets dominated by road haulage. This would bring an effective modal shift from land transport to water.[15] In the UK and Ireland, however, the (previously perceived as) "captive trades" have also been prone to road haulage competition. Examples include, petroleum movements on the Thames, grain flows on the Severn and soda-ash exports on the Weaver which have been replaced by road haulage. In these examples the intrinsic cost advantages of bulk movements by shipping have lost out to economic pressures from the just-in-time logistics economy. The second point of contention is that Britain and Ireland lag some way behind Northern European trading partners – France, Belgium, Holland, Germany - in the utilisation of coastal and river shipping. Similarly, the Scandinavians – Denmark, Sweden, Norway, Finland – and Southern European Community members – Greece, Italy – divert a higher share of their freight flows to water than Britain and Ireland. Although the UK's domestic tonnage figures for coastal shipping are by far the highest in Europe, the overwhelming influence of large tanker crude oil movements from the North Sea oil fields needs to recognised. Coastwise and one-port oil and petroleum movements – primarily from Scottish oil fields – accounted for 78% of total UK waterborne freight in 2005.[16]

Britain's oil resources provide significant opportunity for tanker shipping. Other than pipeline, there is no alternative to tanker shipping in linking the oil fields with the refineries. However, when oil movements are taken out of the statistics, a vastly different picture emerges, revealing the low use of coastal shipping for dry cargo coastal and inland movements. Table 1 provides comparative tkm figures for leading North European nations' inland shipping. The weak position of the UK can clearly be recognised with its year 2000 total of 0.2btkm dwarfed by Germany's 66.5btkm in the same year.[17]

Whilst road journeys in the congested regions of Britain and Ireland suffer increased transit times (resulting in declining vehicle and driver productivity) the shipping alternative has largely been ignored. Coastal shipping which had been in long-run relative decline, suffered absolute decline in the 1960-70 period as a result of the emergence of the motorway age. Since that period the utilisation of shipping on such intensive routes as London-Newcastle has only recently been pursued. Before considering decline in coastal shipping the demise of canal and river shipping is next discussed. Inland shipping expert, Dr. David Hilling, has questioned the endemic neglect of inland shipping mode in the UK which can be traced from the decline of the canal system:

> With the virtual extinction in the 1960s of freight carrying on Britain's canals, there was clearly a widespread feeling that this was the end of inland water transport. On the part of the politicians, the public and transport planners there has since been a largely dismissive attitude towards this mode.[18]

In Figure 3, the recent disappointing performance of UK inland shipping performance is contrasted with the more positive continental performance.

Table 1: Comparative European Inland Waterway, 1970-2002, BTKM						
	1970	1980	1990	1995	2002	2002
Belgium	6.7	5.9	5.4	5.8	6.3	8.5
Finland	0.5	0.7	0.4	0.4	0.5	0.1
France	12.2	10.9	7.2	5.9	7.3	8.4
Germany	48.8	51.4	54.8	64.0	66.5	63.7
Netherlands	30.6	33.5	35.7	35.5	41.3	43.1
UK	0.3	0.4	0.3	0.2	0.2	0.2
Source: EC DG for Energy and Transport(2002)						

11

**Figure 3: Comparative European Inland
Waterway Tonne-km Performances, 1970-2004**

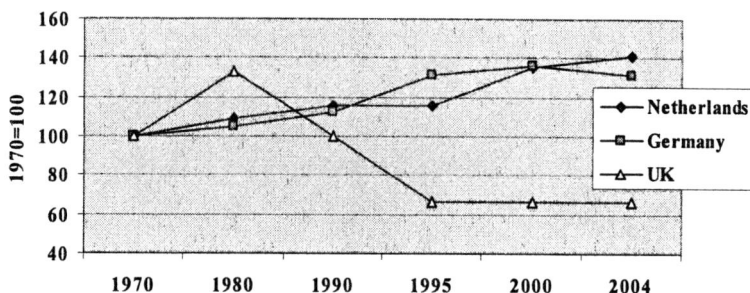

Source: EC (2005) *EU Energy and Transport in Figures: Statistical
Pocketbook 2005.* Luxembourg; EC

1.1.1 The Arrested Development of Canals

In comparison with continental Europe, questions over canals and river
navigation utilisation in Britain and Ireland are raised in the Green Highway
agenda. The network of canals rapidly developed in 18th century. The industrial
revolution in Britain was facilitated by the emergence of efficient low cost canal
and river transportation for key industrial traffics such as coal and iron ore. The
Bridgewater Canal had an immediate impact by linking Manchester's growing
textile industry with the coalfields of Lancashire. By reducing the price of coal
and greatly increasing the volumes moved, the canal was a prime factor in the
creation of the Manchester "Cottonopolis" industrial giant.[19] However, the size
specifications to which the canals were built were a competitive response to the
performance of 18th century horse drawn goods traffic; the Railway Age, let alone
the motorway age, was not envisaged! During the Canal Age competition on
trunk routes was vigorous. In 1830 a number of common carrier operators
competed on the 69 services out of Birmingham. Table 2 sets out some of the key
routes from Birmingham in 1830.

12

Table 2: Key Fly Boat Services ex Birmingham, 1830	
Huddersfield	3
Oxford	6
Leeds	12
London	15
Leicester	18
Source: Osborne, P. (2005) "Pickfords on the waterway," www.upthecut.co.uk	

The economic shortcomings of 45 tonne payload narrow boat pairs in competition with firstly 19th century rail, then 1930s road haulage, were to become patently evident. The problem of atrophied canal development in the 20th century has precluded any prospects of competitive canal barge services. The failure to achieve economies of scale can be viewed as the death knell of the British and Irish canals. The early years of entrepreneurialism and innovation in the post 1750 Canal Age were not sustainable as modal competition emerged. An early innovative approach to canal based logistics was provided by the transport operator, Pickfords. This company has had a long pedigree as a goods aggregator using the most expedient mode of transport, ranging in time from the horse drawn wagons to canal barges, to rail and finally, trunk road haulage. Pickfords can claim to be Britain's oldest road haulage company. Formed in 1756 as a common carrier between Manchester and London, Pickfords found the canal network attractive.[20] During the canal heyday before the mid 1800s upsurge in the rail activity, Pickfords provided regular barge services emanating from London and the Midlands. Phil Osborne's history, "Pickfords on the Waterway" has traced the rise and fall of the company's canal business.[21] By 1838 the fleet of boats numbered in excess of 120. By the 1850s, however, the switch to rail operations was complete.

The contrasting approach to inland waterway development between Britain and Benelux Countries was discussed at the 1999 Birmingham Conference, "Britain's Water Highways: A New Agenda for Freight".[22] Comparison was made between the respective fate of UK's Gloucester and Sharpness Canal and the Netherlands/Belgium Ghent Canal. Both have similar distances to inland ports from the sea, both were constructed to similar specifications in the 19th century. The British Waterways canal has suffered from poor maintenance, particularly lack of dredging and vessel sizes have become restricted. As a result the canal has become increasing unattractive to shipping activity. A rare visitor to the canal in June 2004, the 743dwt German owned coaster, *Kormoran*, had some difficulties in navigating the restricted (undredged) water levels.[23]

By way of contrast, continual developments on the Ghent Canal have not only encouraged direct water access location of industry, but also accommodated large panamax size bulk carriers of 65,000dwt – around 80 times the cargo capacity of the *Kormoran*! As a consequence, Ghent has become a major logistics centre for automobiles, grains, coal, ores and even concentrated orange juice![24] The new Millennium did seem to bring a fresh approach to Britain's canal network. In March 2002 a new "canal age" was announced by British Waterways, facilitated by a £500m cash injection into selected canal revitalisation projects. Major redevelopment schemes were announced indicating the Government's willingness to financially support the renaissance of British canals. *The Times* went as far as to claim that the nine schemes constituted "...the first big investment in the system since the Manchester Ship Canal opened on New Year's day in 1894".[25] The emphasis, however, was on the tourist/heritage role of the waterways to the exclusion of the freight carrying function. Most of the industrial traffics had been lost to the canals by the 1960s. British Waterways new "canal age" does not appear to extend to any significant revival of commercial activity. Projects such as the restoration of the 1875 Anderton Boat Lift and the extension of the Lancaster Canal into the Lake District are two examples of the predilection for the heritage/tourist function.

However, opportunities still do exist, especially where linkages between canals and river system/seaways are in place, where larger vessels can be accommodated. The Manchester Ship Canal and the Gloucester and Sharpness Ship Canal are two examples where, if maintained, the infrastructure permits the passage of sea-going vessels. Ideally, canal systems need to accommodate craft with a carrying capacity of at least 350 tonnes. However, there have been recent examples of where barge operators have been successful in niche trades with 20 tonne payload narrow boats. In the context of the Green Highway, the systems identified in Table 3 offer opportunities for commercial activity.

1.2 Inland Shipping Opportunities

Major trunk systems such as the London to Birmingham Grand Union Canal and the Trent and Mersey geographically parallel key North-South motorway and railway routes. The Leeds-Liverpool canal offers a Trans-Pennine, East West, Humber-Mersey linkage. Whilst these systems were very much at the heart of the industrial revolution, their size limitations prevented sustained competition in the motorway age. Additionally, geographic demands required the building of a large number of lock gate systems on the canal network in order to raise or lower the water level. For example, a barge moving the 200km distance between London and Birmingham would have to negotiate around a 160 locks. This would drastically impede competitive transit times and lead to increased costs. However, the current gridlock crisis in Greater London has led to a positive re-assessment of canal potential. In July 2003 British Waterways signed contracts with aggregates providers, Harleyford Aggregates and Hanson Aggregates for the movement of 450,000 tonnes along the Grand Union Canal in the West Drayton area of Greater London.[26]

Table 3: British Selected Inland Waterway Systems	
System	Vessel Size DWT
Manchester Ship Canal	10,000
Upper Thames (Wandsworth)	1,800 (low air draft)
Gloucester Ship Canal	1,000
River Weaver Navigation	900
River Trent	700
South Yorkshire Navigation	700
Aire and Calder Navigation	700
Caledonian Canal	450
Source: derived from DEFRA (2002), *Freight on Water*. London: DEFRA.	

The move was welcomed by Buckinghamshire County Council as the first major British Waterway's canal contract in thirty years and as an environmentally sustainable alternative to some 45,000 heavy truck journeys on the area's roads.[27] This example demonstrates that a 100-tonne capacity barge can provide competitive services with road haulage, given the willingness of freight users to combine economic and environmental criteria in modal choice. In the case of this aggregates freight flow, the large volumes, the close location of the quarry to the canal side and similarly, the un-loading point to the final destination of the traffic – Heathrow Airport's, Terminal 5 construction site – were key factors in shaping the decision to use water. Limited road transhipment is required, therefore the point-to-point cost advantages of water transport are realised. This demonstrates that in cases where the supply and demand factors interlock with environmental concerns, the Green Highway's extension to inland waterways can prove to be a viable alternative to road.

Such developments provide a highly selective and limited reversal of the long term decline of canal traffics. It can be accepted that the severity of the gridlock problem is forcing a rethink of how freight is moved. As part of this growing awareness, the 2002 Report, *Freight on Water: A New Perspective*,[28] identified significant potential traffics on UK rivers and canals. These were as follows:

- Tidal River Thames, London canals: waste and recyclates, aggregates, construction materials, scrap, containers.
- River Mersey, River Weaver, Manchester Ship Canal: bulk liquids, aggregates, minerals, scrap.
- Aire and Calder Navigation: aggregates, waste, petroleum, chemicals;
- Sheffield & South Yorkshire Navigation: steel products, waste, petroleum, chemicals, fertiliser.
- River Trent: aggregates, petroleum, chemicals.
- River Ouse: aggregates, waste, timber.
- Calder & Hebble Navigation: aggregates.[29]

The potential of these underused waterways is based on their ability to accommodate craft of a size which provides for competitive economies of scale *vis-à-vis* road haulage. It is difficult for the majority of Britain's narrow gauge, shallow depth, canals to facilitate competitive services. The narrow boat canal limits payloads to just twenty five tonnes, a payload similar to an eight wheel tipper truck. By way of contrast the 500 tonne aggregate barges operating on the Trent/South Yorkshire Navigation network each take around 40-45 truck trips off the roads. Where the waterway is capable of handling seagoing vessels, the economies of scale are even more attractive. For instance, the regular French grain trades to the Manchester Ship Canal are carried in ships in the 3-5000dwt range – an equivalent of up to 400 truck round trips. Recognition of the commercial potential of the inland network, when matched with possible freight flows, offers opportunities for freight transfer to water. Awareness of the potential of the 638 kilometres of navigable canal and river navigations[30] forming Britain's inland waterways does prove complementary to the nation's extensive coastline. The inland system open to commercially viable shipping is obviously geographically limited in comparison with continental inland systems. Despite the historic atrophy of the inland system it is also evident that selected waterways do offer opportunities for increased Green Highway activities.

1.3 The Green Highway of the Coast?

The physical limitations of the UK and Irish canal network, combined with the national reluctance to modernise, goes a long way to explaining the low participation of shipping in inland trades. However, the significant coastlines of both countries offer opportunities for a Green Highway of the coast. The question why the UK and Ireland lag behind European trading partners in domestic shipping will be considered within the context of economic, geographic, cultural and environmental factors. The Inland Shipping Group (ISG) has identified the contrast between Britain's neglect of inland waterways with the more progressive continental approach:

> As long ago as 1876 the national waterway strategy was developed in France, providing for standard vessels of 350 tonnes cargo capacity. From 1899, Germany adopted a standard vessel size of 1000 tonnes capacity.[31]

It is clearly evident that Britain and Ireland do not possess such natural river assets as the Rhine, Scheldte, Maas, Seine, Rhone. However, waterways capable of supporting viable ship and barge trades do exist in Britain and Ireland, including the rivers Humber, Liffey, Ouse, Thames, Trent, Severn, Shannon, and the Manchester Ship Canal. Moreover, both countries possess extensive coast lines which serve key industrial and population areas. From this context, the Green Highway offers a coastal alternative to the congested land transport networks. As early as 1950s the decline in UK coastal shipping was promoting comparison with continental inland systems: Southampton academics, Ford and Bound argued that, Germany has a very short coastline for a very large hinterland, while Britain is fortunate in possessing a very long coastline compared with its land area, the German rivers and canals are in fact performing functions which in Britain are carried out by the coasting trade.[32]

Given the potential of inland waterways and extensive coastal opportunities, this study will discuss and appraise areas of opportunity for shipping – where sufficient traffic potentials and navigational infrastructures exist to achieve continental standards of operation. Partly the British and Irish problem is one of acute under valuation of the water option and its potential. It is argued here that a negative perception of shipping's potential has prevailed. This study sets out to challenge this dated view by providing a fresh approach to a shipping legacy that has been allowed to atrophy in recent decades.

1.4 Transport Trends

Despite the maritime history, tradition and culture of the British Isles, the domestic shipping option came to be ignored by politicians, planners and, most importantly, freight movers. The Republic of Ireland appears to be following the British preoccupation with road transport, at the expense of alternative modes. The public perception of coastal and inland shipping has been allowed to become dated and inaccurate: a romantic picture of slow-moving, unreliable and inefficient ships and barges has materialised. The history of domestic freight transport in industrial Britain can be viewed within the context of a succession of dominant modal trends. This is evident in the investment surges associated with the canal age, the railway age and the motorway age. To some extent, each new modal network has destroyed the business of its predecessor mode. Somewhere between the zenith of the railway age and the up-surge of the motorway age, coastal shipping reached its peak. One outcome of these modal surges is exclusive attention to the modern whilst ignoring and abandoning the older mode. This historic process in many instances is unavoidable as improved technological innovation gives the new mode competitive advantage over the older mode. A point not immediately apparent in these surges, however, is that each mode has its own characteristics and niche advantages in the market. Recognition of these advantages tends to be ignored, given the desire to switch to the modern. The older mode ends up being consigned to history, perceived as old-fashioned, out-dated and inefficient. During the "railway mania" of the mid 1850s canal traffics were abandoned indiscriminately. Similarly, the motorway age has witnessed traffic lost from rail and water to road. In the case studies provided in Chapter 7 it will be seen how traffics were switched without serious scrutiny of the long-term impact. For example, the building of the M62 motorway led to Liverpool-Manchester grain traffics being diverted to road despite the inherent advantages of direct inland shipping linkages. During WW2, the need for the rational allocation of transport modes was accepted as vital for the national interest. The Ministry of Transport argued that it was desirable to end "cut-throat" competition between modes and to,

> to establish as great a degree of co-ordination as possible among the various forms of transport...so as to ensure that each form of transport is used to the greatest national advantage and that through co-ordination, each form of transport will tend to carry those traffics to which it is best suited.[33]

Whilst today's emergency may not be comparable with the exigencies of world war, it can be argued that pressing concerns over congestion and pollution demand radical action, that overt reliance on transport competition, on market forces, will not be able to deliver environmental improvement. In order for shipping to fulfil its potential, therefore, the stigma of its dated image must be faced. The problem of shipping's negative image was demonstrated by a late 1990s sample study of the perceptions of 700 shippers. The study highlighted entrenched prejudices that short sea shipping was slow and unreliable.[34] The late 19th century poet, John Masefield,[35] created a vivid impression of a "Dirty British coaster with a salt-caked smoke stack..." with its cargo of Tyne coal and road-rail and pig-lead and a range of cargoes from an earlier era of British industry. This poetic vision of small steamships struggling around the British and Irish coasts seems to be closer to the public perception than the reality of modern motorships providing vital and reliable deliveries of petroleum, chemicals, steel, grain, aggregates and container traffics. Helping to change this dated, albeit romantic, view of shipping is the challenge accepted here. The intention is not to impede innovation and development in the science of transport but to carefully consider the capabilities of shipping *vis-à-vis* road haulage. Sound and sustainable transport economics must be about optimising modes, fully utilising the attributes of each in the supply chain. However, in order for shipping to realise its full potential in the transport network, attention needs to be given to its dated image, the poor perception of quality. Key decision makers need full information in order to make modal choices. This entails awareness of the strides in technological innovation and business efficiency made by modern shipping organisation.

1.5 The Coastline Case

The extensive coastlines of Britain, (>7,000 kilometres) and Ireland, (>3,000 kilometres) provide significant shipping opportunities. The furthest point from the sea in Britain is Church Flatts Farm, Derbyshire, which is 106 kilometres to the Wash port of Fosdyke, Lincolnshire.[36] Furthermore, the inland tidal waterways of the Trent at Newark can be reached by a 500 tonne barge, just 72 kilometres from this central point. In his evidence to the UK Government's 2000 *Inquiry into Inland Waterways*, University Research Fellow, Frank Worsford detailed the potential for coastal shipping in the UK with its,

- 7,240 kilometres of coastline;
- 1,548 kilometres of coastal waterways;
- 373 kilometres of major estuaries;
- 578 kilometres of tidal navigation;
- 300 ports.[37]

Whilst it is inevitable that given the short distance Dover Straits (21nautical miles (nm)) crossing, with its relatively close proximity to London and South East England, continental traffics will funnel intensively through this corridor.

However the sustainable alternative for traffics generated by markets both within and outside the London and South East region, the Green Highway offers the environmental option. The ever-increasing UK dependence on imports from the Far East, particularly China, necessitates a revised approach to the supply chain. The 20-25 day deepsea haul from the Far East extends supply both in terms of distance and time. The arrival of large >9000 twenty foot equivalent unit (teu) container ships in the Southern England ports, Southampton, Thamesport and Felixstowe presents a logistical challenge for port operators and shipping lines.

The growth of container trades with the Far East has led to the phenomena of gridlock not only in UK ports, but worldwide, including Rotterdam and Los Angeles. The potential for coastal container feeder services around the UK coastline becomes increasingly evident as an alternative to road and rail congestion in hinterland routes. In some instances the 45 hour coastal voyage to Scotland may compare favourably to the road alternative, particularly when a similar period of time is spent with the freight held in the port's container stack - awaiting truck collection!

The Irish coastline also represents opportunities for shipping. In many ways the location and strategic importance of Dublin and Cork almost mirrors that of Southampton, Dover and Felixstowe. Whilst these ports directly serve important economic and population centres, they also act as funnels for long distance haulage legs. At the 2002 IMDO seminar, "Shipping Challenges for Ireland 2002-2012,"[38] the Dublin Castle audience heard the case for an improved shipping based supply chain. Given the important role of shipping in the Irish economy, the need for an improved supply chain was viewed as vital. Mr. Dermot Ahern TD, Minister for Communications, Marine and Natural Resources, outlined the increased emphasis on Ireland's maritime strategy. Attention was to be concentrated on:

- port bottlenecks and infrastructure deficiencies;
- enhanced maritime education and training;
- managing and maintaining maritime "know how;"
- achieving increased modal shift from road to water, pipeline and rail;
- increased door-to-door integration in transport services.

The role of the Ministerial Task Force on Transport Logistics was also defined and the focus on diverting traffics to regional ports was outlined. This strategy becomes integral to the prospects for developing traffics through such ports as Greenore and Drogheda on the East Coast, and Foynes and Galway on West Coast. By dispersing shortsea movements to the regional ports, congestion pressure is decreased in the central ports and their road infra-structures. Additionally, road tonne-kilometres are reduced, also fuel consumption and carbon emissions. Therefore, the environmental interest is better served.

1.6 Roads to Water: The Obstacles?

Post-1990s UKgovernmental concern over the road problem led to the commissioning of transport consultant, Jonathan Packer, producing the "Roads to Water" Study.[39] This resulted in a debate on the prospects for freight transfer from trucks to ships in the UK. The report's findings endorsed the extent of the challenge facing shipping in winning traffics from road. Generally, the findings were not optimistic with patterns of decline in core coastal trades – petroleum, dry bulks – identified. A major obstacle to coastal shipping recognised was the geographic concentration of economic activity in the UK. This led to: "... a high proportion of inland freight movements within a central triangle of London-Teeside-Liverpool – distances of no greater than 400km..."[40]

Packer's concern was that the major share of freight flows were too short for shipping's low tonne-kilometre cost advantage. As a consequence, the majority of UK traffic flows were not of sufficient distance for shipping to prove competitive, given that:

> on current cost structures, coastal unit load shipping is not generally competitive with road haulage direct over comparable distances below 800 km and coastal bulk is generally not competitive below 400 km where the consignee's depot is at the discharge port and 600 km where delivery is inland.[41]

The distance factor will become evident as a major factor in modal choice. Table 4 shows the comparatively low averages of truck journeys between 1990 and 2003. It can be seen that all goods vehicles only average around 92 kilometres; larger vehicles, >33 tonnes averaged around 135 kilometres.

Table 4: Average Goods Vehicle Journeys, Kilometres 1990-2003				
Vehicles	1990	1995	2000	2003
All Vehicles	79	89	94	92
>33 Tonne Vehicles	129	137	135	133
Source: DLTR				

In assessing the viability of coastal shipping *vis-à-vis* road haulage, distance is obviously an important factor in determining modal choice. However, other factors need to be considered. These include the volumes involved, the time sensitivity of the freight and the cost of storage. In addition, the problem of growing road congestion on European roads and the impact of rising haulage costs need to be considered. The situation the haulage industry found itself in was one of extreme difficulty during the early years of the Millennium. A growing shortage of drivers, the looming European Working Time Directive and high fuel duties have led to many truck operator/owners experiencing financial difficulties.

Such conditions increasingly force freight movers to consider alternative transport modes. A less quantifiable aspect of modal choice is the growing sensitivity of commerce to the "green issue." Increasingly, as the image and environmental integrity of business is scrutinised, the logistics strategy is becoming more associated with sustainable production and distribution.

Nine case studies have been developed and analysed in Chapter 7 in order to demonstrate the many examples where shipping is competitive with road haulage over distances much less than those stipulated in the "Roads to Water" report. The evidence provided here allows for analysis of the critical balance between distance, volumes and comparative transport costs. The scheme of work developed takes into account the many factors involved in realising the potential of the Green Highway.

1.7 The Scheme of Work

The scheme of work here is constructed from a mixture of historical evidence, the contemporary context, the profile of trades, ships and shipping companies, economics, logistical aspects and finally, the environmental integrity of the Green Highway is appraised.

1.7.1 The Historic Approach

Following on from this introduction, Chapter 2 examines the historic reasons for the decline of British and Irish coastal and inland shipping. It is contended strongly that providing understanding of the reasons behind decline is integral to any contemplation of shipping revival. It will become apparent in this Chapter 2 that a range of factors have contributed to the diminished share of shipping in domestic freight movements. Explanations range from, de-industrialisation, the restrictions of the highly regulated port industry pre-1980s, to shifts in business location, the rise of just-in-time logistics, the development of the motorway system and the growth of road haulage. For inland shipping, the geographic restrictions of British and Irish rivers and canals have limited the size of vessels and thus denied the owners the competitive advantages inherent in the economies of scale.

The intention here is to appraise the historical determinants of decline as a learning exercise. The contemporary context is of a progressive and efficient shipping industry, an industry revived in order to serve the needs of modern industry and environment. Achieving this may require some re-learning of the lessons of the past, however, when coastal shipping played a more prominent role in the economy.

1.7.2 The Context

Chapter 3 provides a broad context from which to view the Green Highway. As public opinion has become increasingly concerned over issues of transport congestion and pollution, as well as declining levels of efficiency, alternative transport modes have been pushed to the forefront. This includes the political context where legislation and policy initiatives have sought to develop shipping's potential. The European Commission's report, *The Future Development of the Common Transport Policy* (1992) has called for "sustainable transport" to become central to the Community's transport networks. The Royal Commission on Environmental Pollution Eighteenth Report, *Transport and the Environment* (1994), also championed the sustainable alternatives to road transport – rail and water. Both reports can be explained as the political response to the European transport problem, particularly given the estimates for traffic growth in the early decades of the Millennium. The gridlock scenario, the desire to reduce carbon emissions and the rise of environmental concerns in the electorate has engendered the beginnings of a new political approach towards sustainable transport. It is incumbent on this study, therefore, to explore the potential contribution of shipping to environmentally sensitive transport policy. European integration impacts on the Green Highway agenda in two ways:

> (1) industrial integration between European firms places emphasis on transport linkages;

> (2) the spread of the *state-of-the-art* practices of continental coastal and inland shipping to the British Isles and Ireland

As firms co-ordinate their production processes across the European continent, the role of shipping becomes increasingly critical. Intra-European mergers, leading to rationalisations and ensuing industrial integration in European steel, chemicals and automobile industries have opened up opportunities for shipping. Particularly pertinent to Britain and Ireland is the higher level of commitment to shipping by continental industry. The sound practice of continental Europe in the field of inland shipping innovation and organisation has positive implications for developing the shipping mode in the British Isles and Ireland. The Single European Market has made it easier for continental collaboration with British operators. The late 1990s joint venture between Kentish and Berlin operators on the Thames/Medway rivers can be seen as leading the way for new initiatives in financing and operating shipping.[42] This Chapter will also focus on the experience and expertise of shipping of continental Europe. Recognition is given to *state-of-the-art* technology and business enterprise that exists on continental waterways. Partly responsible for the low utilisation of British domestic and continental shipping is the historic trading patterns of the British Empire which placed emphasis on the large vessel deepsea trades. The switch in trade direction engendered by European integration requires small ship operations with inland trading capabilities. German operators have been particularly successful in the development of the sea-river vessel.

This hybrid combines the river penetrating capabilities of the modern barge with the sea trading attributes of the coastal vessel, thus extending the tkm capability of shipping. The attributes of the sea-river vessel make it a champion of the Green Highway. Complementing the technology is the innovative way the owners have gained access to investment finance. Other areas of continental expertise are in the movements of containers, automobiles, petroleum and even wine and beers by inland shipping. Finally, the progressive management and development of waterway infrastructure of French, German and Benelux countries has much to offer. This is particularly the case given the contrast with the neglected systems of Britain and Ireland. The January 2000 purchase of the UK's largest tugboat group, Cory Towage, by the Netherlands based, Wijsmuller Group points to the continental interest in British maritime industries.[43] It is becoming apparent that developments in shipping innovation, organisation and financing are becoming pan-European. The launching of the two sea-river ships, *Crescent Rhine* and *Crescent Seine,* brought welcome new dry cargo tonnage onto the UK registry, particularly given the dearth of British investment in this sector. The collaboration between the vessels' German owners, Netherlands shipbuilders and UK operators, Crescent Shipping, demonstrates an Intra-European division of labour, capital and management in shortsea shipping.[44]

The shipping context is also shaped by changes in the ownership and operation of ports. The deregulation and privatisation of British and Irish ports has boosted competitiveness. Additionally, many ports – enhancing their "green profile" – are promoting the shortsea option for transhipped goods as an alternative to road haulage. Deepsea Container trade expansion at Felixstowe, Thamesport, Liverpool, Tilbury and Southampton has raised the profile of feeder ship linkages as a green alternative to road haulage distribution.

The "green transport" issue is increasingly becoming part of the business strategy of principal freight generators. For example, the Anglo-Dutch P&O-

Nedlloyd (taken over by Maersk Line in 2005) container shipping group has demonstrated a high level of commitment to shipping and rail for coastal and inland distribution, with over 50% of the Line's extensive Southampton traffics moving inland by rail. Other examples of sustainable transport commitment in the early years of the Millennium include retail giants, Marks and Spencer, Asda and Safeway, aggregate suppliers, Lafarge, and even Scottish hauliers, Malcolm Group, have diversified into rail trunk haul. The entrance of the innovative Greek ferry operator, Super Fast, on the newly created Rosyth-Zeebrugge ro-pax route has had considerable impact on Green Highway thinking. The diagonal, 17.5 hour, route has been welcomed, both as Scotland's first direct link to continental Europe and as a sustainable alternative to Anglo-Scottish road trunking to English ferry ports.[45] Finally, the context for a shipping revival can draw some positive energy from the experience of the privatised, open access, UK railfreight network.

The two principal operators, Freightliner and English Welsh and Scottish Rail(EWSR) have broken free from the mould of inefficiency and decline and have been joined by new entrant companies, Direct Rail Services and GB Railfreight. These companies have successfully challenged the perception of rail as outmoded and uncompetitive with road haulage. Surprisingly, the long term decline in rail tonne-kilometres has been reversed and rail is now competing over distances hitherto regarded as too short for rail economics. The lessons for shipping are considerable as a new transport paradigm is sought, with alternatives to road haulage being considered utilising economic and/or environmental criteria.

1.7.3. UK & Irish Shipping Renaissance?

Chapter 4 discusses the Green Highway idea within the parameters of a renaissance in the British merchant fleet. After several decades of decline a convergence of political, fiscal, organisational and environmental factors have combined to not only reverse the trend of decline, but also to achieve significant growth under the British and Irish flags. Of particular interest here is the impact of the respective Tonnage Taxes as a catalyst for revival.

The implications of a revived and vibrant national fleet will be appraised as a positive contribution to the transfer of freight from roads to water. The revival of British flagged tonnage can now be explained, partly, as a result of UK Government initiatives in the registration, taxation and safety management of ships. Additionally, reforms in the Maritime Coastguard Agency (MCA) have reduced the bureaucratic burden of registering ships under the British flag; the implementation of the Tonnage Tax has provided a fiscal incentive to register ships in Britain, making the "Red Duster" attractive to the global investor. The stringent ship inspection by the MCA in UK ports, under the aegis of the International Maritime Organisation's (IMO) Paris Memorandum on Port State Control, has made it increasingly difficult for substandard ships to trade to UK ports. The setting up of the Irish Maritime Development Organisation (IMDO) has also had a positive impact on the Irish flag. The signs are encouraging for a quality focused, Green Highway.

1.7.4 The Trades

Chapter 5 provides a profile of the principal traffic flows moving around the British and Irish coasts. The statistics of tonnage movements are outlined. Also, the main sectors are identified, their particular technical and economic characteristics analysed. The survey provided here (see Appendix 1) of domestic and Irish Sea traffics in February 2002 will be utilised in order to identify the cargoes, distance and volumes of trade around the British and Irish coastlines, as well as movements between the two countries. The recognition of the main freight flows is essential to the success of the Green Highway. It will become evident that a significant proportion of traffics are moving relatively short distances. This evidence is utilised to challenge the view that shipping can only compete over long distances.

1.7.5. The Ships and their Owners

The aim of Chapter 6 is to outline the basic "tools of the trade." This is achieved by profiling the business - ship types, their routes and cargoes, patterns of organisation and management. It will become apparent that shipping within the coastal and inland ambit is diverse in its technology, operation and ownership. The technology range stretches from the 120,000 tonne "shuttle" tanker operating between the North Sea oil fields and the oil terminals of the British Isles, as well as Cork's Whitegate Refinery and the 500 tonne barge moving sand down the River Trent in Central England. For the Green Highway to succeed it will be necessary to match the particular features of each shipping sub-sector to the specific demand factors in each. Ownership is also likely to cover a wide spectrum. In the above example, the large tanker is probably owned (or chartered to) by a multinational oil major; the sand barge may be owned by the master of the two or three person crew! However, the gap between the two extremes may not be as wide as it initially appears. A synergetic relationship between inland shipping and the deepsea sector was identified by the Green Award organisation[*] in the early 2000s. Within the context of improved environmental standards, the organisation recognised that much of the expertise gained by inland barge management and crews in the hazardous cargoes sector was transferable to large tanker operations.[46] Many of the leading European shortsea operators have organisational linkages with the inland sector. Three of Britain's largest shortsea fleets have a pedigree that stretches back to the river creek and estuarial traditions of the Thames and Medway sailing barges.

---

[*] The Green Award is a rating scheme for assessing the ship's adherence to safe and environmentally sensitive standards. In order to attain the award a rigorous operational audit is required. See: www.greenaward.com

An interesting dimension of the Green Highway issue is the entrepreneurial stance of British and Irish shortsea shipowners. Contradicting the seemingly irreversible trends of a declining British and Irish deepsea industry, a number of the traditional owners in coastal and shortsea shipping have increased their fleets and enhanced their technological base in recent decades. Neither have the small ship owners been reluctant to lobby parliament. In 1988, the predominantly shortsea, British Motor Shipowners' Association, argued the case for a level playing field in fiscal regimes:

> ...research in West Germany has shown that operating costs of a new UK shortsea vessel are competitive with those of West Germany in all areas under the direct control of the shipowner... These costs amount to 40% of the total costs. The other 60% concerns the financing of the vessel and is influenced by the UK Government's fiscal regime. Here we are hopelessly uncompetitive. In other words, British coastal operators have got their proportion of operating costs right, but the Government has got the share of costs under its control badly wrong.[47]

Whilst these owners have retained or improved their competitiveness against the modern fleets of Germany, Belgium and the Netherlands, they have remained largely attached to their trading history. This has meant continued focus on the dry bulk trades – aggregates, grain, steel, scrap, coal, minerals – and the tanker trades – oil products, chemicals. To a large extent, the expanding fast moving consumer goods (FMCG's), container and roll on-roll off (Ro-Ro) road haulage movements have been overlooked by the traditional British and Irish owners. Likewise it will become evident that the opportunities of moving large volumes of North Sea crude oil have not attracted British tanker owners. The challenge of the Millennium is for these owners to attain and channel diversification of their skills and expertise into new areas of opportunity.

1.7.6. Economics and Logistics

Economics and logistics are integral to the competitiveness of shipping. Chapter 7 will concentrate on the factors that shape the market (and potential market) for shipping. The supply chain forces of volume, speed, distance, location and storage that condition modal choice will be identified. Included are the principal trades and their routes. Also, patterns of industrial and agricultural demand are discussed. Within the context of demand, such important factors as transport and inventory costs, distance, time sensitivity and volume factors are acknowledged. These will be viewed as instrumental in the choice of transport mode. The economic advantage of water transport lies in its extremely low tonne-kilometre cost. However, competitive advantage can be destroyed by the additional costs of cargo handling, storage and transhipment to inland transport from the port to the final delivery point. Attention will be given to this critical area of modal competition. It is intended to examine many of the hitherto accepted assumptions on modal choice, particularly the impact of distance, volume and timing factors.

The supply of shipping is influenced by a mix of capital, operational and voyage costs faced by the shipowner. Also impacting on the cost structure are the terms of operation inherent in the various types of charter available. These include the demise, voyage and time charters. Each requires a differing cost framework. The supply dimension is made up of any number of firms in the market. Whilst the shipping product may be fairly homogeneous in that vessels tend to be of standard designs, cost competitiveness can be affected by such factors as crew nationality, port of registry and its tax regime.

Particularly relevant in determining new shipping ventures is the high capital cost of business entry. The problem facing the shipping entrepreneur is how to survive these cost penalties whilst faced with the slow build up of revenue flows from a new service, particularly in shuttle, feeder and liner trades. However, if the owners have secured a long term charter for the new vessel these problems are diminished; therefore market stability is accepted as conducive to an expanded Green Highway.

Influencing the economics of the Green Highway are two important factors: (1) the economies of scale and (2) the support of the state. These two areas were formalised as the "Delft Paradox" and the "Vouliagmeni Paradox" at the 1994 and 1996 Short Sea Roundtable Conferences.[48] The "Delft Paradox" places emphasis on the size of vessels; and this has implications for both small ships and the size restricted regional ports. Essentially, this highlights the paradox of larger, low tkm cost, vessels (which benefit from the economies of scale) and the flexibility of smaller vessels and their ability to serve restricted ports and inland waterways. In order for vessels to realise their full competitive advantage against road haulage it is evident that a certain critical size needs to be attained. This, however, needs to be weighed against the logistical and environmental advantages of the smaller vessel's capability to reach a point closer to the final destination of the cargo. The "Delft Paradox" has big implications for the smaller ports. Such size restricted ports as Wicklow, Glasson Dock and Wisbech, provide niche services for shippers. However, they face intense competition from larger ports which can facilitate the economies of scale of larger vessels. The same paradox applies to the inland waterways systems of the Trent, Severn and Weaver rivers. If the objective is to maximise water tonne-kilometres then small ships become integral. The final inland destination point may only be reached by a 750dwt vessel. However, lower costs may be achieved by the utilisation of a combination of a fully loaded 2500dwt vessel and road haulage from a larger coastal port situated at greater distance from the delivery point. The emphasis of the EU's Trans European Transport Network (TEN-T) is on major transport flows. These are likely to support larger vessels. For instance, the Benelux-UK-Eire TEN-T route focuses on the shortsea crossing between the Hook of Holland

and East Anglia. Whilst this route is a main freight thoroughfare, the use of RoRo ferries tends to minimise the distance of the sea crossing, ergo the road leg becomes maximised. Conversely, the use of lift on-lift off (LoLo) shipping will extend the sealeg and minimise the tonne-kilometres of the roadleg. As an example the shortest crossing, Dover-Calais, is just 21nm. This route features intensive RoRo operations and generates large volumes of road haulage in Nord Pas de Calais and Kent. By way of contrast, the Rotterdam-Tilbury route is 170nm and the service is provided by LoLo ships.

The Vouliagmeni Paradox was derived from the complex issue of state involvement in transport operations. It has been made apparent that some shipping trades are marginally competitive with road haulage, particularly in the early days of a new service when the shipowner will struggle to achieve a modest rate of return. In the break-bulk and container sectors, support from freight forwarders is traditionally slow to build up as the new shipping service remains untested and is particularly vulnerable to predatory pricing by the hauliers. Given that the paradox is drawn from the desire of European governments to encourage more freight by water and the seeming inability of the free market to achieve this objective, the role of the state becomes paramount. On one hand it can be seen that some degree of state support is necessary to supplement entrepreneurial risk in shipping, on the other this infringes the European Union's commitment to free, unhindered markets. Such state encouragement as the Freight Facilities Grant supplied by British Government is clearly fundamental to this debate. Similarly, the "Marco Polo" European Commission initiative is accepted as a measure of the political will to shift freight movements to rail and water within the European Community.[49]

Chapter 7 also seeks to examine the potential for shipping, given the pattern of industrial and commercial development in the new Millennium. Spatial shifts towards out-of-town production, storage and distribution centres have marginalised dependency on traditional transport provision, namely shipping and railways. As a consequence, ports and railheads have been replaced by motorway connections as prime generators of business location. The focus on road networks, in conjunction with the desire to achieve the low inventory costs integral to just-in-time haulage based supply, has precluded the use of shipping. The rise of fast moving consumer goods (FMCGs) has enhanced the switch to road. Likewise, the decline of heavy industry in the de-industrialisation process has destroyed many of the staple domestic shipping markets – coal, cement, chemicals. Within the context of the restructured European economy, the challenge facing the Green Highway is just how well it meets the new patterns of demand. This requires attention to such concepts as door-to-door, intermodal movements, just-in-time logistics, vertical integration and fast ship technology. Attention to marketing and electronic business communications is an implicit ingredient of logistics success in the new Millennium. This becomes particularly salient given shipping's somewhat dated, low technology, image!

It is evident that significant examples of shipping fitting into the modern supply chain already exist. Nine case studies have been researched by the author and a synopsis of their findings within the Green Highway context are provided in Chapter 7. Coastal movements of large volumes of stone by one of Europe's quarry industry leaders, Foster Yeoman, demonstrate the value of shipping in a vertically integrated supply chain. North Sea LoLo services are identified as intermodal linkages between the British and continental rail and inland waterway networks, providing a reliable, cost effective alternative to the Channel Tunnel The flow of containerised chemical traffics from North West England and continental steel through the Port of Boston is complemented by just-in-time railfreight connections. Direct loading of sea-river ships in steel plants in Liege and Bremen allows for cost effective intermodal integration in the steel supply chain. The idea of a North-South "Marine Motorway" forms a case study analysis based on the existing and future prospects of fast coastal and shortsea RoRo

36

operations. It will be seen that the switch to higher speed vessels has significant potential but also faces operational and cost obstacles. The development of coastal deepsea feeder traffic ex the Port of Southampton is identified as a precursor for growth, particularly given the leading involvement of port-owners in the trade.   The re-emergence of Lighter Aboard Ship (LASH) activities in UK waters in the 1998 marked a significant development in the Green Highway. The flexibility of LASH in combining deepsea shipping with inland distribution adds an important dimension to the competitiveness of shipping, particularly when the floating containers provide the option of a seamless linkage between such up-river locations as Mississippi ports with wharves on the Yorkshire Ouse. A case study on barge movements in and around UK ports been undertaken in order to demonstrate the flexibility of such water-borne services as oil fuel supplies, waste disposal and victualling of deepsea ships. FFG support of aggregate flows on the River Trent are highlighted in a successful roads-to-water freight shift. Similarly, concentration on the Scottish timber trades allows for consideration of the mix of technological developments in cargo handling, a committed port operator and a supportive government start up package, in the form of a Freight Facilities Grant (FFG). The flow of grain along the Manchester Ship Canal was selected as an example of water winning back traffic from road over a relatively short distance.

The 9 case studies provided give insight into the vital factors that determine the success or failure of Green Highway ventures, affording a benchmark for assessing potential routes and freight flows.

1.7.7. Testing the Green Highway

Chapter 8 considers the role of shipping within the context of environmental apprehension. European Union transport policy, particularly the sustainable mobility framework, has identified shipping's attributes. The twin advantages of low tonne-km cost and low emissions of carbon, *vis-à-vis* road haulage, has led to the advocacy of shipping by European policy makers. Additionally, awareness of the link between commercial success and green credibility has necessitated closer attention to environmental issues by business. It is apparent that many progressive firms are seeking to use rail and water modes as a "greener" alternative to roads.

Shipping enjoys an important position in the European Commission's sustainable mobility strategy; however it would be remiss to ignore the negative sides of shipping in this critical evaluation. For shipping to fulfil its "green" potential the industry must fully embrace a number of quality standards. Critical areas will need to be recognised and acted upon. These include the environmental issues of: anti-fouling hull paint, engine exhaust emissions, oil tank wash and other waste discharges and the fuel oil and cargo pollution caused by groundings, collisions and foundering. As well as the technical condition of the vessel, the human relations issues of recruitment, training standards and employment conditions need to be considered. Fatigue and stress are particularly pertinent to the coastal and shortsea trades. Such environmental disasters as the feeder ship, *Cita's* 1997 loss on Newfoundland Isle, off the Scilly Isles' grouping and the more serious 1999 break up of the tanker, *Erika,*[50] do much to undermine the Green Highway. Both vessels were operating on intra-European routes; and it is apparent that both vessels failed to match up to the exacting standards required. The examination of shipping's "green" potential provided here will focus on quality benchmarks and what needs to be done to ensure that these standards are attained by all operators.

1.7.8. Establishing the Green Highway

Finally, Chapter 9 will provide summary and conclusion on the prospects for the Green Highway. By this stage it will become possible to provide a critical analysis of the prospects for shipping. It is clearly evident that there are geographic and logistical limits on just how much traffic can be carried by water, in preference to road. However, it is also apparent that a range of political, environmental, innovatory and logistical forces are combining in favour of shipping. The question that this study seeks to answer is under what circumstances can shipping exploit the opportunity and fulfil its potential as a contributor to the transport challenges facing Britain and Ireland within the context of European integration and sustainable mobility.

1.8 Chapter 1: Summary & Conclusion

This Chapter has sought to provide introduction and structure to the study. The rationale has been identified as the need to develop sustainable alternatives to road transport. The direction pursued is that of critical analysis of the Green Highway's attributes and potential. The following chapter concentrates on the lessons of history, the lessons that can be drawn from the decline of coastal and canal traffics, post WW1.

CHAPTER 1: ENDNOTES

[1] Brewer, J. (1992) "A special report on the UK Maritime industries: A wet roadway awaiting to be used." *Lloyd's List.* 20.5.92.
[2] *Loc.cit*
[3] "An idea whose time has come," *Lloyd's List.* 21.4.05.
[4] Dupin, C. "Coastal shipping: can it be revived?" *Journal of Commerce.* 9.12.02.
[5] Lichfield, J. "300,000 Seabirds dead. Only now can Europe count the cost of sea of Filth." *The Independent.* 8.1.00.
[6] Osler, D. " A saga of single hulls, double standards and too many flags of convenience," *The Independent.* 20.11.02
[7] "£30m cargo lost as ship sinks," http://news.bbc.co.uk 15.12.02. 09:03 GMT.
[8] Stock, S (2005) Letter to the Editor: "Hunt for information on careers at sea shows need for a new approach," Numast, *The Telegraph.* August 2005. p.16.
[9] "People and Places: Floored by the Duster", *Lloyd's List.* 21.9.00.
[10] Lapthorn, D. (2001) Letter to the Editor: "Festival of the Sea creates a ripple of interest for next four years." *Lloyd's List.* 7.9.01.
[11] Whitelegg, J. (1993) *Transport for a Sustainable Future: The Case for Europe.* Chichester: Wiley and Sons. p.1.
[12] McLaughlin,J. "Schubert composes a set of variations," *Lloyd's List.* 15.8.03. p.5.
[13] Matson, L. *et.al* (2006) *CPRE Beyond Transport Infrastructure: Lessons for the Future from Recent Road Projects.* London: CPRE.
[14] Musso, E. Marchese, U. (2002) "Economics of Shortsea Shipping," in Grammenos, T.H. *The Handbook of Maritime Economics and Business.* London: LLP. pp.285.
[15] *Ibid* p.280.
[16] Department of Transport (2006) *Statistics Bulletin: Waterborne Freight in the United Kingdom 2005.* London: DfT.
[17] European Commission Directortate-General for Energy and Transport, (2002*) EU Energy and Transport in Figures: Statistical Pocketbook 2002.* EC: Luxembourg.
[18] Hilling, D. (2001) "Waterborne Freight; The Neglected Mode," *Logistics and Transport Focus.* Vol.3, No.8, Oct 2001. Corby: The Institute of Logistics and Transport. pp.30-33.
[19] Hadfield,C. (1971) *The Canal Age* London: Pan Books. pp.11-16.
[20] Armstrong, J . Aldridge,J. Boyes,G. Mustoe,G. Storey,R. (2003). *Companion to British Road Haulage History.* London: Science Museum. p.297.
[21] Osborne, P. (2005) "Pickfords on the waterway," www.upthecut.co.uk
[22] "Britain's Water Highways: A New Agenda for Freight". Birmingham, 19.10.99. www.publications.parliament.uk/pa/cm200001/cmselect/cmenvtra/317/317ap05.htm
[23] www.gloucesterdocks.me.uk/vessels. Accessed 27.7.05.
[24] Hilling, D, (1993) "British ports in a changing Europe," *Geofile.* No.209. January 1993.
[25] Webster, B. (2002) "Canals to be revived by a £500m flow of cash", *The Times.* 19.3.02. p.8.
[26] " British Waterways Aggregates Deal," *World Cargo On-Line News.* July 2003.
[27] "Transport Minister launches new barging scheme," Buckinghamshire County Council Press Release, 1.7.03.
[28] Freight Study Group (2002) *Freight on Water: A New Perspective.* London: DEFRA.
[29] *Ibid.* pp.28-9.
[30] Worsford,F. (2000) Memorandum to the Select Committee on Environment, Transport and Regional Affairs, *Inquiry into Inland Waterways,* 18.9.00.
[31] The Inland Waterways Association, Inland Shipping Group (1996) *UK Freight Waterways: A Blueprint for the Future.* London: IWA. p.3.
[32] Ford, P. Bound,J.A. (1951) *Coastwise Shipping and the Small Ports.* Oxford: Blackwell. p.1

40

[33] Bagwell,P.S. (1974) *The Transport Revolution from 1770*. London: Batsford. P.108

[34] Zachcial, M. (2001) "Short Sea Shipping and Intermodal Transport", in European Conference of Ministers of Transport Report: *Short Sea Shipping in Europe*. Paris ECMT. p.26.

[35] Masefield, J. *"Cargoes"* in Masefield, J. (1924) *Salt Water Ballads* (10ᵗʰ ed). London: Elkin Mathews.

[36] Haran,B. (2003)http://news.bbc.co.uk/1/hi/england/derbyshire/3090539.stm 23.7.03. Accessed 27.7.03.

[37] Worsford, F. *Op.cit.*

[38] IMDO Shipping Challenges for Ireland 2002-2012. A Seminar held at Dublin Castle, 7.11.02.

[39] Packer, J.L.(1995) "UK Roads to Water Initiative: A Focusing Study", annotated in Wiljnost,I.N.;Peeters,D.C. (1995) *European Shortsea Shipping: Proceedings from the Second European Research Roundtable Conference on Shortsea Shipping.* Delft/London: Delft University Press/Lloyd's of London Press. pp. 502-511.

[40] Packer .*Op.cit.* p.504.

[41] *Ibid.* p.507.

[42] Gaston, J. "The German pusher tug, Billy". *Lloyd's List.* 18.5.95

[43] "Cory deal is just the start for acquisitive Wijsmuller". *Lloyd's List* 25.1.00. p.7.

[44] "Seine and Rhine added to Crescent Cargo Division," *Lloyd's List.* 1.3.01.

[45] Scottish Enterprise, "Superfast Ferries" www.scottish-enterprise.com Accessed 26.11.05.

[46] Parker, C.J. (2001) "Setting the Standard: The Nautical Institute and the Green Award", *Seaways: The International Journal of the Nautical Institute,* February 2001. pp.6-7.

[47] British Motor Shipowners' Association, Memorandum to House of Commons Transport Committee, Session 1987-88, *Decline in the UK Registered Merchant Fleet,* Vol.2 pp.172-5.

[48] Wiljnost,I.N.;Peeters,D.C. (1995) *European Shortsea Shipping: Proceedings from the Second European Research Roundtable Conference on Shortsea Shipping.* Delft/London: Delft University Press/Lloyd's of London Press.

[49] http://europa.eu.int/comm/transport/marcopolo

[50] "Erika disaster may put squeeze on older ships," *Lloyd's List* 3.2.00. p.16.

CHAPTER 2

The Disguised Decline of Coastal and Inland Shipping

This Chapter will examine the historic decline of shipping in the British domestic and Irish trades. The role of canals in the early industrial revolution was discussed in Chapter 1; the vital role that coastal shipping played in both the pre and post railway boom of the mid 1800s is recognised here. In focusing on the historical dimension the intention is to identify the factors that shaped demand and ultimately led to decline. In order to explore future potential, the history of the Green Highways of the past provides important lessons. What can be learned from the rise and fall of shipping in the domestic economy?

Considering current trades, acknowledgement has already been made of the dominance of North Sea crude oil movements, how they inflate the tonnage figures for shipping moving around the British coast. The large crude oil volumes can also be seen to disguise the long term decline of coastal shipping. It will become evident that European integration has stimulated demand on the shortsea routes. This growth, however, has been mainly attained in the RoRo trades and as such is conducive to road haulage expansion. Furthermore, non-oil domestic traffics have been in decline since the WW1 period.

2.1 The Green Highway in the 1950s.

The post WW2 period brought dramatic decline for UK coastal shipping. It was only the impact of North Sea oil demand that led to a recovery in the post-1970 period. Decline was not immediately noticeable in this era. In the 1950s, the Green Highway profile was of a major industry with a vital role at the heart of Britain's industrial economy. Large volumes of coal still moved down the East Coast from the mining areas of the Tees, Wear and Tyne regions. The electricity generating power stations and gas works of the Thames, Medway and South Coast provided massive demand for fleets of collier ships. At least seven carriers provided fleets for this trade. In addition, coal users such as the North Thames Gas Board operated their own "flat iron" fleets of vessels in the 3500 dwt range. On the West Coast the Irish coal trades of Liverpool, Glasgow and South Wales provided work for collier fleets. Another major Irish trade was the movement of livestock to the markets of Liverpool and Glasgow.

In the 1950s steam and motor vessels were still facing competition with sailing barges in the agricultural and cement trades of East Anglia and the Thames Estuary. In addition to the bulk trades, regular liner (timetabled) services ran along the coastline. Such lines as Coast Lines and the Dundee, Perth and London Shipping Co Ltd ran regular scheduled services, even accommodating passengers. Inland shipping was still a major force in the transport economy. The entreports of London, Liverpool and Hull were dependent on large fleets of tugs and barges for deliveries to up-stream wharves. The Thames-Grand Union Canal interchange at Brentford was a hive of activity. On the Grand Union Canal and the River Lee, Greater London industry was served by convoys of barges. In the potteries region, narrow boats were a major element in the industrial supplies of coal and china clay. All major rivers – Avon, Clyde, Medway, Mersey, Severn, Tyne, Tees, Weaver, Wear – supported sizeable barge traffics. In Ireland the important Guinness trade was serviced by fleets of barges linking the malt and barley growing regions with the Dublin Brewery via the River Liffey. As with coastal shipping, the canals were heavily dependent on the coal trades. Major industrial systems such as the Leeds and Liverpool Canal went rapidly into heavy loss-making in the 1950s as coal traffics disappeared.[1]

The Scottish West Coast and its islands were very much dependent on fleets of "Para Handy" type puffers for shipments of wheat, barley, coal and household supplies inward and outward flows of timber and whisky. The early promise of containerisation was heralded by the use of intermodal boxes by

British Railways and its Cross-Channel and Irish Sea steamer fleets. The use of converted landing craft vessels as RoRo ships was a pointer to the shortsea ferry revolution that was to occur on Irish Sea and continental routes.

Despite the apparent high levels of activity in the 1950s, in retrospect it is now evident that a decline in both relative and absolute terms was then incipient. It will be noticeable that the process of relative decline was already in train in the post WW1 period. In the post WW2 absolute decline was to occur.

2.2 Explaining Decline

In Chapter 1 some discussion was made on the sweeping changes, the modal shifts, that have occurred in the transport economy. The switch from a water and rail transport preoccupation in the European transport economy to that of road and air has occurred at such an intense pace as to blur the edges of history. Coastal shipping expert, Dr. Alfred Baird, found that the enduring impression held by British freight movers was of a dated nature, with a perception that coastal shipping was slow, unreliable and only appropriate for low-value, non-time sensitive goods.[2] To some extent, the once important role of (non-oil) coastal , river and canal networks has been "air-brushed" out of the common perception. The re-evaluation of coastal shipping involves reversing this process of negative perception.

Amongst the causes of decline the impact of de-industrialisation and industrial re-location will be acknowledged as a major element. Similarly, the rapid growth of road haulage in the inter-war years will be offered as a key factor in the modal-shift from water to road – helping to re-shape the British economy and ultimately leading to the demise of domestic shipping. In addition to these two dominant causes of decline, post WW2, subsidiary factors can be identified. These include the problem of port efficiency pre de-regulation and, more latterly, the ubiquitous emergence of a gentrification process. This has led to housing development in the port areas, culminating in the crowding out of cargo handling activities. In the shortsea trades to Ireland and continental Europe, the rise of the RoRo ferry has been very much at the expense of liner services. As a consequence, RoRo shipping has contributed to the fall in shipping tonne-kilometres (tkm) : primarily these services seek to minimise sea journey legs, thus maximising road journey legs. For instance, the Paris-Manchester liner service disappeared in the 1960s, a period of early motorway and RoRo ferry development. Three major sectors have been selected to illustrate patterns of demand and the changes that brought about decline:

- the North East England-Thames Collier Trades;
- the Thames Estuary Barge Trades;
- the Liner and Tramp Trades of the UK West Coast and Irish Sea.

2.3 The Impact of North Sea Oil

In raising the question of decline it is important to identify the specific characteristics of the domestic trades. The contention here is that the dramatic rise in North Sea oil movements has disguised the underlying decline of national shipping tonnages. Figure 4 initially shows an increase in domestic shipping from the 1970s onwards. Once again, it is evident that the driving force behind this growth is the rise of North Sea oil flows from the late 1960s onwards. Figure 5 shows the extent of the oil trades accounting for around 70% of tkm movements. The movement of oil is an obvious and largely uncontested market target for maritime transportation. The off-shore loading of oil tankers precludes competition with any other transport mode, excepting pipeline. Terminal locations, such as Scapa Flow, Flotta, Hound Point, Tees-Port, served by pipelines (from the North Sea and Atlantic Fields), are selected for their accessibility by large crude carriers.

Figure 4: Domestic Shipping BTKM, 1955-2004

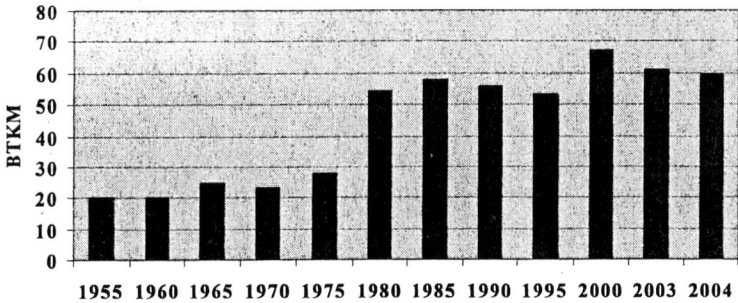

Source: www.DfT.gov.uk

Figure 5: Total & Non-Oil UK Domestic Tonnages Lifted, 1955-2004.

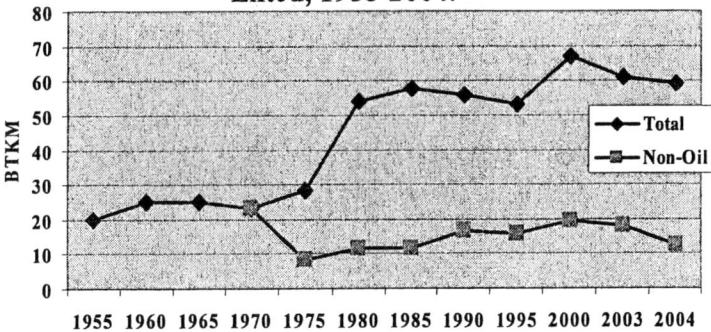

Source: www.DfT.gov.uk

Figure 6: North Sea Oil Flows.

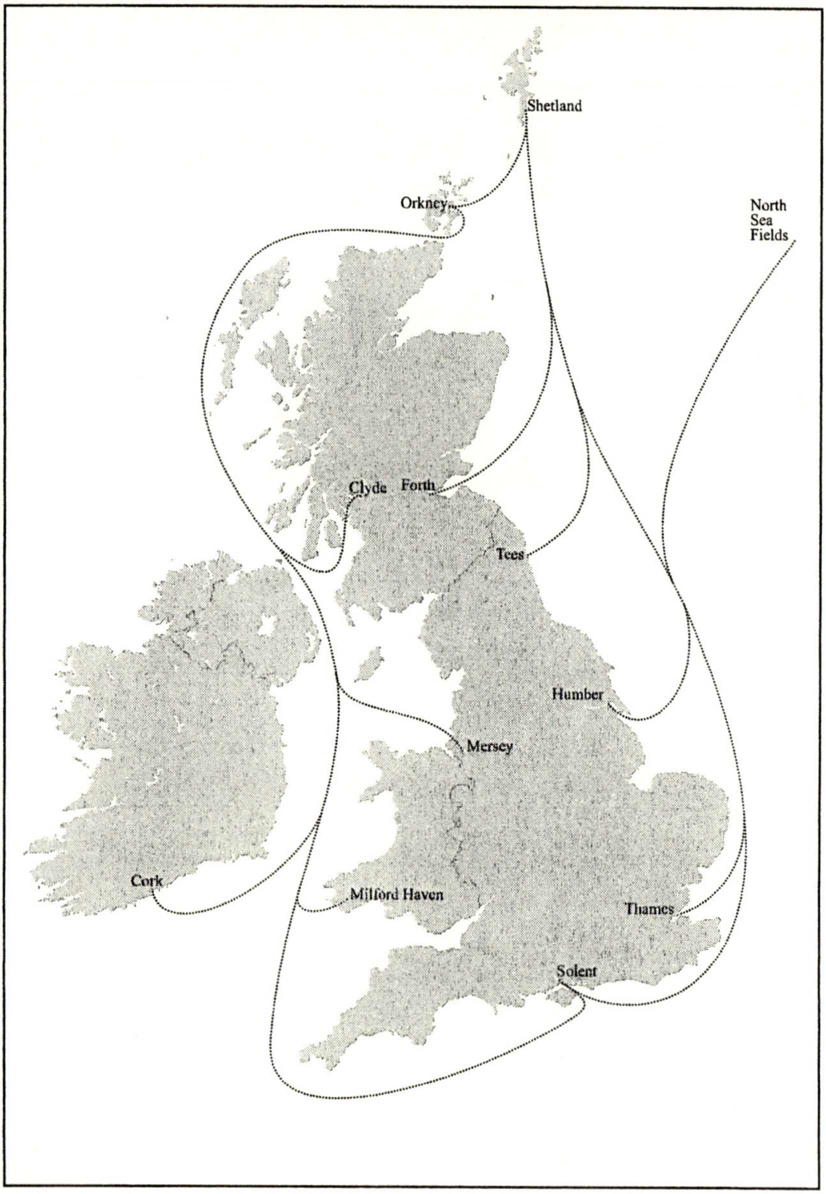

Essentially, the logistics of North Sea oil are inextricably linked to the tanker trade by sea. Figure 6 illustrates the main trunk of the North Sea crude oil tanker supply chain. To its credit, the tanker industry has responded to the demands of large volumes of crude oil. Furthermore, the challenges of the operationally difficult North Sea have been met with innovation in the form of purpose built shuttle tankers. However, it is difficult to envisage any other mode of transport competing for the large volumes involved. Without this oil traffic, the participation of domestic shipping is considerably diminished. A second reason for focusing on the non-oil figures is the reality that North Sea oil has reached its zenith point and predicted to suffer rapid decreases in output in the forthcoming decades. Additionally, the United Kingdom Oil Operators Association (UKOOA) have expressed concern that North Sea oil operators face increasing extraction (geographic) obstacles, ergo rising costs, as the law of diminishing returns intensifies.[3]

Figure 7 shows the pattern of decline of UK North Sea oil output. With daily output set to fall by up to 2.5 million barrels (mpd) between 2000 and 2010, the implications are that the share of shipping in the UK domestic trades could collapse from 24% to around 10% of tkm unless a shipping revival is engendered in non-oil trades.

In the pre-1914 period, railways, canals and coastal shipping were the prime movers in the British and Irish transport economies. Figure 8 shows the predominance of shipping in the pre-motorised road haulage transport economy. By the inter-war years the shares of water and rail were rapidly diminished by the rapid growth of road haulage. Figure 9 shows the rise of road haulage to 64% of all freight movements and the 24% of water's share in UK traffics by 2003. However, by extracting the large volumes of oil traffics, shown in Figure 10, the share of water is diminished to around 8%. This shows the massive importance of

48

North Sea oil movements to the statistics of the Green Highway. Moreover, it is evident the large volumes of oil traffics have served to disguise decline in UK coastal shipping.

Figure 7: UK North Sea Oil Actual & Forecast, 1980-2010

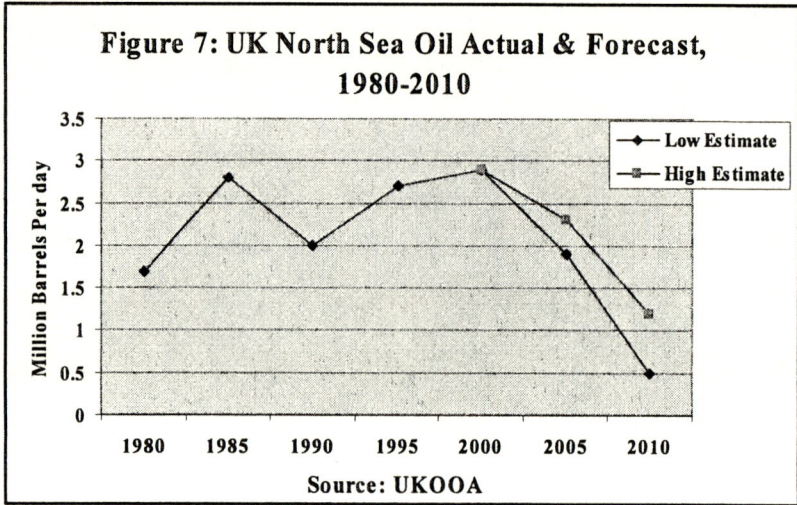

Source: UKOOA

2.4 Shipping in the Industrial Revolution Process

Britain's transport history and the early industrial revolution it helped to create was shaped by water transport in the pre-railway period. The coastline became the major trade route for such important commodities as wheat, barley, timber and coal. The growth of the principal urban centres was facilitated by a mixture of shipping routes and canal networks. An early impetus to the development of the City of Dublin came from the completion of the first new canal outside of continental Europe, the Newry Canal. Pre-dating the more historically famous Bridgewater Canal, the 1742 Newry Canal linked the coalfields of Tyrone with the port of Newry, enabling regular coastal shipments of coal to Dublin. This linkage provided the Irish coal owners with the opportunity to compete with English, Welsh and Scottish coal.[4]

49

Figure 8: UK Tkm Market Share
Rail and Water in 1910.

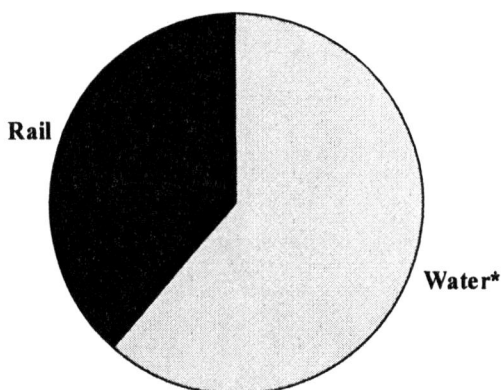

Rail

Water*

Source: Armstrong, J (1987) "The Role of Coastal Shipping in UK Transport:
An Estimate of Comparative Transport Movements in 1910." *Journal
of Transport History*, Vol.8. pp.164-78.

Evidence of a sizeable coastal trade can be traced back to at least the 1600s.
Before the development of the canal system in the 1700s, coastal shipping was the
only effective way of moving heavy goods to the growing industrial and
population centres. The movement of essential freight cargoes around the UK
coast was a key factor in the industrial revolution and the rise of major urban
centres, London in particular. Port cities like Liverpool and Hull were served by
canal and river systems which integrated with the deepsea trades in the ports. The
Leeds and Liverpool and the Trent and Mersey canals linked Liverpool deepsea,
shortsea and coastal routes with the industrial heartlands of Northern England and
the Midlands. The waterways of South Yorkshire, plus the River Trent Navigation
linked the Yorkshire coal fields and steel industry with Hull's deepsea and coastal
services. The industrial growth of cities and their rapidly increasing populations

created major demand for the movement of the predominant energy source, coal. This led to the coastal linkage of the coalfields of Tyneside, Wearside and Humberside with London.

2.5 De-industrialisation and Shipping Demand

The historic growth of coastal and inland shipping can be viewed as a result of development in heavy industries. Such industrial staples as coal, coke, pit props, ores, steel, aggregates and cement provided the economic foundations for the sector. This was followed later by crude oil and petroleum products. Given this perspective, de-industrialisation, post 1960 was bound to have serious repercussions for shipping.

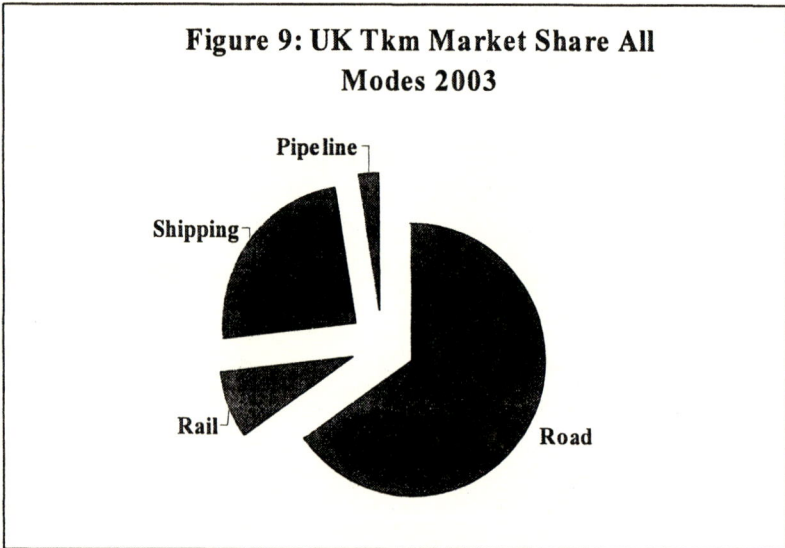

Figure 9: UK Tkm Market Share All Modes 2003

Source: www.DfT.gov.uk

51

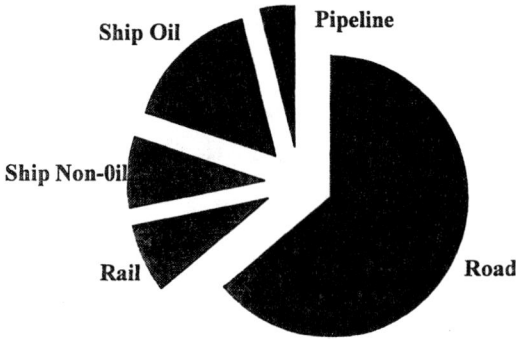

Figure 10: UK Tkm Market Share All Modes & Shipping Total & Non-Oil, 2003.

Source: www.dfT.gov.uk, and *DfT Waterborne Freight in the UK*.

Large volume trades such as coal from North East England, also South Wales, to London and the South East disappeared. The closure or rationalisation of waterside steel plants on the Clyde, Manchester Ship Canal, Dee (Shotton) and also the canal-served Sheffield steel industry, all contributed to big reductions in demand for the carriage of ore, furnace coal, fuel oil and their steel products. Sizeable cement, bulk chemicals and iron ore trades were also lost to coastal shipping as de-industrialisation intensified. In addition to de-industrialisation, rationalisations in the gas and electricity generation industry, led to a massive reduction in waterside served power stations. Later came rationalisations in the oil refining and distribution business; the closure of many of the smaller installations led to the loss of significant small tanker trades.

2.5 1 Industrial Relocation and Restructuring

A fundamental of transport economics is that the demand for transportation services is derived. The demand for freight movement is therefore a function of the volume and spatial spread of economic activity. In the early industrial revolution, industry was dependent on canals, rivers, ports and railheads. Access to these transport networks determined the geographic position of industry. Later came the geographical spread of industry, distribution and population away from (or indifferent to) these networks. During the post WW2 period, major users of coastal and shortsea shipping relocated away from the coastline. In the energy generation sector, even new coal fired power stations were located inland and away from canals – Didcot, Oxfordshire, Fiddlers Ferry, Cheshire, Ratcliffe and West Burton, Nottinghamshire, Rugeley, Staffordshire.

When the American auto-giant Ford first moved to the UK in the post 1920 period, production sites were chosen close to ports. Trafford Park on the banks of the Manchester Ship Canal was to be eventually followed by plants in the ports of Swansea, Dagenham, Liverpool, Southampton. When major global automobile producers opened plants in the UK, post 1970, the trend was to locate inland – Honda in Swindon, Toyota in Derby and Deeside, Peugeot in Coventry. Such developments would not have been possible without progress in road haulage technology and performance enjoying a symbiotic relationship with the strides in road infrastructure development. It has been made evident that in the pre WW2 economy, industry, distribution and population centres were still highly dependent upon water or railway linkages. Developments in the motorway age were to substantially reverse this.

2.6 The Motorway Age

The great industrial centres of the 19th century were either port cities such as Cardiff, Dublin, Glasgow, Liverpool, Manchester and Newcastle or rail and canal served cities – Sheffield, Leeds, Birmingham, Nottingham. By way of contrast, the economic hot spots of the 20th century were motorway served regions such as the M4 corridor between London and Bristol, including growth towns - Slough, Swindon, Reading, Newbury. The trend in the newer industries, post 1960s, was for location away from the congested urban areas to new greenfield sites. Britain's most modern city, Milton Keynes, despite being situated on the West Coast Main Line (WCML), lacks direct railfreight access; it is also located close to the Grand Union Canal, however, the only water activity in the designer city is that of leisure. As light engineering industries and sectors in advanced technology, retail and distribution developed outside of traditional urban industrial, areas the switch to road haulage became paramount. Business parks were often located away from the quayside, close to Motorway connections. In such instances the use of bulk or LoLo container shipping would require a costly and time consuming transfer between ship and truck. The programme[5] for motorway construction in the early 1970s had six main aims:

(1) to alleviate a large number of towns from the trunk route traffics;

(2) to promote economic growth via a strategic road network;

(3) to link remote, less well developed, areas with the more prosperous regions;

(4) to ensure all major towns and cities with populations in excess of 250,000 had motorway access;

(5) to serve all major ports and airports;

(6) to relieve historic towns from the burden of trunk road traffic.

It can be appreciated that these objectives are partly economic and partly social. The early motorways offered great productivity gains to hauliers. Access to the motorway network promoted road haulage growth in two ways:(1) by facilitating efficiency and increased competitiveness; (2) accelerating the pace of industrial relocation.

The trunk roads suffered from acute congestion in urban bottlenecks. The first section of motorway construction in the UK was in fact the Preston by-pass in 1958. Preston had become infamous for its traffic tailbacks as Anglo-Scottish heavy goods movements and tourist traffic to Blackpool and the Lake District converged in the town. By alleviating such haulage hold-ups, driver productivity could be increased by as much as 50%. This meant that long haul routes could be scheduled within the drivers' normal working hours. London-Irish traffic could be routed via the short sea crossing at Stranraer. Increased productivity on such routes as return Liverpool-London hauls could be achieved, when previously this run would have necessitated the driver lodging out in order to comply with the driver's hours legislation. Exampling the impact that these gains had for road haulage *vis-à-vis* shipping is the reduction of the ICI coastal fleet. The vertical integration between the two waterfront located chemical plants at Runcorn and Fleetwood had been maintained by coastal shipping up until the motorway age. Motorway development allowed one driver to complete 2x120 mile round trips in a 12 hour shift, a 100% increase in productivity in the movement of hazardous freights including vinyl chloride.[6] Such just-in-time developments facilitated a swift transition from water to road and ultimately led to the demise of the ICI coaster and barge fleet. In the 1960s, ICI owned a fleet of 26 vessels in the 150-1000dwt category; by the late 1970s, the fleet had been largely divested. In the West of England, oil traffics on the Gloucester-Sharpness Canal were lost as a result of the construction of the M5 and M50.[7]

In March 1960, only 160km of motorway existed in the UK; by 1970 this had grown to 1056kms, with over 560km under construction.[8] Motorway development instigated corridor growth along its perimeters. Towns and cities promoted and vaunted their motorway linkages: Leeds at the cross roads of the North-South M1 and the East-West M62, proclaimed itself the "motorway city". Manchester became the "motorway port". Regional authorities the length and breadth of the country encouraged industry to locate on the strength of motorway linkages. Emphasis on motorway access resulted in shifts in the location of industrial and retail activity away from the traditional industrial towns, towards motorway intersections. Greenfield sites were developed without regard to any water or rail freight linkages. The M4 "Golden Corridor," attracted business as a result of its motorway links between London, the Thames Valley and Heathrow Airport. Many of the globally oriented high technology businesses located to the corridor in the motorway age, viewing this location as the only possible choice in the UK.[9] If London and Liverpool Docks had been the fulcrum of England's economic activity in the industrial age, the Golden Corridor enjoyed predominance in the information technology era. As business activity located away from quaysides the use of shipping became increasingly problematic, involving costly transhipment from road to water.

2.6.1 The Growth of Road Haulage

Enjoying a symbiotic relationship with the processes of industrial relocation and de-industrialisation, growth in the road haulage industry had a detrimental impact on domestic and shortsea shipping. Developments in road haulage were integral to the way industrial and retail sectors were evolving. The attributes of road haulage logistics provide flexibility and significant competitive advantages *vis-à-vis* shipping and railways. The 2002 Freight Study Group

56

Report, *Freight on Water: A New Perspective,* [10] identified the crucial differences
between road haulage and water transport within the context of customer needs:

Road transport provides:
- small loads;
- frequent deliveries;
- fast deliveries;
- competitive prices;
- low stockholding/inventory costs;
- flexibility and convenience.

Water transport provides:
- large deliveries;
- infrequent deliveries;
- slow deliveries;
- limited flexibility;
- higher prices;
- higher stockholding/inventory costs.

What the customer tends to want:
- small or just-in-time deliveries;
- flexibility;
- low prices;
- low stockholding/inventory costs;
- high service levels.

From this focus on supply and demand factors, it is evident that road haulage
attributes have proved to be highly compatible with what customers want. This
helps explain the shift away from rail and shipping to road haulage from the inter-
war period onwards. The rapid growth of road haulage can be clearly detected as
a transport step-change in the inter-war years. Transport historian, Derek
Aldcroft, saw WW1 as a "watershed" in the history of transport, with the new
modes of road transport and civil aviation developing rapidly and the old
established modes – railways, canals, shipping, tramways – in decline. [11] The
move towards faster, more frequent, smaller unit deliveries was facilitated by
developments in road haulage organisation. One leading coastal shipping
operator was at the forefront of these changes in the supply chain. In 1914 the

Manchester based company, Fisher Renwick Manchester-London Steamers, had the second highest annual performance in the UK coastal trades at close to 0.9btkm.[12] Transport historian, Gordon Mustoe's work, *Fisher Renwick: A Transport Saga, 1874-1972,*[13] traces the evolution of this shipping company into trunk road haulage operation. The liner company was an early user of the Manchester Ship Canal, following its opening in 1894, providing a liner service to Shadwell Basin in London. The surplus of army trucks post WW1 provided the opportunity for the line to expand a road fleet for its port connections. Improvements in truck technology, with the Ford T models and later Scammells, allowed the line to diversify into trunk haulage.

In the 1920s the line initiated trunk road services between Manchester and London and in 1934 they were able to offer an overnight service which featured a driver changeover system at the journey halfway point in Meriden. As a consequence of this co-ordination, driver efficiency was maximised and the drivers' domestic life was not disrupted by lodging away from home. This can now be recognised as an early example of road based just-in-time logistics. The business connection with the innovatory US truck manufacturer was consolidated by the line's family owner, Major George Renwick, becoming a Director of Scammell in 1926. The logistics lessons of WW1 and rapid advances in truck performance led to more and more of the traffics being diverted to road trunk operations at the expense of the shipping fleet. Initially the higher value freights, including chests of tea and margarine, were diverted to the "continuous" overnight service, which was viewed as favourable to the 2.5 days coastal sealeg. The introduction of eight wheel Scammell's, with their increased carrying capacity, brought economies of scale. This contributed to the company's withdrawal from shipping in the late 1930s, with the remaining vessels being sold to Coast Lines.

The switch to road haulage operations can readily be understood as facilitating the decentralised trends in business location. The development of business activity outside of the traditional Dublin port area typifies this trend. The new technology industries have located up to 65kms outside of the city. The supply chain to Europe that this generated is oriented towards truck and RoRo ferry combinations. The road tkm generated by this process is often maximised by the preference for the Northern route by many hauliers. This entails the long haul North from the Dublin region to the ports of Warren Point, Belfast and Larne, in order to seek the shortsea passage to Scotland. Similar developments in the predominantly water-based agricultural trades of Kent, Essex and East Anglia led to the London bound produce being diverted from shipping to road haulage. This process also involved diversification from shipowning into road haulage.[14] The move by shipping companies into haulage can now be recognised as a contributory factor in the decline of domestic and shortsea shipping. In fact, many of today's leading transport and logistics companies have their roots in shipping. The culmination of Fisher Renwick's diversification process from shipping into road haulage was completed when its 600 strong vehicle fleet became part of the world's largest truck hire company, the US based Ryder Group in 1973. Similarly, the Leith based whaling and coastal shipping operator, Christian Salvesen, built on its expertise to manage frozen foodstuffs to become one of Europe's leading logistics providers for food products. This entailed leaving the coal trades in the 1980s, selling all its vessels and even surrendering the secure income of the management of Central Electricity Generating Board colliers.

One of Britain's fastest growing haulage groupings in the early motorway years, Transport Development Group, had its pedigree in the Thames and Humber based tug and barge operating company, General Lighterage Co. The company demonstrated business acumen in its inter-war period list of company acquisitions, including wharfage, warehousing and road haulage as well as tug

59

and barge fleets.[15]   The diversion of shipping traffic away from the Port of London in WW2 enhanced the growth of road haulage.   This direction was aided in the post-war period by the continuing labour problems on the docks which affected lighterage operations.   Denationalisation of road haulage and the construction of a national motorway network, 1950-70s provided increased opportunities.   By 1969 the group operated 4,500 lorries, as opposed to 150 in 1950.[16]   Coast Lines provided another example of diversification into haulage.   In 1971 Coast Lines was purchased by the UKs leading shipowner, P&O, who consolidated a fleet of 6,000 trucks, including trailer services to Ireland and the European Continent.[17]

2.6.2 Development in Truck Performance.

Improvements in truck performance has made trunk haulage increasingly competitive with shipping.   Developments in road surfacing, vehicle suspension, tyres and braking all contributed to increased speeds and, therefore, performance. Progressive lifting of regulatory speed limits was successfully promoted by early road lobbyists such as the 1895 formed, Self-Propelled Traffic Association.[18]   The consistently raised speed limit trends up to the motorway age are presented in Table 5.   The enhanced carrying capacity of trucks is reflected in the up-grading of the UK legislation on vehicle weights.   Table 6 shows a constantly increasing permitted weight. The increases in carrying capacity and speeds were to boost modal competitiveness as tkm costs were reduced and driver and fuel efficiency maximised.   For the haulage operator this meant that more tkm could be covered with fewer trucks and drivers.[19]

2.6.3 The Road Haulage Lobby

The rise in permitted truck size and speed can also be perceived as a result of successful lobbying.   The development of road haulage in the UK has been accompanied by a free enterprise ideology and lobbying stance. From the early days of motor lorries the ethos has been very much one of enterprise, with antipathy toward state involvement and trade union organisation. The opportunities afforded by the 1926 General Strike, (when the rail and port network was closed for a week) gave the industry a foothold in the nation's freight markets. The post WW2 nationalisation programme, leading to the state take-over of trunk haulage in 1948, was to become a cause célèbre of the industry. Harper and Birch's history of the Road Haulage Association, *On the Move,*[20] traces the campaigns of the lobby group. These range from a virulent anti-nationalisation stance, to lorry drivers' hours, vehicle weights and speeds, road tax and fuel excise duty, plus dockgate delays as a result of trade labour unrest. The haulage lobby has proved to be a powerful voice in Westminster, exerting consistent pressure on government for favourable regulation

Table 5: UK Heavy Truck Speed Limits, 1905-2005.	
Year	Speed Limit MPH
1905	5
1922	12
1928	20
1957	30
1967	70 Motorways
1984	60 Motorways
1992	60/56 Motorways*
Source: Armstrong, J .et.al. (2003) *Companion to the British Road Haulage Industry*. London: Science Museum. p.367	

*From 1992 all new trucks over 12 tonnes gross were fitted with speed limitors in accordance with EC regulations. Initially these were set at 60 mph but a 90kph/56mph limit was later phased in.

Table 6: UK Haulage Weights Limits, 1905-2001		
		Gross Weights
Year	Rigid + Trailer	Articulated
1905	20.0	
1922	22.0	18.5
1947	32.0	22.0
1955	32.0	24
1983	32.52	38
1993	35.0	38
1999	40.0	40
2001	44**	44*
Source: ARMSTRONG, J .et.al. (2003) *Companion to the British Road Haulage Industry.* London: Science Museum. pp.353-4.		

** from 1994, 44 tonne gross weight were permitted when dealing with road-rail intermodal movements.[21]

2.6.4 Road Haulage Attains An Unassailable Position?

The dramatic rise of road haulage in the post 1945 period eclipsed both rail and shipping as the premier freight transport mode. Increases in the size and speed of lorries, accompanied by fuel efficiency gains and a comprehensive road building programme, have all boosted the attraction of the road mode. The enduring levels of competition stimulated by the relative ease of market entry has ensured that price competition is always vigorous. The trunk trades between Northern and Southern Britain have increased at the expense of railfreight and coastal shipping. Reliability, flexibility and just-in-time logistics has helped to facilitate road's dominance. In the 1960s, a round trip between Dundee and London would require at least seven days to complete by road (at least legally!).

By the 1980s, it would have been possible to make the round trip in 2.5 days. Every road improvement scheme has leant itself to improving road efficiency and been to the detriment of shipping. For example, road upgrades to the South West of Bristol made it feasible for road tankers to complete a round trip, within the permitted nine hours driving, between the Milford Haven refinery and the petrol stations of Somerset and North Devon. Such factors were instrumental in the closure of a number of coastal shipping served petroleum distribution depots. The steady increase in vehicle payloads and improvements in fuel efficiency has also improved road haulage efficiency and competitiveness. It also became evident in the high unemployment years of the 1980s and early 1990s that the supply of drivers, boosted by stocks of temporary agency staff, had brought about a fiercely cost competitive and highly flexible labour force. The economic pressure of a dynamic road haulage sector has in several instances stifled new shipping initiatives in recent years. There is some evidence to show that competing lorry firms act in concert when faced with modal-competition. By reducing rates, the hauliers make life difficult for the new entrant. This can be accepted as aggressive, piranha like market behaviour.

2.6.5 The Piranha Thesis?

The development of this thesis is a result of the author's study of competitive behaviour between road hauliers and new shipping and rail ventures. The ability of lorry firms to adjust their rates downwards has served as a barrier to alternative transport modes. The early experience of the Port of Boston's rail-sea inter-modal steel transhipment was marred somewhat by intensive road competition, with hauliers cutting rates by up to £1.50 per tonne.[22] In June 1994 optimism was reported for a new container feeder service linking the West Country port, Falmouth with the deepsea hub, Thamesport. The intention was for a weekly service to integrate with the round the world container liner services of the major Taiwanese carrier, Evergreen Line. Falmouth port director, Mike Deeks, heralded the initiative, claiming that the service:

> ...has enormous potential in Cornwall and Devon, which for many years have been disadvantaged by the very high costs of transporting containers by road to the deepsea ports.[23]

Two staple Cornish export traffics were identified as the core for the estimated break-even point of 30 containers: powdered China Clay and Bottled Steam Beer from the Redruth Brewery. Despite the apparent demand the service failed after only six weeks; the required traffic levels had failed to materialise. Shippers preferred to keep their contracts with hauliers, fearing increased haulage rates if the feeder venture proved unsuccessful. The problem of concerted competitive pressure from hauliers is a European wide phenomena. Between 2000 and 2005 a number of new European short sea and feeder services failed after a short market life. These include:

- Southampton-Bayonne;
- Toulon-Livorno;
- Sete-Majorca.
- Zeebrugge-Le.Havre-Bristol,
- Cork-Liverpool.[24]

Such failures can partly be understood as the failure of shipping to adequately compete with road haulage. Also, the problem is trying to convince shippers that a viable alternative to road haulage exists. Mr.Willy Deckers of the Belgium Short Sea Promotion Centre referred to a slow but steady increase in shortsea shipping in Flemish ports in 2002, adding that:

> There will not be a boom; there will be steady growth. The shipper is the one who has to decide how he wants to ship his cargo. We need to change mentalities from a truck reflex to an inter-modal reflex.[25]

64

It can be accepted that achieving modal switch to coastal domestic shipping faces formidable barriers. The same can also be said of European shortsea LoLo shipping attempting to compete with RoRo shipping

2.7 The Development of RoRo Shipping

Somewhat complementary to the growth of roadhaulage is the rise of shortsea RoRo shipping on the Irish Sea, North Sea and Channel routes. The impact of RoRo shipping has been to totally re-shape the pattern of trade between continental Europe, the British Isles and Ireland. At its most intense the Dover-Calais schedule offers a turn up and go service at 30 minute intervals. The North Channel shortsea route, displayed in Table 7, between Scotland and Northern Ireland attracts road traffic on the strength of its short crossing times. British Railways early ventures into RoRo shipping in 1956 focused on the market attributes of "the shortest sea route" to Ireland , with an "open sea passage – 70 minutes". [26]

Table 7: North Channel Ferry Intensity, Summer 2005.		
Line	Route	Daily Frequency
Stena Line	Belfast-Stranraer	6
P&0 Irish Sea	Troon-Larne	2
P&0 Irish Sea	Cairnryan-Larne	7
Source: www.directferriesfreight.com		

This gave road haulage operators the ultimate flexibility in combining their schedules with ferry sailings. The upsurge in RoRo traffic in the Dover Straits and such East Coast ports as Harwich, Ipswich, Hull and Immingham, can be understood very much in correlation with the shift in the direction of trade brought about by European integration. Concentration on East Coast ports minimised the sea-leg to Europe, ergo the road leg was maximised.

The pattern of RoRo ferry development has been one of concentration on the shortest crossing route, a factor that maximises the road haulage length. As a consequence, such short-sea services as Dover-Calais and Stranraer-Larne have prospered at the expense of LoLo shortsea shipping. An early casualty of the switch to RoRo activity was the Manchester-Amsterdam express liner service. The linking of these two inland ports by small vessels had been a successful example of sea-river shipping. However, the development of large RoRo ferries and the complementary growth of motorway networks on both sides of the Channel contributed to the demise of the service. An extended form of this pattern became evident in the early 1990s in the trades between the Irish Republic and continental Europe. The 1992 publication, *Green Links to Europe,*[27] reported the rapid growth in truck movements via the long haul UK landbridge passage to continental per year. By the Millennium around 1.5mt per annum of Irish freight crossed the UK landbridge, via French,Belgium and Netherlands' ports.[28]

The 1998 failure of the short-lived East Coast Ferries venture shows the difficulties facing operators offering a diagonal alternative to the shortest crossing route. The new entrant line attempted the operation of a scheduled RoRo freight service between Hull and Dunkerque. The harsh reality discovered by the operator was that hauliers preferred to maximise the road leg and minimise the sea leg, not the opposite! Loadings were poor and the new venture quickly ran into irredeemable cash flow difficulties.[29] In Chapter 7 similar problems facing the Rosyth-Zeebrugge RoRo service in the early Millennium will be discussed. The original RoRo Cross-Channel services were carried out by converted WW2 landing craft from 1946 onwards. The lessons learned from the exigencies of WW2 military logistics was found to have a peace-time attraction.[30] A number of factors have contributed to the rise of the intensive shortsea RoRo routes. Initially it was the vertical integration of the vessels into the railway timetable that provided the catalyst for growth. Gradually, as the development in RoRo technology matched the inexorable rise in road transport, the once rail oriented business evolved towards road linkages. The ability to combine foot passengers emanating from the rail system with cars, coaches and heavy goods vehicles provided a lucrative business opportunity for the ferry companies. New entrant competition with the British Rail ferries, Sealink, only served to intensify this trend. Road development and up-grade schemes such as the Anglo-Scottish M6 motorway and A75 trunk road (Carlisle-Stranraer), as well as similar road schemes in Ulster and the Irish Republic, have proved conducive to increased road haulage tkms.

The diversification of Coast Lines into haulage and RoRo operations typifies the trends in the 1960s. Gradually liner services to Ireland from such ports as Bristol, Southampton, Manchester and Glasgow were replaced by short crossing RoRo services from Preston and Liverpool.[31] The net result of the growth of shortsea ferry linkages to and from Ulster/Eire, France, Belgium and the Netherlands has been to relatively reduce the tkm of LoLo shipping. Examples include the transfer of traffics between West Coast UK and the Netherlands from coastal liner services to road haulage-RoRo linkages utilising the Dover Straits crossing. In 1996 it was established that of the total wheeled traffic between Germany and Britain, only 35% was dispatched directly from/to German ports; the remaining 65% was via Dutch (24%), Belgium (32%) and French (44%) ports.[32] It can be noted here how the road haulage leg is maximised and the sea leg minimised, with the French ferry ports situated furthest away from Germany. Figure 11 portrays the high growth rate of RoRo freight through the Port of Dover. It is shown that between 1985 and 2004, road haulage movements via Dover increased by 171%, whilst the average growth rate for all UK port volumes was 24% in the same period. In 2005 Dover announced its highest

Figure 11: Comparative Growth - Dover RoRo Freight and UK Total Port Volumes (1985=100).

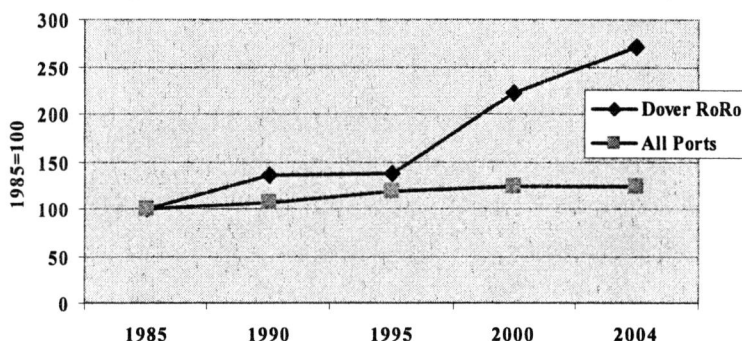

Source: www.doverport.co.uk and DfT Transport Statistics

freight vehicles passing through the Port. Furthermore, the occasion was marked by Dover's Chief Executive, Bob Goldfield's prediction that traffic was set to double within a thirty year period.[33] Economic growth in the Irish Republic has induced a surge in shortsea RoRo shipping to Dublin.

Table 8 : Central Route Dublin RoRo Services, Summer 2005		
Destination	Line	Sailings Per Day
Holyhead	Stena Line	5
Holyhead	Irish Ferries	5
Liverpool	P&O Irish Sea Ferries	1
Birkenhead	Norse-Merchant Ferries	2
Heysham	Norse-Merchant Ferries	2
Source: www.directferriesfreight.com		

It was reported in July 2000 that, "The port's buoyant transformation has been a result of the booming Irish economy which has spurred a massive surge in unitised traffic. This now accounts for 74% of total throughput, with RoRo handling accounting for 52% of the overall volumes. The capacity utilisation rate for RoRo traffic was, according to a KPMG study prepared for the Dublin Chamber of Commerce, on target to increase by110% in 2007."[34] Table 8 details the intensity of Dublin's Irish Sea RoRo services in summer 2005.

One well established shortsea tanker service to be undermined by the rise of RoRo shipping was the bulk movement of Guinness beer from Dublin to the Runcorn bottling and canning plant. The purpose built 1732 dwt, *Miranda Guinness*, was replaced in the early 1990s by road tankers using the RoRo service to Liverpool, generating at least 260 weekly round road trips over the congested Widnes-Runcorn Bridge. In the Scottish Islands trades the switch to truck-RoRo combinations was to have a similar detrimental impact on the Clyde Puffer services. For over a 100 years the Isle of Islay, Caol Ila Whisky distillery, was served by Clyde Puffer ships. Malted barley, coal and empty casks were all carried to the island by the small coastal trading Puffers. The end product, malt whisky, was carried back to Glasgow for both domestic consumption and the export trades. Developments in RoRo shipping and truck technology allowed the distillery to be served direct by road hauliers, bringing the demise of this trade for the Puffers, post 1960s.[35]

The regulatory controls on EU drivers' hours have an impact on determining ferry crossing route decisions. Where distances make it difficult to achieve arrival at the Dover Straits ferry terminals within the HGV legal driving time (9/10 hours driving maximum in one shift) alternatives to trunk-road haulage may be considered. This is the rationale of the Scottish Office promoted Rosyth-Zeebrugge service. The location of significant light industry and computer assembly in the Scottish lowland – "Silicon Glen" – has provided opportunities for transportation to Northern Europe. Part of the transport problem, however, is the long trunk leg of 750 kilometres to the intensive ferry services of the Dover Straits. The rationale behind the development of the Rosyth-Zeebrugge RoRo service was originally to offer daily sailings, with door-to-door journey times compatible with road haulage flows using the shorter Dover Straits and Humber crossings. In Chapter 7 it will be seen that such ventures face considerable barriers when challenging the shorter crossing routes.

2.7.1 The Troubled Port Industry

The development of the UK port structure and organisation post 1945 did not prove conducive to a dynamic shipping industry. Many of the major ports suffered from acute under investment, congestion and poor industrial relations. The National Dock Labour Scheme (NDLS) may have provided job security for stevedores, but it also loaded up excessive labour costs on the ports, shipowners and ultimately the shippers. Maritime historian, Alan Jamieson, has identified the problems of a fragmented, under invested, inert, backward looking port sector, marred by polarised industrial relations.[36] On the River Thames barge operations were subject to NDLS labour provision and conditions. Many ports restricted their normal working hours to daylight Monday-Saturday mid-day. In retrospect, the scheme can now be acknowledged as an attempt to historically redress the excesses of casual labour exploitation on the docks. The need to supply dignified, skilled work under regulated, safe working conditions was an admirable objective of the socialist planners of the post 1945 Labour Government. However, what was not envisaged was the negative competitive impact the scheme was to have on port efficiency, shortsea and coastal shipping in particular.

Ports that remained outside of the scheme were able to gain competitive advantage by providing lower cost, flexible and reliable services (see Port of Felixstowe, see below, pp.133-35). Moreover, road haulage competition with coastal shipping was regularly boosted by the endemic labour problems of the scheme ports, resulting in strikes, over-time bans and go-slows. At a time when road haulage was benefiting from vast leaps in productivity, atrophy in the ports could only serve to the detriment of domestic shipping. In 1955, for example, the newly de-regulated haulage industry benefited from the coastal shipping disruptions brought about by 112 strikes in UK ports, leading to 693,209 working days lost, as UK dockers became the nation's most strike prone workforce.[37] In addition to the labour problems, the nationalised scheme ports which formed the British Transport Ports Group, faced the problem of limited access to investment finances. Treasury restraints led to limitations on capital funding. This meant that developments in cargo handling technology were denied. The result was that the ports had to persevere with antiquated labour intensive equipment and worsening productivity. For example, the round trip between Duisburg and the Hull would take an average of 14 days in the 1960s with further cargo handling delays proving commonplace.[38] Currently the round-trip between the two ports is feasible in 4-5days. This reflects a 9 to 10 day saving, primarily as a result of improved port performance. In the British Waterways sector, state control failed to achieve development of such river systems as the Severn, Trent and Weaver, with limited network maintenance, let alone improvements in the vital task of dredging in order to maintain navigable channels.

The Thames barge and wharfage operator, General Lighterage (Holdings), made the diversification into road transport holdings partly as a result of the continuing labour problems in the London Docks, post 1950. With 1,200 barges and 16 wharves on the Thames the group found itself vulnerable to strikes which paralysed its assets. The diversification into road haulage holdings in the denationalised and deregulated market post 1951, was a way of avoiding the risks associated with labour strife.[39]

2.7.2 The Gentrification of Port Areas

One unexpected outcome of the mix of de-industrialisation and industrial relocation has been the transformation of port areas into desirable residential quarters. The marketing of properties, accompanied by rising prices, has forced a reassessment of the waterfront, its use and its valuation. On the Thames, Manchester Ship Canal and at Gloucester Basin the property interest has developed an often haughty and unsympathetic stance towards shipping. The process of "gentrification" evident in the London Borough of Greenwich's once industrial waterfront has led to opposition to the continued handling of grain traffics in the close proximity of the new housing. Some 25 working wharves were lost to shipping activity up-river of the Thames Barrier between 1987 and 1997[40] Likewise, it is highly apparent that throughout the 1980s, the Manchester Ship Canal Company was more enthusiastic about developing such prestigious retail projects as the Trafford Centre along its banks than pursuing new shipping businesses. As a consequence, Britain's only sizeable canal faced the prospects of closure. At this juncture, it must also be stated that in recent years, the current owners of the canal, Peel Holdings, have been much more proactive in promoting shipping[41].

A similar detrimental effect has been created by the rise of the water leisure business. As canals and rivers have attracted leisure seekers in large numbers, the dependence on commercial shipping has diminished. A particular criticism of the waterways custodian, British Waterways, has been the focus on leisure and environment at the expense of freight shipping. Pleasure boating is popular, brings in considerable revenues and does not require the high level of infrastructure expenditure that shipping demands, obviating much of the cost of dredging. The deterioration of the River Weaver's water level has jeopardised coastal tanker services to the chemical industries of Mid-Cheshire. By the late 1990s the tanker vessel, *St Kearan*, which was purpose built for the River Weaver, was finding it increasingly difficult to load beyond 50% capacity. Draft restrictions forced loading from road tankers to take place some 24kms downstream. The additional delay and expense that this transhipment process necessitated eventually destroyed any advantages that the coastal tanker option enjoyed over road haulage for bulk deliveries to the Scottish West Coast. The tank freight was lost to the Green Highway and an estimated 25 million tkm was added to the UKs roads, including the rural lanes of Cheshire and the winding roads of the West Highlands of Scotland. The *St. Kearan* was sold in 2001, renamed *Georgie* and transferred to the Russian flag.

The condition of the River Weaver, which links the industrial Mid-Cheshire area with the Manchester Ship Canal (ultimately the River Mersey and the Irish Sea) became the subject of the Parliamentary Committee on the Environment, Transport and Regional Affairs (2000-1). Evidence submitted referred to the neglected state of the River, leading to the loss of traffic. The evidence was taken from a number of interested parties including two shipowners, the river pilot and the transport manager of one of the Mid-Cheshire area's chemical industries.[42] Concern expressed by these stakeholders was that British Waterways was not fulfilling its obligation to dredge the River. The river pilot was particularly concerned by the risk of doing serious damage to the *St. Kearan* due to constant groundings on the loaded outward voyage. The situation that small ports and inland shipping now face can be seen as a result of the high property prices that waterside developments generate. The emphasis on residential, office and leisure investments is obviously a factor in the decline of domestic shipping.

A number of historic forces shaping the demand for the Green Highway have now been examined. The factors that led to a rise in demand in the Industrial Revolution have been identified. Conversely, the decline in demand has been associated with the changes in transport and distribution in the Post-Industrial Age. It next remains to consider the nature of shipping supply and demand in three selected, contrasting, shipping sections: (1) the East Coast Collier Trades, (2) the Thames Sailing Barge Trades, (3) The Irish Sea Trades.

2.8 Route One:The East Coast Coal Trade.

The importance of the East Coast collier trade cannot be understated in the development of the Green Highway. It will become evident how the technical developments in the logistics of the trade have had positive implications for modern shipping. The current predominance of North Sea oil flows can now be accepted as a contemporary parallel to the pre-1970s dominance of the coal trades. North Sea oil has returned the East Coast of Britain to its premier, "route one" status in the British coastal shipping hierarchy. Whilst today large shuttle tankers ply their 100,000 tonne cargoes of North Sea crude oils down the East Coast to Scottish, English, Welsh and Irish refineries, historically large volumes of coal traffic dominated on the East Coast route. The growth of London as a major metropolis was made possible by the vast amounts of coastal traffics that served the energy demands of the city. Figure 12 represents the main trunk route of the East Coast collier trades into the Thames and Medway. The coal traffics from the North along with the wheat and barley traffics of Kent, Essex, Suffolk and Norfolk provided the basic prerequisites of economic growth, energy, heat and foodstuffs.

There is some evidence to support the view that the Romans started the coal trade and the first documented records from the 12th century show a Tyneside-London flow well developed.[43] From the 17th century onwards improvements in both the technology and efficiency of sailing ships and the ports they served led to a supply side spur to economic growth. The coal trades were at the heart of industrial progress in the eighteenth century. Important industries were dependent upon coal, especially iron working, glass making, brewing, distilling, sugar baking, soap boiling, dying, calico printing, lime burning, brick making, engineering and steam powered industry.[44] Ville's paper on the link between shipping productivity and the supply of North East coal[45] provides a clear picture of a dynamic innovative industry between 1700 and 1850. 45,000 seamen were employed in the East Coast collier trades (1830) serving on an estimated 1,400 vessels (1824). The sector was not only an important source of regional seafaring employment but also proved a valuable training ground for the demands of the Royal Navy. The Stuart Kings came to regard the collier fleet as the backbone of their Navy. In 1615 it was reported that the trades served as a nursery school of seamen; and exemplifying this point, in 1746, the famous British navigator, Captain Cook, began his seagoing career as an apprentice in the collier trades.[46]

Before the emergence of steam propulsion in the mid-late 1800s, sailing ship design and operations enjoyed significant improvement. In the 1700s vessels averaged eight round trips between the North East and the Thames per year. By the end of the century this had increased to nine or ten and by the 1830s some sailing colliers were reported to be making up to fourteen round trips as more and more voyages were attempted in the winter months.[47]

In this period the North East coal trade bore many of the operational challenges that the modern shipping and transport operator would recognise. The emphasis on improved loading and discharge techniques not only reduced labour costs but also served the need to improve vessel turn around time. Early intermodal linkages were provided by horse drawn rail wagonways which served the loading staithes. On the River Wear primitive (but visionary) attempts at containerisation were developed with coal being transhipped from barges to ships in chaldron tubs. Low bridges across the Thames led to problem of accessing the river's upper reaches. This problem was eventually solved by vessels with hinged masts that dropped down to deck level, thus proving to the precursor for the "flat iron" steam collier and the modern low air-draft profile sea-river ship. The intense North Sea highway even developed the equivalent of the modern motorway truck stop with the improvement of harbour havens of shelter in Bridlington, Seaton, Whitby, Scarborough and Burlington.[48] Between 1821 and 1836, 117 vessels, which would otherwise have been at risk to storm conditions, took shelter in the haven of Scarborough harbour.[49] Not only did these havens shelter the colliers but also allowed crews to take on food provisions and fresh water. Safety was also aided by the development of steam tugs post 1830s. Tugs could also offer time-saving towage services to vessels when arriving or departing in bad weather conditions. Before tug assistance, the problem of an Easterly winter gale could trap vessels in the rivers and harbours of the North East for periods up to four weeks. The concerns of the modern logistician to minimize stock levels were already latent in the eighteenth century with efficiency in the operation of colliers equating to a more secure supply chain of coal, resulting in less need to stockpile, especially in the winter months. Before the advent of steam tugs, sailing colliers over the 240 tons size were faced with a transhipment process in the Tyne Estuary; steam tugs assisted 400 tonners up into the City Quays of Newcastle, thus engendering economies of scale. [50]

The rapidly increased traffic demand in the Port of London led to congestion and delays in the eighteenth century; and this was a problem with which many transport operators today would emphasise. Collier operators had to take turns with London's deepsea traders in waiting for discharge berths. The solution lay in the separation of traffics by the building of the West and East India Docks network in the early 1800s. The non-tidal docks provided berths for the deepsea general merchandise trades. This left the tidal wharves and jetties free for the bulk discharge of coal. The rapid development of steam technology in the mid-eighteenth century had major implications for the coastal trades. The first practical steamship was the 10hp tug, *Charlotte Dundas*, of 1802, which had some early success on the Forth-Clyde canal towing barges. The canal had been intended as an East-West short cut and safe alternative to the stormy Pentland

Firth of the North Scottish coastline. Sailing vessels up to 100 tons could transit the canal but were dependent on wind conditions. Steam towage was potentially a major time-saving advantage for sailing ships. However, the canal's proprietors were more concerned by the potential damage to the canal banks from the steamer's wash, feeling repair costs would outweigh the tugs' revenue earning potential. The Duke of Bridgewater was to show more imagination, spotting the future potential of steam towage as a replacement for horse-drawn barges, the Duke immediately ordered eight steam tugs for his canal system.[51] The Swansea steam tug, *Monarch*, symbolised the state-of-art and was immortalised as the mighty tug towing the *Fighting Temeraire* in Turner's famous painting of 1838.

The advantages of steam propulsion quickly spread to the coal trades. During the mid 1850s steam colliers were making significant inroads into the market. By providing a more reliable service – less impeded by tide and weather conditions - the steamers were able to increase productivity. In the 1860s the steamers were managing 57 round trips; this was four times greater than the annual round trips of the sailing colliers. Improvements in vessel and cargo handling technology brought about an average of 70 roundtrips by 1895.[52] The consistent improvement in the economics of steam colliers ensured competitiveness with rail. By the mid-1850s Palmer's Jarrow shipyard on Tyneside was leading the way in pioneering the specialised shipbuilding of standard colliers. A local joke of the time was that Palmers built the steamers by the mile and cut them off as required![53] Market integration and concentration also brought the economies of scale and enabled the colliers to sustain competitiveness. In 1896, a grouping of eight separate shipowners and London coal merchants amalgamated into the William Cory & Son company, leading to Cory's control of 70% of London coal imports.[54]

Economic Historian, John Armstrong, has contended that coastal shipping in this period made a positive contribution to economic growth and welfare:

> The continued evolution of urbanisation and industrialisation – dependent almost wholly on coal for heat, light and power – would likely have been retarded if the operating costs of coastal ships had not been reduced so drastically.[55]

Coastal shipping efficiencies contributed to the falling price of delivered coal. Table 9 shows the correlation between decreasing collier rates and coal prices.

Table 9: Collier Rates & London Coal Price Indices 1870-1913		
Period	London Coal Price index	Collier Rate Index
1870-1874	100	100
1875-1879	84.0	85.8
1880-1884	70.1	69.2
1885-1889	68.7	61.3
1890-1894	77.1	56.9
1895-1899	67.4	54.6
1900-1904	78.8	53.6
1905-1909	72.6	49.7
1910-1913	81.3	54.6
Source: Armstrong, J. "Late Nineteenth-Century Freight Rates Revisited: Some Evidence from the British Coastal Coal trade." *International Journal of Maritime History*, V1, No.2 . December. 1994. pp.45-81.		

In 1948 24.7mt of coal was moved around the UK coast, 84% of total coastal tonnages.[56] The long decline of King Coal was becoming evident in the late 1950s as alternative fuels were used in industry, on the railways and as a source of domestic heating. By the 1990s the last cargoes of Newcastle coal were shipped.

Figure 12: Route One, East Coast Collier Trade

The coal fired power stations that remained were dependent on imported coal. As a consequence, the coastal trading of coal had all but disappeared.

This short review of the North East-Thames coal trades provides an early example of "Route One" in the British supply chain. The massive demand for coal in the Industrial Revolution and up until the 1970s was met by a constant up-rating of shipping scale and performance, enabling costs to be consistently reduced. The close location of coal mines to river and coast loading terminals facilitated relatively easy and cost effective transfer of coal to the colliers. Similarly, the riverside siting of power stations and gasworks along the banks of the Thames leant for seamless discharge directly to stockpiles. Under such conditions the premier position of the colliers was unassailable by modal competition.[57] It can be accepted that it was the shift in energy strategy that was to have a significant and detrimental impact on the trade. As such, the major decline in coastal shipping activity, measured in terms of tkm, is explained as a result of dramatic changes in energy consumption.

2.9 The Thames Barge Tradition

If the East Coast collier trades were characterised by their concentrated high volume routes serving urban demand, the trades of the Thames sailing (and motorised) barges can now be appreciated as low volume carriers supplying a fragmented, often rural, market. Linking the agricultural regions with the demands of London, fleets of sailing barges worked the East Coast and the Thames and Medway estuaries. These vessels proved to be exceptional survivors as they continued to trade long after sail had disappeared from all other trades. The last sailing barge was built in 1930. Well before the upsurge of steam and motor powered coastal tonnage, these two/three man crew barges had served important freight flows. The creation of London as a major population centre and world city was dependent upon supplies of coal, wheat, aggregates and cement.

The Thames sailing barge was at the forefront of domestic trades linking the country and the city, rural and urban areas stretching from Portland to the Humber. These 25-150 tonne vessels connected London with a wide and varied range of ports, including those of the creeks of Kent, Essex, Suffolk and Norfolk, where limited shipping access was common. *The Essex Chronicle* in March 1829 considered the lack of harbours along the Essex coast:

> Along this coastline from Tilbury Fort to Harwich, an extent of nearly 100 miles, there does not exist a single harbour.[58]

The barges could obviate the harbour shortage problem in Essex by grounding in shallow waters and maintaining cargo operations in the creeks and on the beaches. The shallow draft of the barges was a design feature specifically for the penetration of just such locations. The sailing barge tradition had helped to keep small creek ports competitive. The vessels were highly flexible in that their shallow drafts and flat keels helped them to penetrate many up-river locations which would otherwise have remained un-served by pre motorised road transport. In addition, many of these craft had the ability to drop their sail masts from the vertical to the horizontal deck level. This facilitated passage to air draft restricted inland ports such as Norwich which had railway bridges whose height would have impeded the passage of fixed mast, high superstructure vessels. The barge, *Cygnet,* could sail up to farmyard locations with a draft of just 18". It was jokingly said that this barge was capable of sailing on wet grass![59] The low cost flexibility of these vessels enabled them to trade under sail up until the 1960s. Although by the inter-war years they had begun to lose market share to steam and motor coasters and, more particularly, the motor lorry.

The work-based autobiography of barge skipper, Bob Roberts, *Coasting Bargemaster*, details the concentrated trading pattern of these vessels and the skills of their crews.[60] Figure 13 illustrates the London and the Thames estuary regions of Kent, Essex and East Anglia, where the barges plied the majority of their trades. Although these vessels were capable of two short-distance cargoes a week in times of good weather, the storms of the East Coast could also severely disrupt their trades. One example of the weather delays incurred, provided by Captain Bob Roberts, is the inter-war trip of the 210 tonne payload barge, *Martinet*.[61] After loading oil-cake in the Port of London, the *Martinet* proceeded to the Norfolk inland port of Wells, with the up-stream passage being aided by a small motor launch acting as a tug. Following the discharge, three weeks were spent alongside, awaiting a favourable wind before the downstream passage could be attempted. Several more weeks were spent in adverse weather conditions returning to the vessel's Thames homeport, Greenhithe, leaving the skipper to reflect on the erratic earnings and accident prone nature of life in the sail trades:

> It had been an unlucky trip all round, for the freightage was very low and having taken six weeks over the job I had practically nothing to come. After paying the crew, buying stores and losing the use of two fingers I had exactly four shillings left for myself at the end of the voyage.[62]

This illustrates not only the hard life of the "sailormen" but also the dependency these vessels had on winds and tides. As such they proved vulnerable to competition from road haulage. The history of the Southend on Sea based barge operating family, Vandervord, contains details of the 34 barge fleet.[63] This and other fleets of agricultural barges, "Hoys," were integral to the Essex maritime trades to London. These sailing barges dominated the Thames and Medway estuaries and East Coast of England up until road competition in the post WW1 period. Kentish, Essex and East Anglia farmers relied on these vessels to get their produce to the London foodstuffs market. The hay barges, with their cargo stacked high above deck level (Stackies) supplied animal feeds for the London horse-drawn cabs and buses and other vehicles. Cut off from the road network, the village pubs of the Thames and Medway estuaries depended on the barges for beer and the London brewery businesses demanded the carriage of hops and barley. The quarries and brickworks of Essex needed barges for the movement of their stone, bricks, flints, sand, timber etc. The company also catered for local population needs: they were involved in the storage and supply of foodstuffs and owned their own granary. In addition to these freight activities, Vandervord's offered passenger services between remote villages and even had a weekly sailing from Southend to the Pickled Herring Wharf in the Pool of London.[64] Many of the brickfield and cement factory owners were also barge owners. John Eastwood being one of them - his company went on to become a national concern and a private limited company in 1872. By the turn of the century 80 barges had passed through that Company's ownership and had transported an average of nearly 70 million bricks a year.[65]

Technology changes were bound to have implications for the sailing barges. Steam and later motor ships brought obvious improvements in carrying capacity and in vessel/crew productivity. Three of today's leading UK owners in the coastal sector – Crescent, Everards, Lapthorns – have their roots in sailing barge trades. The *Cambria* carried the last cargo under sail in 1968. Some of the barges were de-rigged and fitted with engines. The wooden barge, *Trilby*, was the last engined barge to operate commercially in 1980.[66] The main cause of the demise of the river and creek trades, however, was the development in motor lorries and a corresponding improvement in road provision.[67] The niche service of the sailing barges was particularly vulnerable to the development of road haulage and the road system in the inter-war period.

Figure 13: The Thames Estuary Sailing Barge Trading Area

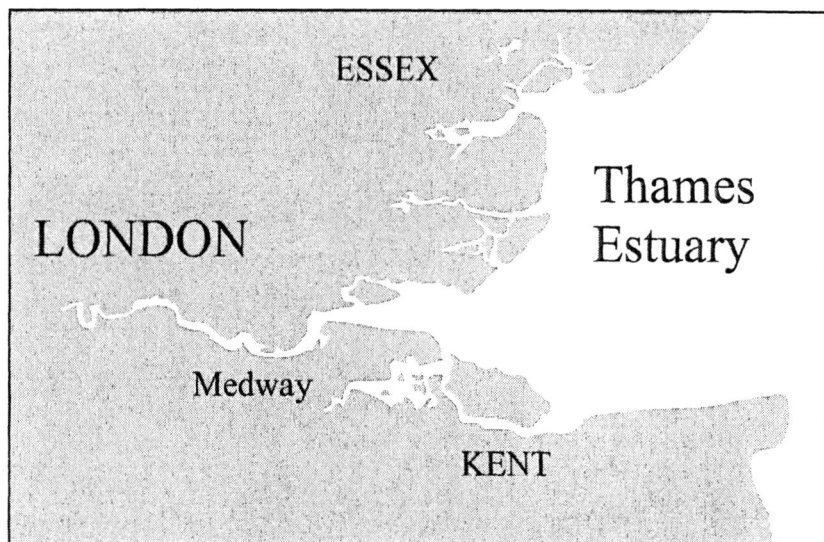

Motor transport brought a demise in the Thames sailing barges in two ways:(1) it replaced horse drawn transport in the towns, thus destroying the demand for the horse hay carried by the stackies; (2) improved technology in trucks and roads opened up the agricultural, beer, brick and cement trades to road haulage.

As truck performance improved, many sailing barge operators and users switched to road. The Kentish cement producer and sailing barge user, Blue Circle, for example, developed a fleet of trucks in the inter-war period for its deliveries in the Greater London area. The Thames-based, wharfinger, J.W. Cook & Co. Ltd, set up the haulage operation, Eastern Roadways, in 1929. This company developed strong links with Essex and East Anglia and such agricultural trades as brewing malt for London breweries were won from the sailing barges.[68]

The sailing barges had served a community which reflected the pastoral age, a period depicted by Constable's 1817 study of Flatford Mill. This can now be understood as an era when rural society was distant in terms of journey times from the urban centres. The spread of urbanisation, facilitated by suburban railways and road systems, was to encroach on this enclave of rural activity. Large parts of Essex and Kent made the transition from low population, agricultural based economies, to commuter based agglomeration. In 1918, some 1650 sailing barges served these areas; by 1939 this had fallen to 600.[69] Some diversification into motorised tonnage was undertaken in the inter-war period. The precursor of Crescent Shipping, London and Rochester Trading Company (LRTC), was a leader in making the switch from sail. By the 1950s the company possessed a fleet of around 80 motorised barges, as well as 48 sailing barges.[70]

Table 10: Barge, Lodella's Cargoes, March 1977.			
Cargo	Tonnage	Loaded	Discharged
Steel	264	Otterham, Kent	London Docks
Timber	119 Bundles	Tilbury	Lowestoft
Grain	300	Tilbury	Ipswich
Maize	250	Tilbury	Ipswich
Maize	250	Tilbury	Ipswich
Wheat	300	Tilbury	Rochester
Tapioca	200	London Docks	Otterham, kent
Steel Rods	395	Strood	London Docks
Francis, D.(2004) *Out of Rochester: Memoirs of a Thames and Medway Barge Skipper*, p.119.			

The motor barges provided improved performance. The sailing barges were hard worked to manage one trip per week; the motor barges managed 2-3 weekly trips. The memoirs of LRTC barge skipper, Duncan Francis, *Out of Rochester: Memoirs of a Thames and Medway Barge Skipper*, have provided a valuable insight into the patterns of motor barge trade, including the 400dwt *Lodella*'s cargo performance in March 1977, shown in Table 10.

Despite the intensity of their cargo trades, plus the long hours worked, the barges faced considerable obstacles. Captain Francis has evidenced the Port of London Authority (PLA) preference for road haulage movements of timber as opposed to barge movements, despite the customer's inclination towards deliveries by the latter. In the case of the Maldon timber wharf, the preference was for barge deliveries as opposed to the random, unpredictable drip-feed arrivals of lorries.[71] However, the enduring strikes in the London Docks disrupted the barge trades. The closure of riverside industries – breweries, steel plants, oil refineries – took away the advantages of direct cargo operations at the customers premises without the need for costly transhipment to road. In the Port Of Felixstowe, antipathy between the (then) owners, the Felixstowe Dock and Railway Company and the port based wheat mill owners, often led to excessive delays. The resulting claims for compensation by the barge owners (demurrage) made it difficult for the barges to compete with road haulage, as barge rates were increased by the delays.[72] Crescent's barge fleet was consistently rationalised and in 1983, despite enjoying plentiful cargoes, barge operations ceased. The last three vessels were withdrawn from the trade; this decision was precipitated by a long and damaging London Docks' strike. The evidence from the Thames estuarial trade is informed by changes in the transport economy. The labyrinth of rivers and creeks of Kent, Essex and East Anglia had proved a barrier to creeping urbanisation. The image of isolationism in the marshlands of the Thames Estuary was a vivid theme of

Charles Dickens', 1861 novel, *Great Expectations.*[73] With their capacity for penetrating the creeks, the sailing barges were integral to the preservation of a rural enclave economy by providing access to the London market.

The rise of road haulage, facilitated by increased truck performance and an extended road network was to doom the barge trades. Road haulage began to access the hitherto impenetrable regions. In addition to road haulage competition, it also should be noted that antipathy from port managers and the disruptive impact of labour unrest in the ports, also contributed to the demise of potentially viable trades. Given the switch to motor barges, it is apparent that a portion of these estuarial/coastal trades could have survived if a more efficient, reliable, port service had been attainable. By the Millennium, the only visible vestiges of the estuarial trades were aggregates from Essex, stone transhipment from the Isle of Grain and London waste disposal.

2.10 Irish Sea Operations

UK West Coast, Irish Sea, coastal and shortsea shipping activity concentrated on the major ports of Glasgow, Liverpool/Manchester, Dublin, Cork, Belfast, Cardiff and Bristol. However, a large number of smaller ports also generated significant cargoes. The South Wales' valleys coal fields provided heavy demand for both coal exports and coastal trade. As well as Cardiff, the ports of Newport, Barry, Swansea and Briton Ferry provided coal traffics for London. The disadvantage of this coal route to London compared to the East Coast route was the perilous passage around Land's End, particularly in the days of sail. The North Wales stone and slate trade to Liverpool and Manchester helped to facilitate urban growth by the supply of building materials. China clay coastal movements from Cornish, Devon and Dorset ports supplied the pottery industries of the Midlands linked with canal barges in the Merseyside ports of Runcorn and Ellesmere Port. A mixture of de-industrialisation and the switch to road haulage was to have a detrimental impact on these trades.

Table 11: The Top Liner Routes in 1914.		
Route	**Monthly Frequency**	**Monthly Cargo Capacity**
London-Manchester	40	70,064
London-Liverpool	45	65,554
Aberdeen-Leith	87	63,267
London-Dundee	N/A	56,310
London-Leith	26	40,784
Hull-Newcastle	19	38,231
London-Newcastle	21	34,639
Glasgow-Liverpool	57	33,379
London-Hull	33	29,689
London-Grangemouth	N/A	28,176
Source: ARMSTRONG, J. CUTLER, J. MUSTOE, G. (1998) "An Estimate of the Importance of the British Coastal Liner Trade in the Early Twentieth Century," *International Journal of Maritime History*, Vol.X, No.2, December 1998, p.48.		

Whereas the East Coast was dominated by the bulk volumes of the coal trades, the West Coast was focused on the coastal liner and Irish shortsea trades. Figure 14 illustrates the Irish Sea region. The Port of Liverpool had a strong presence in the liner trades to Dublin, London and Glasgow. In 1914 Liverpool's monthly coastal liner tonnage capacity approximated to 442,474, over four times that of Newcastle's coastal liner trades.[74] Table 11 shows the importance of the West Coast trades, particularly London-Liverpool/Manchester, which accounted for 30% of the UK coastal liner trades in 1914. In the steamship era the Port of Bristol provided a pivotal role in co-ordinating North-South coastal services with Irish linkages. Table 12 shows the comprehensive extent of these regular services.

In the inter-war period, West Coast activity was somewhat dominated by the growth of Coast Lines. The Liverpool based liner grouping developed rapidly as a result of mergers and takeovers in the difficult trading years post 1920. Over 50 shipping, warehousing and cartage firms formed the group and by 1955 Coast Lines had 110 vessels and could claim to own the largest coasting fleet in the world.[75] Up until the 1960s the itinerary of Coast Line's passenger and freight services included: Liverpool, Belfast, Dublin, Cork, Southampton and London. The passenger embarkation time for London sailings was advertised as 18.30hrs Friday and this promised a Liverpool arrival of Wednesday morning.[76] In the inter-war years and post 1945, the line operated two weekly sailings between Dundee and London, plus a regular Scottish whisky export linkage service to Southampton.[77] Hardy travellers were offered the opportunity to cruise with Coast Lines between Liverpool and London via Dublin, Cork, Plymouth and Southampton.

Continental liner services also operated: Manchester had regular scheduled services to Paris, Amsterdam and Hamburg. Market concentration was viewed as the solution to the falling margins in the coastal liner and ferry trades; and Coast Lines could claim success in balancing cargo flows with passenger carriage. For example, the Liverpool-London service offered accommodation for 78 passengers for the ten day cruise via Dublin, Falmouth and Southampton.[78] The story of Coast Lines is very much one of the demise of shortsea liner shipping in Britain and Ireland. Although the company enjoyed rapid growth in the inter-war period, this can now be accepted as a symptom of the industry's problems. The slump in demand resulting in over-tonnaging and the collapse of freight rates in the inter-war period eased the moves towards market concentration under Coast Lines ownership. As smaller lines found it increasingly difficult to survive competition within the short-sea market, also with rail and the increasingly efficient road haulage sector, mergers and take-over were viewed as the key to survival.

Figure 14: Irish Sea Ferry Routes, 2005

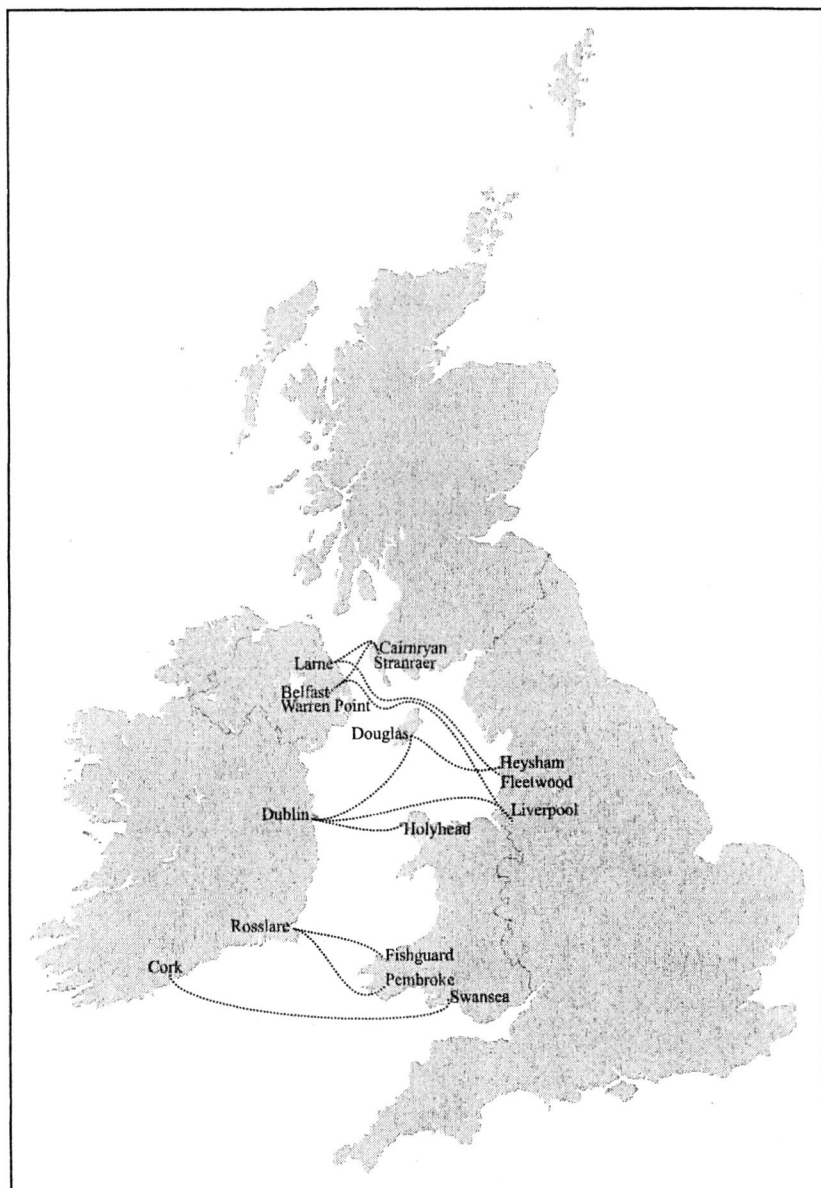

Table 12: Port of Bristol Coastal Liner Services 1935		
Port	Operator	Frequency
Aberdeen	Coast Lines	Tuesday
Belfast	William Sloan	Tues & Friday
Bideford	Robert Gilchrist	Every 4 days
Cardiff	Robert Gilchrist & P & A Campbell	Both Daily
Carmarthen	Banker & Norman	Weekly
Dartmouth	Coast Lines	As Required
Dublin	Bristol Steam Nav	Weekly
Dundee	Coast Lines	Weekly
Falmouth & Southampton	Coast Lines	Weekly
Glasgow & Greenock	William Sloan	Twice Weekly
Hayle	Robert Gilchrist	Weekly
Hull	Coast Lines	Weekly
Ilfracombe	Robert Gilchrist	Every 4 days
Kirkcaldy	Coast Lines	Weekly
King's Lynn	Coast Lines	As Required
Leith	Coast Lines	Weekly
Liverpool	Robert Gilchrist & Coast Lines	Weekly/Twice Weekly
Llanelly	Coast Lines	Weekly
London	Coast Lines	Weekly
Middlesbrough	Coast Lines	As Required
Milford Haven	Coast Lines	As Required
Newcastle	Coast Lines	Weekly
Newport	Robert Gilchrist	Daily
Penzance	Coast Lines	Weekly
Plymouth	Coast Lines & P & A Campbell	Weekly/Daily
Swansea	Coast Lines & P & A Campbell	Weekly/Daily
Torquay	Coast Lines & P & A Campbell	As required/Daily
Waterford	Clyde Shipping	Weekly
Source: *Journal of Commerce*		

The outcome of Coast Line's market concentration was the rationalisation of services. The focus was placed upon intensively used central core routes. The current (2007) Irish Sea ferry routes are illustrated in Figure 14. The fast Irish Sea passenger steamers, owned by the railway companies, were already concentrated on the short-crossing routes: Fishguard-Rosslare, Holyhead-Dun Laoghaire, Heysham-Belfast, Stranraer-Larne. This was an obvious strategy of vertical integration as it maximised the time savings of express rail services. By way of contrast, the freight routes, provided by Coast Line's predecessors, were more geographically dispersed. The need to move cargoes nearer to the point of final destination was more important than attaining the shortest sea passage. Coast Line's route rationalisation strategy was to reverse this freight routing strategy. This had dramatic implications for services across the Irish Sea, which were often of a relatively long diagonal sea-leg. The Clyde Shipping Company had specialised in Glasgow-Cork and Waterford services. Such diagonal routes maximised the sea leg of the journey, thus minimising the need for land transport. These trades enjoyed prosperity in the pre WW1 boom conditions. Whilst watching the frenetic port activity of shortsea liner operations, when four of his vessels were being worked simultaneously in the Port of Waterford, a Director of Clyde Shipping was humorously entreated to the opinion of one local wit: "It's getting more like London everyday!"[79]

Clyde Shipping's Irish connections also included a coastal liner service in the South West of Ireland. Prior to the building of the railway extension to Dingle, the town was somewhat isolated. Being 48kms from Tralee, the nearest railhead and market town, the Dingle Peninsula would have lacked integration with Irish and British markets, had it not been for the company's service provided by the small vessel *Rio Formosa*. This vessel provided a service every 5-6 days, linking Dingle with Cork, via the ports of Valencia, Kenmore, Bantry, Schull, and Kinsale. Initially there had been a small public service subsidy for this route, including the maintenance of port channels, quaysides and warehousing. It was reported that the withdrawal of the subsidy, pre-empting the ending of the service in 1905 was met by public protest in the Dingle region. Clyde Shipping biographer, A.D. Cuthbert, writing in 1956, likened the protest to the opposition registered in Britain when British Railways opted for a branch line closure.[80] The rationalisation of the diagonal shortsea and Irish coastal liner services in the inter-war years resulted in increased emphasis on the main ports and economic centres of Dublin, Cork and Belfast. From this perspective it is perceptible that Coast Line's rationalisation strategy was the precursor for intensive short-crossing RoRo services.

The West Coast trampship owners concentrated around the Liverpool and Merseyside region were committed to the coal trades to Ireland. The Zillah Shipping Company, which evolved from Warrington's sailing barges, typified the West Coast tramp owners. In addition to the staple traffic, coals to Ireland, the itineraries of Zillah's ships demonstrated the heavy industry economy of Northern England. Industrial slag from the Manchester steel industry, Partington to the Continent, was balanced by back cargoes of silver sand from Antwerp to Garston for the St. Helens' glass industry. Potash from Holland and Belgium was carried for the Mersey Basin chemicals industry. China clay ex Fowey to Runcorn was for the pottery industry of the Stoke-on-Trent region. Ammonia sulphate was carried from ICI plants on Merseyside to Fison's fertiliser plant in Avonmouth.[81]

The reliance on primary and heavy industry was to prove difficult in the de-industrialisation period. In 1890, around 0.5mt of slate was shipped out of North Wales ports for coastal dispatch.[82] This trade suffered a long decline in the 20th century; a major loss to the coastal tramp fleets of the West Coast. Additionally, the dependence on the Irish coal trades caused some difficulties in the coal strike of 1955. With shortages and UK prices rising, Zillah and other

West Coast tramp shipping companies found that they lost business when Irish importers switched to supplies from USA and Poland.

Roy Fenton's 1997 work, *Mersey Rovers: The Coastal and Tramp Shipowners of Liverpool and the Mersey*,[83] has provided a rigorous analysis of the decline of this sector. In addition to the coal trade dislocations, bad weather affected the French grain harvest in 1955 and a warm winter reduced the demand for the carriage of coal. The harsher winter of 1956-7 brought a standstill to Baltic timber trades and continental river and canal movements as freezing over occurred. Many Dutch coasters were forced onto the British coast to look for cargoes. This caused consternation amongst the Liverpool owners as it was felt that the Dutch vessels were accepting break-even freight rates. The problems were further compounded when the English China Clay company announced its 1959 acquisition of a lorry fleet, thus taking 40,000 tons of traffic off the coastal trades per annum. The difficulties facing the owners were exacerbated by the reluctance of these traditional owners to modernise into more economic diesel powered vessels. Ambitious shipowners, particularly Dutch owners, had pioneered the diesel coaster in the inter-war period. It was the chemicals giant, ICI, not the traditional shipowner, that led the way on the West Coast with the 1943 built motor coaster, *Cerium*. However, it was not until the late 1950s that the West Coast tramp owners began to make the transition to motor ships. Economics made this inevitable. In 1955 it was reported that motor coaster owners were making a profit of £54 per day, whist steamship owners made just £4 per day.[84]

The reservations and delays over the decision to switch from steam in the inter-war years may be explained by conservatism by the owners, but some rationality may have applied as steam technology had improved and the abundance of cheap coal on the West Coast kept fuel costs down. Additionally, many operators felt a commitment to the coal industry as a major customer - switching from steam to motor may have been interpreted as an affront to the coal sellers! The costs of investment were also a consideration, with depressed freight rates not proving conducive to building new motor ships. This problem was to endure. In 1985 the traditional Glasgow coastal and shortsea shipping operator, J&A Gardner, was concerned by the over-tonnaging crisis in the sector, with freight rates forced down to below 20% of viability, thus precluding investment in new tonnage.[85] By way of contrast, lorry fleets could be gradually built up unit by unit. When the North West England road haulage giant, Eddie Stobart, bought his first truck in 1960 it cost him £450, second hand. A new Ford Thames followed at £1,450, facilitated by a loan secured by a deposit of just £135.[86] The investment conditions for incremental growth were conducive to the haulier, whilst shipowners deferred expenditure in new tonnage awaiting improved market conditions.

The forces that brought decline on the West Coast can now be acknowledged as a combination of de-industrialisation, the switch to road haulage and depressed freight rates impeding investment in efficient new tonnage. In the Irish Sea trades, the concentration on intensive RoRo road and passenger services on central core routes proved detrimental to freight services. As a consequence, British-Irish trade flows were funnelled into the shorter crossings and sea tkm were decreased; conversely, road tkm were increased.

2.11 Examining Decline

The collapse of coastal shipping post World War 1 can now be explained as part of the re-shaping of the British transport structure. The process of decline began dramatically with the dislocations caused by the 1914-18 war. For much of the 19th century the UK coastal tonnages had exceeded those of the deepsea trades.[87] In 1910, total coastal tonnages amounted to 81.5 mt and tkms stood at 32.64b. By 1948, tkm had reduced to 14.1b, 86% of which was accruable to the collier trade.[88] Armstong *et.al*[89] found that this decline was partly explained by the impact of Irish independence. This had the effect of reducing coastal trade figures as the Irish trades became classed as foreign after 1924. But even more influential in the decline process was the collapse of the general cargo and coastal liner trades:

> The staple industries, which provided much of the bulk cargoes for coasters, had declined, and road haulage was taking away the more valuable commodities which had been carried previously by the coastal liners.[90]

Whilst post WW2 collier traffics were roughly the same as in the immediate pre WW1 period, Ford and Bound found that the year 1914 was to prove the turning point for coastal shipping in general. After a century of trade expansion, "not only was growth arrested but a disastrous decline and a depression so prolonged that the coastwise trade had not recovered by 1938."[91] Figure 15 illustrates the sharp fall in coastal tonnages post 1914. During the WW1 period, state direction of railways and shipping had occurred as a means of co-ordinating the logistics of the war effort. The vessel losses and dislocations of the war led to British shipping losing its dominant status in the world market. It has been estimated that over 7.25mgt of British shipping, 38% of the total pre-war fleet was lost as a result of enemy action. [92] Economic historian, Derek Aldcroft also found that "Coastal shipping and the canals suffered an even greater set back" with canal traffic falling by a third and coastal shipping volume by half.[93] Water transport found itself under threat from the dual threat of rail and road competition. Wartime economic control over the railways had obviously been more vigorous than that of coastal shipping. Intensified competition brought about by the freezing of railway freight charges was to have a detrimental impact on the coastwise trade, impeding recovery up until the verge of WW2.[94] In some cases, coastal freight rates which had been highly competitive with rail pre 1914, had

96

risen to as high as 100% of the rail freight rates by 1918. [95]   By 1921, half the UK coastal fleet was surplus, in "lay up" and a number of reports by the Railway

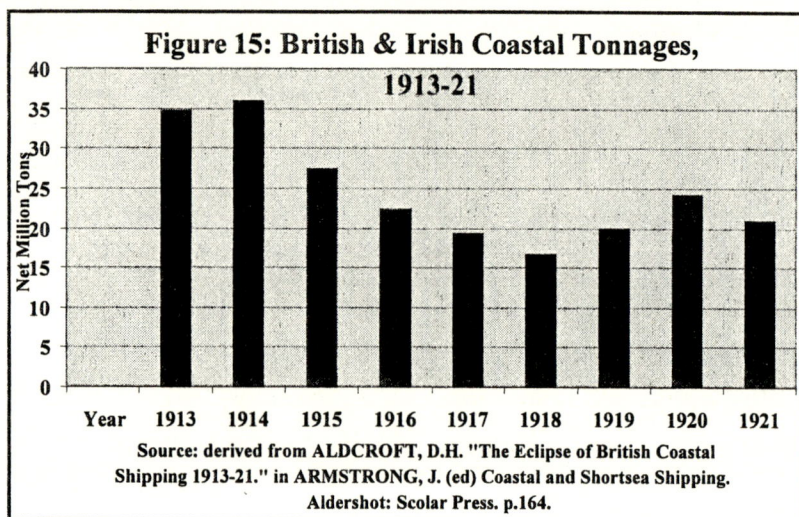

Figure 15: British & Irish Coastal Tonnages, 1913-21

Source: derived from ALDCROFT, D.H. "The Eclipse of British Coastal Shipping 1913-21." in ARMSTRONG, J. (ed) Coastal and Shortsea Shipping. Aldershot: Scolar Press. p.164.

Rates Advisory Committee considered the plight of depressed coastal shipping and its impact on the supply chain. The low railfreight rates had the effect of creating congestion not only on the rail network but also in the ports and warehousing as the system grid-locked.[96]   In addition, the growth of road haulage in the post war period began to attack canal and coastal shipping. The Great War had a highly positive impact on the development of road haulage technology. The petrol engine had proved itself during the war. The diesel engine followed bringing even more efficiencies; road haulage rapidly became the dominant force in British and Irish freight movement. In the post WW2 period the previous high levels of Green Highway activity were not sustainable, given the imminent decline of coal and the start of the motorway age. Continuing labour problems in the docks and in some cases, the antipathy of port management only served to exacerbate the problems of maintaining competitiveness for shipowners.   Coal had proved an ideal traffic for coastal shipping. As with the current flows of North Sea oil, the competitive position the colliers enjoyed was unassailable *vis-à-vis* other modes. The coal could be loaded directly from coastal situated mines and the final destination point, primarily the energy industry, was located in riversides and coastal locations. The high costs of cargo transhipment were thus obviated. It is evident that by 2000, dramatic changes in the economy had completely changed the pattern of demand. "King Coal" was only a shadow of its former self and many of the riverside wharves had made the transition to sites of desirable housing, office space and leisure/retail complexes.

2.12 Chapter 2: Summary & Conclusion

A number of factors have been identified in this Chapter as determinants of decline. Firstly, the demise of coal as a major energy source was bound to have irrevocable consequences for shipping. The close resemblance of the North Sea oil trades with the East Coast coal trades – as dominant Green Highway traffics - holds a salutary lesson. The reduction in oil traffics has the potential to marginalize shipping in the transport statistics of the UK – an outcome similar to the immediate collapse of coal in the post 1960 period.

The development of road haulage efficiency looms large in the modal switch to road. Additionally, other factors include de-industrialisation, industrial restructuring and relocation, port inefficiency and the gentrification of port areas. In the intra-European trades, the spectacular growth of shortsea RoRo shipping post 1970s resulted from the increased demand of road haulage in preference to LoLo shipping.

This Chapter initially set out to de-couple the large volumes of the crude oil trades from the pattern of long-term decline. The role of shipping in the industrial revolution process, was identified. The heavy demand for bulk commodities, primarily coal, as well as iron ore, china clay, salt, bulk chemicals and slate provided buoyant markets for coastal shipping. The de-industrialisation process was bound to reduce demand in these trades as the staple industries declined, particularly coal. The relocation of industry also had a detrimental impact, as firms sought sites away from coastal ports and inland waterways. This development was clearly a factor in the Thames estuary barge trades. The rise of road haulage has been identified as a major factor in causing relative decline. Advances in the speed and load limits have served to consistently up-grade haulage performance. The liner trades of the West Coast were particularly susceptible to the competitive impact of road haulage flexibility and improved performance from the inter-war period onwards. Unlike the direct loading and discharge processes in the collier trades, the liner services were dependent on transhipment to road haulage.

The resulting costs and delays of transhipment made road haulage increasingly attractive. The switch from shipping to road haulage by liner firms, such as the Manchester-London operator, Fisher Renwick, can be explained as a desire to reap the tangible benefits of the modern mode, road haulage. On the Bridgewater Canal, the sharp demise of traffics post 1950 was partly attributable to the canal owners switching from barge owning to lorry owning operations. Subsidiary causes of decline have been identified as port delays in the era of labour unrest. More latterly, the rise of a gentrification process in the port regions has proved unfriendly towards cargo handling activities. In the shortsea trades, the emergence of RoRo ferries has undermined the role of LoLo shipping. The concentration of RoRo ferries on short crossings has served to minimise tkm by sea whilst maximising by road.

Having discussed the historic decline of water transport in the UK and Irish economies, the following Chapter will critically examine the broad range of factors that are currently providing optimistic grounds for recovery. It will become evident that a combination of changing European political priorities, improved port performance, growing environmental awareness and declining haulage efficiency (resulting from congestion), are all engendering a fresh look at the Green Highway.

100

CHAPTER 2: ENDNOTES

Hadfield, C. (revised by Boughey, J.) (1998) *Hadfield's British Canal's* 8th edition. Stroud: Budding Books.pp.278-9.
[2] Baird,A.J. "Coastal RoRo freight ferry services: An alternative to trunk road haulage in the UK," *Transport Logistics.* Vol.1. No.2. June 1997. pp.103-113.
[3] Urquhart, F. "Oil industry warns North Sea tide show signs of turning," Business Scotsman.com. 19.3.07.
[4] Hadfield,C. (1971) *The Canal Age.* London: Pan Books. p.7.
[5] Department of the Environment 1972) *Roads in England 1971.* London: HMSO.
[6] Conversation with ex ICI tanker driver, Harold Dunning, Runcorn, Cheshire.
[7] Hadfield, *Op.cit.* p.275.
[8] Charlesworth, G. (1984) *A History of British Motorways.* London: Thomas Telford. p.50.
[9] Hall,P. Breheny,M. Mcquaid,R.W. Hart,D. (1987) *Western Sunrise –the Genesis and Growth of Britain's Major High-Tech Corridor.* London: Allen & Unwin .
[10] Freight Study Group (2002) *Freight on Water: A New Perspective.* London: DEFRA.p.27
[11] *Op.cit* p.30.
[12] Armstrong,J. Cutler,J. Mustoe,G.(1998). "An Estimate of the Importance of the British Coastal Liner Trade in the Early Twentieth Century." *International Journal of Maritime History.* Vol.X. No.2. December 1998. pp.41-63.
[13] Mustoe, G. (1997) *Fisher Renwick: A Transport Saga, 1874-1972,* Nynehead: Roundoak.
[14] Armstrong, J .et.al. (2003) *Companion to the British Road Haulage Industry.* London: Science Museum. pp.96-7
[15] *Op.cit.* p. 405.
[16] Armstrong, J .et.al. p.405.
[17] *Op.cit.* p.284.
[18] *Op.cit.* p.353-4
[19] *Op.cit.* p.143
[20] Harper, L. Birch, C. (1995) *On the Move: The Road Haulage Association, 1945-1994.* London: Baron Birch.
[21] Armstrong, J .et.al. (2003) *Companion to the British Road Haulage Industry.* London: Science Museum. p.428.
[22] "Hauliers derail UK port plan," *Lloyd's List.* 16.10.97.
[23] "First Falmouth call for Evergreen today," *Lloyd's List.* 13.6.94.
[24] Spurrier, A. (2002) "Silent army fighting battle for shortsea", *Lloyd's List* . 14.3.02. p.7.
[25] *Ibid.*p.7
[26] Forsythe, R.N. (2002) *Irish Sea Shipping Publicised.* Stroud: Tempus. p.40.
[27] Rowlinson, M. Salveson, P. (1992) *Green Links to Europe.* Manchester: CLES.
[28] www.imdo.ie
[29] Mott, D. "Failed ferry firm needed £1m," *Lloyd's List.* 3.3.99.
[30] Cowsill, M (1990) *By Road Across the Sea: The History of the Atlantic Steam Navigation Company Ltd.* Kilgetty: Ferry Publications. pp.4-5.
[31] Middlemiss,N.L. (1998) *Coast Lines.* Gateshead. Shields Publications. p.68.
[32] Zachcial, M. (1997) "Land/Sea Transport Flows in Europe." In Peeters, D & Wergeland, T. *European Shortsea Shipping: Proceedings from the Third European Research Roundtable Conference on Shortsea Shipping.* Bergen, 20-21 June 1996. Delft: Delft University Press.. p.40.
[33] "Two million up." *Lloyd's List.* 21.12.05.
[34] "Traffic surge pressure on Dublin", *Lloyd's List.* 20.7.00.
[35] "The history of Caol Ila Distillery," www.discovering-distilleries.com accessed 22.12.05.
[36] Jamieson, A.G. ((2003) *Ebb Tide in the British Maritime Industries: Change and Adaptation, 1918-1990.* Exeter: University of Exeter. pp.84-125.

101

[37] *Op.cit.* p.99.
[38] Macdonald, M. (1997) "German Coastal Shipping since 1945 – Part 2", *Ships Monthly,* December 1997. p.33.
[39] Armstrong, J. *Op.cit* . p.405.
[40] Ibid. p.37.
[41] Landon, F. "Manchester Ship Canal unveils Port of Salford container complex plan. *Lloyd's List.* 15.10.03.
[42] Evidence given to the Environment and Regional affairs Committee by the Author.
[43] Wheatley,K. (1990) *National Maritime Guide to Maritime Britain.* Exeter: Webb & Bower. p.37.
[44] *Loc.cit*
[45] Ville, S. (1986) "Total factor Productivity in the English Shipping Industry: The North East coal trade, 1700-1850." *Economic History Review* 2nd ser. XXXIX. pp.355-370.
[46] Wheatley. *Op.cit.* p.50.
[47] Ville. *Op.cit.*
[48] *Ibid.* p.365.
[49] *Loc.cit.*
[50] Nicholson, T (1990) *Take the Strain.* London: The Alexandra Towing Company Ltd.. p.13.
[51] *Loc cit.*
[52] Armstrong, J.(1994) "Late Nineteenth-Century Freight Rates Revisited: Some Evidence from the British Coastal Coal Trade," *International Journal of Maritime History,* VI, No.2. December 1994, pp.45-81.
[53] Wheatley. *Op.cit.* p.41.
[54] Armstrong, J. *Op.cit* . p. 49.
[55] *Op.cit.* p.68.
[56] Ford, P. Bound, J.A.(1951) *Coastwise Shipping and the Small Ports,* Oxford: Basil Blackwell. p.16.
[57] Armstrong, J. *Op.cit.* pp.68-9.
[58] "Vandervords: Hoymen of Essex," www.mmhistory.org.uk/vandervord.
[59] "A Brief look at the history of the Thames sailing barge," www.thames-barge-art.co.uk accessed 23.9.05.
[60] Roberts, R. (1984) *Coasting Bargemaster.* Lavenham, Suffolk: Lavenham Press.
[61] *Ibid.* pp.86-7.
[62] *Ibid.* p.87.
[63] Vanerdervords: Hoymen of Essex," *Op.cit.*
[64] *Loc.cit.*
[65] *Loc.cit.*
[66] "A Brief look at the history of the Thames sailing barge." *Op.cit.*
[67] *Loc.cit.*
[68] Armstrong, J. *Op.cit.* p.141.
[69] "A Brief look at the history of the Thames sailing barge." *Op.cit.*
[70] Francis, D. (2004) *Out of Rochester: Memoirs of a Thames and Medway Barge Skipper.* Unpublished. pp.4-5.
[71] *Op.cit.* p.125.
[72] Francis, D. *Op.cit.* pp.120-21.
[73] Dickens, C. (1965) *Great Expectations.* Harmondsworth: Penguin.
[74] Armstrong, J. *et.al* "An Estimate of the Importance of the British Coastal Liner Trade in the Early Twentieth Century." *International Journal of Maritime History, Vol.*X, No.2 December 1998. pp 41-63.
[75] Middlemiss, N.L. *Op cit.*
[76] Collard, I. (2000) *Coastal Shipping: The Twilight Years* . Stroud, Gloucester: Tempus. p.109.

102

[77] Somner, G (1999) *D.P.L: A History of the Dundee, Perth and London Shipping Company Ltd and Associated Shipping Companies*. Kendal: WSS. p.35 & p.63.

[78] *Op.cit.* p.37.

[79] Cuthbert, A.D. (1956) *Clyde Shipping Company Limited*. Glasgow: University Press, Glasgow. p.83.

[80] *Op.cit* p.79.

[81] Fenton, R. (1997) *Mersey Rovers: The Coastal and Tramp Shipowners of Liverpool and the Mersey*. Gravesend: WSS. p.279.

[82] The Slate Industry of North and Mid-Wales: A Brief History of the Welsh Slate History. www.penmorfa.com accessed, 21.9.05.

[83] Fenton, R. *Ibid.*

[84] *Ibid.* p.278.

[85] McClelland, A.H. (1991) "British Small Bulk Carriers," A Second Merseyside Maritime History Lecture. Liverpool Nautical Research Society.

[86] Davies,H. (2001) *The Eddie Stobart Story*. London: Harper Collins. p.15.

[87] Aldcroft, D.H. (1996) "The Eclipse of British Coastal Shipping, 1913-21", in Armsrtrong, J. ed (1996) *Coastal and Shortsea Shipping*. Aldershot: Scolar Press. pp.163-177.

[88] Armstrong, J. *Op.cit.* pp.48-9.

[89] *Loc.cit.*

[90] *Loc.cit.*

[91] Ford, P. Bound, J.A. (1951) *Op.cit.* p.1.

[92] Aldcroft, D.H.(1975) *British Transport Since 1914*. Newton Abbot: David & Charles.p.18.

[93] *Loc.cit.*

[94] Ford, P. Bound, J.A. (1951) *Op.cit.* p.1.

[95] *Op.cit.* p.19.

[96] Armstrong, J. *Op.cit.* pp.48-9.

[96] Ford, P. Bound, J.A. (1951) *Op.cit.* p.3

CHAPTER 3:

The Green Highway Context

Having discussed the many factors that led to the historic decline of domestic and shortsea shipping in the UK and Ireland, it is now pertinent to examine the contemporary context. A number of elements can be observed which are potentially conducive to a revival of shipping activity. It is apposite, therefore, to examine these factors within the context of a growing interest in sustainable transport. In the early days of the new Millennium, shipping is increasingly seen as a potential alternative to road haulage in certain trades. A number of forces ranging from economic change to political and environmental strategies can be identified as positive in the moves towards an expanded Green Highway. Specifically, this chapter sets out to critically examine the impact of six key areas valued as pertinent to the Green Highway:

(1) the dynamics of European business;
(2) the rise of the Celtic Tiger;
(3) the impact of port deregulation;
(4) the desire of businesses to become associated with "greener" forms of transport;
(5) the impact of favourable transport policy;
(6) the emergence of a water transport lobby.

3.1. The Dynamics of Euro-Business - not only Heineken can do this!

If Heineken Breweries can successfully operate barges over short distances in the Rotterdam area, then it must be feasible that British and Irish operators can emulate. The clear contrast that manifests when comparing both Britain and Ireland with Germany, France and the Benelux countries, was made in chapter One. Whilst these continental nations lack the coastal opportunities of an island nation, their inland shipping has continued to prosper in many trades, particularly on the Rhine and its tributaries. An obvious difference between the two island nations and the continental nations is the geography and scale of the latter's developed river and canal network. Lacking the opportunities for long distance barge traffic flows, Britain and Ireland enjoy only a minimal share of inland shipping. As well as the distance factor, the continental river sizes permit far higher tonnage ranges than could be contemplated on the restricted waterways of Britain and Ireland. However, it can also be noted that not all intra-European traffics are long distance, large volumes; small shipments over short distances also exist. The Dutch brewer, Heineken, has been a particularly active proponent of barge and shortsea operations over short distances.[1] Such experience is pertinent to the Green Highway in Britain and Ireland. If Heineken and other operators can do this, why not British and Irish equivalents? Making the contrast is of value therefore, as it reveals that distance and volume are not the only determinants to be found influencing the choice of mode. For instance some of the barge services on the Rhine, Maas and Seine are of distances compatible with those attainable on the Manchester Ship Canal and the Rivers Thames, Trent, Severn and Shannon. Likewise, in some instances, the sizes of mainland European operations are of similar or of lower tonnage than those found on British inland waterways. A few recent examples of low distance small/medium size inland operations from the Continent are:

- Bremen-Bremerhaven container links;
- River Seine automobile distribution;
- Berlin, city reconstruction flows;
- Heineken, raw material and beer flows in the Rotterdam   region;
- Ikea, packaged furniture flows River Rhone.

In answering the question of why barges can operate on such short distance trades on continental rivers but not in Britain and Ireland, a number of factors need to be considered. These include considering European entrepreneurial and investment culture. Also, the constant up-grading of technology. This is supported by the positive perception that shipping exudes on the Continent. Partly, this positive image may be explained as the result of an active water transport lobby in France, Benelux and Germany.

Comparative evidence drawn from contrasting the Dutch/Belgium Ghent Canal with the Gloucester and Sharpness Canal illustrates clearly the disparity in the national importance of water transport. Both canal systems have a similar early history. From their 19th century inceptions, the development paths of the two canals have totally diverged. Whereas the Gloucester Canal size specifications have actually reduced, due to low levels of investment and poor maintenance, the Ghent Canal and its port have consistently improved, with vessel sizes increasing from 1000dwt to 65,000dwt. Table 13 presents the sharp contrast between a dynamic and a moribund canal.

Table 13: Comparison: Ghent and Gloucester & Sharpness Canals		
	Ghent Canal	Gloucester & Sharpness Canal
Opening Date	1827	1827
Distance	19 miles/31.75 km	16 miles/25.75km
Tonnages Handled 2004	>40 milllion tonnes	<1000 tonnes
Vessel Size Limits	65,000dwt	<1200dwt.
Source: derived from www.waterways.org and www.portofghent.com		

In the Netherlands, the development of barge traffic has consistently progressed. In 2002 some 340mt of traffic was dispatched by barge and this was predicted to reach 500mt by 2020.[2] Additionally, container traffic by barge rose from 2.3mteu to 3.91m teu between 1998 and 2002.[3] Also in 2002, France pledged to double river traffic by 2010. It was also reported in October 2002 that after two years of discussions between professional operators and Government agencies a "contract of growth" had been finalised.[4] Included in this accord is the doubling of grain movements from 12mt (2002) to 24mt (2010). Navigational improvements, including the Seine above Rouen and on the Rhone in Southern France were being targeted. The initiatives were welcomed by the International Grains Council as it would lower costs and thus make French agriculture more competitive.[5]

One area that UK and Irish owners could perhaps emulate lies in the organisational structure of continental shipping. In the UK the tradition of intense competition and rivalry in a declining market has served against co-operation. In Germany and the Netherlands, collaboration is more typical. Large companies such as Rhein-Maas-und See (RMS), Peter Döhle Schiffahrts and Wagenborg Shipping, have a major impact on the market, providing an operating framework and guidance for many small owners.[6]

This allows the smaller shipowners, including the captain-owners of sea-river ships, to benefit from the organisational economies of scale bestowed from their involvement in the larger umbrella type network. In 1988 the Department of Transport report, *Short Sea Bulk Shipping: An Analysis of UK Performance*[7] considered the advantages that the German management pooling system gave their home fleet over UK competition. By providing a commercial management umbrella, covering the fixing of cargoes and the co-ordination of voyage patterns, the small owners were able to gain entry to important markets.[8] Access to investment funds can also be perceived as an advantage enjoyed by continental shipowners. The German bank, Deutsche Schiffsbank, has focused on shipping loans and investment generating KG Financing schemes. Table 14 shows a 51% increase in the former and 49% in the latter between 2003 and 2005.

Table 14: Deutsche Schiffsbank Shipping Loans 2003-05 (000€)			
	2003	2004	2005
Loan Advances	2,285	2,683	3,461
KG Finance	770	887	1,144
Source: Deutsche Schiffsbank *Annual Reports*			

Given this access to investment funding, the small and highly entrepreneurial German owners quickly took market leadership in fast, flexible and compact feeder ships. Tinsley has found that:

> ...for the tightly-knit communities of small-shipowners in Germany, the by-word continues to be flexibility, and this manifests itself in a leaning towards optimised, multi-purpose cargo and container carrying designs and in a corresponding reluctance to invest in more specialised vessel forms such as ro-ros.[9]

A particular feature of German investment in shipping has been the KG system of limited partnerships, formed by such professional groupings as doctors and dentists, who are able to reduce their tax liabilities by investing in containerships. The so-called "Dettorney Ships" are financed by professionals seeking to avoid the high-income tax rates of Germany by off-setting their tax payments against shipping. The system allows for hundreds of investors to have shares in vessels under the aegis of a specialist investors company. These firms have specialist market knowledge; they arrange for an investor to cover about half the new building's capital cost. The balance is then allotted to share ownership for the numerous investors.[10] Although the scheme has had its critics – that it fuelled a new building boom – Deutsche Schiffsbank records show that all new tonnage was absorbed in the growth markets.[11] In addition to the KG system, the Landesbanken, which are the municipally-owned banks, have traditionally offered cheap loans to shipping. However, the easy credit terms made available by the

Landesbank has been viewed with some suspicion by the European Commission, anxious to prevent any strategies that are incompatible with the European axiom of the idea of free and open competition.[12] The local shipowning community is a particular strength of German shortsea shipping, with operational and investment strongholds in Duisburg, Haren-Ems and Hamburg. A predominantly effective aspect of the German sea-river fleet based in the Rhine logistics hub-port, Duisburg, is the financial support of the local investment community.

By pooling investment, the Duisburg shipowners, many of whom are masters of their own vessels, have been able to secure a market leadership in the sea-river trades. A study undertaken by consultants, Peat Marwick McLintock, has demonstrated that under the limited partnership K/S scheme, a high income German investor ploughing £10,000 into the scheme will generate tax savings of some £8400.[13] On the waterways of the Benelux countries family owned and operated barges are a dynamic element of the river tradition. Typical of the way of life is the Hoekeyns family, who were featured in a 1999 edition of *Lloyd's List*. The family life style was based around the movement of containers from the deep-sea ports of Antwerp and Rotterdam to Rhine destinations as far up-stream as Frankfurt. Their home was the 192teu barge, *Acropolis,* chartered to a P&O-Nedlloyd subsidiary, Rhenania.[14] Such evidence points not only to the entrepreneurial tradition of continental waterways but also to the ability of inland shipping to compete with intensive rail and road competition in a time sensitive container logistics market. The European dimension works on two fronts, both favourable to the Green Highway:

(1)   trends towards Pan-European business activity and integration;

(2)   the spread of European shipping enterprise, innovation and culture to Britain and Ireland.

3.1.1 European Economic Integration

As business activity becomes more Pan-European in its outlook and the trends of industrial organisation intensify, demand for transport linkages will increase. The choices facing the shipper are: truck-RoRo ferry/Channel Tunnel Shuttle combinations, rail-intermodal via the Channel Tunnel and shortsea shipping. Unless customers are directly connected to waterway networks, it is inevitable that the shortsea option will be provided in conjunction with road or rail services. European opportunities do exist for shipping in vertically integrated industrial flow operations in the steel, automobile and chemical industries; also, where cargoes can be consolidated, as in container and break-bulk operations. In 2001 it was possible to observe the export and import of Ford Transits through British ports: Southampton built models were being exported from the Port of Southampton whilst Genk built models were imported through Harwich!

Rationalisations in the European steel industry in the 1980s led to return shipments across the North Sea. Slab steel produced in South Wales and at Scunthorpe prior to the run down of British Steel in the mid 1980s, would have been rolled and pressed in the South Yorkshire/North Lincolnshire region. The run down and closure of steelmaking in the UK led to this product being shipped to Bremen and other German steel rolling mill regions for finishing. Frequently the rolled steel is returned to the UK via such ports as Goole, Boston, Sutton Bridge and Poole. Thus the steel making process involves crossing the North Sea twice. The sea-river linkage of Corus' (former British Steel) steel flow exports from Llanwern and Port Talbot to the up-river (Seine) Paris distribution centre, Gennevilliers, has served as a prime example. The 1999 formation of Corus following the merger between British Steel and the Dutch steel producer, Hoogovens – with its likelihood of further rationalisations – offered increased opportunities for steel supply chain shipping. Industrial concentration in

European automobile production is partly the result of a division of labour based on plant specialisation.

One graphic example of the impact of UK de-industrialisation was provided by the imports of German steel for the new Wembley Stadium, under construction in 2004-7. In 2005 the Port of Duisburg very proudly announced its role in the construction of England's football folklore, by the loading of steel in the up-river German port for passage to Dagenham on the River Thames.[15] Similarly, chemical industry integration has focused on specialisation and rationalisation. The impact on the transport industry is one of increased demand. A side-effect of UK de-industrialisation is that increased amounts of manufactured goods have to be imported into the nation. Whilst this is bad news for the manufacturing industry and its workers, it does provide greater opportunities for the transport industries.

As with industrial production, the transport industry is becoming more Pan-European in its outlook and operations. The 1996 merger between P&0 and Nedlloyd brought the two largest deepsea container shipping companies in Britain and Holland, respectively, together. The successful franchise bid of the utilities group, Companie Generale des Eaux (CGEA), for Network South East Kent and Central rail passenger franchises led to French ownership of one of Britain's largest rail concentrations, Connex. In the railfreight sector, the major deepsea liner company, Mediterranean Shipping Company (MSC), has started its own freight container service between Felixstowe and Birmingham, in conjunction with GB Railfreight.[16] Also, the Swiss Stock Market listed world logistics player Kuehne and Nagel, has been a leading advocate of the switch from road to rail/water in their global container movements.[17] In road haulage, UK and Irish owners have been pressurised by continental operators in domestic markets. The threat of British operators to "flag out" their haulage fleets to mainland locations – in order to avoid high vehicle and fuel tax burdens – points to the Pan-European trend.[18] The 2005 takeover of the UKs biggest logistics provider, Exel Logistics by Deutsche Post AG, is further evidence of European concentration.[19] In shortsea and inland shipping similar trends are evident. The Seacon grouping displays a mix of British and German capital, warehousing, freight forwarding, vessel ownership and operation in trades between the Thames and the Rhine. Both Arklow Shipping and Carisbrooke Shipping have connections with Netherlands operators in the shortsea sector.

Continental innovation in ship design and operation also has important implications. In chapter Two the incursions of the Dutch fleet in UK trades was alluded to. In the 1950s and 1960s it was the 499 gross registered ton Dutch motor coaster that had set the pace in design, forcing many British owners to up-date from their steam age thinking. The low air draft ships of the 1980s and 1990s added a new dimension to coastal shipping allowing vessels to combine the trading advantages of the river barge with the sea keeping attributes of the coastal vessel. Refinements of the generic sea-river ship include self discharging capabilities and customisation to facilitate specialised cargoes – steel, paper, cement. Leading British and Irish owners – Crescent Shipping, Lapthorns, Union Transport and Arklow Shipping – have benefited from the extension of the continental sea-river innovation to the trades of the British Isles. The 1990s brought the Rhine barge-tug combinations onto the Mersey-Manchester Ship Canal and Medway-Thames and Humber-Ouse systems, with traffics in ormulsion, paper, steel, aggregates and rice.

The 2001 newbuildings *Crescent Rhine* and *Crescent Seine* typified the potential of Trans-European collaborations. The vessels built for the German owner, Reederei Shipcom, were then turned over to the management of Crescent Shipping of Southampton on a ten year bareboat charter option. Being designed with sea-river trading in mind the loaded draft of 4.05m and air draft of 5.2m enables the sisters to trade in the industrial heartlands, passing under restricted height bridges of France, Germany, Belgium and the Netherlands. The box hold construction of the vessels provides for the carriage of steel coils – a staple of the sea-river sector – and also the major European bulk flow, grain.[20]

Complementary to the spread of continental technical innovation to the British Isles has been the recognition of alternative ways of financing vessels. The growth of Isle of Wight based, Carisbrooke Shipping, has been facilitated by a tie with Dutch shipyards, which has provided access to capital funding for Carisbrooke's new buildings. Similarly the financing of Merchant Ferries new RoRo vessels for the Liverpool-Dublin route was achieved by a collaboration with the Italian state builder, Fincantieri. As a consequence, the two *state-of-the-art* ferries arrived on the central, Dublin-Liverpool Irish Sea route flying the Italian flag, registered in Chioggia and employing an Italian crew. This proved a novel example of European integration impacting on Irish Sea operations.

The use of fast RoRo shipping on continental coastlines offers alternatives to long distance haulage. Italian "Autostrade Del Mare" North-South liner services between such ports as Genoa-Naples/Palermo and Venice-Bari, allow lorry operators the opportunity to avoid Italy's congested coastal roads. In 1992 the Italian state owned ferry company, Finmare, set up a subsidiary, Viamare, to operate a Genoa-Sicily service.[21] The idea here was to provide a fast, reliable, low cost alternative to the long North-South road leg along Italy's congested trunk roads. A major focus was placed on the needs of hauliers; this includes simplified and rapid check-in processes. Also, the attempt was made to secure return trailer workings for drivers delivering to the terminals for unaccompanied dispatch. This helped to ensure that hauliers benefited from revenue earning on both the outward and inward legs of their journey. The culinary needs of the Sicilian *padnrocini* (owner drivers) are even catered for by chefs with specific skills in regional dishes. In the first two years of operation the service had won 16% of the road haulage market between Northern Italy and Sicily.[22]

The setting up of the Strade Blue Line service in 2001 between Genoa and Palermo has also enjoyed success, with the two ships on the route accounting for the carriage of some 2,500 trucks per month. Strade Blue Line, which enjoys the investment support of the famous fashion house, Benetton, has claimed that truckers can make cost savings of between 15 and 35% by using the sea option.[23] Similarly, the Genoa-Barcelona fast ferry linkage avoids the congested and environmentally sensitive Alpine and Pyrenees routes. The tragic fire in the Mont Blanc road tunnel in 1999 caused 41 fatalities and provoked a serious debate on the impact of heavy lorries on the delicate Alpine environment.[24] Increasingly, the coastal highway is seen as a viable alternative to such congested and vulnerable road routes.

3.1.2 Shipbuilding in Europe?

The survival and revival of specific parts of the European shipbuilding industry has considerable implications for the Green Highway. The irreversible demise of shipbuilding on the British mainland, in Belfast and also in Cork, has ensured that owners will need to look overseas for standard new buildings. However, a small number of niche projects lend themselves to construction nearer to home. Interestingly the construction of the giant airliner, Airbus 380, has created demand for a dedicated barge, capable of transporting large wing sections down river. The Chester located construction plant has close access to the River Dee. The 58m, 800 tonne dwt barge, *Afon Dyfrdwy*, was constructed in 2004 by Merseyside's McTay shipyard, specifically to move the wing sections to the Dee estuary or Port of Liverpool, enabling transhipment for further aircraft construction in Toulouse.[25] An early Millennium Pan European division of labour was demonstrated by the designing and building of the specialist heavy lift, sea-going, barge, *Terra Marique*. Built to the specifications of the Staffordshire based heavy lift specialist, Robert Wynn and Sons, *Terra Marque*, was financed by a UK

Department of Transport (DfT), Freight Facilities Grant(FFG) designed in Southampton and built in Romania to the specifications of the Dutch shipbuilder, Damen.[26]

In continental Europe, shipbuilding rationalisation has occurred, although Germany, France and Italy still have the capacity to be build large deepsea ships. In the Netherlands there has been renewed emphasis on buildings for the shortsea sector. A clear division of labour can be detected with the low cost, low technology, aspects of ship construction being contracted out to yards in Poland and Romania. This cost saving strategy then entails the towage of the vessel's hull to the North European yard for the high value finishing off process. Traditional European shipyards such as Damen, have close linkages with their Eastern European partners. The UK coastal tanker operator, James Fisher Tankships, has recently taken advantage of this west-east, technology-labour collaboration by having two 5,000 dwt tankers built by Damen's Galati Yard in Romania.[27]

This collaboration offers a halfway house solution to the cost options accessible within the global economy. In addition to the economics of East-West European collaborations, the financial packages offered can also prove attractive to shipowners. In 1998, Arklow's decision to build and flag in the Netherlands was partly a result of the investment that could be channelled into the ship from Dutch small investor circles. Isle of Wight based operator, Carisbrooke Shipping has also participated in Dutch investment schemes. This scheme provided capital for the 4,650dwt general cargo vessels, *Janet C* and *Johanna C* built in Holland, financed by Dutch investors but allowed Carisbrooke to operate the sisterships with a 17% share in ownership.[28]

The perceived benefits of the Green Highway have also been recognised in Southern Europe shipyards. In 2002 the president of the Vigo based, Barreras shipyard welcomed the prospects of increased ship building activity in an area where European yards still enjoy comparative advantage: "The focus on inter-modal traffic and logistics can only serve to reinforce the contribution of shipyards such as ours within the European community".[29] It can be seen that shortsea and small ship building is a niche area of opportunity, given the precarious position of shipbuilding in Western Europe. Moreover, the collaboration between West and East fits nicely with the vision of an expanded Europe.

3.1.3 Inland Ports

A strength of European shortsea shipping lies in its ability to access a network of sizeable inland ports, many of which have attained status as logistical hubs. The top three inland ports in Northern Europe are Duisburg on the River Rhine, the Port of Paris at Limay and Gennevilliers on the River Seine, and Liege on the River Maas. All three offer excellent prospects for linkages to UK and Irish ports. Inland ports provide significant potential for minimising road tkms and maximising sea-river tkms. They provide a more sustainable alternative to road haulage-RoRo ferry combinations. Moreover, they offer a clear example of how the Green Highway can be integrated into the supply chain, with shipping legs maximised, road legs minimised. Figure 16 identifies the extensive European inland network

3.1.4 The Port Of Duisburg

Duisburg has enjoyed particular success as a major inland hub-logistics centre. The port has a unique position in European logistics. It is positioned, 300 kilometres up-stream from the North Sea, at the confluence of the Rhine and Ruhr rivers and at the centre of the Federal State of North Rhine-Westphalia. This region forms the powerhouse of the German economy, contributing to 22% of the national economy. Some 30m inhabitants live within 150 kilometres of the port, which attracts up to 2000 (4,500dwt max) sea-river ships per year.[30] The large volumes moving by ship through the public port and adjoining private wharves, around 50mt per annum, make the inland port a major player in European tonnages. In 2004, Duisburg ranked as 13th in European port volume tables, a considerable achievement for a port so far up-stream. The importance of the port to the macro-economy is reflected in its composite ownership, divided equally between the Federal Government, State Government and the City of Duisburg Council. The port has also been at the forefront of industrial change. The diversification of the regional economy from its traditional heavy industrial base to warehousing, distribution and logistics, provides opportunities for inland shipping. In 2002 it was announced that Duisburg planned to double container capacity within five years.[31] P&O Ports became a major shareholder in the new Duisburg Intermodal Terminal which opened in September 2002 with an initial capacity for 200,000teu.[32]

Japanese shipping giant, NYK Logistics, has commissioned a 10,000sqm warehouse within the port. Additionally, the Port of Duisburg has invested into the Antwerp Gateway Terminal project, securing a strategic link between P&O Ports in Duisburg with its deep-sea terminals in Antwerp. The need to increase capacity in the Duisburg-Antwerp corridor has led to the reinstatement of the 174 km Iron Rhine rail project.[33] This will reopen the freight artery between Europe's second largest deep-sea port with its premier inland port. The 19th century line was closed in 1916 as a result of the disruptions of WW1. The rationale for the railway is to alleviate road congestion in the rapidly growing Belgian port as well as enhancing the inter-modal connections of the Duisburg hub. The port has

117

Figure 16: European Inland Waterway Networks.

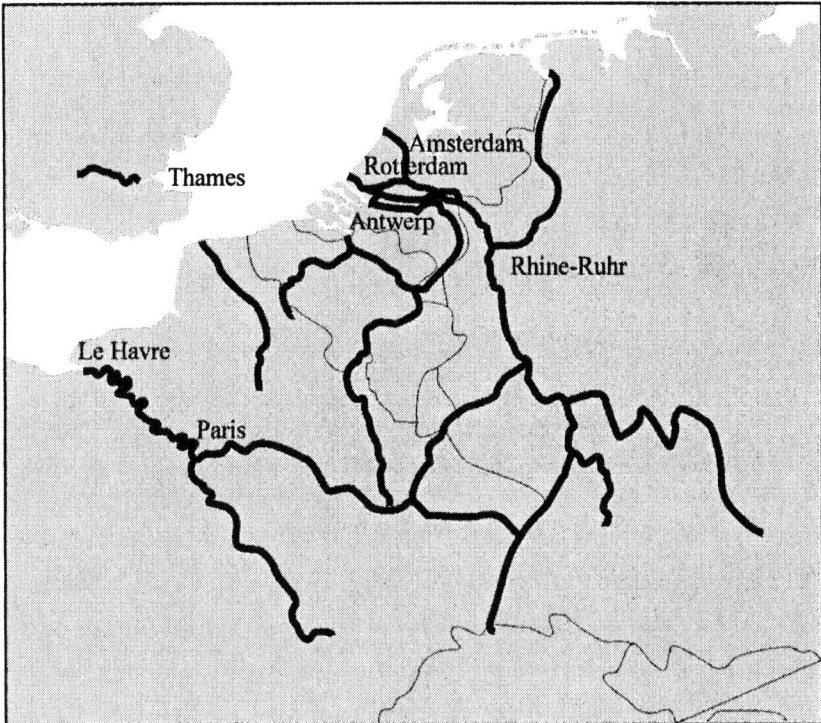

identified the new paradigm challenge as it moves into inter-modal operations: rail-ship transfers are prized as integral to the port's logistical mission, with 21.2mt of cargo being transferred between the two modes in the public and private terminals. Figure 17 presents the 42mt of traffic handled by the public port in 2004, made up of 19.6mt by road, 14.0mt by water and 8.4mt by rail. In addition, the Duisburg-Vienna rail shuttle service, commenced in 2003, has been championed by the port as a major contributor to modal shift, with the service meeting its target to take 10,000 truck loads off the road in the first year of operation.[34]

118

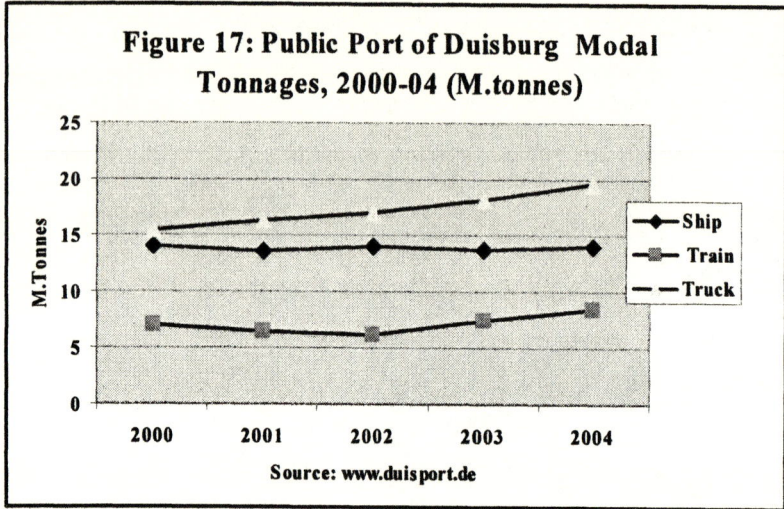

Figure 17: Public Port of Duisburg Modal Tonnages, 2000-04 (M.tonnes)

Source: www.duisport.de

The two-year project to dismantle the giant Krupp steelworks at Dortmund has provided regular cargoes via the Duisburg hub. The large volumes generated by the dismantling of the plant provided welcome backhaul cargoes from Duisburg and it was anticipated that the critical mass of volume reached would lead to a continuance of traffic after the cessation of the scrap traffics.[35] This shows the potential for utilising water transport in transforming the economy. The shift to container operations was proving highly successful in the early years of the Millennium. Figure 18 shows the 46.0% increase in containers handled in the public terminals between 2002-4. In June 2004, Duisburg welcomed a new river service in the form of Cobelfret's purpose built RoRo ship, *Waterways 3*, which loaded 500 Ford Fiestas for the UK market.[36] The German road toll on heavy lorries, LKW-Maut, which came into force in January 2005 has proved an extra cost incentive to use Duisburg's sea-river and barge services. Along with the Working Time Directive and its impact on road haulage productivity, the imposition of the LKW-Maut road tax (to be introduced to all EU motorways in 2010) on German motorways has influenced modal transfer.

119

Figure 18: Duisburg Public Terminals, Container Volumes, 2002-4

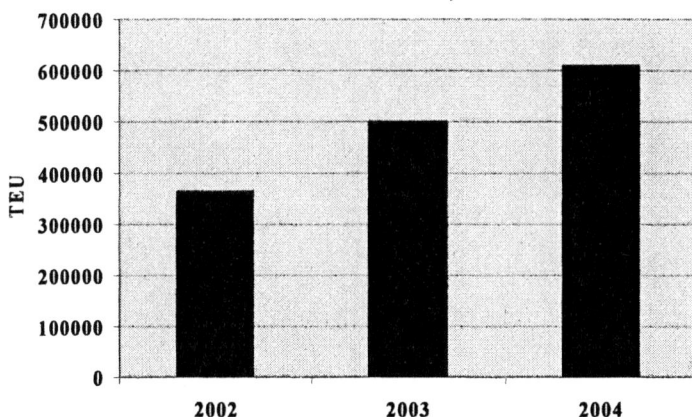

Source: www.duisport.de

Both factors proved instrumental in leading shortsea and inter-modal operator Geest Line North Sea's 2004 decision to instigate a dedicated Duisburg-Rotterdam barge service to feed its shortsea services.[37]

3.1.5 The Port of Paris

The Port of Paris has attained considerable growth in recent decades. Improvements to the River Seine infrastructure has facilitated growth and provided for larger vessel sizes. The mission statement of the publicly owned Port of Paris Authority, which claims the position of Europe's number two river port, is to serve as a catalyst for economic development in the Île-de-France Region.[38] With its 70 public berths, 200 private industrial berths and 500km of waterways, the Seine focuses on steel, grain, construction materials and fertilisers in the dry bulk sector, with 5000 tonne tug-pusher barge combinations providing economies of scale. In the unitised trades, the Seine has seen successful container shipping and RoRo innovations. The joint venture between terminal operators

120

and barge operators, Logiseine, has enjoyed increased container volumes on the 30 hour river corridor passage between Le Havre and the Port of Gennevilliers (situated 6km from Paris), with movements rising from 6000teu in 1995 to 22,800 in 2000.[39] The company, with its own haulage fleet, provides intermodal coverage within a 100km radius of Gennevilliers, thus demonstrating the advantages of door-to-door integrated transportation. Inter-modal operations are also offered by the Port's daily rail shuttle to Milan. The Renault logistics subsidiary, GAT, has been successful in utilising barge traffics, with around 150,000 vehicles moving along the Seine to Le Havre per year.[40] The movement of building materials into Paris has been a strategic objective of the City. Between 10-12% of the City's cement is distributed by river transport. Re-development contracts for the City's prestigious public buildings have generated large volumes of materials and site clearance rubble for river barges. These include:

- Musée des Arts Premiers: 200,000 tonnes;
- Stade de France: 130,000 tonnes:
- Meteor Metro Line: 560,000 tonnes;
- Bibliothèque de France Library: 900,000 tonnes.[41]

The global aggregates leader, Lafarge, with its 14 river berths and 5 riverside depots has proved a particular champion of river traffics. The €9m investment in a 7 km conveyor system at the Muids-Doubeuf gravel pit has facilitated barge loadings and, as a consequence, 120,000 annual truck trips are taken off the City's roads. The Seine Ports, Gennevilliers and Limay, offer facilities for sea-river ships up to 2500dwt. Sea-river volumes average between 500-700,000 tonnes annually, with a further 150,000 generated by private wharves. Selected shortsea passage times offered are: Southampton, 1.5 days, Dublin, 3 days.[42]

3.1.6 The Port Of Liege

The Port of Liege is strategically situated in the industrial heartlands of Northern Europe. Barges can steam the 310km to Rotterdam in 20 hours. The barge routes are supplemented additionally by two shuttle trains per day to the Dutch hub. Heading in a westerly direction, the canal corridor of 362km to the French industrial port, Dunkerque, has been up-graded from 300dwt to 1350dwt barge size. Liege which is accessed from the North Sea via the Scheldt or Rhine connections, the 129km long Albert Canal and the River Maas, has traditionally generated significant volumes of quality finished steels. Despite the large number of low bridges, sea-river ships can penetrate the inland network. Regular steel services from Liege serve such ports as Poole, Northfleet, Sutton Bridge, Boston, Goole and Seaham. These services have become increasingly important, given the decline of UK steel manufacturing.

In 2004, the Port Of Liege achieved a tonnage record of 15.1mt handled.[43] However, by 2005 Liege was facing a massive rationalisation of its steel making capacity and, therefore, the port faces a similar challenge as Duisburg's in assisting with transforming the regional economy.

3.1.7 Routes to the East

The collapse of Communism and its consequences, the opening up of Europe for East-West trade, has greatly increased inland shipping opportunities. The Rhine-Danube link with its potential to move vast quantities of low cost bulk materials between East and West Europe offers significant shipping opportunities. Likewise, the Saimaa Canal, which links the inland Finnish forestry belt with the Baltic ports via Russian territories and the Gulf of Finland. The inland route to the Middle East also provides potential. In 1992, history was created when a cargo of china clay from Fowey in Cornwall took the inland route to Bandar

Anzali in Iran. This fourteen day voyage by a 2,500dwt *Sormovskiy* class ship, which went up into the Baltic via the Kiel Canal, passing St Petersburg and into the River Neva, then through the Volga-Balt system of North Russia to Volograd and finally entering the Caspian Sea.[44] The inland route is conducive to use by the extensive river barge fleets of the ex Soviet Union..

It has been made evident how the continental inland waterways and ports network offers opportunities for the Green Highway to link Britain and Ireland to the industrial and logistical heartlands of the European economy. The important role of the inland ports has been shown as fundamental to the economy (and its transformation) in the respective local region. In addition, the new entrant nations of Eastern Europe are becoming increasingly accessible. Furthermore, the consistent up-grading of European waterways is facilitating increased vessel sizes (thus lowering shipping costs) and allowing for improved transit times.

3.2 The Celtic Tiger Impact.

The recent dynamic growth in the Irish economy has emphasised the importance of the nation's European trade links. In addition, moves towards a favourable shipping policy, resulting in a strengthening of shipping enterprise, have raised the profile of the Irish Registry. However, economic growth brings its own problems. Road congestion is part of the price to pay. Given the concentration of traffics on the main ports, Dublin, Cork and Belfast, there is scope for spreading shortsea and coastal trades to the less congested regions.

The Irish shortsea trades provide significant prospects for the Green Highway in three major areas:

    (1)   the traditional importance of the large LoLo volumes between Britain and Ireland;
    (2)   the burgeoning RoRo passenger and freight trades;
    (3)   the rise in Irish services directly servicing continental ports.

Liner services from such ports as Bristol, Cardiff, Liverpool and Glasgow have traditionally operated to Cork, Dublin and Belfast. The growth of road traffics and developments in RoRo shipping post 1960s, however, has led to the dominance of this mode. This has placed emphasis on such short crossings as Holyhead-Dublin/Dun Laoghaire, Stranraer-Larne and Fishguard/Pembroke-Rosslaire. The emergence of fast catamaran ferries on all major routes in the 1990s has provided passenger and freight customer with a rapid crossing option.

Integration into the European economy has brought substantial trading opportunities for Ireland. One of the leading forces in 1980-90s European LoLo trades was the Netherlands-Irish joint venture, Bell Lines. The linkage between Rotterdam and Dublin via the Port of Waterford provided an early example of inter-modal logistics. The hatchless container ship, *Bell Pioneer,* brought express, fast turnaround services, to the route and was integrated with Bell Lines container train service to Dublin. This enabled fast transit times to Dublin. In addition, ferry services from Le Havre, Cherbourg and St. Malo have unlocked Irish trades with the Continent.

The economic and environmental pressures associated with rapid economic growth in Ireland have placed emphasis on the transport system. The economic "hotspots" of greater Dublin and the Cork region have induced increasing amounts of road traffic. The historic role of Ireland as an agriculturally based economy, aligned to the UK economy, has given way to a modern world trading economy, focusing on high growth sectors – electronics, pharmaceuticals, information technology and financial services. The challenge facing shipping is how much of this trading activity can be diverted from the road system to the Green Highway? The concentration of RoRo trades on Cork, Dublin and Belfast has led to large road haulage volumes in these cities. Meanwhile, smaller regional ports have been restricted to peripheral activities, particularly on the West Coast. The West Coast exception, however, is Shannon-Foynes Ports. Port expansion, including the early Millennium development of a weekly container service to Rotterdam, has significant potential for reducing road haulage tkm on Irish roads.[45]

The major element of the Irish flag fleet is composed of Arklow Shipping's vessels. The modern green hulled fleet of mainly bulk vessels in the 2,000-15,000dwt range is well known throughout Europe. In 2005 the company operated 37 vessels under the Irish and Netherlands flags.[46] The importance of the company to the Irish maritime economy was revealed in December 2001 when the threatened re-flagging of some 27 vessels from the Irish to the Netherlands flag was prevented by the Irish Government's reform of the tax regime.[47] Following the success of such off-shore tax regimes as the Danish and Norwegian international registries and tonnage tax schemes in Germany, Holland and the UK, it became obvious that the Irish Government would have to respond with a similar scheme or run the risk of losing its largest fleet.

3.2.1 The International Maritime Development Office (IMDO)

The need to stop the latent demise of Irish shipping was met by a positive response: the setting up of the IMDO in 2001. A number of initiatives were developed, as the Irish Government began to appreciate the importance of shipping. With the IMDO as the catalyst, investment was directed at training, education and employment generation. The Irish Tonnage Tax was set up in order to prevent the loss of further tonnage, namely, Arklow Shipping and Irish Continental Group's, Irish Ferries, but also to attract new tonnage. The announcement of the Irish Tonnage Tax, Christmas 2002, was timely as these companies were considering leaving the home registry. Previously, Arklow Shipping had demonstrated its concern over the Irish tax regime by flagging out the 3,000dwt, *Arklow Sand* to the Netherlands flag in 1998 with Irish seafarer jobs lost to Dutch and Indonesian Officers and ratings.[48]

Up until the new Millennium, the boom years of the Celtic Tiger economy generated significant maritime trade. The boom, however, had somehow by-passed Irish Shipping. Eventually a gradual awareness of the opportunities in attracting global shipping capital emerged. Ireland had enjoyed particular success in attracting overseas investment: international banking, investment fund management and insurance have become strong contributors to the financial services sector. The compatibility of a maritime cluster with these industries was to become apparent in 2003 when the Bank of Ireland led a shift in banking strategy towards maritime finance, realising the opportunities that came with the Irish Tonnage Tax. The new regime was particularly timely and much welcomed: *Lloyd's List,* after interviewing a leading Irish shipowner, ran the heading: "Cavalry arrives in the form of new tonnage tax regime,"[49] and also quoted IMDO director, Glenn Murphy:

> The Irish maritime industry was on the brink of collapse...many of our larger owners would have been compelled to lower the Irish flag and relocate their core business structures to another country.[50]

In the first two years of the scheme, which offers a notional corporation tax rate of 12.5%, Irish tonnage grew by 68%.[51] The IMDO promoted the €58m investment in a National Maritime Centre in Cork which brought world class maritime training standards to Ireland, providing 750 students from both the domestic and global labour market with state-of-the-art facilities. Government training schemes have focused on Cadet recruitment and training. Also, seafarer tax relief and refunds in social insurance for employers of Irish crews have been implemented as a means to encourage a revival of Irish seafaring. Despite the positive moves towards developing maritime business in Ireland, events in November 2005 were dominated by a serious and damaging labour dispute. The attempts by management at replacing Irish nationality crew on Irish Ferries, Dublin-Holyhead and Rosslare-Pembroke services, with lower wage East European seafarers led to the ships becoming occupied by the incumbent crew and ferry services temporarily suspended.[52] This illustrates the global pressures placed upon seafarers in Northern Europe.

At the Dublin Castle launch of the IMDO in 2002, Mr. Dermot Ahern T.D. Minister for Communications, Marine and Natural Resources, outlined the new maritime strategy, "Shipping Challenges for Ireland 2002-2012." The importance of the shortsea sector was acknowledged and commitment to modal shift based on quality, frequency, as well as safety, was stressed. The need to integrate shipping in door-to-door transport services was made evident.[53] The growth of the Irish economy is illustrated by Figure 19 which shows the €86.9b value of Irish export trade in 2004, a 87% money growth on the 1994 value. In the same period, the value of imports is shown to have grown by 52.0% to €50b. Figure 20 illustrates the tonnage increases in Irish maritime trade. Although these volumes do not achieve the same high growth rates as the money values of the Irish trades, the figure of 47.7mt in 2005 represents a substantial 31.3% growth in the 1997-2005 period. With 40% of total Irish freight tonnages accruing to the UK trades, and 73% within the European Union,[54] it is evident that shortsea shipping's role is paramount. Of particular interest to the Green Highway debate are the 10.21mt of RoRo freight in 2005, approximating to 21.0% of total Irish maritime volumes. Figure 21 details the composition of Irish maritime trades and identifies the high

Figure 19: Irish Trades by Value, 1997-2005.

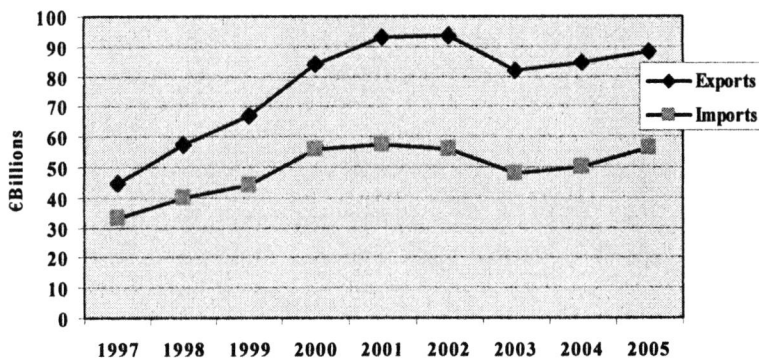

Source: IMDO, *Irish Maritime Transport Economist*.

Figure 20: Irish Maritime Tonnages, 1997-2005.

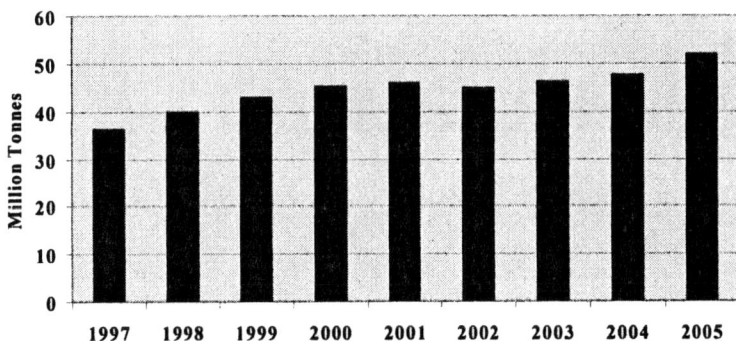

Source: www.cso.ie

growth rate of RoRo shipping, 1997-2005. The intensity of RoRo corridors, with 186 weekly sailings, between Ireland and Great Britain, is measured by the 9.97mt of freight (>94% of Irish RoRo traffics) wheeled traffics crossing the Irish Sea in 2005.The convergence of these traffics on the short crossing routes leads to high lorry tkm. Traffic concentration on Dublin, as the engine-house of the Irish economy, is obviously a major factor in the predominance of RoRo linkages. However, opportunities exists for transferring an increased portion of this freight to LoLo container and break-bulk shipping, away from the central corridors, utilising the regional ports on either side of the Irish Sea. In 2004, of the 10.21mt of Irish RoRo freight, 7.88mt[55] (77%) passed through the Port of

Figure 21: Irish Maritime Trades by Tonnage & Sectors, 1997-2005.

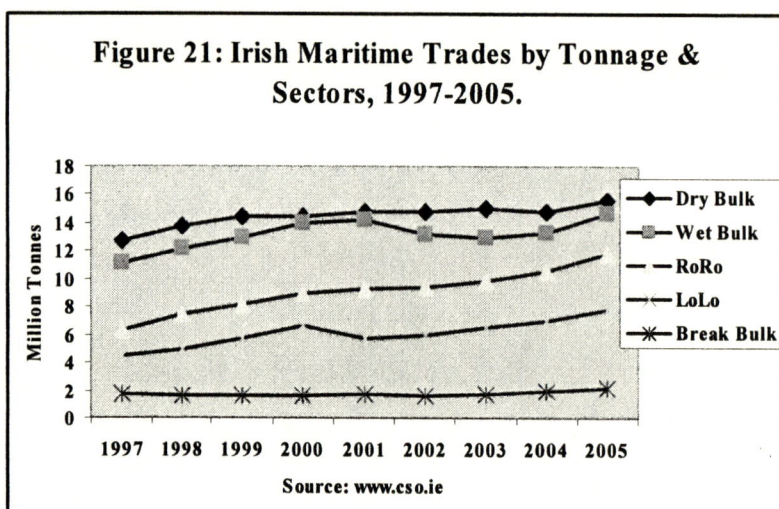

Source: www.cso.ie

Dublin. The IMDO Trans European Network (TENS) strategy, "Irish Motorways of the Sea," includes the objectives of:

- minimising the peripheral island nature of the Irish economy;
- achieving sustainable sea-freight connections;
- eliminating transport bottlenecks;
- reducing dependence on the UK landbridge.[56]

The evidence drawn here from the growing Irish trades, suggests that there are opportunities to extend the Green Highway to regional Irish ports, to question the dependence on RoRo services and to reduce the UK landbridge. The current re-emphasis on shipping and the commitment to the Irish flag bodes well; as does the continued growth of one of Europe's major players in the shortsea bulk trades, Arklow Shipping, as a domiciled Irish company, with its head office in the historic Irish port of its namesake.

3.3. The Impact of Port Deregulation

In chapter 2, the problem of an inefficient, backward looking ports industry was identified as a factor in the decline of domestic and shortsea shipping. The twin obstacles of low investment (thus poor productivity) and labour unrest beset many ports and rendered the shipping option unreliable and uncompetitive. Many regulated ports were unable or unwilling to offer flexibility in cargo handling services, often closing down for evenings and weekends. One outcome of this deregulation in the ports' sector has been the revival of such traditional ports as Tilbury, Hull, Southampton and Liverpool. The historic industrial relations problems, coupled with restrictions on investment funding of these ports led to the loss of trade to less regulated, often smaller ports in the 1960-90 period. For example, the enduring problems of Tilbury in the 1980s led to a concentration of London's newsprint handling at the up-stream (Thames) Convoys Wharf (now closed). Likewise, the dramatic growth of the container port, Felixstowe, was greatly assisted by enduring labour problems at Southampton, Liverpool and Tilbury. Since de-regulation, productivity gains and significant investment in handling and storage at Tilbury have led to the newsprint traffic returning and the impending run-down of Convoy's Wharf.[57] Southampton, Tilbury and Liverpool have revived and now provide competition with Felixstowe. On the River Humber/Trent/Ouse privatisation and deregulation has brought intense competition between Associated British ports (ABP) Hull,

130

Grimsby, Immingham, Goole and the River wharves - Howdendyke, Flixborough, Neap House, Grove Wharf, Keadby, Gunness Wharf, New Holland and Killingholme.

If the decline of domestic and shortsea shipping in the British and Irish trades can partially be apportioned to the historic problems of the port industry, the impact of port deregulation has been to re-introduce competitiveness and to secure investment in cargo handling and storage technology. A prime example was the 1991 re-opening of the Hull Container Terminal, which had closed in the late 1980s, after a decade of uncertainty and under-utilisation. Unable to operate reliable services due to acute labour problems, the nationalised British Transport Commission's managed port felt that the only option was closure.[58] The labour politics of the National Dock Labour Scheme led to a complete dialogue failure with management. As a result shortsea container services to Netherlands and German ports were withdrawn. The mixture of port privatisation (1983) and the abolition of the Dock Labour Scheme (1989) provided the conditions for the re-opening of the Hull terminal and the reinstatement of European and Scandinavian container services.[59]

The net impact of deregulation can also be witnessed in the improvement in port efficiency, providing shipowners with a 24 hour x 7 day service. This gives shipping a competitive edge and allows for a full utilisation of vessels. Another port to benefit from deregulation is Dublin. In July 2000, it was reported that "... Dublin is fast becoming a victim of its own success, with demand placing considerable pressure on the port's existing infrastructure and access arrangements."[60] This can now be accepted as a sign of considerable progress from the uncertainties of the 1980s and early 1990s, when restrictive practices and other industrial relations' problems, tainted the commercial perception of the port, leading to the loss of traffics.

European port policy has promoted the opening up of port services to competition via the EU Port Services Directive. European Union ports' policy is based on the need to promote competitive, unsubsidised ports. In 2001, European transport commissioner, (the late) Loyola de Palacio, called for increased deregulation and competitiveness, arguing that:

> ...outmoded practices have to be changed in order for all to benefit fully. In addition, our ports will be called upon to play an increasing role in attempts to transfer more goods and passengers to the environmentally less damaging and less congested sea transport mode, encouraging intermodal transport and making it less costly.[61]

The question of competition and the level of port dues is integral to the issues of port deregulation and privatisation. Expressing shipowner concern over port costs and "restrictive practices", leading shipping director, Mr. Emanuele Grimaldi, has called for more competition in European ports.[62] The shift since the early 1980s privatisation strategy in the UK has been towards deregulation in Europe's ports. Given that the freedom to provide services is enshrined in the Four Freedoms of European Unity – free movement of people, capital, goods, services – there has been a constant legislative pressure on ports to liberalise. Therefore, the provision of port services has become increasingly open to competition.

In the Antwerp-Hamburg range competition and the traditional cross-border rivalry has intensified as a result of moves towards deregulation. In November 2001 the Rotterdam Municipal Council responded to the competitive pressures in the shortsea and feeder container trades by introducing a reduced tariff for ships lower than 6500gt in these highly cost sensitive trades.[63]

One unpredicted – but highly conducive to the Green Highway – aspect of port privatisation and de-regulation is the move of ports into shipping services. The Mersey Docks and Harbour owners (now Peel Ports) of the Port of Liverpool have expanded their investment portfolio by setting up three shipping lines with container services in the Irish and North Seas – BG Shipping, Coastal Container Lines and Concorde Container Lines. The Glasgow based Clydeport, has expanded into bulk and container feeder services. Integration between these services and the regions they serve became strengthened in 2005 when Mersey, Manchester and Clyde ports were assimilated under the control of Peel Holdings.[64] More attention is given to these ventures in chapter 5, which will link shipping and port business organisation with the Green Highway. It next remains to consider the progress of the Port of Felixstowe, which has enjoyed growth outside of the politics and strife of the mature ports.

3.3.1 The Rise of Felixstowe

The development of the port of Felixstowe serves as a clear example of the benefits of deregulation. The containerisation revolution enabled a small agricultural port, with extremely limited port infrastructure and rail and road links to race ahead of the giants of UK deepwater ports – Tilbury, Southampton, Liverpool. These three ports were somewhat restricted by political intervention and the National Dock Labour Scheme (NDLS).

Napier University's maritime researcher, Professor Alfred Baird, has traced the growth of the port in the post-war period.[65] The Port developed from humble beginnings. Promoted as the Felixstowe Dock and Railway Company in 1879, it never really fulfilled its early promise and suffered declining traffics in the inter-war years. In 1951 the port was bought by a local grain merchant for £50,000 and some modernisation occurred. Burgeoning developments in European trades involving RoRo and container shipping provided viable traffics for Felixstowe. The growth of the port invoked the interest of Government and in 1960 a decision was taken on whether Felixstowe should be entered into the NDLS. Professor Baird has recognised the Minister of Labour's decision to allow the port to remain outside of the scheme as fundamental to future success: "Felixstowe thus avoided the high costs and restrictive practices associated with the NDLS."[66] The port had enjoyed investment, growth and good industrial relations in the post 1960 period in marked contrast to its older rivals. Felixstowe's development provided a sharp contrast with the general pattern in UK ports. Between 1983 and 1992 the UK ports industry shed 20,000 employees, representing a 40% reduction, whilst Felixstowe was enjoying an almost 300% growth in employment.[67] Recognition in 1991 by the leading Hong Kong port operator, Hutchinson Whampoa, of Felixstowe's container potential, can now be seen as part of a global strategy. Spreading from one of the world's leading container ports, Hong Kong, where Hutchinson Whampoa hold a dominant position, the group has become a major global terminal operator: 44 terminals, with 236 berths and corresponding facilities now form part of the group's global portfolio of ports, including 11 in the Peoples Republic of China (PRC), 6 in Northern Europe and 11 in Northern and Central America.[68] The Green Highway is well served by Felixstowe with a high frequency of domestic container feeder services to Teesport, Newcastle and Grangemouth. Table 15 shows the evolving ownership of the port – a clear example of how ports are traded in the de-regulated/privatised environment.

Table 15: The Evolving Ownership of the Port of Felixstowe

Ownership	Date Purchased	Purchase Price
Felixstowe Dock & Railway Company 1879	Port Opens 1886	
Gordon Palmer (Grain Merchant)	1951	£50,000
European Ferries/P&O Group	1976/1987	£6.8m
Hutchinson Whampoa	1991	£108m
Source: Port of Felixstowe		

What this evidence of Felixstowe's growth shows is that given the right mix of location, geographic factors and managerial enterprise, ports can provide excellent service in both the deepsea and coastal sectors. The potential of the port has proved attractive to overseas investors and the contrast with the more established ports is highly apparent. At this juncture, however, it is apposite to draw attention to the fact that since privatisation and de-regulation, the more mature ports have made significant progress on improving efficiency. In December 1996, port performance was discussed in Parliament. The Port of Tilbury was proclaimed as an example of the new spirit of enterprise in the industry:

> At one time damned by an image of crumbling infrastructure and fractious labour relations, Tilbury has emerged over the past few years to maintain increasing challenge to its more recently developed competitors at Felixstowe and the Isle of Grain. Those dramatic changes have served to revolutionise the culture and business attitudes of the past...[69]

In 2005, the success of Tilbury in the shortsea container trades was endorsed by the introduction of a Geest Line container rail freight service, Tilbury-Birmingham, to link with the company's intensive Rotterdam shipping service.[70] Further evidence of revival was presented by the 2005 opening of the fully automated £36m Enterprise Distribution Centre at Tilbury, linking intensive Scandinavian sea linkages with a rail-dock.[71] This evidence reform in the British and Irish ports industry bodes well for the Green Highway. With increased emphasis on competition and choice, the coastal and shortsea ship operator benefits from improved reliability and vessel turnaround time. Enhanced vessel performance – leading to increased revenues – provides for improved Green Highway competitiveness with road haulage.

3.4. Shipping: the Green Business Choice?

The growing awareness of environmental issues is beginning to prove conducive to shipping. As businesses become increasingly focused upon becoming "good neighbours" and projecting a caring image, the shipping choice becomes more attractive. A major turning point in the thinking of global business strategy came about with the off-shore crude oil loading platform Brent Spar controversy in the early 1990s. Shell International decommissioned the large platform in 1991, after 15 years service in the North Sea. Decisions on the disposal of the platform were influenced by costs; the lowest cost option appeared to be to tow out the platform to a deep Atlantic trench and consign it to the ocean floor. Shell, however, were surprised to learn of the widespread public hostility to what was widely perceived as an environmentally damaging act. In Northern Europe, campaigning orchestrated by Greenpeace, promoted widespread aversion to Shell. In several countries this translated into the boycotting of Shell petrol stations. The aftermath of the controversy brought about a shift in emphasis at Shell: a more environmentally acceptable scrapping solution was selected, costing the multinational a further £39m. Moreover, greater attention was given to business ethics, sustainability, social auditing and environment concern.[72] The "sea-change" at Shell was heralded by the Institute of Social and Ethical Account Ability's chief executive, Dr. Simon Zaldek, as smart, positive and ethical strategy towards environmental issues.[73]

As well as leading the concern over Brent Spar, the Scandinavian and Northern European nations have been active in their promotion of sustainable transport. The leading Swedish vehicle producer, Volvo, has been an advocate of greener alternatives to road haulage based logistics. Volvo's transport operators have the logistics task of distributing the parent company's production of 162,311 trucks, 17,867 buses and 38,417 construction machines (2005-6 figures).[74] The commitment of Volvo to environmental concern is evident in the following statement by transport executive, Kerstin Bergvist:

> Environmental concern is very important to Volvo and Volvo Transport. We have achieved an ISO 14001- certificate as a base for our actions...we have included environmental awareness in our Supplier's Assessment and we make yearly surveys to measure awareness as well as actually follow up on emissions of Nox, Sox, CO_2 and Particles.[75]

Shortsea transportation has been a key feature of Volvo's pan-European logistics, particularly the utilisation of Grimaldi Line's RoRo service linking Northern and Southern Europe. In 2005, the German white goods giant, Bosch, demonstrated its commitment to sustainable transport via the use of barges and shortsea shipping. By switching from high sided mega-trailer services, some 60mtkm of UK bound white goods were on target to be transferred to shipping by 2007.[76] In all, Bosch has targeted a total of 334btkm of freight transfer, given the ability of specialised shipping to compete with road haulage, whilst enabling the multinational manufacturer to implement its environmental strategy which states:

> ...respect for peoples' health and safety, for an economic use of resources and a natural and clean environment are basic principles of our business policy.[77]

The French furniture chain, Conforma, has proved a high profile advocate of using river barges on the River Rhone, linking the Port of Marseilles with their inland distribution centre in Lyon. Conforma has not only benefited from cost savings by switching from roads to water, but has also been able to claim environmental credibility by achieving significant cuts in carbon emissions.[78] Although business in continental Europe and Scandinavia has been more pro-active in developing environmental strategies, British and Irish businesses are beginning to follow suit. The use of shipping as an alternative to road haulage enables the transport user to become more aligned with the cause of environmental sensitivity. The annual transfer of 23,000 tonnes of lubrication oil movements between Hull and Rotherham from road to inland waterway, allowed the transport user, Exol/Green Line Lubricants, to extol the virtues of reducing road traffic. On the inaugural arrival at the Rotherham installation of Whitaker Tankship's 500 tonne barge, *Humber Energy*, the oil company's MD, Mr. Steve Everitt, welcomed the return to water and, moreover, the reduction of a 1000 annual loaded road tanker journeys off the roads of Humberside and South Yorkshire.[79] In new industrial and commercial developments, shipping connections may become integral to the planning agenda.

Container feeder shipping, for example, became increasingly important to the controversial debate on the proposed construction of Southampton's Dibden Bay container terminal. The issue of road traffic generated by the New Forest fringe terminal fuelled environmental concern in the Solent region. The response of the port owners, Associated British Ports (ABP), was to advocate the rail and coastal shipping alternatives to road as a way of moving deep-sea containers domestically (the Dibden Bay scheme was ruled out by Government in 2004 on environmental grounds). The 2004 launch of Shannon-Foynes Port's first container service was lauded by the port not only for the linkages it provided Western Ireland with the mega port, Rotterdam, but also for its environmental positives: some 2mtkm of freight would be immediately taken off Irish roads.[80] The shift towards environmental sensitivity in business strategy holds obvious benefits for the Green Highway. Increasingly as concern over environmental issues and road congestion intensifies, the case for alternative transport modes to road strengthens.

3.5 The Impact of Transport Policy

The growing awareness of transport pollution in the last two decades of the 20th Century has led to alternative modes to road haulage being championed in the political arena. EU Common Transport Policy (CTP) has advocated an enhanced role for shipping in the sustainable mobility strategy of European transport policy. The CTP's perception of a sustainable European Transport network can be recognised as conducive to water transport and freight transfer. In addition to the environmentally driven policies, developments in maritime policy have also proved conducive to the Green Highway. After many years of indifference, policy makers in the UK have reassessed their perception of shipping's value to the economic, as well as environmental welfare of the nation. The impact of a positive Irish maritime policy has already been discussed; the following chapter will consider the influence of a pro-active maritime policy on British shipping and its role in the Green Highway.

The importance of some degree of supportive public policy was recognised at the outset of this book. Having outlined the obstacles to be overcome in gaining freight transfer in the UK, the future implementation of European transport policy will favour water transport. The two critical areas are:

(1) the carbon tax imposition;
(2) the identification of the externally
generated environmental costs of transport.

Both policy areas are likely to serve to the detriment of road haulage economics. Given the sharp contrast in energy efficiency per tkm between road and water, the imposition of such "green" taxes can only serve to benefit the latter transport mode. The end result of such policy helps reduce the critical distance/volume thresholds where water transport becomes competitive with road haulage. The twin problems of road congestion and vehicle fuel emissions are seen as a threat to the concept of an economically integrated and environmentally discerning European Community. Worsening journey transit times and the economic inefficiency of lorries delayed by congestion are now evident – the dominance of road haulage is now being challenged. In chapter 2, the dramatic growth of road haulage in the 20th century was highlighted. From the seemingly unassailable supremacy of the mode it is now questionable if this dominance can be sustained! For the first time in the short history of the motor lorry its supremacy is beginning to be questioned in the world of European politics and logistics. Partly this can be accepted as the result of the critical levels of rapidly increasing road congestion. To a large extent the market has failed to ensure a workable solution to the transport problem.

The preoccupation with private cars has been at the expense of public transport, buses and passenger trains; the emphasis on road haulage has proved detrimental to inland and coastal shipping and railfreight. The desire of European policymakers is recognisable as an attempt to divert some traffic away from roads. The EU has recognised that three modes have the spare capacity to achieve a significant shift away from road haulage – railways, inland shipping, coastal and shortsea shipping.[81] In 1995, in order to facilitate this shift the Commission adopted three areas of action, all conducive to the Green Highway:

(1)   to improve the quality and efficiency of short-sea transport;
(2)   to improve ports and infrastructures;
(3)   the inclusion of short-sea shipping within the Common
         Transport Policy (CTP) external relations framework.[82]

The 2001 European Commission's White Paper, *European Transport Policy for 2010: Time to Decide*[83] outlined a number of strategies for curtailing the growth of road haulage in Europe, whilst promoting rail and water alternatives. The recognition of the need to target road haulage for the external costs it generates per tkm is based upon the "polluter pays principle." The equalisation of external cost recovery is a prime EU transport objective for facilitating the modal transfer of freight to rail and water. In addition, more attention paid to the enforcement of regulations on driver hours, more scrutiny of driver training and qualification and Community parity on weekend bans, all lead to a higher cost, albeit professionally improved, haulage sector. Integral to the modal shift strategy is the revitalisation of the European rail network, the integration of rail and shipping, including inland shipping and the promotion of Marine Motorways. The opportunities offered by the Community's inland waterways and its 25,000km of coastline for intra-European traffics are valued as part of the solution for inland congestion and road traffic pollution:

> Intra-Community maritime transport and inland waterway transport are two key components of intermodality which must provide a means of coping with the growing congestion of road and rail infrastructure and of tackling air pollution. [84]

The 2001 European Conference of Ministers of Transport report, *Short Sea Shipping in Europe* has identified the importance of shipping within the context of European cohesion in the way it,

- promotes European trade competitiveness;
- maintains vital transport links;
- decreases unit costs of transport;
- facilitates Eastern European integration;
- relieves congestion from land based networks.[85]

Additionally, the EU Commission's Marco Polo Project has allocated funds of €115M to its objective of diverting some 12 btkm of intra-European freight from road to coastal and inland shipping.[86] The Royal Commission on Environmental Pollution's Eighteenth Report, *Transport and the Environment* (1994), is an important milepost in the direction of British policy making. The Committee's warnings of high traffic growth in the first decades of the new Millennium have focused attention on the gridlock scenario, the inevitability of an unsustainable road dominated economy. The problem facing the policymakers, however, is how best to ensure that traffic is diverted to water and rail. The political approach in the UK appears to be working on two mutually compatible fronts: (a) raising the profile of shipping in the national transport agenda; (b) financially supporting schemes which lead to shipping securing or retaining traffics which would otherwise have been lost to road haulage (without the financial assistance). Such capital projects as the chemical handling and storage facilities at the Manchester Ship Canal based Huntsman Chemical Company, have been financially supported both by the Department of Transport and the Regions. The shortsea-inland movement of chemicals in this example has been applauded as a successful shipping alternative to road, reducing heavy road tanker chemical movements by 6000 per annum.[87]

For the Green Highway to achieve anything like its potential, the problem of disappearing riverside wharfage needs to be addressed. Pressure from property developers is intense, particularly on the Thames, but also in a number of regional UK ports. The desirability of waterfront property, both as residential and as office space, has already been identified as a factor contributing to lost markets for shipping. Realisation is dawning that it is paramount to policy objectives on shipping promotion that wharves and quaysides are protected. At a regional and local level, planning guidance is beginning to take cognisance of the need to protect cargo wharves from property speculation. The Regional Planning Guidance Note, RPG3B, *Strategic Planning Guidance for the River Thames* was issued in February 1997. Key paragraph of this Note, 3.57, requires relevant authorities to:

> adopt policies in their development plans to encourage the use of the river for the transport of freight, including waste, aggregate and other goods; identify in development plans sites suitable for the loading and unloading of water-borne freight in furtherance of these policies, and adopt policies to protect these sites against permanent development which could jeopardise the future for these purposes.[88]

In Summer 2005, UK Government declared its support for the Mayor of London's policy for safeguarding 50 Thames wharves.[89] This news came as relief to the operators currently using the Thames and also signals to new entrants in the future that port infrastructure will be retained. With the huge demands for bulk site clearance and the supply chain of building materials generated by the London Olympics in 2012, the safeguarding of riverside cargo handling facilities is essential if water transport is to be significantly employed. It can be accepted that transport policy is beginning to have a positive impact on promoting domestic and shortsea shipping. One area where Government has actively (financially) promoted modal transfer from roads to water is with the Freight Facilities Grant (FFG), particularly the simplified application process, post 1997.

3.5.1 Reforming the Freight Facilities Grant

The Freight Facilities Grant was first enacted by Government in the UK for rail freight 1974. In 1981 the FFG was extended to waterways with the express objective of securing increased use of inland shipping. The capital grant to shipowners, shippers and port facility operators who could utilise the funding in order to secure traffics from road haulage initially had a disappointing take up response. Figure 22 illustrates the sudden surge in successful grant applications that followed the FFG reforms in 1997-8. It can be seen that between 1983 and

1998 only 9 applications proved successful; between 1998 and 1999 11 grants were awarded! Basically, the system was made more user friendly with the administering Civil Servants playing a more supportive role to applicants. Previously the tedious process of applying had proved something of a barrier with only the most determined, persistent applicants pursuing their claims. In addition to the inland waterway conditions of application, reforms have also extended the FFG to coastal shipping operations. Grants have been awarded to operators on the Mersey, the Manchester Ship Canal, River Trent, South Yorkshire Navigation, River Severn, River Thames and also in the Western Isles timber trades.

Post-Graduate research at Southampton Institute/Solent University has identified a number of cases where a successful and sustainable, transfer of freight from roads to water has been achieved under the aegis of the FFG.[90]

Figure 22: UK Freight Facilities Grants to Shipping, 1983-2004

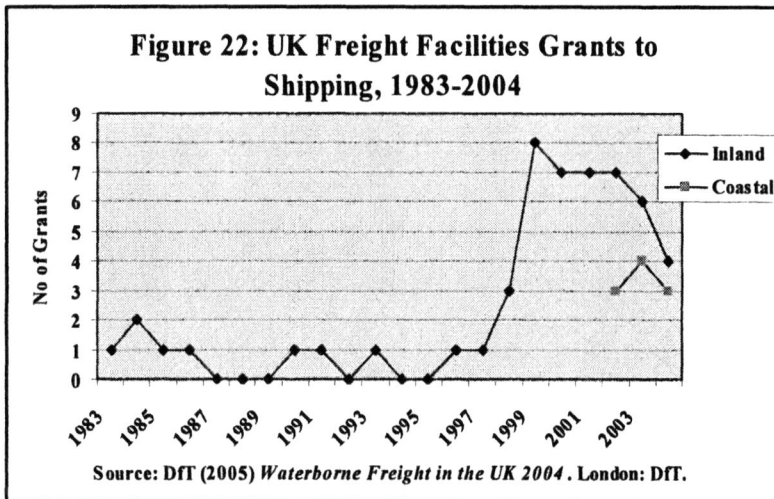

Source: DfT (2005) *Waterborne Freight in the UK 2004*. London: DfT.

By co-ordinating shipping enterprise, economic rigour and environmental integrity, the successful FFG applications have achieved a long term viability. The £8.5m FFG awarded to heavy goods specialist, Robert Wynn and Sons, in

2002 (see below pp.345-6) was supported by the (then) Minister of Shipping, David Jamieson, as a positive, but realistic contribution to sustainable transport:

> We accept that there will be no return to the age of the narrow, historical canals reopening for freight, but we can look for increases in freight traffic on larger canals, rivers and tidal waters.[91]

The importance of the FFG has been to tip the balance in a shipping investment decision. Where the relative costs of a shipping operation are marginal *vis-à-vis* road haulage, the FFG can help to off-set risk. The transfer from roads to water, as implemented by Lafarge Aggregate in 2001/2, would not have been financially viable without FFG support for a loading conveyor system. The switch resulted in around 300,000 tonnes of aggregates per annum being secured for barge operations in the East Midlands, Humberside and Mid Yorkshire for a 10-15 year period, equating to some 1.3mtkm (See below pp.371-4).

It is evident that the Green Highway has achieved a significant boost in the post 1997 period, with a number of shipping operations achieving a business maturity which would have proved unattainable without the FFG's support. Despite the success of the FFG, the planned £10m reduction of the grant budget in 2007-8 made available to rail and water operators by around £10m has been criticised by the Rail Freight Group.[92] This illustrates the sporadic nature of transport policy.

3.6 Promoting and Informing the Green Highway

The apparent emergence of shortsea and inland shipping in the European political agenda has induced a number of organisations that serve as promoters, political lobbyists and information providers for the industry. The development of a water transport lobby is clearly an important dynamic of the Green Highway. In the following chapter it will be made evident how UK shortsea operators have become leading members of the UK shipping industry trade association, the Chamber of Shipping. Renewed Government attention to inland shipping issues was reflected by the award of the Member of the British Empire (MBE) medal to Dr. David Hilling in 2003. Dr. Hilling was involved in the setting up of the Sea and Water organisation (see below, p.147) and has devoted over forty years of academic and administrative contribution to the promotion of inland shipping. Within the European context, inland shipping is represented by European River Sea Transport Union (of which Dr. Hilling is the UK Vice President). Coastal and shortsea shipping has the European Shortsea Network as its co-ordinating agency. The role of these bodies is to actively promote the shipping alternative.

3.6.1 The European River Sea Transport Union (ERSTU)

The Berlin based European River Sea Transport Union (ERSTU) was launched in 1997, with 17 members from five countries but has now grown to over 80 members from 13 West and East European countries. The Union represents the owners of some 8mt of shortsea and inland shipping tonnage.[93] With over 600 vessels, the ex German Democratic Republic barge operator, Deutsche Binnenreederei, has been a major contributor and as a consequence the ERSTU has focused on East-West European traffics, extending into Russia and the CIS states. However, the ERSTU is now (early Millennium years) extending its membership and influence in Western Europe including Belgium, the Netherlands and Britain. In Britain the link with the ERSTU has been with the Inland Shipping Group which has consistently argued the case for more effective integration of inland shipping and inland ports into the supply chain. Such integration is particularly pertinent to the UK, given that over 50% of Britain's inland waterway freight is foreign traffic, predominantly carried in sea-river ships. The ERSTU has campaigned for Britain's inland waterways to be recognised by Government, in order to achieve closer integration of West and East Europe inland systems. Recognising that sea-river transport has great potential for freight transfer from road, the ERSTU has pushed for harmonisation of the conditions for competition between modes. With 12,000km of navigable waterways, the ERSTU has argued that the European Union has great scope for increasing the use of water transport. [94]

The ERSTU has progressed beyond a barge operators' organisation by pushing for new members amongst coastal, shortsea and inland shipping companies and any other organisation in favour of expanding inland shipping operations, within the context of sustainable mobility. The starting point for integration has been the "purposeful connection" of significant European regions with sea-river operations, such as exists on the Rhine and Danube corridors. Countries identified with future potential include: France, Britain, Finland, Sweden and Russia.[95]

3.6.2 The European Short Sea Network

One aspect of European integration has been the significant development of shortsea shipping information and promotion. The shifting emphasis towards a sustainable transport strategy in Europe has required a proliferation of information and an effective exercise in raising the profile of shipping. The needs of the shipping industry to share information on trade flows, on vessel design and on technical and crewing operations have required a forum approach. The dated perception of shipping that has prevailed in the minds of transport users and policy decision makers has necessitated a more positive image. The Shortsea Shipping Bureaux set up in the EU 15 (also Norway) have also sought to respond to these challenges within the framework of the European Shortsea Network (ESN). In Ireland the IMDO has actively promoted the shortsea sector. The flow of information on cargo opportunities can be most useful to operators and shippers, particularly when it provides the opportunity to "back load" a vessel.

The Irish Shortsea Bureau has identified the role of shipping in tackling the problems of road haulage growth and congestion: it can help curb the forecasted substantial increase in HGV traffic and rebalance the modal shares and offer a sustainable marine alternative by-pass to land transport bottlenecks.[96]

It was the need to raise the profile of shortsea shipping in the European Union that helped to create the European Short Sea Network (ESN). Throughout the late 1990s Short Sea promotional groups emerged in the Netherlands, Belgium, Sweden, Italy, Denmark and Greece. By 2004, some 14 European countries had started to participate in the organisation, although British participation had been delayed by deliberations between interested parties, including port agencies and shipowners, also divisions between inland and coastal shipping representatives. This provided difficulties in reaching agreement within the UK Government's framework.[97] However, the creation of the UK's Bureau, Sea and Water, provided for an integrated promotion of shortsea, coastal and inland operations. The Sea and Water organisation was set up in 2003. With forums held in Manchester, Hull, Birmingham and London, Sea and Water has championed many aspects of shortsea and inland shipping.

The benefits of such unions and bureaux are that they allow for improved communication and an enhanced business and environmental image of shipping. In Britain, shortsea operators have traditionally practised an intense competitive rivalry that has precluded much in the way of industrial collaboration. Whilst it is obvious that there has been little weakening of the competitive thrust in the British owners, as well as their customers' demands, the Sea and Water Bureau provides a forum for a range of technical, trade and political issues. Whilst partly financed by UK Government, Sea and Water operates at arm's length. However, the link between Government transport policy and shipping is strengthened by the organisation. Raising the profile of the shipping alternative is prized as a major priority. Within the European context, the ESN seeks to co-ordinate the national bureaux by serving as an information conduit. Additionally, the ESN, along with the ERSTU, serves to link shipping with such related interest groups as the European Community Shipowners' Association (ECSA) and the European Sea Ports Organisation (ESPO) and the European Federation of Inland Ports.

3.7 Chapter 3: Summary & Conclusion

This chapter set out to identify and examine the changing context for the development of the Green Highway. In chapter 2, the forces that led to the decline of domestic shipping in the coastal trades were identified. In this chapter, the focus has been on a number of forces currently exerting a positive influence on the Green Highway. The historic changes, set in train towards the late years of the old Millennium, have begun to generate a "sea change" in the way the shipping alternative is now perceived

The European dimension has been demonstrated as a major positive in not only developing intra-community trade but also in the very dynamics of how shipping operates. Concentration in industrial activity, whilst bringing rationalisations throughout Europe, has also increased the demand for transport. European integration has induced direct access from British and Irish ports to the inland waterway networks of Europe and, moreover, such major, dynamic, inland port hubs as Duisburg, Liege and Paris. The spectacular rise in the Irish economy, the "Celtic Tiger," has led to a shortsea boom, but also brought its own growth pains, traffic congestion in particular proving intractable. The Green Highway has a well defined opportunity to spread some of the traffic flow away from central routes. As a consequence, road tkm could be reduced by shipping links with Ireland's regional ports. Additionally, growth in the Green Highway can assist in aiding the integration of new access nations into the European Community via shipbuilding collaborations. The main challenge the Green Highway faces here is, given European integration and the rise of the Irish economy, from road haulage-RoRo ferry combinations. The growth of Dover Straits and central Irish Sea RoRo routes has already been acknowledged. The Green Highway offers a more sustainable link to European integration, particularly for the economic peripheries. However, a successful shift towards sustainable transport means de-coupling the strong correlation between economic activity and road haulage dependency. From this perspective, it is apparent that the continental propensity for waterborne freight needs to prevail against the British and Irish predilection for road haulage.

The de-regulation of European ports does offer increased opportunities for shipping. Port inefficiencies, together with enduring labour problems, were shown in chapter 2 as militating against domestic and shortsea shipping operations. The movement of logistics activities away from the waterfront may have been a rational response – given the high costs associated with port delays – but this was dependent mainly on road haulage linkages, thus proving detrimental to a shipping connections in the supply chain. Given the moves towards an open market, opportunities exist for a more dynamic port industry, one that is receptive to the niche needs of the Green Highway. Examples of ports, including ABP, Mersey Docks and Harbour and Clydeport, becoming actively involved in coastal and shortsea operations is a pointer to future supply chain integration in the Green Highway. Where concerns over port de-regulation could possibly emerge lies in the competitive process. If smaller periphery ports were to lose out to larger, more centralised ports, this could prove detrimental to the Green Highway. In 2002, ABP withdrew from one of its smaller ports, the Yorkshire Coast Port of Whitby.[98] Although port services are still maintained by the local municipality, Whitby, situated between the much larger Humberside and Teeside port complexes, was deemed not viable by ABP. If such centralisation strategies were to become a trend, the "Delft Paradox" (see above p.33) would materialise – where small ports are competitively over-whelmed by more powerful larger ports.

150

The net result would be increased tkm road haulage as traffics became funnelled through centralised ports.

The desire of businesses to be viewed as environmentally responsible is also a factor in promoting European shipping. As congestion and carbon emissions are becoming increasingly recognised as a symptom of road haulage dependency, the shipping alternative offers some degree of environmental credibility. It has been demonstrated here that transport is one area where producers can move tangibly towards sustainability without output being affected. The considerable reduction in tkm achieved by a modal switch from roads to water can certainly enhance the environmental component of a company's mission statement. From this perspective, the Green Highway becomes a positive and marketable image associated with environmental sensitivity. The continued and increased commitment of business to sustainable transport will be dependent upon the willingness of business to support sustainable transport and, conversely, the ability of the latter to provide economically viable services. The 2005 decision by CMA-CGM Line to withdraw its Bristol feeder services was a result of rising vessel charter rates. Business cannot be expected to underwrite the sustainable option without financial consideration.

The rise of transport and environmental issues in the European political agenda has provided encouragement for the Green Highway. The intensifying congestion problem of road traffic growth and its association with carbon emissions has forced the search for alternatives. Rail has obviously a large part to play here; however, problems in capacity, in matching up pan-European network practices and business culture, have necessitated an increased focus on the Green Highway. In Ireland, the desire of the network operator, CIE, to rationalise freight services has increased road haulage activity.[99] As a consequence, even more importance has been attached to the Green Highway around Irish coastlines. The Marco Polo initiative has been targeted on intra-European freight flows. The project was allocated a budget of €100, 2003-6 and this will be extended to €740, 2007-13.[100] It has already been shown how in the UK the FFG, was initially aimed at rail freight, followed by inland shipping. The Transport Act 2000 extended the FFG to the coastal and shortsea sector. The FFG has offered financial support to operators and/or shipping users. Such initiatives have an important role in nurturing modal shift when comparative road-water costs are marginal. Although it is obvious such initiatives are at the behest of government decision making and political will, the situation in early 2007 remained most positive regarding public support.

Finally, the re-emergence of shipping in the taxonomy of the British and Irish transport economy has been synonymous with the rise of a supportive lobby. The role of such bodies as the ERSTU and the ESN has been recognised as paramount in developing ideas, information and in raising the profile of the Green Highway. The extent of the challenge facing these forums, however, cannot be understated. During the first full year (2004) of the UK's Sea and Water Bureau, domestic shipping tonnages fell by 4%, freight moved fell by 2%. In the inland waterway trades the decline was even more pronounced, 6% and 7%, respectively.[101]

On balance, the conclusions to be drawn from the context provided in this chapter can be accepted as encouraging for the development of the Green Highway. Realistically, it has been shown that this objective will not be easy. Conversely, it is apparent that the current conditions are conducive towards a revival of shipping activity in the British and Irish trades given the logistical viability and environmental integrity of the Green Highway. In chapter 7 the prospects of the Green Highway within the context of the contemporary and future logistics trends are discussed. Chapter 8 will appraise the environmental integrity of the Green Highway. The possibilities of adding further momentum to the Green Highway are next considered. In the following chapter the renaissance of British shipping in the post 1998 period is appraised as a potential accelerator of Green Highway development.

CHAPTER 3 ENDNOTES

[1] Thuermer, K "As Europe Changes, so do Logistics Options." www.expansionmangement.com accessed 25.12.05.

[2] Netelenbos, T. (2002) "Europe's Wet Infrastructure", *Dredging and Port Construction* April 2002. pp. 20-1.

[3] *Loc.cit*

[4] Field, F. "French grain trade increase gets green light", *Lloyd's List* 1.10.02. p.4.

[5] *Loc.cit.*

[6] Tinsley, D. (1991) *Short-Sea Shipping: A Review of the North European Coastal Bulk Trades.* London: LLP. p. 6.

[7] Department of Transport (1988), *Short Sea Bulk Shipping: An Analysis of UK Performance.* London: Department of Transport. pp. 37-8.

[8] *Loc.cit.*

[9] Tinsley, D. (1991*), Op.cit.* p. 7.

[10] "Flags of (tax) convenience," *Fairplay.* 6.1.00.

[11] "Mortgage-lending sets sail," *The Baltic*, September 2000, p. 58.

[12] *Loc.cit.*

[13] Tinsley, D. (1991*). Op.cit.* p. 8.

[14] "For this busy waterborne family home is where the barge is," *Lloyd's List.* 3.8.99. p. 9.

[15] www.duisport.de Accessed 3.8.05.

[16] GB railfreight, "GB Railfreight is to double the number of trains it runs from the Port of Felixstowe for shipping giant, Medite Shipping." www.gbrailfreight.com/news accessed 29.12.05.

[17] "K&N extends use of inter-modal rail." www.worldcargonews.com accessed 29.12.05.

[18] Road Haulage Association, "University of Ulster finds no fair play for hauliers." www.rha.net/public/news 7.3.00.

[19] Deutsche Post, "Deutsche Post, World Net completes acquisition of Exel. www.dpn.de 14.12.05.

[20] "Flexible new tonnage for Crescent Shipping", *Fairplay* 5.4.01.

[21] Baird, A. (1997) "The Marine Motorway: Opportunities for Coastal Freight Ferry Services", In Peeters, D & Wergeland, T. *European Shortsea Shipping: Proceedings from the Third European Research Roundtable Conference on Shortsea Shipping.* Bergen, 20-21 June 1996. Delft: Delft University Press. pp. 352-3.

[22] *Ibid.* p. 353.

[23] "Let the sea lane take the strain", *Lloyd's List.* 10.6.02. p. 20.

[24] www.atmb.net. accessed 3.10.05.

[25] Hilling, D. "Wings down the Dee," www.waterways.org.uk accessed 4.10.05.

[26] O'Mahony, H. "A very special craft takes to the water." *Lloyd's List.* 30.3.04.

[27] "James Fisher unveils latest state-of-the art product tankers," *Lloyd's List.* 29.9.05.

[28] Speares, S. "Dutch finance for Carisbrooke ," *Lloyd's List* 8.6.98.

[29] "EU shortsea boost will have knock-on benefits", *Lloyd's List.* 11.8.02. p. 13.

[30] www.duisport.de. Accessed 3.8.05.

[31] "Logistics-German seaports come under fire for poor links to inland terminals," *Lloyd's List.* 30.7.02.

[32] *Ibid.*

[33] *Port of Antwerp Annual Report, 2002.*

[34] Press statement: "One hundredth departure of the South Eastern Europe Shuttle Train". 27.7.04. www.duisport.de

[35] "Barge link traffic increases as plant dismantled." *Lloyd's List.* 19.11.02. p. 13.

[36] Press Release: "First arrival of new Roll-on Roll-off Freighter," 8.6.04. www.duisport.de

[37] "Dedicated barge gives Geest double benefits," *Lloyd's List.* 25.2.05.

[38] www.paris-ports.fr Accessed 5.8.05.

[39] *Loc.cit*

154

[40] *Loc.cit.*
[41] www.paris-port.fr Accessed 6.8.05.
[42] *Loc.cit.*
[43] www.liege.port-autonome.be accessed 31.12.05.
[44] Spruyt, J.(1993) "The Last Word: the romance of little ships and tiny ports," *Lloyd's List.* 21.6.93.
[45] "Shannon Foynes invests in ambitious projects to boost estuary port facilities. *Lloyd's List.* 13.7.06.
[46] www.isl.ie accessed 8.10.05.
[47] Frank, J. (2001) "Tonnage tax proposal averts 'disaster' for Irish companies", *Lloyd's List.* 7.12.01.
[48] Macsweeney, T. Osler,D. (1998) "Arklow flags out vessel in tax protest," *Lloyd's List.* 31.1.98.
[49] "Cavalry arrives in form of a new tonnage tax regime," *Lloyd's List.* 6.2.02.
[50] *Loc.cit.*
[51] IMDO Press Release: "Statement from the IMDO" 2.12.03. www.imdo.ie Accessed 15.8.05.
[52] "Sailings suspended as ferry dispute intensifies," *The Irish Times.* 26.11.05.
[53] Ahern, D. (T.D.) "Out of Sight, Out of Mind: Shipping Challenges for Ireland". Seminar, Dublin Castle, 7.11.02.
[54] CSO, Dublin: *Statistics of Port Traffic, 2004.* www.cso.ie 30.6.05.
[55] CSO, Dublin *Op.cit.*
[56] IMDO: *TENS and the Irish Motorways of the Sea.* www.imdo.ie/tens Accessed 15.8.05.
[57] "Convoys Thames wharf closes as paper imports plummet," *Lloyd's List.* 20.6.00. p. 3.
[58] Moloney, S. "Boost for Hull as UTL returns,". *Lloyd's List.* 16.7.91.
[59] *Loc.cit*
[60] "Traffic surge pressure on Dublin", *Lloyd's List.* 20.7.00., p. 11.
[61] "Ports get ultimatum to spur competition", *Lloyd's List* 15.2.01. p. 1.
[62] Porter, J. "Grimaldi in stinging attack on 'overpaid' European dockworkers." *Lloyd's List.* 24.10.02. p. 14.
[63] "Rotterdam keeps port dues down," *Fairplay* 20.11.01.
[64] Dixon, G "Mersey docks agrees takeover," *Tradewinds.* 9.6.05.
[65] Baird, A. M. (1998) "The Port Of Felixstowe," in Kreukels, T. Wever, E. (eds) *North Sea Ports in Transition: Changing Tides.* Assen: Van Gorcum. pp. 95-120.
[66] *Ibid.,* p. 96.
[67] *Ibid.,* p. 99.
[68] www.hutchinson-whampoa.com
[69] http://www.parliament.the-stationery-office.co.uk/pa/cm199697/cmhansrd/vo961205/debtext/61205-09.htm
[70] "Geest launches rail service," World Cargo News. www.worldcargonews.com accessed. 31.12.05.
[71] http://www.total-logistics.eu.com/clients/port-of-tilbury.pdf accessed 31.3.07.
[72] Hainsworth, K. "A question of ethics", Office Hours, *The Guardian.* 19.8.02. p. 4.
[73] *Loc.cit.*
[74] Volvo Annual Reports: http://www.volvo.com/logistics/global/en-gb accessed 6.11.06.
[75] "Volvo's Environmental-friendly approach," *Grimaldi Euro-Med News.* The Quarterly Publication of the Grimaldi Group. Issue 6 – Jan/March 2000. p. 3.
[76] Sea and Water Press release:"Bosch moves white goods by water,." www.seaandwater.org/news, 12.7.05.
[77] *Bosch: Global Responsibility Environmental Report, 2003-4.* www.bosch-umwelt.de. Accessed 14.9.05.
[78] "Better by Rhone than Road," www.seaandwater.org.news 6.10.05.
[79] Waugh, I "Off the Road and on to the water for oil delivery," *Yorkshire Post,* 5.5.04.
[80] Macsweeney, T. "First container service starting in Shannon Estuary," *Lloyd's List.* 15.11.04.

[81] CEC 1993. "The Future Development of the Common Transport Policy. (1993) A Global Approach to the Construction of a Community Framework for Sustainable Mobility." *Bulletin of the European Communities, Supplement 3/93.* Luxembourg: OOPEC, p. 24.

[82] Ross, F.L. (1998) *Linking Europe: Transport Policies and Politics in the European Union.* Westport: Praeger. P.168.

[83] European Commission White Paper (2001) *European Transport Policy for 2010: Time to Decide.* Luxembourg. EC.

[84] *Ibid.* p.41.

[85] Papadimitriou, S (2001) in European Conference of Ministers of Transport Report: *Short Sea Shipping in Europe.* Paris ECMT. p. 10.

[86] http://europa.eu.int/comm/transport/marcopolo/index_en.htm

[87] DETR (1998) *Inland Waterway Freight Grants.* London: DETR. p. 8.

[88] The Freight Study Group. (2002) *Freight on Water: A New Perspective.* London: DEFRA. p.37.

[89] "Government backs policy to protect Thames wharves," *Port of London News.* September/October 2005. Vol. No.5.

[90] McNamara, T. PhD (2005) The Waterborne Freight Alternative to Road Transport in the UK and its Role in Sustainable Mobility. Southampton Solent University

[91] O'Mahony, H. "UK funds pontoons to take large loads off the roads", *Lloyd's List.* 12.6.02. p. 24.

[92] "Government fails sustainable transport – rail freight grants merged with water and road budget slashed," www.rfg.org.news accessed 25.10.05.

[93] www.erstu.com accessed 24.10.05.

[94] Hilling, D. (1998) "New push on advantages of Europe's inland waterways," *Lloyd's List.* 10.11.98.

[95] *Loc.cit.*

[96] www.shortsea.ie accessed 24.10.05.

[97] Spurrier, A. (2002) "Silent army fighting battle for shortsea", *Lloyd's List.* 14.3.02. p. 7.

[98] Landon, F. "ABP pulls out of Whitby," *Lloyd's List.* 12.3.02.

[99] Macsweeney, T. "Irish Rail Axes containers *Lloyd's List.* 1.8.05.

[100] http://europa.eu.int/comm/transport/marcopolo

[101] DfT: (2005) *WaterborneFreight in the United Kingdom 2004.* London: DfT.

CHAPTER 4

The Renaissance of the Red Ensign?

This chapter will discuss the link between the Green Highway and the revival of the UK flag. In the early years of the New Millennium British owned and registered shipping underwent a surprising revival. Furthermore, the increase in fleet size has been accompanied by a raised profile. After a long sunset period of decline, the British shipping industry is beginning to recover some of its former dynamism and status. Moreover, the revival of British shipping can be appreciated within the context of commitment to quality, safety and environmental integrity, particularly in the tanker sector. If the 1975-1995 period was about cost competition in the free market, the following decade has brought more focus on quality factors, supported by a selective amount of state encouragement.

The implications for the Green Highway can only be encouraging. This chapter will examine the changes that have occurred in both shipping policy and in the business behaviour of shipping companies. Four British tanker companies will be identified as emerging champions of the Green Highway. Additionally, it will be made apparent that there is a symbiotic linkage between the revived flag and national interest in shipping – this bodes well for the Green Highway. Finally, the composition and characteristics of the rejuvenated UK fleet will be critically examined. It will become evident that the current fleet composition and character is not a complete return to the status of the pre 1970s world leader – not all UK maritime observers are enamoured by the recovery! Questions have been asked regarding the quality of operations under the revived flag. Additionally, the break up of P&O's shipping empire raises questions over the commitment of the British investment community towards shipping.

Between 1975 - the high-water mark of the British fleet, with over 50m dwt on the UK registry – and 1998, aggregate tonnages collapsed to 2.69m dwt, a decline of more than 94%. That a number of leading British shortsea shipping lines have not only survived this competitive onslaught, but also achieved growth and a qualitative shift upwards in enhancing their fleets, is testimony to their entrepreneurial vitality. Moreover, the economic resilience of the shortsea owners has brought about a relative shift in their importance *vis-à-vis* the deepsea sector. This factor, coupled to the shift in trade route emphasis from deepsea to shortsea, as the British economy realigned itself within the European market, has seen the shortsea owners taking a higher profile in the UK merchant marine hierarchy. The 2001 appearance of the 2000dwt coastal bulker, *Hoo Falcon,* at the International Festival of the Sea was referred to in chapter 1 (see above p.6). That such a small "workhorse" coastal vessel could take centre stage alongside the pride of the Royal Navy in its own home port, Portsmouth, is a measure of the enhanced profile of the shortsea sector, its elevation from the "dirty British coaster" image!

The success of leading coastal operators needs to be viewed within the larger context of the remarkable recovery of the UK fleet from the late 1990s onwards. The culmination of a favourable maritime policy and a resilient strain of shipping ownership and organisation, has facilitated a surprising rise in the British flagged fleet. The reversal of the long term – seemingly irreversible – trend of decline following the introduction of the 1999 Tonnage Tax, begs some discussion and analysis. In addition, the active promotion of the Freight Facilities Grant (FFG), post 1997, has proved conducive to an up-surge in inland shipping activity.

In examining the apparent revival of UK shipping, it is pertinent to explore the link between shipping industry behaviour and the political context. The traditions of UK shipping – owning, management, seafaring – were somewhat threatened by the economic forces of globalisation, post 1970s. In the de-industrialisation era, traditions and skills wax and wane in the global economy as capital and labour become fluid. British shipping proved no exception to this trend, post 1975. Following the downturn in the global economy, late 1970s, demand for shipping has grown consistently, accelerating from the late 1980s onwards. However, supply has increasingly been met by ships flying the flags of Liberia, Panama, Cyprus, Antigua, Bahamas, Bermuda and the Vincent and Grenadine Islands and with the crews of developing nations, particularly the Philippines, India, China and also Eastern Europe. The future for traditional maritime nation shipping was seen as time expired – the omens for British flagged shipping were not good! Towards the end of the Millennium, however, changes in UK maritime policy, accompanied by increased concern over the maritime environment, were to initiate a reversal of decline.

4.1 Outlining the Recovery

By 1998 the Government paper, *British Shipping: Charting a New Course* stated that, "The Government does not accept that the long decline in the British Merchant Navy should simply be allowed to continue."[1] The shift from a market led to a moderately interventionist Government strategy, has proved to be the catalyst for revival in the UK flagged fleet. From 1998 onwards, ships began to join the UK flag; some companies returning to the UK register after an absence of a decade or more. By November 2000, the fleet had grown by 22% measured in deadweight tonnage terms (dwt), from 2.69mdwt to 3.3mdwt. This represented some 17 companies and 160 vessels joining the UK flag.[2] The pace was to increase. Figure 23 shows the growth of the UK flagged fleet from 2.7mdwt to 11.15mdwt between late 1999 and Summer 2005, a rise of 306%. It can also be noted how the UK owned (as opposed to flagged) fleet has grown from 7.1mdwt to 16.9mdwt, a increase of 135%. The surprising reversal in the fortunes of the

160

UK flag begs attention. At the heart of this seeming revival is the convergence of three key factors:

(1) the re-positioning of Government thinking on shipping, from a free market to a selectively interventionist approach;

(2) increased recognition that a strong UK fleet would provide strategic and environmental benefits as well as generate significant national income;

(3) the changing business behaviour of the shipping industry and its customers in relation to safety and environmental integrity.

Firstly, in order to evaluate this surprising recovery of UK shipping activity it will be necessary to concentrate on the collapse of the fleet, post 1975.

4.2 Decline and the Free Market Approach, 1975-1995

The decline of the UK fleet in the post 1975 period corresponds to an era of economic instability and a dominant adherence to the principles of free trade and open markets in the UK political economy. In 1990 the Department of Transport responded to concerns over the decline of UK flag shipping by reiterating the principles of the market. The 1990s Department of Transport report, *British Shipping Challenges and Opportunities,*[3] argued the case for a competitive, non-interventionist, response from UK shipping given that,

> ...the shipping market approximates to the textbook ideal of competitive markets. Entry and exit to and from shipping markets is usually relatively easy. There are not many natural barriers to competition.[4]

Given the entrenched faith in market economics by successive Conservative Governments, post 1979, it was to be competitive forces that influenced the scale and shape of the UK fleet in the 1980s.

Figure 23: UK Flag & Owned Fleet, 1999-2005

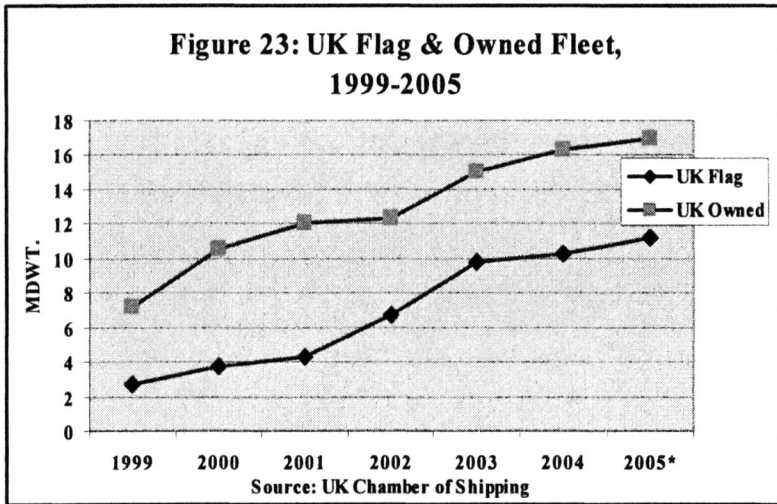

Source: UK Chamber of Shipping

The assumption was that the open market, based upon the principles of comparative advantage, would resolve the problem of global allocation of shipping resources. This is clearly evident in the influential writings of leading maritime economist, Professor Goss:

> International shipping services are commonly bought and sold in competitive markets which lead to the lowest private costs...the relevant principle is that of comparative advantage.[5]

From this perspective, the negative impact of its relatively high costs was bound to have serious implications for the UK fleet. In the last two decades it became apparent that the declining number of ships and corresponding demise of seafaring opportunities was of a permanent nature, in accordance with free market economics. UK economic trends of the 1970s and 1980s were somewhat dominated by industrial decline and restructuring. Traditional labour intensive industries either gave way to services or were exported to the newly developing nations, particularly the Asian Tiger Nations. Merchant shipping, as a traditional

UK industry, appeared to be sharing the same fate as shipbuilding, coal mining, steel production, textiles and automobiles. This seemed to fit with the "mature economy" thesis, that UK shipping was a low profit, low added value, industry with no place in the new post-industrial economy.

The market economics perspective, which held great influence during this period, had a ready-made explanation for this decline, namely that it was the result of global market forces. As lower cost nations entered into the open shipping market, it was seen as inevitable that the higher cost nations – USA, Germany, Norway, Holland – as well as the UK, would suffer a decline. Merchant shipping was accepted as an element of Britain's industrial past but not of the future - service industries in finance, leisure and higher technologies. Shipping lines – many of which had become components of large conglomerates – decided to cut their losses and leave the shipping market.

The market protagonists of this period were able to direct some criticism at British innovation and competitiveness. Whilst British shipping had made some progress in modernisation, its critics were quick to point out that it was essentially a backward looking, conservative industry. Sturmey was a major critic of the British shipowners in the 1960s. In *British Shipping and World Competition*,[6] Sturmey argued that the traditional owners were slow to respond to the market potential of larger and more technical ships. The thesis, outlined by Sturmey, provided some ammunition for the pro-market advocates of the 1980s. This approach engendered a "sink or swim" strategy towards the UK shipping industry, along with other traditional industries – either compete globally or leave the market! Deregulation in capital markets and the withdrawal of the capital allowances on new ships in the 1980s led to a global flight in shipping investment. In response, the General Council of British Shipping (GCBS) had argued that capital allowances were conducive to investment in new UK flag ships, citing the 12mdwt of new vessels joining the registry between 1975 and 1984.[7] However,

Chancellor Lawson's view was that such tax break systems would lead to inefficiency by penalising "...profit and success and blunting the cutting edge of enterprise".[8] Prime Minister Thatcher rejected the industry's calls for a supportive policy:

> I do not believe it would be right to conclude that the time has come for us to abandon free trade principles...Were Government to embark on a round of protectionism and subsidy for shipping it could only be to the detriment of the UK industry.[9]

The emphasis on a free market economics policy induced a declining level of commitment to national shipping in the UK. One solution to the market axiom of global comparative costs was to switch vessel registration from the UK flag to open registry operations. During the 1980s the sharp contrast in costs between UK flag/crew and flag of convenience operations highlighted the difficulties of British shipping. This change in direction became manifest in the financing and ownership of shipping in two major ways: (1) the flagging out and crewing out option; (2) divestment and diversification away from shipping. Table 16 shows how crew costs could be slashed by flagging out to "flags of convenience." Such evidence strengthened the market view that UK shipping could not be sustained in the global market. From this perspective, the flagging out option becomes a rational response to free market competition.

Table 16: Comparative Crew Costs (Tanker) 1986/7		
Flag	Ratings	Annual Crew Costs ($000)
UK	British	908
Liberia	Korean	490
Bermuda	Filipino	480
Hong Kong	Hong Kong	396
Source: *House of Commons Transport Committee, Session 1986/7. Interim Report: Decline in the UK Registered Fleet*, London: HMSO, p.8		

The deregulation of capital markets and the abolition of overseas capital movements made it increasingly easy to move investments out of Britain. The option to "flag out" British ships under the open registry "flags of convenience" of such nations as Panama, Liberia and Cyprus enabled British shipowners to reduce their costs, as well as the tax burden.[10] For those shipowners intent upon retaining some link with the home country, the British Commonwealth and dependency countries – Bahamas, Bermuda, Cayman Islands, Hong Kong, Malta - provided opportunities. The rise of the Isle of Man off-shore registry in the 1990s offered the closest resemblance of British standards, with the important exception that it featured the attraction of lower corporation tax.

Post 1974, global shipping suffered a decade of over-capacity as world trade declined following the oil crisis. The ensuing slow down in world trade brought about a massive slump in shipping markets as supply outstripped demand. Freight rates fell considerably and owners sought options to reduce costs. By flagging out, owners could avoid corporation tax and in some instances attain lower costs from the lower quality standard threshold pertaining in the open registries.[11] Typically, the flagging out process was accompanied by a crewing out process. Owners took the opportunity to replace national crew with the much lower cost crews of third world countries. The abandonment of BP's directly owned tanker fleet and the setting up of the "arms length" BP Shipping organisation, featured a switch to the Bahamas and Hong Kong registries and the replacement of British nationals with Filipino and Polish seafarers. A phased, albeit unplanned, process of flagging out occurred post 1975, commencing chronologically with the lowest cost, lowest market entry barrier, sectors:

- The deepsea drybulk tramp fleet;
- the deepsea tanker fleet;
- container shipping;
- cruise shipping;`
- shortsea shipping.

The earliest casualties of the shipping slump were the tramp owners. With major industrial markets in decline the demand for the shipments of coal and iron ore reduced, the steel products markets collapsed. Many of the British tramp shipowners had strong regional and family connections. The development of the coal export trades in the Tyne, Wear and Tees and also the Cardiff and South Wales regions had induced a cluster of family owners. These owners found themselves increasingly exposed at a time of falling freight rates. Leading trampship owners had recently embarked upon investment into new, larger vessels, in order to provide better economies.[12] In the early years of the oil price rise crisis, the industrial nations had little option than to remain committed to oil consumption. As demand for oil made the transition from price inelasticity to price elasticity, the need for oil tankers decreased. Whole fleets of ships were forced into lay-up. Tankers on long haul routes were forced to "slow steam" in order to conserve fuel oil consumption and also to slow down the oil supply chain.[13]

The container market had been acknowledged as a premium high value, high speed sector, but as the demand for manufactured goods faltered, container rates suffered. The severity of the slump saw even Japanese owners flagging out and crewing out. Previously the ethics of Japanese business had ensured job security but economic circumstances led to the replacement of Japanese ratings with Filipino crews. Major world container sector leaders, Hapag-Lloyd of Germany, Maersk of Denmark, Ned-Lloyd of the Netherlands and Britain's P&O, followed suit. As the flagging out and crewing out process intensified, such bastions of the UK merchant fleet as *QE.2* were affected. British catering (and later deck) ratings on the flagship were replaced by crews drawn from the global pool of labour[14]. Additionally, the practice came nearer to home. The privatised ex British Rail Sealink ferry fleet was reflagged in the Bahamas and some P&O ferries were reflagged and re-crewed. The Swansea-Cork ferry also followed the flagging out, crewing out process. The coastal shipping sector was not immune

166

from these forces. The British coastline had always offered an open market opportunity to foreign ships but traditionally British owned ships flew the British flag, the "Red Duster". The flags of Gibraltar, Malta, Antigua and Barbuda, Cyprus and St. Vincent and Grenadines, were just some of the flags that became evident in UK and Irish coastal/shortsea trades as British firms flagged out.

The decline in maritime activity had a detrimental impact upon seafaring as an attractive career. The historical identity of the British merchant fleet was shaped by a fiercely independent and proud commitment to the ethos of each line. Premier lines such as Union-Castle and the New Zealand Shipping Co had inculcated a company culture. For officer cadets articled to such famous lines this meant a guaranteed career structure through to Master or Chief Engineer. Many lines found that following mergers forced about by economic circumstances, the intra-company rivalry persisted to the extent that fellow crew members were reluctant to even talk to the "other lot."[15] Even more traumatic for the loyal company seafarer ethos came the shock of redundancy. The institution of a safe professional career was devastated as seafaring became a mercenary occupation, with crew hired and fired in accordance with the short term needs of the company.

As a result of these dramatic changes, the attraction of seafaring rapidly diminished. School and college career advisors began to counsel against joining a declining insecure industry. A number of maritime training centres including the Merchant Navy College, City of London Polytechnic, Plymouth Polytechnic, Liverpool Polytechnic and Cardiff Maritime School all ceased their training activities. The world renowned Warsash Maritime Centre in Southampton narrowly avoided closure, remaining open as an academy of deck and engine-room training. The shortsea sector found itself influenced by these shock waves. Increasingly, the industry suffered from an ageing crew population as new entrants were discouraged from joining the merchant service. Naturally, the comprehensive decline in UK ships was detrimental to career opportunities for

British nationals. The apparent lack of future career prospects in the Merchant Navy has led to low recruitment. This led to an increasing average age of the seafaring population. In 2004 it was found that almost 70% of active British officers were aged 40 and above.[16] As a result the switch to Third World and East European crews became as much a desire to tap much needed labour supplies as it was to gain economies in labour costs.

From an investor's perspective, the image of shipping was tainted by the pattern of retardation and decline. The opportunity costs of shipping investment were weighed as unacceptably high in contrast to other, more lucrative, business and commercial sectors. Small ship entrepreneurs suffered due to the reluctance of the investment community to support what was viewed as high risk ventures. This was mainly the fate of the 1980s Business Expansion Scheme (BES). Although the scheme did facilitate some new shipping developments, including Bromley Shipping and Edinburgh Tankers, generally the response of the investment community to this enterprise scheme was disappointing.[17] In particular, the perception of shipping at policy making level had shifted. The operations of shipping were perceived merely as a function of the forces of supply and demand in the years when market forces informed the dominant economic doctrine. Under these conditions, competitive forces were acknowledged as the arbiter of both what was demanded and which shipping companies provided the supply of ships. In short, if British and Irish owners could no longer achieve cost competitiveness in the global market they would have to admit defeat and withdraw.

The coastal waters of Britain and Ireland offered no respite from the forces of global competition. Increasingly in the post-1945 period, trades around both Islands have been open to all comers. This has led to a wide variety of flags appearing on the coastal and shortsea trades. Dutch, German and Norwegian shipping entrepreneurs were early challengers. Gradually, lower cost flags priced their way into the market post 1970s, including China, Cyprus, Gibraltar, Liberia, Malta, Ukraine, Panama, St. Vincent and Grenadines.

4.3 Post 1975: UK Fleet from High-Water to Ebb Tide

The profile of the UK fleet at its highest ever tonnage level in 1975 was dominated by three major sectors: (1) Crude Oil Tankers;(2) Large Dry-Bulk Carriers; (3) Container Ships. To some extent the UK fleet had diversified towards larger and more modern ships by 1975. Very Large Crude Oil Carriers (VLCC) and Ultra Large Crude Oil Carriers (ULCC) tankers had been added to the UK flag, replacing smaller vessels. Small trampships had been replaced by Panamax and Capesize bulk carriers. The container ship sector was valued as a more promising investment target. The transition from labour intensive cargo liners to capital intensive container ships was well progressed by 1975 on the major trade lanes – North Atlantic, Northern Europe – Far East, Trans-Pacific. Also in train was a process of capital concentration as lines formed consortia or merged. The culmination of this was to be the world's second largest container fleet brought about by the Anglo-Dutch, P&O-Nedlloyd merger in 1996 (acquired by Maersk-Moller Line in 2005).[18]

UK fleet decline post 1975 occurred in all sectors with the exception of RoRo ferries and oil rig support vessels servicing the rapidly growing North Sea oil market. However, the loss of tonnage was most pronounced in the crude oil and dry bulk sectors. Figure 24 illustrates the sudden reversal of tonnage totals following the oil shocks of the mid 1970s. From the tonnage peak in 1975 of > 50m dwt, the UK fleet continued to fall to 2.7m dwt in 1998.[19] In the tanker trades the upheavals in the global oil market brought about a fleet rationalisation in the fleets of the oil majors. The large UK flagged fleets of BP, Shell and Esso were affected by a mixture of flagging out and contracting out strategies.

Between 1975 and 1990 the BP UK flagged fleet fell from > 5m dwt to around 0.2m dwt.[20] A significant Green Highway component of the statistics of decline is the 27% reduction in the shortsea UK flag tanker fleet. Between 1980 and 1985 tonnage in this sector fell from 364,000 to 267,000 dwt.[21]

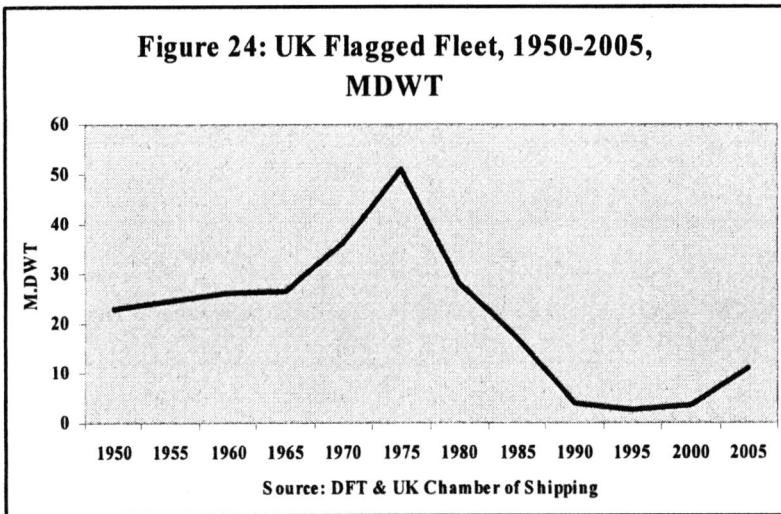

Figure 24: UK Flagged Fleet, 1950-2005, MDWT

Source: DFT & UK Chamber of Shipping

Similar events unfolded in the dry bulk sectors with the enduring over capacity of vessels and ensuing slump freight rates. The approach adopted by the traditional tramp ship owners was to either flag out or sell the fleet completely. By flagging out, the UK owners could retain control of their vessels whilst enjoying the lower tax and cost levels of the open registers. The firms that sold out their ships pursued diversification. Some retained the maritime ambit by offering their skills as ship managers in the global market. Others preferred a complete divestment from the industry.

The rationale of British companies either divesting away from shipping or switching to open registry operations is theoretically supported by free market ideology. The comparative costs of British shipping were regarded as prohibitive in the de-regulated global market. Questions of less quantifiable factors such as supply chain security, maritime safety and environmental integrity were not so easily addressed by free market thinking. These have proved to be essential factors in evaluating the Green Highway.

4.4 Issues of Decline: The Quality Angle?

The decline of the UK fleet posed many questions over the British nation's custodial role of her coastal waters. A spate of environmental disasters in British, French and Spanish waters had raised the question of maritime management. It was becoming apparent that the free market approach was not compatible with the maritime trading demands of the European Community. Additionally, the emergence of new registries into the extended Community placed a premium on maritime standards and their leadership. Significant challenges faced the UK maritime regime. By the 1990s, the academic case against the free market approach had strengthened. The opposite perspective to the comparative cost approach on British shipping sprang from the broader, national interest view. University of Plymouth academics, Ledger and Roe, proved visionary in their 1992 case for a proactive approach to shipping, one that extended beyond the narrower confines of the free market approach. Their argument was that:

> A UK shipping policy is important to provide direction to an economically and strategically vital industry.[22]

The basis of this contention rests upon the following perceived advantages of a UK merchant fleet:

- the preservation of maritime expertise;
- the development of new trade;
- savings for the Balance of Payments;
- strategic interest during times of conflict;
- environmental protection.[23]

It is apparent that Ledger and Roe's contention broadens the evaluation of shipping beyond the free market perspective. The concentration on such factors as maritime expertise, developing new trade and balance of payments savings, endorses the importance of the British shipping fleet to the UK macro economy. The strategic interest is informed by the historic reliance that Britain, as an island nation, has placed upon both deepsea and shortsea shipping. The need for environmental protection stems from the dawning realisation that the quality of shipping, ergo its environmental integrity, was strongly correlated to the flag of the ship. From the Green Highway perspective, the need to nurture and retain maritime expertise and the imperative of environmental protection are not only inseparable, but also integral to the renaissance of British shipping.

Major tanker oil spill disasters in UK and European waters have forced a rethink on the importance of the quality of shipping and, therefore, raised the question of reviving the national fleet. In 2000, the World Wildlife Fund (WWF) critically pointed to the increase in major tanker pollution incidents along the UK coastline, rising from 17 in 1992 to 22 in 1999.[24] The emergence of North Sea oil fields as a major oil source brought a significant change in tanker routing and, consequently, an increased risk to the British Isles and Ireland. Prior to the 1970s development of the North Sea, the tanker supply chain was primarily focused on the exports of the Persian Gulf States to Japan, North America and Northern Europe. The volume of oil traffics generated in Northern Europe was beginning to register in the oil pollution disasters as the switch in the geography of oil extraction occurred.

The Loss of the *Braer* and its cargo of Norwegian crude oil on Shetland raised concerns nationally on the state of preparedness of the UK Coastguard and emergency response services.[25] Also, the practice of tankers passing close to the UK coastline in bad weather conditions became a cause of consternation. The *Braer,* disaster prompted the following headline in *The Scotsman,* "Shetland's Oil

Nightmare Comes True,"[26] A particularly vexing question over the accident was the tanker had drifted helplessly, without engines for six hours before a rescue salvage tug could be attached. Despite the heroic actions of the tug crew, events were to render their actions too late to save the ship and the spillage of 84,700 tonnes of Norwegian crude oil on the Shetland coastline.[27] Table 17 details the major tanker incidents occurring between 1992 and 2002. With Scotland, Russia and Norway being identified as crude oil loading regions, the implications for the UK, France, Spain and Portugal become apparent as increased south bound tanker flows pass along their respective coastlines. A second and related factor in these accidents is the prevalence of open registry operations. The only exception here is that of the Greek flagged, *Aegean Sea*.

In addition to tanker disasters, the British nation had suffered the tragedy of the loss of the Dover-Zeebrugge RoRo ferry, *Herald of Free Enterprise*, in 1987. The salutary lessons of the "Herald" disaster in Zeebrugge harbour were that safe standards were ignored in a shortsea market where competition had taken

Table 17: North European Tanker Wrecks, 1992-2002					
Tanker	Flag	Date of Incident	Loading Port	Incident Location	Oil Spill Tonnes
Aegean Sea	Greek	1992	Sullom Voe, Shetland	La Corunna, Spain	74000
Braer	Liberia	1993	Mongstad, Norway	Shetland, Scotland	85000
Sea Empress	Liberia	1996	Hound Point, Scotland	Milford Haven, Wales	72000
Erika	Malta	1999	Dunkirk, France	Brittany, France	37000
Prestige	Bahamas	2002	Ventspils, Latvia	Galicia, Spain	63000
Source: The International Tanker Owners' Pollution Fund (ITOPF)					

precedence over safe standards. The subsequent accident report proved scathing of a management that ignored the principles of professional seamanship whilst focusing on the need to increase market share against Cross-Channel Ferry rivals, Sealink. The Herald's (previous) owners, Townsend Thoresen, were found wanting. Following on from this investigation legislation was enacted on ferry safety standards – the free market was beginning to give way to the need for safe standards. The 1996 *Sea Empress* disaster on the Pembrokeshire coastline intensified the pressure on maritime operators. Following the 2003 Shetland Isles wreck of the *Braer*, the grounding and eventual loss of the tanker, *Sea Empress,* in the environmentally sensitive waters of Milford Haven led to the authoritative "Donaldson Report", *Safer Ships, Cleaner Seas.*[28] In Europe the environmental sensitivity of large stretches of coastline has focused attention on the quality of operations, including imposing increased responsibilities on charterers to vet the quality of the ships they are hiring. In addition, safety standards, such as ISO 9000 and the International Safety Management Code have placed responsibilities not only on management systems of the operators but also those of the charterers.

The *Erika* disaster proved to be a catalyst in European thinking on tanker safety. The US had suffered the 1989 *Exxon Valdez* disaster in Alaska and this resulted in increased scrutiny of oil tankers operating in US coastal waters. Many maritime experts inferred that this scrutiny resulted in a "dumping" from the US trades of older, sub-standard ships to the European trades. The 25 year old *Erika,* certainly fitted the description of an ageing, corroded, poorly maintained and inadequately inspected tanker. The *Erika* disaster motivated European pressure on the UN Agency, International Maritime Organisation (IMO) to act on tankers. The resulting MARPOL legislation led to a phasing out of ageing single hull tankers. Attention to critical attributes focused on two key areas:(1) segregated ballast tanks;(2) double hulls.

174

In the US, it has long been recognised that the users of shipping services, the charterers, have an important and influential role in monitoring safety and environmental standards in the ships they hire. Large chartering companies, including the oil majors, have been identified in terms of liability for accidents and pollution incidents. This has been seen by the US Coastguard as a deterrent to substandard operations. This approach spread to Europe, particularly after the *Erika* and *Prestige* environmental disasters. The *Erika* oil spill exposed numerous weak spots in not only the ageing ship problem but also the way these vessels are vetted. Critical attention has been focused on the procedures that enabled a vessel with apparently severe structural defects to remain in service. The quality tanker operators forum, International Association of Independent Tanker Owners (Intertanko) endorsed the importance of the chain of responsibilities, including the role and performance of shipowners, charterers, flag states, classification societies, port state controllers, insurers, terminal operators and port authorities. In addition, Intertanko noted that an immediate impact of the accident was the changes in the chartering behaviour of the oil majors. Wishing to avoid further bad publicity, the "overnight" change in policy towards ageing vessels left many responsible shipowners with quality tonnage over 15 years old without secure employment.[29] The *Prestige* disaster only served to accelerate the need to act. Further European legislation was implemented on the immediate phasing out of ageing, single hull tankers. From this perspective it can be accepted that there is considerable potential for the Green Highway to become "greener."

Following these failings, more attention was given to quality. From this perspective the higher costs of British shipping could be balanced against the inherent higher standards of a well managed fleet and a regulated flag. The "*Erika* Effect" was a condition actively sought by British owners. The calls for more restrictions on substandard operators were appreciated by British owners who were keen to benefit from increased emphasis on the quality oriented standards of the UK flag. In 2000, James Fisher Tankships, M.D. Angus Buchanan, claimed:

> Most importantly, there needs to be universal rejection of substandard tonnage, no matter what the age, and recognition of those operators who have made a commitment to quality.[30]

In addition to the impetus towards quality made by Fisher Tankships, there has also been the contribution of family owned coastal operator, F.T. Everard, in the debate on standards. In 2005, incoming UK Chamber of Shipping President, William Everard, chairman of Everard's, called for a proactive approach to environmental integrity. Commitment to high standards here would differentiate between quality and sub-standard ship operators. Giving his inaugural speech to the Chamber, William Everard said that "a responsible approach to the environment" would be highlighted during his presidential year.[31] Furthermore, he praised the more advanced proponents of quality shipping management and challenged the critical view that shipping had to be "dragged into the future" over environmental issues. Quality and the long term view on standards was advocated by the new Chamber of Shipping President who predicted that the extra investment in hardware and planning, designed to reduce and manage risk "will be repaid many times over during the lifetime of the ship".[32]

As company chairman, Mr. Everard was able to demonstrate commitment to quality environmental management with the news that his tanker fleet was taking delivery of sophisticated newbuildings, featuring advanced systems in twin propulsion and computer controlled cargo handling. Mr. Everard also cited other British flag shipping companies which have moved beyond regulatory criteria in their approach to the environment: P&O-Nedlloyd had reduced its generated wastes by more than 32% and its ozone depleting Chloroflourcarbons (CFC) emissions by 82% between 2001 and 2003. Meanwhile, BP Marine and P&O had financed the Eco-Silencer System which was also being trialled by P&O Ferries.

The system has the potential to reduce harmful emissions by scrubbing exhaust gases. In addition, the leading container line and major recruit to the UK Tonnage Tax scheme, Hatsu Marine, was fitting double skinned bunker tanks to their newbuilding containerships, thus reducing the risk of pollution from heavy fuel oil spills.[33]

Attention to the importance of environmental standards is valued as integral to the revival of the UK fleet. In the changing shipping environment post *Erika* and *Prestige*, British shipping was beginning to market itself as an ambassador of quality operations, safety and environmental integrity. The shift in business behaviour here lies in demands in terms of quality as well as costs! Also, leading the moves towards improved safety standards, William Everard's brother, Michael has argued that "charterers should take responsibilities for the ships they charter". Michael Everard's thesis is that it is not only the shipowner that is culpable for sub-standard operations.[34] The recognition of the importance of the charterers influence on standards can now be acknowledged as a signpost for the moves towards intensified scrutiny of shipping standards. The oil majors embarked upon an immediate post-*Erika*, strategy on maritime safety. The *Erika,* after much investigation, was found to be an ageing (25 years old), poorly maintained and inspected tanker, Italian owned and Maltese flagged, on charter to the French oil major, TotalFina. The BBC referred to the lack of transparency and the apparent lack of concern over safe standards as "The Scandal of the 25 years old *Erika,*"[35] Blame was passed to the captain, the shipowners, the ship inspection classification society, Rina, the Maltese Registry and the charterers, TotalFina.[36] The environmental pressure group, Friends of the Earth, were particularly scathing in their criticism of the French oil major. Other oil companies had refused to charter *Erika* for safety reasons but TotalFina "preferred to use a cheaper, older tanker to transport its fuel."[37] The conservation group, Birdlife, directed concern to: "Europe's worst ever Atlantic coast oil spill disaster,"[38]

In the Paris High Court in 2004, TotalFina faced a charge of "Endangering human life, causing marine pollution and deliberately failing to take measures to avoid a casualty."[39] The implications for oil majors employing ageing substandard tankers could not have been made more obvious.

4.5 BP Returns to Shipping Leadership

The spotlight on oil tanker practice following the *Exxon Valdez*, *Erika* and *Prestige* coastal pollution disasters can be recognised as a factor in the changing business behaviour of global oil major, BP. The return of BP to large scale shipping operations has considerable implications for the emphasis on quality, ergo the Green Highway. Expansion programmes have projected BP into pole position as the UK's most dynamic ship operator, an amazing "sea change" in strategic behaviour from the tanker fleet rationalisations of the 1980-90s.

Given the increased commitment to environmental scrutiny in the oil trades, BP's rationalisation of its tanker fleet post 1975 began to prove problematic. BP's tanker vetting system had already rendered two thirds of the independent, third party world tanker fleet ineligible for charter on safety standards in the early New Millennium years.[40] Given that BP had retained a core of in-house maritime expertise, the decision was made to manage risk rather than delegate its responsibilities to a third party tanker operator.

The changing direction of the oil supply chain also had some bearing on BP's decision. In addition to the cataclysmic impact of tanker disasters on the European coastline, the recognition of maritime hot spots in the new Europe has placed emphasis on shipping quality.[41] The exploitation of the vast oil reserves in Russia's Northern Seas raises many questions over the potentially damaging impact on the environmentally sensitive permafrost.

In addition, the long haul down the Norwegian coastline into the North Sea and English Channel is of particular concern for environmentalists. BP, with its global business expansion strategy, found itself and its shipping strategy at the centre of the ensuing debate. The wreck of the *Prestige* off the coast of Galicia prompted questions over the safety of Russian oil exports. The *Prestige* had loaded Russian crude oil out of the Latvian port of Ventspils and steamed through the environmentally sensitive and navigationally demanding Baltic/Kattegat region. Moving down the North Sea coastlines of Denmark, Germany, Holland, Belgium, France, England and negotiating the intensive maritime traffics of the Dover Straits, the ageing vessel was an accident waiting to happen on any number of coastlines. In the aftermath of the pollution disaster, Russian chartering procedure was castigated. It was established that the Russian/Swiss company responsible for chartering the *Prestige* deliberately targeted lower cost ageing tankers – a practice which provided cost savings of £5,000 per day over a more modern tanker![42] Also, it is of interest to note that the *Prestige* was one of the tankers that BP's Chartering department had previously rejected.[43]

As well as the oil trades out of the Baltic, exploration developments in the Arctic Northern Seas regions has helped to promote Russia to number two in world oil supplies, second only to Saudi Arabia. The ice free Port of Murmansk has achieved a focal role as a transhipment port for oil transfer from the small, shortsea vessels capable of serving the Northern Seas oil fields. Murmansk is able to load 100,000dwt Aframax tankers. In March 2005 trade analysts Bloomberg reported that Murmansk, Russia's largest Arctic oil port, had plans to boost exports of crude oil and oil products to Europe and the US by as much as 60% within the year as pumping more oil to the region increased. This would result in the Kola Peninsula port loading around 10m tonnes in 2005, up from 6.3m tons in 2004.[44] Smaller oil tankers deliver crude from the ports of Vitino and Arkhangelsk on the White Sea coast to discharge into the Bergesen-controlled ULCC storage ship, *Belokamenka*, or the handysize, *Che Guevara*.[45]

Murmansk has become a logistics centre for oil transhipment. Such developments place BP's tanker management at the heart of an environmentally sensitive supply chain. BP's joint venture with Russia's Tyumen Oil, TNK-BP, has provided access to Siberian oil supplies via Murmansk. The $18bn joint venture in 2003 proved to be Russia's largest ever corporate deal and made BP the second largest private sector oil producer in the world. The strategic and political importance of the merger was endorsed by the presence of the UK Premier, Tony Blair and Russian Federation President, Vladimir Putin at the signing of the deal in London in 2003. The *New York Times* saw the merger as a desire to inject some corporate discipline into Russian enterprise following the corruption debacle surrounding the collapse of the state oil corporation, Yukos, the jailing of its executives and the seizure of its oil field assets.[46] The immediate impact of the deal was to raise the capitalization of the Russian oil assets by $7.5b.[47] In 2003, TNK-BP, in collaboration with Lukoil, Yukos Oiland Sibneft declared the intention to build a $4.5bn oil pipeline to link Siberian fields with Murmansk.

Tanker market leadership had been at the forefront of BP's shipping strategy up until the oil crisis of the late 1970s. The pace of tanker divestment was accelerated following the corporate traumas brought about by the *Exxon Valdez* oil pollution disaster in 1989. It appears that BP followed ExxonMobil's lead in moving out of fleet ownership. The risks associated with a large scale tanker pollution incident – political, legal and financial – as well as the damage to corporate reputation, were seen as too high. Divesting from direct fleet ownership was prized as a way of avoiding these risks. By 2001 the BP tanker fleet was down to just 18 vessels (in 1975 BP owned 88 tankers).[48] Two factors were, however, to bring a change to BP's strategy. First, the 1998-9 mergers with US oil majors, Arco and Amoco had increased the logistical demands on the merged company – the volume of petroleum products to be moved by sea quadrupled to 6m bpd.[49] Secondly, the French coast sinking of the *Erika* in 1999, had demonstrated that oil majors could not distance themselves from pollution disasters, irrespective of ownership. The foundation of maritime expertise that had allowed BP to build up its fleet up until the late 1970s still offered the opportunity to reverse the strategy on ownership and the in-house management of maritime risk. It was felt that the reputation of the oil giant was safer in the hands of BP's own professionals.[50]

Increased participation in the logistics of Russian oil and renewed attention to shipping issues by BP has brought about a qualitative extension of the Green Highway. With environmental concern directed to Northern seas by the International Maritime Organisation (IMO), BP's re-commitment to shipping is timely. However, commercial objectives are also evident in the corporation's investments in purpose built, ice strengthened tankers. In 2004, BP's spokesman had concluded that there would be growing opportunities for ice strengthened ships around the Baltic Sea. "There will not be many ships around with this capability and we are looking to take advantage," adding that "Rather than going into the market, why not build them ourselves?"[51] This demonstrates commitment to the longer term objective of environmental sustainability, as well as a pragmatic desire to benefit from market leadership in the quality focused ice-strengthened tanker markets. Ice strengthened tankers reduce risk of ice damage, ergo oil spillages, but also cost an extra 30% in construction costs.

From 2002 onwards, the BP reversal in fleet ownership has accelerated with the fleet planned to expand to 80 vessels by 2007. Table 18 contains details of BP's order book in 2004. In 2004 the oil major's fleet totalled more than 40 vessels, including double-hulled crude carriers, product carriers and liquefied natural gas carriers (LNG), as well as some single-hulled coastal tankers. The scale of BP's commitment to the newbuilding market in the early years of the New Millennium has restored BP as a major world shipping operator. The extensive building programme saw the group take delivery of 15 ships in 2003, with a further 43 vessels on order in the 2000-7 period, including four high cost

US builds for the Alaskan Trades. It was been reported in 2004 that at any one time BP has 500 cargoes "on the water", 300 of which are deepsea traffics. This includes vessels in its own fleet, chartered tonnage and cargoes purchased on a cost insurance freight basis. With the remaining average of 200 cargoes moving daily around coastlines and inland, BP is now a major global Green Highway, as well as deepsea, player. The corporation finds itself in prime position to measure their efforts to improve safety by playing a more active role in ship operations. In April 2004, BP Shipping were able to claim that its directly operated fleet had "achieved a new level of industry leading performance", with no reportable personal injuries or environmental pollution incidents in a 20 months period. During this time, the officers and crew accumulated 10m hours on board, with more than 1,400 voyages safely completed, 2.7m.nm travelled and about 38mt of cargo carried.[52]

The link between the leading oil majors and the UK fleet has proved beneficial to established tanker owners. Crescent Tankships of Southampton has built up a long term working relationship with the oil majors, BP in particular. In 2003, Crescent Tankships, who operate ships' bunker oil services for BP in many ports, was awarded the coveted, BP Golden Barge Award. Such business relationships have enabled the company to embark upon an ambitious fleet renewal programme. With a rolling programme of six 3500dwt coastal tankers Crescent's investment risk is off-set by a series of long-term charter agreements with BP and other oil majors.[53] Attaining the long-term security of vessel employment is an important pre-requisite of expanding the Green Highway. With

182

a significant portion of its new tanker fleet under the Isle of Man flag, the return of BP to fleet ownership has proved to be a large boost to (Red Ensign) shipping.

Table 18: BP's £3b Tanker Order Resurrection, 2004		
Order	Builder	DWT/Volume
10 Product Carriers	Hyundai. S. Korea	46,000
8 Aframax Tankers	Samsung, S.Korea	105,000
4 Suezmax Tankers	NASSCO, USA	185,000
3 Product Carriers	Damen, Netherlands	2,200-3800
10 Product Carriers	Miura, Japan	1,550-5000
4 LPG Carriers	Mitsubishi, Japan	83,000m^2
4 Platform Support Vessels	Yantai, China	N/A
Source: "Why a Super Major ordered a sea change," *Fairplay International Shipping Weekly*, 19.8.04.		

Given the focus on Baltic and Northern Seas oil trades, traffics around the British and Irish coastlines will involve increasing amounts of BP tonnage. From this perspective, the corporation has stated its intention to provide quality oil logistics – a tangible contribution to the Green Highway.

The following section will examine how such policy initiatives as the Tonnage Tax and the restructuring of the Maritime and Coastguard Agency (MCA) has facilitated further positive developments in UK shipping. The increased emphasis on quality in the tanker trades has featured a leading role by British companies.

The bigger picture of British fleet growth has a mixture of quality and fiscal incentives at its centre. The radical changes in UK shipping policy are now discussed as the catalyst for growth.

4.6 Maritime Policy Changes: Towards a Re-assessment of the UK Fleet

The Merchant Fleet has been traditionally known as "the fourth arm" of Britain's military defence. In both world wars merchant shipping played a vital role in maintaining food and military supplies and was integral to the logistics supply chain for the Falklands War Campaign - ultimately military success. By the time of the Gulf War in 1990-1, the run down in the UK fleet had left a shortage of available tonnage. As a consequence, the nation became dependent on chartered tonnage. The excessively high charter rates paid by the British Ministry of Defence, ultimately the tax-payer, helped to place merchant shipping back on the political agenda (see below, p.188).

The renaissance of British shipping can be traced to a significant shift away from the free market approach in the late 1990s. The emergence of a Labour Government in 1997 signalled a reversal of policy towards shipping. The implications for the Green Highway are considerable in that the policy changes have facilitated national interest in matters of national maritime security and safety. Historically, UK shipping, along with other traditional maritime nations – Denmark, Germany Holland, Norway – has been regarded as a quality operation. Having one of the world's lowest casualty ratios, the British registry compares favourably to the flag of convenience registers. This approach introduces the qualitative dimension as opposed to the quantitative comparative cost angle. Perceptions on the role and value of the UK fleet has been polarised by these two positions. However, it is apparent that there has been a move away from the purely cost-led approach towards the broader evaluation.

The 1998 DETR policy paper, *British Shipping Charting a New Course*,[54] set out the strategy for the reversal of the decline of the UK fleet, a decline which had continued unabated from 1975 onwards. The recovery of both UK flagged and UK managed shipping coincides firstly with this strategy paper which explored ways which could lead to a revival of UK shipping, also seafarer employment. In this DETR paper the commitment to shortsea and inland shipping is clearly in evidence. Examples include adherence to the European Commission's shortsea shipping proposals – fostering competitiveness, improving port efficiency, removing the administrative burden, undertaking new market initiatives, promoting the use of information technology.[55] The European Commission's, *Common Transport Policy* (CTP) provided some focus on the competitiveness of shipping, *vis-à-vis* road haulage. The question of road haulage avoiding the full burden of the environmental costs it generates was identified as critical in the sustainable development debate. The DfT has followed this idea through with targeting of Vehicle Excise Duty rates as a compensatory factor.[56] A second initiative has been the extension of the Freight Facilities Grant to coastal and shortsea shipping.[57]

The extension of the Freight Facilities Grant to coastal and shortsea shipping is recognition of the trading opportunities that exist on the UK coastline. The resumption of grain traffics on the Manchester Ship Canal in 1999 was facilitated by the support of a FFG. This contributed to the purchase of the 984dwt coastal barge *Gina D* as well as cargo discharging equipment. The introduction of the UK Tonnage marked a shift in attitude by Government in 2000. There was a recognised need for a tax regime that would allow UK shipping to competitively trade on its reputation for quality and at the same time to promote training of officer cadets. Specifically, the objectives set out for the UK Tonnage Tax were:

> to help arrest (and reverse) the decline in the UK shipping industry by increasing direct ownership of shipping by companies within the UK, and increasing the UK merchant marines workforce – officers and ratings.[58]

Companies electing to enter the Tonnage Tax scheme would have their earnings assessed on the size of vessels, measured in tonnage terms.[59] The extent of the changing national evaluation of shipping was endorsed by the evolution of Conservative Party thinking. The role of Government *vis-à-vis* shipping was questioned in 1999 when amendments to the Finance Bill incorporating a UK Tonnage Tax were tabled by the Conservative Party Shadow Transport Minister, Bernard Jenkin. The pledge followed strong criticism from Mr Jenkin of the Government's failure to propose a Tonnage Tax in the Budget. It had been anticipated by Britain's maritime industry that Chancellor of the Exchequer, Gordon Brown, would introduce a radical overhaul of the way shipping companies were taxed. Instead, he proposed a study into the implications of a Tonnage Tax. Mr. Jenkin charged that the shipping industry "is teetering on the edge of final despair with the present tax regime, adding,

> come what may, the Conservatives are seeking advice on the tabling of amendments to promote the Tonnage Tax for discussion during considerations of the Finance Bill.[60]

The urgency of the Conservatives to provide supportive legislation to shipping marked the significant reversal of political approaches towards the industry. The "Tonnage Tax" and the restructuring of the Maritime Coastguard Agency (MCA) were both outcomes of *British Shipping Charting a New Course*. Also, the strategy paper prompted the broader evaluation of shipping including the link between vessel, seafarer and maritime businesses – maritime law, hull classification, insurance. The policy emphasis on quality tonnage and crews favours higher cost UK operators, after what can at best be called a few decades of UK Government indifference to shipping. In the shortsea/inland sector, renewed impetus followed the 1994 *Royal Commission on Environmental Pollution Eighteenth Report, Transport and the Environment*.[61] The report concentrated on the environmental damage caused by road transport. The roles of shortsea, coastal and inland shipping in reducing dependence on road haulage were identified as key green strategies .

In addition to the re-evaluation of British shipping, the painful shrinkage process that the UK fleet had undertaken in the last three decades had in relative terms left the shortsea sector in a much stronger position *vis-à-vis* the deepsea sector. As a consequence, the outcome of this resurgence of interest in shipping is seen as highly conducive to the Green Highway.

4.7 Shipping, the Tonnage Tax and Great Britain Plc?

The revival of the UK fleet can partly be explained as a re-evaluation of the strategic and economic importance of shipping. This includes the link between a national shipping fleet and shore-based employment in the maritime services sector. In 2000, it was estimated that combined UK overseas earnings in the banking, insurance and legal services of the maritime sector was around £1b per year.[62] The earnings potential of maritime expertise has brought about a reassessment of the seafaring profession and its foundation link to a career in maritime services. It has been established that some 17,000 ex-seafarers are employed in maritime services in the UK.[63]

In 1999, David Cobb, the then President of the UK Chamber of Shipping and Chief Executive of the major UK coastal shipping and maritime services operator, James Fisher Group, urged the UK government to implement a Tonnage

Tax sooner rather than later, in his speech at the Institute of Marine Engineers Annual Dinner.[64] An initiative on the tax regime had been anticipated by the UK shipowning community but Government had deferred decision making. Chancellor Gordon Brown was singled out for criticism for erring on the side of caution, delaying the go-ahead until 2000.

In the March 1999 Budget Speech, the Chancellor announced that the Government had asked Lord Alexander Weedon to undertake an independent, neutral study on the national and international implications of a Tonnage Tax (a corporation tax based on the vessel's tonnage of ships). It was obvious that this delay had disappointed those in the British shipping community keen to develop activities under the UK flag. Many companies had been eagerly awaiting the Budget in order to take decisions on ship ownership, employment, financing and registration. David Cobb was to add: "the delay is therefore disappointing, since it puts off the time when industry can start renewing its fleet and contributing to the British economy in an even higher gear than in recent years."[65] The delay in the decision was also of some concern to the 1996 merged British-Dutch P&O-Nedlloyd Group, particularly given the availability of a Tonnage Tax under the Netherlands flag

Tonnage Tax schemes within the European Union had been assessed by the UK Chamber of Shipping. The schemes in place in Greece, the Netherlands, Norway and Germany, all met EU guidelines and appeared to be having some success in restoring tonnage under the respective national registries. The Netherlands had already implemented a Tonnage Tax regime in 1996 and its impact was instantaneously positive in terms of ships and tonnage joining the registry, maritime employment and shipbuilding. Table 19 shows the positive contribution that the Netherland's Tonnage Tax made to the national economy. With a 37.0% increase in ships under the Netherland's flag, a 23.0% rise in seafaring employment and, significantly, a 400% boost to Dutch shipbuilding orders, the Tonnage Tax proved overnight success.

Following the success of the scheme in the Netherlands, the case for a Tonnage Tax was made not just in the interests of the British shipping companies but also of "Great Britain plc", including shipbuilding and repair yards, marine equipment manufacturers, ports and the financial and other maritime-related services in the City of London.[66]

Table 19: The Impact of the 1996 Netherlands Tonnage Tax		
	1995	1998
Number of Ships on Dutch register	383	525
Million gt	2.8	3.9
Employment in the shipping industry (1994)	22,781	28,000
Number of Dutch orders at Dutch shipyards	33	166
Million dwt	0.15	0.64
Source: H.M. Treasury. (1999) *Independent Enquiry into a Tonnage Tax: A Report by Lord Alexander Weedon, QC*. London: HMSO.		

The Independent Enquiry into the Tonnage Tax[67] in 1999 commissioned by HM Treasury presented evidence from Britain's (then) largest shipping group, P&O. At the time P&O owned 40% of UK tonnage. The desire to retain the UK link whilst enhancing competitive advantage was instrumental in P&O's support for the UK Tonnage Tax. During a period of global mergers and fleet rationalisations business location was becoming paramount to competitive success. P&O's 1996 merger with the leading Netherlands container operator, Royal Nedlloyd, was forcing a global outlook: the desire to avoid full corporation tax was viewed as instrumental to global competitiveness.

Without a Tonnage Tax regime there was a risk that the merged market leaders would transfer their ships into fiscally favourable registries. The prerequisite for the merged group was to find a tax structure that would ensure global competitiveness.[68] In 1999, Lord Sterling, P&O's chairman, declared that his group would immediately place 49 vessels under the UK flag, thus increasing UK tonnage by 75%. Additionally, P&O's UK training programme would expand from 170 to 310 Cadets. By the end of the Millennium P&O-Nedlloyd had taken delivery of four of the world's largest container vessels and the large cruise ships *Arcadia, Oriana* and *Aurora* had been added to the fleet. The historic role of the British Merchant Navy and P&O's leading role within the fleet engendered a "UK" plc approach towards fleet registration:

> There is great pride in this country in our maritime history and we in P&O are very conscious of the role of the UK fleet as the'fourth arm of defence'. As we enter the new millennium, we now have the opportunity of rebuilding our maritime heritage and ensuring that the younger generation is as proud of the Red Ensign as their forebearers.[69]

Lord Sterling, who proved to be the champion of a revived UK merchant fleet, outlined the case for a Tonnage Tax before a large enthusiastic London audience, pointing out that a positive government decision would bring benefits in terms of increased earnings, GDP growth, high-value training and skills, employment, inward investment and defence. The spirited defence of the UK Merchant Navy and its traditional role as the Fourth Arm of the nation's defence took on a broad rationale – the economic case for a stronger UK fleet - became interwoven with the defence issue. Partly this can be explained as a reaction to the logistics crisis of the 1991-2 Gulf War. The demand for suitable tonnage to serve the logistical needs of the British armed forces could not be met by a depleted UK flagged fleet. Unlike in the 1982 Falklands War, when 153 UK ships were requisitioned for the campaign in the South Atlantic, during the Gulf War only 8 out of a total of 143 MOD chartered vessels flew the Red Ensign.[70] Moreover, financial impropriety was revealed after the war by the UK National Audit Office (NAO). As a result of the NAO's investigations, by 1993 it had become obvious that the nation had paid an unreasonably high charter rate for many of the foreign flag vessels, to the sum of £38m.[71] In addition to the Tonnage Tax, the Green Highway was given a boost in 2003 when shortsea shipping was brought into the European guidelines for state aid and tax concessions for the first time. This resulted in shipping operators producing a verifiable business plan, one which featured a modal switch from road haulage, receiving state aid for up to three years.[72]

The resurgence of economic activity under the UK flag has important implications for the Green Highway. The revived British Red Ensign has served as a reminder that shipping has a future in Britain. Moreover, it will become evident that UK coastal shipping companies, particularly Everard's of Greenhithe, Kent, Carisbrooke Shipping of the Isle of Wight, and Fisher's of Barrow, Cumbria, have played an integral role in the revival process. If UK shipping had been condemned as a sunset industry in the 1980s period of painful de-industrialisation, the reversal of its long-term decline at the closing of the 20th century has provoked a re-assessment of the role of shipping in the economy. UK flagged shipping had been in free-fall from 1975 onwards. However, a shift in perception at the policy making level has brought about a re-valuation of the importance of quality oriented shipping.

Two main dynamics may be identified in the revival process:(1) Enhanced concern over standards of maritime safety and environmental protection; (2) The financial benefits of the 2000 implemented Tonnage Tax. In 2004, the UK Chamber of Shipping was able to report a 250% increase in UK flagged tonnage since the 2000 implementation of the Tonnage Tax[73] and in 2005 the Chamber supported its claim that "The UK owned merchant fleet is one of the most efficient and diverse in the world," by stating that the UK fleet:

- takes over 4% of the world's shipping business with only 1.7% of the world fleet;

- is the fifth largest earner in the UK services sector – ahead of telecommunications, film and television and computer services;

- has a core of highly competent British seafarers, respected worldwide that provides essential skills and core business for marine related business ashore;

- provides over half the business of British shipbuilders and marine equipment suppliers.[74]

The Tonnage Tax along with its recruitment and training initiatives was a major element in the Government's policy direction. P&O Director, Graeme Dunlop has responded to the challenge of the new opportunities for UK shipping and seafaring:

> What we have to get across to young people is that a career at sea can be very attractive…It is all a question of creating an ambience of a sunrise rather than a sunset industry and the tonnage tax gives us the chance to do that.[75]

In mid summer 2000, the UK owner's forum, the UK Chamber of Shipping, benefited from the renewed membership of Canadian Pacific's (CP Ships). With 25 directly owned vessels and a further 50 chartered vessels, CP Ships instantly became one of the Chamber's leading companies.[76] The attractions of the Tonnage Tax to a globally footloose shipping industry were becoming obvious. Following the lead that shortsea specialist, James Fisher, had taken earlier in campaigning for the Tonnage Tax, the company proved to be an early beneficiary of the scheme. In September 2000 profits of $4.6m were announced, boosted by a reduction in the corporation tax burden of $200,000.[77] The favourable level of tax burden on owners utilising the Tonnage Tax regime has been calculated by chartered accountants, Moore Stephens.

Table 20 shows the tax liability for a 10,000 net tonnes containership under selected flags. The conditions of the Tonnage Tax can be accepted as an attempt to stimulate British shipping operations. On 12th August 1999, Deputy Prime Minister John Prescott announced the scheme, claiming it "as the most important day for British shipping for generations."[78] Although registration under the UK flag is not a pre-condition of the regime, vessels that are strategically and commercially managed in the United Kingdom are accepted:

> The scheme has implications for UK seafarer employment as it provides the recipient company with the obligation of recruiting one new officer cadet per annum for every 15 officers employed.[79]

It has been shown that the Tonnage Tax is obviously an incentive to registration under the UK flag. Companies signing up for this fiscal package can avoid corporation tax. The main proviso is that they agree to recruit and train British nationals as cadets. It is apparent that without some degree of state encouragement the UK flag sector has only limited prospects. The laissez faire approach of the 1980s proved to be disastrous for UK flag shipping. The favourable and immediate response by the industry to the modest support offered by Government suggests that it has responded positively to public acclaim, the recognition of its vital role in serving the economic interests of the nation. Lower cost operations can be achieved outside of the UK registry: global combinations of developed nation capital and expertise and developing nation labour and flag of convenience registries – Panama, Liberia, Cyprus, Malta – have a comparative advantage against British flag and crewed ships. Even so, lines are returning to the UK flag and demand for UK seafaring is increasing rapidly.

Table 20: Selective North European Tax Payable on 10,000 Net Tonne Containership	
Tonnage Tax Regime	Tax Payable
Netherlands	$8,554
Norway	$27,104
Germany	$16,292
United Kingdom	$7,738
Source: "British tonnage tax lower than rivals", *Lloyd's List*. 7.7.00, p. 18.	

From this perspective the notion of a mercenary, globally footloose, business is replaced by one which is influenced by qualitative as well as quantitative forces. Under these conditions the hostile aspects of the global market are softened by supportive Government policy. It will be recognised that shipping enterprise can re-emerge in this environment. If the stance of maritime policy in the 1980-mid 1990s was very much conditioned by the supremacy of market forces, strategy from the late 1990s onwards has been one of creating an investment environment conducive to maritime revival. In attempting to explain the revival of UK shipping it is necessary to search beyond the market view of comparative cost. The wider spread of analysis includes a number of factors:

- the link between shipping enterprise and favourable maritime policy;

- the recognition of the importance of the UK fleet in sustaining the broader maritime commercial and technical industries;

- the role of UK shipping in improving maritime safety standards;

- the role of UK shipping in the sustainable mobility strategy of transferring freight from the congested road system.

The paramount importance of shipping to the UK economy is universally recognised. Around 95% of the UK's trade tonnage is by sea. The UK manages 1500 ships, employing some 25,000 British seafarers.[80] During the 1980s much discussion took place on the future of the UK fleet. The debate hinged around the role of Government. On the one hand, there was a strong case for a favourable fiscal regime which would induce new buildings for the UK flag; on the other hand, the case for a non-interventionist approach was based upon the rationale of market efficiency.

4.8 Restructuring and Reforming the MCA

At the heart of the up-turn in UK shipping is the shift in the way Government policy and regulation is implemented. The transition from a market driven to a proactive approach has been facilitated by the rationalisation and re-organisation of the regulatory inspectorate. The setting up of the Maritime and Coastguard Agency (MCA) in 1997-8 brought together disparate arms of safety and regulatory agencies. The long held view of UK shipowners had been that the authorities were rule bound, bureaucratic and obstructive; that the registering of ships was a painful exercise in over zealous vessel inspection and form filling. The service provided was not conducive to registering under the UK flag. The reorganisation process, which coincided with the opening of the purpose built directorate headquarters in Southampton, brought a shift in culture. Required service standards to customers have been identified and delivered, with the emphasis upon becoming more accessible, with a 24 hour, 365 day desk cover. Electronic communications have been developed and all personnel have undertaken "Investors in People" training and accreditation.[81] This has helped to transform the culture of the MCA from that of a uniformed, hierarchical organisation to that of a modern flat management structure with an emphasis on service provision.

The shift to a customer focus is very much appreciated by shipowners as it provides for an efficient registry and regulatory service.[82] It is evident that such a "user friendly" restructuring of the MCA has helped to encourage tonnage back to the UK registry, whilst retaining standards of inspection and regulation. In 2001, Chief Executive Maurice Storey, summarised the balance between maintaining effective safety standards and business communications: "We are still prepared to say no to shipowners, but now they understand why we say no".[83] The changes in attitude at the MCA bodes well for new shipping investment and therefore, the Green Highway. The more user-friendly approach allows for new entrant businesses to develop trades, whilst simultaneously retaining the high operational standards integral to the UK flag.

4.9 The Fleet at the Start of the New Millennium

Figure 24 illustrated the post WW2 growth in the UK fleet tonnage up until the mid-1970s, when the oil crisis had a crippling impact on world trade and ergo, the decline in demand for shipping. The much depleted 1999 UK fleet was dominated by the P&O group fleets – container ships, ferries and cruise ships. Few large crude tankers flew the UK flag, a handful of North Sea shuttle tankers proving the exception. The large, former British Rail, Sealink ferry fleet, was re-flagged to the Bahamas flag early into the privatisation process of the 1980s. By 1990, the deep sea dry bulk sector was virtually non-existent, although British companies continued to own and/or manage vessels off-shore. One of the brighter sectors of UK shipping was that of coastal and shortsea.

Traditional British companies from coastal regions: Everard's of Greenhithe, Kent; Lapthorn's of Rochester, Kent; Union Transport of Bromley, Kent; Fisher's of Barrow in Furness, Cumbria; Carisbrooke Shipping of Cowes and Crescent Shipping of Southampton - had been able to retain (in some cases increase) their market share whilst still remaining under the British flag. In particular, they have been successful in the highly competitive, quality oriented clean petroleum products (CPP) market. Crescent Tankships, F.T. Everard and Fisher Tankships have attained sizeable long term contracts with oil majors for the dispatch of oil products ex-refinery. From this perspective, the British owners in the shortsea sector have proved their mettle in the most difficult of trading periods. The end of the century brought a significant developments in the UK merchant fleet. In addition to P&O's large expansion in both container and cruise shipping, (see above p.187) even more surprising was the early Millennium declaration by the Cunard Line that it was to build a new, British flag, *Queen Mary 2* for the North Atlantic passenger service |(summer only). The rise in the cruise ship market brought a reversal in passenger shipping which had been in decline since the early days of jumbo jets. This decision was particularly welcomed by the Solent regional daily, *Southern Daily Echo*, as it would allow Cunard to operate a two ship service on the "Blue Riband", Southampton-New York run for the first time in over 30 years.[84]

The qualitative dimension is evident in the type of vessel attracted to the UK flag, post 1998. Overwhelmingly, the trend is for ships in the higher added value sectors. These include ferries, cruise ships, container ships, product tankers, oil rig support vessels/anchor handling tugs and specialist project ships. Spearheading diversity in UK shipping, the traditional owner, James Fisher and Sons Plc have spread their assets from dry bulk and oil products tankers trading in European waters to a diverse portfolio of cable ships, nuclear fuel carriers, heavy lift ships and Royal Fleet Auxiliary (RFA) tankers. By 2002, Fisher's chairman, Tim Harris, announcing a 62% rise in pre-tax profit, was evidently keen to re-brand the company away from simply conventional shipowning to that of a provider of a wide range of maritime services.[85]

The reverse side of the move towards quality operations is the divestment from low value sectors. Demonstrating the difficulties of trading in the low value bulk sector was the 2002 announcements of both Crescent Shipping and Fisher's of their withdrawal from the dry bulk sector. Although Crescent still continued to manage dry cargo vessels – as well as Irish Sea freight ferries – the companies directly owned vessels were to be dedicated solely to the CPP trades. Also 2002 saw the setting up of the joint venture drawn from Union Transport and F.T. Everard's dry bulk fleet.[86] The announcement meant that effectively Everards had withdrawn from the dry market, with Union Transport taking over the operational role. Everard's had consistently reduced their exposure to the risky dry bulk market in the previous decade and focused on the CPP sector. By 2002 it directly owned just two vessels in the dry sector; however, a further eleven managed and nine time chartered vessels were transferred to the joint venture. The evidence from the dry-bulk trades in the early Millennium was that foreign flagged and crewed vessels had supplanted British ships in the market. Appendix 3 shows the dearth of British flagged vessels and the complete dominance of East European crewed vessels arriving in the Port of Bideford to load brick-clay.

4.10 A Revived Fleet – but not as we know it!

The revival of shipping activity under the British flag is viewed as a positive trend by many. Speaking at the Chamber of Shipping in January 2004, Transport Minister, Alistair Darling, made much of the registering of the *Queen.Mary.2* under the British flag. The Minister referred to the success of British shipping's recovery. The speech took place just a few weeks after the naming ceremony of the *Queen Mary 2,* which the Minister claimed as the largest, most expensive passenger ship in the world, sailing under the Red Ensign and registered in Cunard's home port of Southampton. In addition, the Minister carried on to praise:

- the largest maritime sector in Europe, with a turnover of £37b;
- London as a world centre of maritime business expertise;
- a UK register which had trebled its tonnage in a period of seven years;
- a Tonnage Tax regime which would lead to 1000 cadets in training. [87]

The UK Chamber of Shipping has been particularly optimistic in envisaging future employment prospect for UK nationals. In 2005, the Chamber's President, William Everard addressed a joint shipping committee between the Chamber and the seafarer unions. Mr. Everard welcomed the new momentum towards increasing the national maritime skills base, particularly addressing the problems of providing opportunities for British junior officers and ratings. Efforts were continuing to encourage and increase employment for British seafarers, said Mr. Everard. An "honest debate", he added, was taking place. [88]

In October 2005, the UK shipping community applauded the success of British shipping in attaining revenues of £10b, a doubling of 2002s earnings. [89] Over-hauling the earnings of the British air industry – the first time in twelve years – Lloyd's List carried the heading, "Revival lifts British Shipping to star status." Mr. Mark Brownrigg of the UK Chamber of Shipping lauded the positive impact of the Tonnage Tax in not only attracting investment, but also encouraging new cadet entrants into the seafaring profession. By providing an internationally competitive fiscal regime, many foreign shipping lines were attracted to the UK register. Additionally, some 600 new recruit cadets had joined the Merchant Service within a two year period. [90]

Heralding one of the UK Tonnage Tax schemes most prestigious new-entrants is the British commitment of the Taiwanese carrier, Evergreen Line. In

June 2004, Evergreen ranked at No.4 in the world container fleet with a total capacity of 683,000 teu.[91] The moves by Evergreen to the UK flag signal a reversal in fates. The rise of such "Asian Tiger" economies as Taiwan has been explained as part of a process which negates industrial activity in the mature western economies. During the post 1970s Evergreen were successful in competing with UK lines in the burgeoning Europe-Far East trades. With a mixture of innovation, investment and intense competitiveness, Evergreen were able to project themselves into the top echelons of container shipping. From this perspective, Evergreen's move to the UK flag marks the extent of the British flag's recovery in global terms.

Having set up its British subsidiary, Hatsu Marine, at the beginning of 2002, Evergreen chairman, Dr Chang was keen for a British national to be put in charge in order to further differentiate the new line from its huge sister company.[92] The setting up of the British based and managed Hatsu Marine subsidiary in Euston, London is valued as a way of both locating closer to British customers and also to enjoy the quality status of the UK flag. By 2004, Hatsu Marine had acquired its own dedicated, 68-strong staff at the European headquarters of Evergreen in Euston.

The parent company, Evergreen, has justified its commitment to the UK registry for Hatsu, praising the British register as a quality flag that is respected around the world. This, in turn, brings in business from customers who feel more comfortable working with a UK line.[93] In addition, Hatsu have claimed a ten year gap in environmental leadership with the delivery of its 2005 built vessel, UK flagged, *Hatsu Shine*, the first of four sisterships.[94] Hatsu have highlighted innovations in engine exhaust pollution, including the ability to switch to low sulphur fuels. Also, increased fuel bunker tank security reduces spill risk and oily water separators are improved to reduce the discharge of polluted bilge waters. When in port the vessel has the ability to close down diesel generators and switch to less polluting shoreside power supplies – a strategy already being advocated by the largest US container port, Los Angeles. Evergreen's Chief Executive and founder, Y.K.Chang, has rationalised the expenditure on environmental welfare:

> Although our market is price-driven and highly competitive, with our customers all seeking to achieve the lowest costs, we know most of them are also very aware of the environmental issues.[95]

In addition to Hatsu's UK collaboration, another "Asian Tiger" in the container sector to join the post 2000 Tonnage Tax and UK flag was the South Korean market leader, Hyundai Merchant Marine. Yet another fillip was given to the UK registry when, in 2003, the Zodiac Group announced it was transferring half of its 140 strong fleet to the UK flag.[96] The move was made as part of Zodiac's strategy to rationalise the number of flags under which its fleet operates, dividing the vessels between the UK and Liberian administrations. Zodiac Maritime is one of the management arms of Ofer International and is regarded as a key operator in London because of its size and the scope of maritime activities undertaken. Its responsibilities cover the complete range of management services from chartering and operating, crewing, maintenance and repair to legal matters and sale and purchase. The transfer of 7 Capesize bulk carriers has added 1.3mdwt to the UK registry and made Zodiac Maritime one of the largest operators under the UK flag in 2003, as well as managing one of the biggest cadet training schemes in the UK. Thus, Zodiac has the placing power of 300 vessels in the insurance market. As a consequence, Zodiac's presence in London is critically important for the maritime business community. *Lloyd's List* has warned, "Should Zodiac ever decide to leave London, it would be a major blow to the city's position as one of the world's premier maritime centres."[97]

Located in Central London, Zodiac was attracted to the City by the huge range of maritime services and expertise on its doorstep. Subsequently, Zodiac is a sizeable employer, with a London staff of about 150 people and between 5,000 and 6,000 seafarers aboard its vessels. These people service a fleet of 50 bulk carriers, a similar number of containerships, 15 chemical tankers, 7 liquefied petroleum gas carriers, as well as some reefer vessels and car carriers.[98] As a management agency, Zodiac has proved to be the conduit for overseas shipping lines to enter the UK registry. As a result of Zodiac and a number of other overseas firms, the 2005 UK fleet composition does not have the same British character as two or three decades earlier. In terms of national ownership, investment and crewing the revived British flag has become much more cosmopolitan.

Despite the apparent success of the Tonnage Tax in attracting tonnage, reservations have been expressed over UK employment levels and the operational quality of some ships flying the Red Ensign. The employment of UK nationals as ratings has become extremely rare. Many of the serving officers are provided by lower wage nations, including India, the Philippines, Russia, Croatia, Ukraine and Poland. Not all in the industry have praised the Tonnage Tax. The ratings union, Railway and Maritime Transport Workers Union (RMT) have issued scathing criticism. As part of their contribution to the World Maritime Day in 2002, the RMT charged that the Tonnage Tax and its accompanying initiatives had done little for UK ratings, adding that the only way seagoing employment could be secured by British nationals was by accepting wages determined by the global labour market.[99]

A Past-Captain of the Southampton Master Mariner's Club, Captain Reg Kelso, a former shipmaster and later Chief Marine Superintendent of a major UK shipping conglomerate, has been a vigorous critic of the fall in standards and (what he sees as) the ambiguous commitment towards training and retaining British nationals as cadets. In a series of "Letters to the Editor" in Lloyd's List, Captain Kelso has warned of the dangers of UK seafarer rates of pay being forced downwards in accordance with the workings of the international labour market and what he recognises as the insistence of the UK shipowners' organisation, the Chamber of Shipping, that UK officers must compete in terms of cost and competency.[100] The concern here is that low pay rates will prove detrimental to UK seafarer recruitment. The thrust of Captain Kelso's argument is that if British nationals are to be enticed into a seafaring vocation, then it is vital, as well as ethical, to ensure a stable, professional career pathway:

> if the UK flag cannot offer our young men and women a worthwhile career then do not entice them into the industry in the first instance. Go for the cheaper option and allow our nationals to take up a more rewarding career.[101]

Furthermore, Captain Kelso links the absence of British crews on British flagged ships with a decline in professional standards, resulting in skill deficiencies and poor operational standards. The 2004 collision case of the British flagged, *Hyundai Dominion*, is cited as an example of sub-standard watch keeping skills on a UK flagged ship with a crew drawn from six nationalities.[102]

Maritime academics Leggate and McConville's 2005 critical appraisal was that the Tonnage Tax was successful in reviving tonnage under the UK flag between 1998 and 2003 but that, "its achievement in relation to the employment of UK seafarers can be seriously questioned…"[103] The concern over UK seafarer shortages is supported by a survey conducted by Southampton's maritime academy, Warsash Maritime Centre. The Centre's survey in 2004 revealed only 17% of school leavers were aware of the existence of a British Merchant Navy.[104] The reality is of a mixture of reluctance to go to sea, the seeming unawareness of the seagoing career opportunities and/or the unwillingness of shipping companies to hire British nationals. This is particularly the case when lower cost alternatives can be easily accessed via the global pool of maritime labour.

In April 2005, the reputation of the revived UK flag was sullied by the assertion that 10% of the UK fleet was deemed "flag of convenience" standard. The global transport workers union, International Transport Workers' Federation (ITF), has charged that sub-standard conditions exist on these vessels.[105] It is evident that there are some concerns over how the Tonnage Tax is implemented. However, by 2005 there were signs that UK cadet recruitment and training was increasing. In October of that year, the Chamber welcomed the second year of over 600 cadets being recruited.[106] In addition, the Chamber, supported by the officers union, NUMAST, has defended its commitment to the employment of UK nationals at a time when many UK firms are moving their production overseas.[107]

In relation to the Green Highway, the central question here is how safety and environmental standards are affected. It has been shown that leading UK tanker companies have spearheaded quality standards, marketing their expertise and commitment to safety and environmental integrity. In chapter 8, further consideration will be given to the environmental credibility of the Green Highway, with particular focus on the lower value end of the market. The question of fatigue and low manning levels in the shortsea sector – another area of concern raised by Captain Kelso – will be addressed.

Despite the renewed optimism surrounding the revival of the UK flag, it should also be mentioned that the behaviour of Britain's largest shipping group has questioned the long-term commitment of British investors towards maritime assets. The 1996 sale of the 14 strong coastal fleet of P&O Tankships now can be accepted as the precursor of total maritime divestment. Between 2003 and 2006, the break up of the three main components of P&O's shipping empire – cruise ships, container ships, ports and ferries – have been merged or sold off. In 2003, the Southampton based P&O Princess Cruises and Miami based Carnival Cruises embarked upon a $5.4b merger, creating a fleet of 66 vessels, plus an order book of a further 17 new vessels.[108]   In 2005, the Anglo-Dutch P&O-Nedlloyd container business, with 162 owned and chartered vessels, was involved in a €2.3b take-over by the Danish based market leader, Maersk.[109]   Finally, the £3.3bn buy out of P&O Ports and Ferries by Dubai Ports (DP) in February 2006, marked the demise of the final component of P&O's asset portfolio. At the Extraordinary General Meeting of P&O Shareholders, held at the Wembley Conference Centre 13.2.06, opinions divided according to the interests of investors.   Whilst the high price attained by the Board was welcomed by shareholders, with a 99.0% vote in favour of the sale to DP, others felt that the British maritime heritage was being negated. Master Mariner, Captain David Hawker summed up this mood:

> ...I never cease to be amazed at the lack of patriotism in this country, Britain. And I am astounded at the ignorance of those that fail to understand the importance of seafaring to the nation.[110]

This evidence reflects the dichotomy between the short-term interests of mercenary investors and the longer term strategic concerns of the defenders of the UK maritime heritage. The sale of P&O Princess Cruises to the US owned Carnival Cruises in 2002, the take-over of P&O-Nedlloyd by the Danish owned Maersk Line in 2005 and the sale of P&O Ports to Dubai Ports in 2006, all point to the footloose nature of British maritime capital. This reflects the financial reality that the Green Highway must endure and serves as a reminder that British shipping has taken on a extremely cosmopolitan characteristic.

4.11 Chapter 4: Summary & Conclusion

This chapter has discussed the issues of firstly, a declining UK fleet and secondly a dramatic revival. The relatively lower rate of decline of the coastal fleet *vis-à-vis* the deepsea fleet has provided for a raised profile of the former. A number of British shortsea companies (considered in chapter 6) including Fisher Tankships, Carisbrooke Shipping and Scot Line, as well as Ireland's Arklow Shipping, have taken advantage of respective national Tonnage Tax schemes. In addition, concerns over environmental risk along European coastlines, corresponding with heavy oil traffic volumes in the North Sea and, increasingly, the Baltic and Northern Seas, has focused attention on coastline movements. It has been shown how the free market approach to shipping was found wanting in delivering safety and environmental standards. Following such close to home pollution disasters as the *Braer, Sea Empress, Erika* and *Prestige* and, furthermore, the national catastrophe of the *Herald of Free Enterprise* sinking, more attention has been paid to quality issues. Given the increased attention to quality and environmental integrity, the higher costs of British and Irish operations can be off-set against risk reduction. This shift in qualitative perception at national levels can only prove conducive to a quality led Green Highway.

The transition in Government policy has been highly successful in encouraging more shipping activity under the UK flag; and this, in conjunction with a change in behaviour of the oil majors, particularly BP, has raised the profile of shipping in the UK. In addition, the broader UK economic interest is served by the location of shipping line offices and insurance placings in the City of London. It has also been made evident that some reservations over the standards of ships exists; more importantly, the standards of the globally sourced crews employed under the UK Tonnage Tax. Against this criticism the potential of the quality operators, primarily in the tanker sector, for spear-heading a critical mass of high standard tonnage and crews must be balanced.   From this perspective, the standards practised by these operators can serve as a benchmark for all other operators to adhere to.   The evolving role of Britain's hitherto maritime leader, P&O demonstrates the ethos to be found in the ownership of the newly revived fleet.   On the one hand, P&O have been able to attain financial benefits from the prestigious heritage, to which the company has made considerable contributions, on the other hand, it is clear that the short-term financial interests of the British investment community take precedence over issues of maritime tradition and national security.

Finally, the re-affirmation of both UK and Irish Government commitment to shipping, corresponding to national concern over coastline management, can only be conducive to the Green Highway as a sustainable alternative to road haulage dependency.   The following chapter will concentrate on the specifics of the ships and their trading patterns around the Irish and British coasts.   This is the test-bed against which the environmental credentials of the Green Highway will be measured!

CHAPTER 4: ENDNOTES

[1] DETR (1998) *British Shipping: Charting a New Course.* London: DETR. p. 1.

[2] Storey, M.; From a talk; "MCA and its Mission in Maritime Management", given by the Director of the MCA at London Guildhall University, 16.10.00.

[3] Department of Transport (1990) *British Shipping Challenges and Opportunities;* London: HMSO.

[4] *Op.cit.* p. 35.

[5] Goss, R. O. (1993) "The Decline of British Shipping: A Case for Action? *Maritime Policy and Management;* Vol. 20, No. 2, pp. 93-100.

[6] Sturmey, S. G. (1962) *British Shipping and World Competition.* Oxford: Athlone Press.

[7] *GCBS Annual Report, 1986-7.* London: GCBS, p. 2.

[8] Chancellor Lawson's Budget Speech, *Hansard,* 13/3.84. Cols. 295-6.

[9] Thatcher, M. (1982) Extract from a letter to the National Union of Seamen's General secretary, Jim Slater. Reproduced in Marsh, A. Ryan, V. (1989) *The Seamen: A History of the National Union of Seamen.* Oxford: Malthouse.

[10] Doganis, R. S. Metaxas, B.(1976) *The Impact of Flags of Convenience.* London: Polytechnic of Central London.

[11] NUMAST (1990) *Information Bulletin, Seafarers Hour's: Time to Act.* London: NUMAST. p.1.

[12] Hope, R. (1990) A New History of British Shipping. London: John Murray. p.450.

[13] House of Commons Transport Committee, Session, 1987-88. *Decline in the UK Registered Merchant Fleet. Minutes of Evidence,* 27.5.88. p.72.

[14] Marsh, A. Ryan.V.(1989) *The Seamen: A History of the National Union of Seamen.* Oxford: Malthouse. p.224

[15] Lane, T. (1986) *The Grey Dawn Breaking: British Seafaring in the Late Twentieth Century.* Manchester: MUP.

[16] Glen, Dowden, J. Wilson, R. (2005) *UK Seafarer Analysis: Report for the Department of Transport.* London: DfT. p. 48.

[17] Rowlinson, M. P. (1995) Doctoral Thesis, "*The Decline of UK Merchant Shipping 1975-90: Beyond the Market View.* City of London Polytechnic/London Guildhall University.

[18] Brooks, M. (2000) *Sea Change in Liner Shipping: Regulation and Managerial Decision-Making in a Global Industry.* Oxford: Pergamon Press. pp. 171-9.

[19] www.dft.gov.uk/transtat/maritime

[20] *Lloyd's Register of Shipping List of Shipowners* (Annual).

[21] Department of Transport (1988) *Short Sea Bulk Shipping: An Analysis of UK Performance.* London: Department of Transport. p. 30.

[22] Ledger, G. Roe, M. (1992) "The Decline of British Shipping: A Case for Action?" *Maritime Policy and Management,* Vol.19, No.3. pp. 239-51.

[23] *Loc.cit.*

[24] WWF Press Statement (2000) "Oil tanker accidents off the UK coastline increasing", London: WWF. 15.2.00.

[25] MAIB (1993) *Report of the Chief Inspector of Marine Accidents into the engine failure and subsequent grounding of the motor tanker, Braer, at Garths Ness, Shetland on January 5th, 1993,* Southampton: MAIB.

[26] Urquhart, F. McLean, A. "Shetland's Oil Nightmare Comes True," *The Scotsman.* 1.6.93.

[27] *Ibid.*

[28] Donaldson, J. F. (1994) *Safer Ships, Cleaner Seas: Report of Lord Donaldson's Inquiry into the Prevention of Pollution from Merchant Shipping. Command Papers, CM 2560* London: HMSO.

[29] Intertanko, (2001) "Safety, quality issues top agenda," *The Tanker Newsletter* Issue 5. May 2001.

[30] "Fisher posed for fleet revival," *Lloyd's List.* 8.9.00.

[31] Grey, M. (2005) "Chamber Chief to push green issues," *Lloyd's List,* 24.3.05.

208

[32] *Loc.cit.*
[33] *Loc.cit.*
[34] Everard, M. (1995) "Rogue Ships: A Shipowner's View." *Maritime Policy and Management.* Vol. 22. No. 3. pp.197-99.
[35] "The Scandal of the *Erika*," www.newsbbc.com , 16.8.00.
[36] *Loc.cit.*
[37] "Totally irresponsible: what the insurance industry should do in the wake of the *Erika* oil spill. www.foe.co.uk. February 2000.
[38] "Europe's worst ever Atlantic coast oil spill disaster,". www.birdlife.net/news. 1.3.00.
[39] Spurrier, A. "Total pursues annulment of *Erika* charges." *Lloyd's List.* 2.4.04.
[40] "Why a Super Major ordered a sea change," *Fairplay International Shipping Weekly,* 19.8.04.
[41] Rowlinson, M. Wixey, S. (2005), "Green Shipping: European Policy and Economic Forces," in Leggate, H. (ed) *International Maritime Transport Perspectives.* London: Routledge. p. 277-88.
[42] "Crown cashes in with older tankers," *Lloyd's List.* 27.11.02.
[43] *Loc.cit*
[44] "Russian gate to the North plans to boost oil exports into Europe and the US," *Lloyd's List.* 27.1.05.
[45] *Loc.cit.*
[46] Arvedlund, E. A. Timmons, H. (2004) "Oil prospects under Kremlin watch," *New York Times,* 29.10.04.
[47] "TNK-BP Capitalization to be increased after merger," *Pravda.* 24.6.03.
[48] *Loc.cit.*
[49] *Loc.cit.*
[50] "Why a Super Major ordered a sea change," *Op.cit.*
[51] O'Mahony,H. "BP shipping converts tankers to ice class," *Lloyd's List.* 2.4.04.
[52] *Loc.cit.*
[53] "Crescent Beaune – first of a new vintage," *Fairplay International Shipping Weekly.* 2.12.04.
[54] DETR (1998) *British Shipping Charting a New Course.* London: DETR.
[55] *Ibid.* para. 131.
[56] *Ibid.* para 133.
[57] *Ibid.* para. 137.
[58] H.M. Revenue and Customs(2000) *Inland Revenue Tonnage Tax Manual TTM01001. Origin and brief chronology of tonnage tax.* www.hmrc.gov.uk/manuals accessed 22.11.05.
[59] "Tonnage Tax Boost for UK Shipping Industry", *Accountancy Age.* 2.5.00.
[60] Osler, D. "Tory shock at tonnage tax hold up: Challenge to Government," *Lloyd's List.* 16.3.99.
[61] Royal Commission in Environmental Pollution Eighteenth Report, (2004) *Transport and the Environment.* London: HMSO.
[62] Mann, M. (2000) "Developments in British Shipping: the Tonnage Tax," A Paper presented to the International Association of Maritime Economists' Annual Conference, Naples, September, 2000.
[63] *Loc.cit*
[64] "Chamber of Shipping President implores government to implement Tonnage Tax", Institute of Marine Engineers Press Release 19.4.99.
[65] *Loc. cit.*
[66] *Loc.cit.*
[67] H.M. Treasury. (1999) *Independent Enquiry into a Tonnage Tax: A Report by Lord Alexander Weedon, QC.* London: HMSO.
[68] *Loc.cit.*
[69] P&O Press release: "P&O Welcomes Government Shipping Initiative," www.prnewswire.co.uk. 12.8.99.
[70] "MOD Charters Condemned," *The Telegraph.* June 1993, p.13.
[71] "NAO urges a more professional approach,"*Lloyd's List.* 10.6.93.

209

72 Hailey, R. (2003) "Shortsea boost in European State Aid Rules," *Lloyd's List*. 31.10.03.
73 Gerber, M. (2005) "Taxman waives the rules for British Shipping," *The Observer*, 16.1.05.
74 www.british-shipping.org. 2005.
75 Mott, D. "Dunlop hails tonnage tax as ending years of decline," *Lloyd's List*. 15.5.00.
76 O'Mahony. H. "CP Ships takes leading role at Chamber of Shipping." *Lloyd's List*. 3.7.00.
77 "Fisher boosted by Tonnage Tax, *Fairplay International Shipping Weekly*. 12.9.00.
78 "UK to adopt tonnage tax regime," *Fairplay International Shipping Weekly*. 12.8.00.
79 HM Inland Revenue (2000) *Tonnage Tax in the UK: A Brief Guide*. London: Inland Revenue Tonnage Tax Unit.
80 DETR Press Release (2000), *Prescott Launches Merchant Navy*. 3.9.00.
81 Storey, M. *Op.cit.*
82 Cobb, D. (2000) From a conversation with David Cobb, Director, James Fisher and Sons, London Office, 16.11.00.
83 "MCA admits culture failings", *Lloyd's List*. 26.1.01. p. 3.
84 "New Queen won't sink QE.2". *Southern Daily Echo*, 10.11.00.
85 Gray, T. (2002) "Fisher Shares soar on 62% profit rise", *Lloyd's List* 13.3.02. p. 22.
86 Grey, M. (2002) "Union Transport and FT Everard link dry bulk fleets". *Lloyd's List*. 13.3.02. p. 1.
87 DfT Press Release, 26.1.04. www.dft.gov.uk.
88 "Chamber Chief to push green issues," *Op.cit.*
89 Frank, J. "Revival lifts British Shipping to star status," *Lloyd's List*. 12.10.05.
90 *Loc.cit.*
91 US Department of Transportation: Maritime Administration, Data & Statistics.
92 "Storey throws his Hatsu into ring," *Lloyd's List*. 27.1.04.
93 *Loc.cit.*
94 O'Mahony, H. "Maiden call for the greenest containership," *Lloyd's List*. 8.11.05.
95 *Loc.cit.*
96 Gray, T. Porter, J. (2003) "Bright future is forecast for Star Quality Zodiac," *Lloyd's List*. 31.7.03.
97 *Loc.cit.*
98 *Loc.cit.*
99 "Left wing Crow puts the fat cat among the pigeons for World Maritime Day", *Lloyd's List*. 27.9.02.
100 Kelso, C. R. Letters to the Editor: "Third world wages won't stem shortages," *Lloyd's List*.1.8.05.
101 Communications with Captain Reg Kelso, Past-Captain Southampton Master Mariners Club. 15.2.06.
102 Kelso, C. R. Letters to the Editor: "End the insistence on cheap labour," *Lloyd's List*. 13.11.05.
103 Leggate, H. McConville, J. "Tonnage Tax is it Working?" *Maritime Policy and Management*, Vol. 32. No.2. April-June, 2005.
104 "So would you go to sea," *Fairplay International Shipping Weekly*. 2.12.04.
105 Osler, D. "British flagged ships given FOC label for first time." *Lloyd's List*. 21.4.5.
106 http://www.british-shipping.org/news/index.htm accessed 24.11.05.
107 Brownrigg, M. Orrell, B. Letters to the Editor: "hands-on approach to jobs needed from UK Government, *Lloyd's List*. 14.7.03.
108 Londner, R. "Stockholders approve Carnival-P&O merger." *South Florida: The Business Journal*. 16.4.03.
109 Klinger, P. Maersk closes in on P&O-Nedlloyd stake," *The Times*, 30.6.05. http://business.timesonline.co.uk/article/0,,9077-1674358,00.html.
110 Macalister, T. "Investors salute P&O as Dubai takes command," *The Guardian* 14.2.06.

CHAPTER 5

Green Highway Traffic Flows

The objectives of this chapter are to profile the essential characteristics of each distinct shipping sector within the Green Highway context. In order to assess the role and potential of shipping it is felt necessary to outline the principal trades and trends involved.

Figure 25: Main Trade, Tonnages Handled UK Ports, 2004

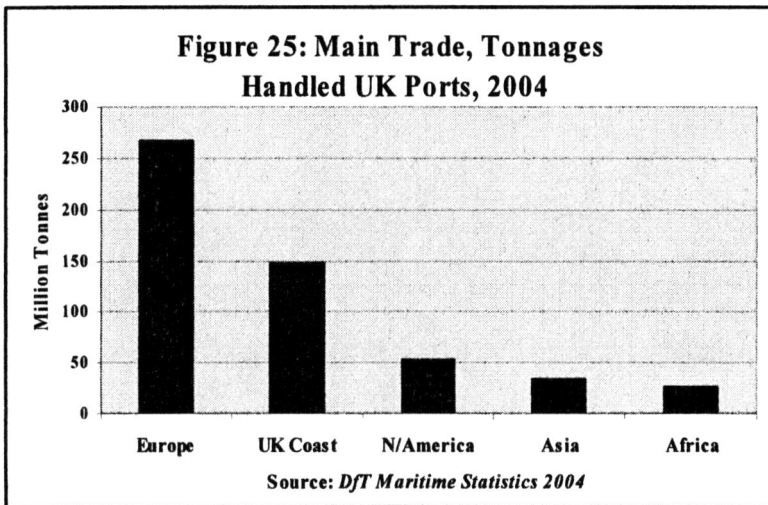

Source: *DfT Maritime Statistics 2004*

Figure 25 demonstrates the importance of UK domestic traffics to total maritime trade and UK ports in particular as coastal cargo is handled twice in the home country. European trades dominate the picture with 266mt handled in 2004, accounting for some 46% of UK maritime trade. The UK's domestic trade was measured as 146.9mt handled in the same year, 25% of the UK's total maritime trade. Starting with the statistics, the macro picture of coastal, one port and inland shipping appears stable when measured in goods lifted between 1995 and 2005. Table 21 shows no great variance in the decade from 1995, with figures of between an 2004 low of 97.2mt and 114.2mt high of 1998. Between 2002 and

2004, however, tonnages fell by 8.5% to 127.2mt. A major cause of this decline has been identified by DfT research as the reduction in one port traffics – off shore oil traffics, sea dredging and sea dumping.[1] Table 22 shows some contrast when distances are considered, with a 16.5% increase in tkm measurements. This is explained by the DfT as a result of a 56% rise in tkm moves in the one port category in the same 10 year period.[2]

5.1 Coastal Movements Sample Survey

In order to gain a clearer picture of the volume, direction and cargo content of coastal flows, a sample survey of traffics is provided in Appendix 1. February 2002 was selected and the survey was limited to UK and Irish domestic traffics and non-ferry traffics between the two islands. The data gives details of the ship by name, flag, dwt; also, the cargo and the sailing and arrival ports. The information gleaned points to first, the large volumes of crude oil passing down the UK coast from the North Sea Oil Fields and the loading terminals, Flotta (Orkney) Sullom Voe (Shetland), Hound Point (Forth) and Tees. The major arrival ports for this trade are Tees (Teesport), Humber (Hull and Immingham), Solent (Fawley), Milford Haven, Whitegate (Cork) and the Mersey (Tranmere). It can be seen that the average shipment for these trades is in the 100,000 tonne region. Around 2mt of crude oil were identified as moving domestically around the UK coast. Secondly, comes the petroleum product flows from the refineries of the Forth, Tees, Humber, Solent, Milford Haven and Merseyside as well as the Whitegate Terminal in Cork. Irish traffics loaded in Milford Haven/Pembroke form a significant portion of these trades. Shipments in these trades tend to be in the 2000-15000 tonne category.

Another important flow is that of stone from the coastal quarries of Glensanda (Western Highlands), Llandulas and Raynes (North Wales) and Dean.

Table 21: Domestic Waterborne Freight Tonnages in the UK, 1995-05. Million Tonnes Lifted

	1995	1996	1997	1998	1999	2000	2001	2002	2003	2004	2005
Internal	6.6	5.7	4.8	4.3	4.3	4.3	4.3	4.0	3.2	2.6	3.4
Coastal	67.7	70.9	71.1	77.3	73.0	63.1	58.5	59.5	58.5	59.8	65.1
One Port	36.4	33.5	31.3	32.6	33.3	39.3	35.1	43.7	39.0	34.8	32.3
Total	110.7	110.1	107.2	114.2	110.6	106.7	97.9	107.2	100.7	97.2	100.8

Source: Derived from DfT, *Waterborne Freight in the UK* London: Dft

Table 22: Domestic Waterborne Freight Tonnages in the UK, 1995-05. Billion Tonnes-Kilometres

	1995	1996	1997	1998	1999	2000	2001	2002	2003	2004	2005
Internal	0.2	0.2	0.2	0.2	0.2	0.2	0.2	0.2	0.2	0.2	0.2
Coastal	41.0	45.4	40.4	45.0	40.6	36.5	34.1	35.1	33.3	35.4	39.4
One port	10.2	7.9	5.7	10.0	16.2	29.7	23.3	30.8	26.4	22.9	20.3
Total	51.4	53.5	46.3	55.2	57.0	66.4	57.6	66.1	59.9	58.5	59.9

Source: Derived fromDfT, *Waterborne Freight in the UK* London: Dft

Quarry (Cornwall). Additionally, Belfast emerges as an important stone loading port. An interesting contrast in the size of shipments exists here with the Glensanda flows to Southern England being dominated by large bulk carriers, up to 97,000dwt, whilst shipments from Belfast, Llanddulas and Dean Quarry tend to be in the 2000-3000dwt category. Grain traffics/malted barley are predominantly from Southern England and East Anglia to the Scottish Highlands and Islands. These include shipments of malted barley for the Scotch whisky business.

Container flows along the UK coast are dominated by the deepwater ports of Southampton, Felixstowe and Thamesport. Southampton's Eurofeeder Link service is to Cork, Dublin, Belfast, Felixstowe and Zeebrugge. The vessels *Tinka* and *Nordsee* provided weekly services to Greenock (Clyde) with one of the vessels calling at Liverpool (since replaced by Manchester call) also Dublin and Belfast. These vessels are in the 3000dwt range, with capacities for between 150

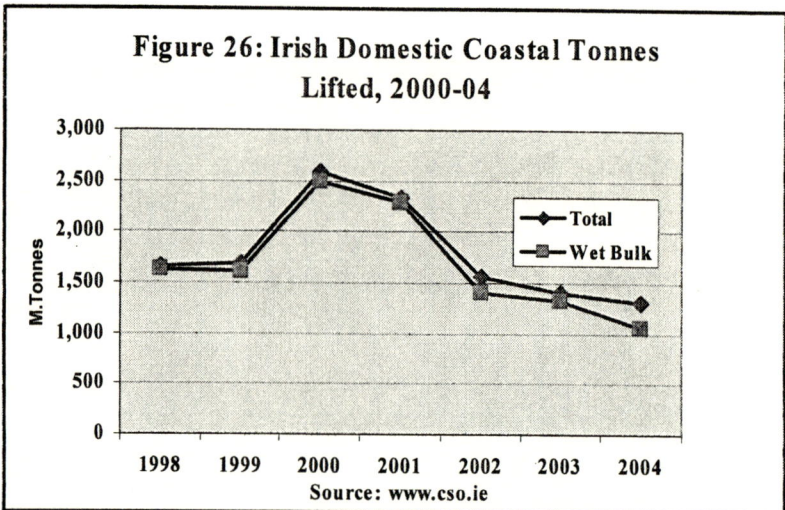

Figure 26: Irish Domestic Coastal Tonnes Lifted, 2000-04

Source: www.cso.ie

and 400teu. The pattern of Irish domestic trades is also dominated by oil products. From Figure 26, it can be seen that of the 2000 high of 2.58mt lifted on the Irish

Coast, 96% were tanker traffics. The sample survey notes the petroleum shuttle of the 1571dwt tanker *Breaksea,* between Cork's Whitegate refinery and Drogheda; also, the 4973dwt *Forth Fisher,* Whitegate-Galway. In order to identify the specific characteristics of the ships and trades of the Green Highway, it is next proposed to profile the distinct shipping sectors:

- Tanker Shipping;
- Dry Bulk Shipping;
- Liner Shipping;
- Feeder Shipping;
- RoRo Shipping;
- One Port Shipping;
- Inland Shipping

5.2 The Tanker Sector

It has been stated many times that the tanker market approximates closely to the economist's model of perfect competition.[3] This suggests lots of buyers and sellers, no barriers to market entry, the shipping firm accepts the market price, the product (ship) is homogeneous and market information is freely available to all participants in the market. The evidence provided in this and the following chapter (chapter 6), however, points to the market becoming increasingly exclusive, with an emphasis on operational quality and environmental standards. In chapter 2, attention was given to the importance of this sector as it generates by far the largest amount of freight movement on the UK coast – almost 80% of tonnes moved in 2004. Primarily, this is a result of the intense oil flow activity, resulting from the North Sea oilfields.

The discovery of oil in UK waters posed the logistical problem of linkages between the oil fields of Shetland, the North Sea, as well as Dorset, to the refineries of the British Isles – Grangemouth, Teesport, Hull and Immingham, Thameshaven and Canvey Island, Southampton, Milford Haven, Ellesmere Port and Cork's Whitegate and installation. Similarly, shuttle tankers operate to refineries in Gothenburg, Wilhelmshaven and Rotterdam. Figure 27 shows the extent of tanker movements, primarily crude oil shipments; it can be seen that in in the early Millennium years traffics fluctuated between 54 and 66mt. Figure 28 illustrates the location of the principal loading and discharge points. As an example, the sample survey detected the Bahamas flag tanker *Hildegaard*, 99,122dwt, loaded crude oil in the Tees for the Merseyside Tranmere Terminal. This 840nm coastal leg would have added around 773m tonne-nautical miles to the Green Highway figures.

Figure 27: UK Domestic Tanker Liftings, 2000-05.

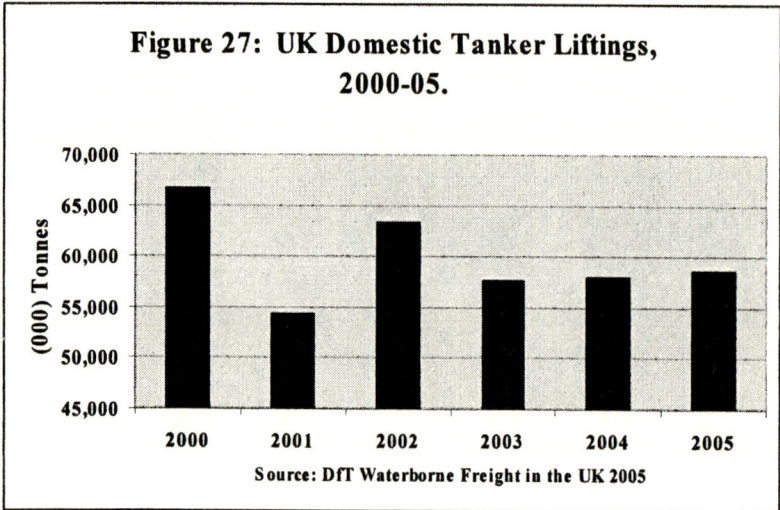

Source: DfT Waterborne Freight in the UK 2005

Shuttle tanker developments reflected a radical re-structuring of oil movements in and out of the UK. Up until the oil shocks of the mid 1970s, when prices trebled within a three year period, the major oil flow into the UK was from the terminals of the Persian Gulf. This trade built up rapidly in the post 1950 period and was drastically affected by the two closures of the Suez Canal in 1956 and 1967-72. The long 11,500nm haul to the UK via the Cape of Good Hope proved to be the

Figure 28: Principal Tanker Ports UK and Ireland

accelerator of oil tanker sizes, up to the > 400,000dwt Ultra Large Crude Carrier (ULCC) level. The emergence of UK oil, however, brought about further changes. Analysis of the changing trends was made by the British Port's Federation/Department of Transport in 1991:

> Until the mid 1970s, the United Kingdom was traditionally a net importer of low value raw materials, and an exporter of smaller tonnages of manufactured goods. With the exploitation of oil from the North Sea, exports increased steadily to reach the same weight as imports between 1981 and 1983.[4]

The scale of North Sea oil movements demanded a radical response from the tanker industry. The requirement was for tankers large enough to move the massive oil volumes but also with the capability to efficiently manoeuvre in the confined and congested waters of the loading zones, including off-shore pipelines. Additionally, the environmental sensitivity of oil movements on the coastlines of the British Isles led to an emphasis on quality tonnage. This has led to concentration on double hulled tankers, which limits the risk of oil egress following groundings and collision. Also, many of the tankers are equipped with dynamic positioning technology. This enables the large tankers to manoeuvre alongside the North Sea loading installations in inclement weather. Typifying the pattern of the shuttle trade is the track of the 94,998dwt, Liberian flag, *Braveheart*. This tanker loaded in the Tees for Cork's Whitegate Terminal. This was followed by a ballast (empty) passage to Scapa Flow to load crude oil for Rotterdam. The North Sea trades of the oil majors have seen a move away from owned to chartered tonnage. In the Norwegian one-port trades, the exclusive emphasis is on the well regulated tonnage of the Norwegian flag. This flag preference contrasts sharply with the tonnage operating in the UK sector which includes the participation of open registries – Liberia, Panama, Cyprus.

A noticeable trend in the ownership and organisation of the crude oil trades post-1975 is the downsizing and divestment of the oil major fleets. From the oil market slump of the mid 1970s the oil majors shed large amounts of tonnage. This has occurred in the fleets of BP, Shell, Esso, Mobil and Chevron. Also, a certain amount of decentralisation has occurred. In chapter 4 it was shown how the creation of BP Shipping led to the rationalised oil major's fleet operating at arm's length from the parent company. This was accompanied by "flagging out" the tanker fleet (from the UK flag) to the Bahamas, Bermuda and Hong Kong flags and the replacement of British crews by lower wage East European and Third World nationals. At the time of writing, the fleet expansion strategy at BP was beginning to radically reverse the "out-sourcing" trend.

5.2.1 The Clean Petroleum Products Sector

Whereas the movement of North Sea crude oil is dependent upon large oil tanker supply (80-120,000dwt), the domestic trades in oil products are open to competition from road, rail and pipelines. The oil refineries are large generators of movements of products – diesel, petroleum, lubricants, fuel oil, bitumen. In addition, the petro-chemical downstream activities lead to the production of such volatile derivatives – liquid petroleum gas (LPG) and liquid natural gas (LNG).[5] Traditionally, coastal regions are served by small tankers in the 500-15,000dwt range.

Typically, the movement of petroleum from Southampton's Esso Fawley refinery to Plymouth, a coastal leg of 80nm (149km) is by weekly 2000 tonne tankers. This in itself keeps at least 80 round trip road tanker journeys off the rural roads of Hampshire, Dorset and Devon per week. The supply of refined products follows the transformation of the long hydrocarbon molecular chains of crude oil by various methods of separating, altering and blending into short hydrocarbon molecular chains of refined. The lightest liquid products with the

220

lowest boiling points are drawn off near the top of the catalyst tower. Shorter hydrocarbon chains are high value white products such as gasoline, jet fuel and gas-oil or middle distillate, sold as diesel fuel and heating oil.

These products form the volatile, higher value products of the coastal trades. A typical coastal/shortsea white products trading diagram was provided in Appendix 1 by the Swedish owned and flagged tanker, *Prospero*:

- Fawley-Pembroke;
- Pembroke-Dublin;
- Dublin-Finnart(Clyde);
- Finnart-Plymouth;
- Plymouth-Pembroke;
- Pembroke-Belfast.

In the black product's trades – lube oil, heavy fuel oil, asphalt, petroleum coke – a similar trading pattern is evident. The 3122dwt British flagged tanker *Crescent Highway*, was detected (Appendix 1) on a regular bitumen shuttle to Belfast and Dublin ex-Fawley. A number of forces, however, have diminished the shipping option in recent years. The rationalisation of such regional distribution centres such as Esso's Manchester and Shell's Caernarfon depots, have meant lost shipping business. Such closures have led to petroleum being transported increasingly longer distances by road from the refinery, direct to the petrol pump. Intensifying the closure rate of regional oil distribution centres has been the impact of the Vapour Recovery Act[6], which called for heavy investment in the terminals. The aim was essentially led by environmental concerns over the loss of petroleum fumes venting into atmosphere. The net result, however, was the closure of the installations as the oil companies sought to avoid this additional cost. A similar impact was registered by changes in the way excise duty was collected. The imposition of excise duty at the point of production has militated against the storage of the volumes necessary for delivery by water.[7] Both areas of policy change led to reduced demand for shipping and increased road tanker movements. To some extent these developments have been facilitated by improvements in road haulage performance, following technical innovation in traction and road improvement schemes. The resulting decrease in timings and tkm costs has led to increasing emphasis on the road option. The response of the leading owners in the coastal tanker sector has been to improve efficiency. The 1997 addition to the Everard tanker fleet of *Asperity* and *Audacity* brought not only increased size but also greatly reduced turnround times – discharge times being completed in around three hours. This is a great advantage when trading with ports with restrictive tidal windows, enabling same tide discharge. *Lloyd's List's* 1997 report on the new sister tankers found that:

> The design and the outfit of the *Asperity* type reflect the increased expectations of shippers and charterers about cargo handling efficiency and flexibility, turnround and schedule keeping. The two new ships will be predominantly employed on various contracts of affreightment. Given the fundamental importance of expeditious turnround in the shortsea tanker trades, where a ship has to be off the berth within a few hours of arrival, every aspect of design relating to cargo loading and discharge has commanded the closest attention.[8]

Such vessels enhance shipping efficiency by allowing as many as three shortcoastal trips per week, providing the oil majors and their distributors with a flexible and speedy service. As an adjunct to agricultural development in Ireland, the Irish fertiliser trade had provided significant loadings for the shortsea and coastal sectors. Irish fertiliser Industries (IFI) has concentrated on three plants, Arklow, Belfast and Cork, producing around 1.5mt of fertiliser, as well as 1.2mt of ammonia per annum.[9] The Cork-Belfast passage (Appendix 1)of the LPG 4298dwt tanker, *Hamilton*, proved to be one of the few movements on the Irish coast detected in the 2002 sample. The fertilizer business in Ireland had supported the long term charter of LPG tankers for shuttles between Irish Fertilizer plants in Cork and Belfast with ammonia shipments.[10] Unfortunately this trade ceased following the financial collapse of the joint Irish state-ICI. Irish Fertilizer Industries (IFI) in Autumn 2002.[11]

Inland product movements have survived on the Humber and the Manchester Ship Canal. However, BP's sizeable Thames fleet was declared redundant by the closure of the up-river installation at Fulham. Similarly, the closure of the inland petroleum depot in Nottingham ended tank-barge traffics on the Trent. As in the crude oil trades, the organisational trend in the clean petroleum products (CPP) market in recent years has been the downsizing of the own account fleets of the oil majors. Shell, Esso and BP-Amoco have all scaled down their CPP fleets. Replacing the own account fleets are those of selected third party carriers such F.T. Everard and Sons, Fisher Tankships and Crescent Tankships, as well as Gothenburg's Brostrum Tankers. The distribution needs of the oil majors are shaped by the need to retain a just-in-time frequency which minimises inventory costs but guarantees supply reliability and integrity in a highly competitive European marketplace. The principal contract arrangement is that of contract of affreightment (COA). This means that the carrier is contracted to carry a specified amount of CPP's within an allotted time, usually two years. For example, eight of Crescent Tankships' fleet were engaged in primarily COA work in the North Sea, English Channel and Irish trades in 2004. Whilst this arrangement provides for security of supply – as opposed to the risks of the spot market – it does exert the pressures of combining a range of products and routes on the operator. In the winter time the problems of the operators are intensified by the delays brought about by stormy weather as well as fog. This places a major emphasis upon operational efficiency and flexibility.

5.3 The Dry Bulk Sector

The staple bulk trades – coal, grain, aggregates, cement, scrap – have traditionally provided heavy demand in the coastal and shortsea trades. Historically, many of the UK's major small ship operators have featured significantly in these trades. These include the Kentish operators – Everard of Greenhithe, Lapthorn's of Hoo St. Werburgh, Crescent of Rainham (moved to Southampton in 2000). Other leading operators are Newcastle's Stephenson Clarke group, Bromley based Union Transport and the Isle of Wight's Carisbrooke Shipping. On the West Coast, Fisher of Barrow combined dry cargo vessels within a diversified maritime asset portfolio. Ireland's Arklow Shipping has demonstrated a prominent position in intra-European grain and steel movements.

The de-industrialisation period post 1980s obviously affected the demand for bulk shipping. Furthermore, the highly competitive nature of dry bulk trades has resulted in three of the above firms leaving the sector – Crescent, Everard, Fisher. The British retreat from the dry-bulk sector is partly explained by the emergence of low cost flags and crews in the traditional trades. As an example, the clay trades of North Devon would have been a staple business for such UK

Figure 29: UK Coastwise Dry Bulk Tonnages, 2000-04.

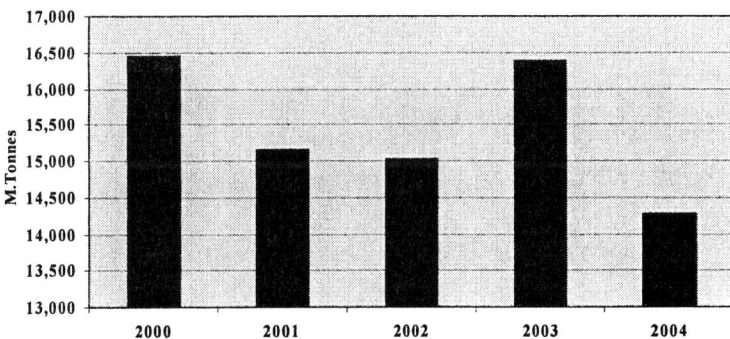

Source: DfT Maritime Statistics

224

firms as Everard's up until the 1970s. This withdrawal from dry-bulk trading strategy will be discussed further in chapter 6. Appendix 3 shows that in a survey of 7 vessels calling to load brick clay in the Port of Bideford in 2005, not one flew the British flag or employed British crews.

The key to economic survival in the low value bulk trades is to minimise empty voyage legs as much as possible. Arklow Shipping's regular grain trade between Western France and Manchester is complemented by return loads of scrap to Pasajes in Northern Spain. This means that the vessels transit the Manchester Ship Canal loaded in both directions and empty running is restricted; in the case of the return from the discharge Port of Pasajaes to the loading port of Bayonne this amounts to less than 30nm (56km) about 1.7% of the 1800nm (3334km) return trip distance. Table 23 represents three months in the hard working life of Carisbrooke Shipping's 3200dwt, Nordstrand.

Table 23: Three Months in the Life of the *Nordstrand*		
Loaded	**Discharged**	**Cargo**
Terneuzen	Southampton	Fertilisers
Southampton	Belfast	Wheat
Barrow	Plymouth	Project Cargo
Mistley	Cork/Dublin	Wheat
Teesport	L'Orient	Potash
La Palice	South Spain	Wheat
Huelva	Drogheda/Dublin	Iron Ore
Shoreham	Drogheda	Barley & Wheat
Mistley	Cork/Dublin	Wheat
Terneuzen	Silloth	Fertiliser
Llandulas	Shoreham	Aggregates
Source: Carisbrooke Shipping		

Other patterns detectable, following freights to Ireland or West Coast Britain, are return cargoes of china clay and stone from the West of England. Following Polish coal traffics to Ireland, stone from Belfast or china clay from Teignmouth provides a regular back-cargo for Union Transport ships returning to the Thames or the Rhine. Also, steel flows to Shoreham and Poole are often counter-balanced by china clay shipments ex-Teignmouth and Fowey. In winning new trades from road haulage it is evident that the sector needs to think outside of the "box". Bulk shipping specialist David Tinsley has suggested that the way forward:

> will be to build its capabilities to offer specialised and high quality services to industry and shippers. The logistics of transportation, storage and distribution are assuming increasing importance for the buyers of raw materials and the producers and suppliers of goods.[12]

Typically sizes are in the 1500-5000dwt range, although new buildings are likely to be nearer to the latter tonnage. This allows for maximum flexibility trading in smaller European ports. Such flexibility is enhanced by the low air draft profiles of many of these vessels, facilitating trade considerable distances inland, without being confined by low height road and rail bridges. Services on such rivers as the Rhine, Maas and Seine are dependent upon these low profile ships. These vessels are referred to generically as sea-river traders.

David Tinsley's reference to sea-river ships as modern "flat irons" serves as a reminder of the up-river tradition precursed by the collier tradition; also in that these "flat irons" represent the shortsea sector's response to the desire to provide sea-river door-to-door services.[13] An interesting example of innovative thinking in the dry bulk trades was provided by leading UK operator, R.D. Lapthorn's 2001 launch of a "takeaway" service for builders.[14] The all-inclusive package of building site spoil disposal offered a real alternative to the large volumes of lorry traffic generated by the construction industry. Lapthorn M.D., David Lapthorn stated that the company were aware of the desperate need for an

226

alternative to the lorry with thousands of tonnes of material leaving the Thames area every day. Possessing self-loading/discharging grab facilities vessels such as Lapthorn's 1412dwt *Hoo Dolphin*, can offer direct bulk services in a range of up-river restricted access locations.

In 1997 it was estimated that there were some 536 vessels in theWest European shortsea/inland shipping sector. The average size of these vessels was 2000dwt. Figure 30 shows the percentage breakdown by flag. The high market share of German flag vessels can be attributed to the effectiveness of the collaboration between the investment and shipping. In German shipping communities - Hamburg, Bremen, Haren-Ems, Duisburg – access to finance via the KG system has proved conducive to growth.

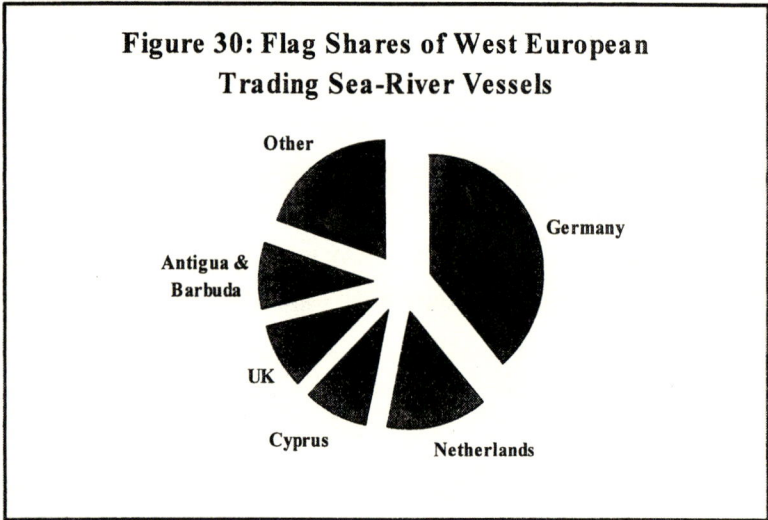

Figure 30: Flag Shares of West European Trading Sea-River Vessels

Source: Stoop, JA. Hengst, S. Dirkse, C. "Integrating Safety into the Shortsea Shipping System", in Peeters, D & Wergeland, T.(1997) *European Shortsea Shipping: Proceedings from the Third European Research Roundtable Conference on Shortsea Shipping.* Bergen, 20-21 June 1996. Delft: Delft University Press. p.389.

In addition to the sea-river size of vessels, it will become evident (chapter 6) that some of the market leaders - Arklow Shipping, Carisbrooke Shipping, Stephenson-Clarke Bulk Shipping - are opting for larger vessels in the 12,000-15,000dwt range. Although the dry-bulk sector has faced a reduction in demand for such staple traffics as coastal coal and cement, two growing export traffics—grain and coastal stone – have emerged, calling for changes in technology and the scale of operation. A mixture of European agricultural integration and the productive success of UK and Irish farmers, has led to a sizeable shortsea grain trade in both imports and exports. The success of Southampton diversification into grain exporting demonstrates the vibrancy of the grain market. Two deepwater terminals were commissioned in 1982-83 and by 1990 1mt per annum were being loaded, mostly in handy sized and panamax sized vessels.[15]

Although the export business has been concentrated on five major ports – London, Immingham, Ipswich, Hull and Southampton – smaller UK and Irish ports still generate large amounts of grain for smaller vessels. Ports such as Wisbech in Cambridgeshire, King's Lynn in Norfolk, Berwick in Northumberland and Arklow in County Wicklow provide opportunities for smaller vessels. The Boston-Inverkeithing passage of the 1394dwt British flag *Hoo Pride,* (Appendix 1) examples the flow of malt barley for the Scottish whisky industry. The Manchester Ship Canal provides opportunities for sea-canal grain flows. In 2000-1, 400,000 tonnes of French maize were shipped up the waterway to Manchester.[16]

Larger sized vessels in the stone trades do provide exceptions to dry-bulk size averages of 2-5000dwt. The stone traffics from Glensanda Quarry to Sheerness and Southampton feature large specialist bulkers. The relatively long distances and large volumes from the Scottish West Coast to Southern England require vessels in the 20,000-96,000dwt range. The Bahamas flagged, 96,772dwt, *Yeoman Bridge* was observed (Appendix 1) as making two trips between

Glensanda and the Foster Yeoman's hub port, Isle of Grain. The Glensanda
terminal provides access to the UK's premier granite reserve. The geographic
constraints of the region preclude rail and road links to the terminal. This makes
the operation totally dependent upon water transport for the movement of around
5mt of stone per annum. An interesting example of this trade, demonstrating the
open market of UK coastal trade, was the stone movements to the Channel Tunnel
construction site in the early 1990s. The charter went to the Chinese owned and
crewed 27,500dwt bulk carrier, *Nan Ji Zhou*.[17]

Changes in the stone trades in recent years reflect economic, political and
environmental concerns. Economic growth, particularly in South East England in
the post-1945 period, created heavy demand for quarry stone, sand and aggregates
for the building trades. Initially supplies were extracted from quarries close to
urban centres. However, environmental concerns, reflected in increasingly
rigorous land planning restrictions, have forced the quarry companies to search
further afield to source their supplies.[18] British Governments have sought to
reconcile the national importance of the construction industry with the
environmental interest. The solution of the 1990s was the "superquarry" option.
The development of the superquarries in the Scottish Highlands and Islands was
seen as an acceptable compromise which simultaneously reduced pressure on land
use in Southern England and promoted economic activity in peripheral, de-
populated, rural locations. Geographer Richard Cowell found that the case for
coastal superquarries such as Glensanda, is based upon the evidence,

> That concentrating extraction into a few high-output
> sites results in lower environmental costs per tonne
> than a larger number of smaller sand and gravel pits,
> that sea transport is environmentally preferable to
> movement by road and that fewer people would be
> directly affected by quarrying operations in remote
> rural locations.[19]

The challenge facing shipping here is to provide efficient, low cost tkm transportation of the raw materials. The positive response of the industry has been to secure economies of scale via the use of large bulk carrier vessels and to achieve flexibility by the provision of self-discharge equipment on the larger vessels. This not only enables the vessels to off-load cargo in remote sites, where fixed cargo handling equipment is not available, but also to limit stevedoring costs in established ports. In the inland trades, the Manchester Ship Canal and River Trent support dry bulk movements. Manchester's Cerestar corn mill is served

Table 24 Key UK & Irish Shortsea & Coastal Dry Bulk Cargo Flows		
Freight	From	To
Stone	Glensanda	Medway/ Southampton
Stone	Belfast	Dagenham
Grain	Brittany Ports	Manchester
Grain	King's Lynn/Humber Ports	Perth,
Malt Barley	King's Lynn/Boston	Scottish Highlands and Islands
Steel	Liege/Ijmuden/Bremen	Poole, Boston, Grimsby,Goole
Scrap	Manchester/Liverpool	Pasajes
Coal	Zeebrugge	Medway/Thames
Coal	Clyde	Warren Point
Coal	Clyde	Ellesmere Port
Cement	Northfleet	Aberdeen
China Clay	Cornish Ports	Thames
Recycled Glass	Southampton	Ellesmere Port
Animal Feeds	Rotterdam	Dublin
Source: deduced from *Lloyd's List* Shipping Movements		

directly by Arklow Shipping and other chartered vessels for the importation of continental grains, usually from Spanish and Brittany ports such as Brest, St. Nazaire and Nantes. Also the Rank-Hovis mill receives, ex-barge, North American grain which is transhipped from panamax bulk carrier in the Port of Liverpool. Barge traffic on the Trent and Ouse is supported by sand and aggregate flows. Table 24 identifies selected key bulk flows around the UK and Irish coasts. Trades that have suffered particularly acute competition with road haulage are coastal movements and river movements of cement, stone and grain. Margins are low in these trades and there is a large supply of cost oriented bulk haulage operators in the market. In such competitive situations the impact of the Freight Facilities Grant becomes pivotal in determining shipping's success. The coastal movement of stone from Cornwall's Lizard Point to Southampton and the up-river movement of cement on the Thames are two examples where the Grant proved conducive to shipping when otherwise the trade would have been won by road hauliers. The steel shuttle service between Ijmuden/Liege and the Dorset port of Poole is an example of the shipping option being maximised in the steel flow to the West Midlands. The provision by the Poole Harbour Commissioners of a weather proof holding shed is of paramount importance to Poole's competitive advantage, given the vulnerability of steel coils to damp conditions.

5.4 The Shortsea Liner Trade

On the regular trades, liner shipping operates intensive shuttle patterns. Discernibly these operations are represented by the RoRo ferries that operate across the English Channel, North Sea and Irish Sea. The development of such services has normally minimised the sea leg crossing distance and, as a consequence, maximised the road haulage leg. Within Europe, three major areas of RoRo operations are located in, the Baltic Sea, North Sea/English Channel/Irish Sea and the Mediterranean and Black Sea. Table 25 illustrates the dominance of RoRo traffics in UK-Europe liner trades.

Table 25: UK Coastal & European Liner Traffics, 2004 (000 Tonnes)			
UK Container	UK RoRo	UK-Euro Container	UK-Euro RoRo
1,106	11,167	20,255	68,933
Source: DfT *Maritime Statistics 2004*			

Shortsea expert, Zachial, has found that in most cases, "…the RoRo transport of lorries, trailers (powered vehicles, unaccompanied trailers) is more or less a short part of a combined land/sea transport…"[20] Figure 31 illustrates the 11-12mt of UK unitised traffics in the early Millennium. It is estimated that around 90% of this traffic is transiting the UK mainland-Northern Ireland corridors. This included traffic moving south into the Republic of Ireland. For example, export traffics moving from the Republic several hundred km north in order to access the short crossing (35nm/57kms) ferry routes out of Larne to Stranraer and Cairnryan. Packer's "*Roads to Water*" report found that logistical concerns were important in determining the routing of freight flows:

> Routing is determined as much by considerations of relative service quality and transit time as by relative transport costs. As a result, much unit load and higher value semi-bulk traffic is carried over longer land routes rather than taking a sea route to port closer to the point of origin or destination.[21]

From the context of the Green Highway the objective here is to reverse this trend, maximising the sea leg. The 2000 inception of RoRo services heading south out of the Scottish port, Rosyth, obviates the long haulage leg to the Dover Straits and leads to a considerable reduction in tkm road traffic. Similar opportunities exist in the Iberian trades. It has been estimated that 67% of Spanish and 38% of Portuguese unit load traffics from the UK are routed via the shorter French crossings.[22]

232

Figure 31: UK Domestic Unitised Liftings, 2000-05.

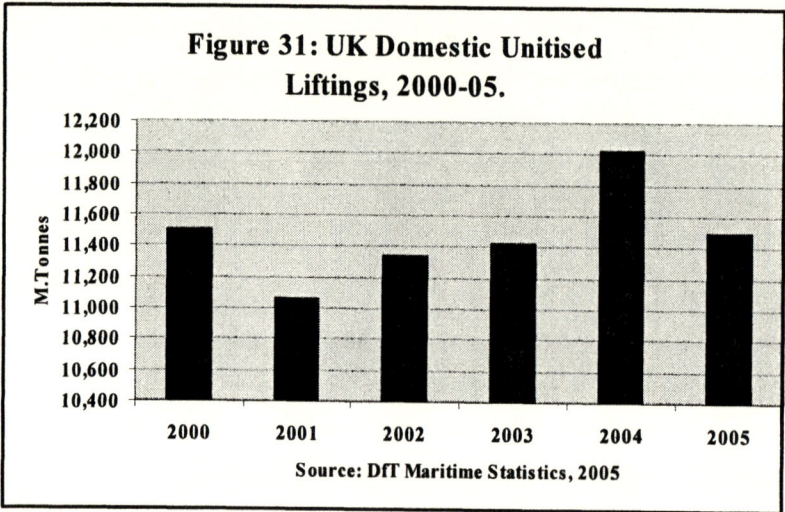

Source: DfT Maritime Statistics, 2005

In addition to RoRo services, LoLo container liner services operate across the Irish Sea, Liverpool-Dublin/Belfast, Cardiff-Dublin. On the North Sea such services operate between Tilbury and Rotterdam, Harwich/Felixstowe and Zeebrugge and the sea-river route between Goole (Humber) and Duisburg (Rhine). The service operated by the RMS Line provides for at least three sailings per week between these inland ports. Setting up new trades in the coastal/shortsea liner sector is particularly vulnerable to predatory road haulage market behaviour. Building up volumes in the new trades can often be a slow process.

5.5 The Coastal/Shortsea RoRo Sector

European freight services by RoRo liners offer haulage users the opportunity of maximising the sea leg and minimising the road leg. For example, the Immingham-Cuxhaven service links with Deutsche Bundesbahn freight trains in the German port. This obviates the long 500 kilometre plus journey from

Northern England to the Dover Straits and a similar road leg from Calais to Northern Germany. Table 26 examples major freight RoRo services to the British Isles.

Table 26: Selected European RoRo Freight Services to Britain			
Southampton/Ipswich	Setubal/Vigo	Suardiaz Line	Weekly
Portbury/Cork/ Southampton	8 Mediterranean Ports	Grimaldi Line	Weekly
Immingham	Cuxhaven	DSR Line	Daily
Killingholme	Hook of Holland	Stena	Daily
Tilbury	Zeebrugge	Cobelfret	Daily
Tees	Zeebrugge	P&O NSF	Daily
Tilbury	Zeebrugge	Stora	Weekly
Source: *Lloyd's Loading List*			

Noticeable in the sample survey (Appendix 1) are the small automobile carriers operating in Scandinavian, North European and Iberian waters. The Norwegian International Registry flagged (NIS), 6670dwt RoRo *Autosun*, was detected shuttling between Emden, Sheerness, Southampton and Dublin. Continental bound, Southampton built Ford Transit vans have been noted (by the Author) using this service in order to tranship to via Sheerness. As a consequence, some 204 kilometres by road are obviated. RoRo services that maximise the sea leg normally have a core cargo on which to build their regular liner services. The examples given of Grimaldi Line and Suardiaz Line have automobiles underpinning their routes. Grimaldi's movement of Fiat cars, buses and trucks from Savona to Portbury and Cork (See Table 27) was balanced by exports of Jaguars, Rover (now defunct) and BMW Mini cars, as well as JCB mechanical shovels from Southampton to Mediterranean ports. Similarly, Suardiaz based

234

their service on Iberian produced cars moving North to Southampton with North European cars on the return South-bound leg.

Table 27: Grimaldi Lines Euro-Med Service Linkages Winter-Early Spring 2006

Port	Grande Europa	Gran Bretagna	Grande Med	Grande Scand	Grande Ellande	Grande Europa
Portbury	20.1.06	27.1.06	3.2.06	10.2.06	17.2.06	24.2.06
Cork	21.1.06	28.1.06	4.2.06	11.2.06	18.2.06	25.2.06
Esbjerg	24.1.06	31.1.06	7.2.06	14.2.06	21.2.06	28.2.06
Wallhamn	25.1.06	1.2.06	8.2.06	15.2.06	22.2.06	1.3.06
Antwerp	27.1.06	3.2.06	10.2.06	17.2.06	24.2.06	3.3.06
Southampton	28.1.06	4.2.06	11.2.06	18.2.06	25.2.06	4.3.06
Salerno	4.2.06	11.2.06	18.2.06	25.2.06	4.3.06	11.3.06
Piraeus	6.2.06	13.2.06	20.2.06	27.2.06	6.3.06	13.3.06
Savona	6.2.06	13.2.06	20.2.06	27.2.06	6.3.06	13.2.06
Valencia	6.2.06	13.2.06	13.2.06	20.2.06	27.2.06	6.3.06
Izmir	7.2.06	14.2.06	21.2.06	28.2.06	7.3.06	14.3.06
Palermo	7.2.06	14.2.06.	21.2.06	28.2.06	7.3.06	14.3.06
Ashdod	9.2.06	16.2.06	23.2.06	2.3.06	9.3.06	16.3.06
Livorno	9.2.06	16.2.06	23.2.06	2.3.06	21.8.00	28.8.00
Tunis	9.2.06	16.2.06	23.2.06	3.3.06	10.3.06	17.3.06
Valetta	10.2.06	17.2.06	24.2.06	4.3.06	11.306	18.3.06
Limasssol	10.2.06	17.2.06	24.2.06	4.3.06	11.306	18.3.06
Alexandria	11.2.06	18.2.06	25.2.06	5.3.06	12.306	19.3.06
Ravenna	13.2.06	20.2.06	27.2.06	6.3.06	13.306	20.3.06
Haifa	13.2.06	20.2.06	27.2.06	6.3.06	13.306	20.3.06
Koper	14.2.06	21..2.06	28.2.06	7.3.06	14.306	21.3.06
Monfalcone	15.2.06	22.2.06	1.3.06	8.3.06	15.306	22.3.06
Tartous	21.2.06	28.2.06	7.3.06	14.3.06	21.306	28.3.06

Source: Grimaldi Line Euromed Schedule 2006

STORA's Scandinavian-Zeebrugge-Tilbury RoRo link has targeted forest products as its base cargo. The advantages of such core freights are that they enable the operator to plan with confidence and to utilise extra, low marginal cost, cargo capacity. As a consequence, such diverse trailer cargoes as chemicals, engineering plant, cocoa beans, wines and citrus fruits are moved, as are containers and wide gauge project cargoes. Antwerp shipping editor, Bernard Van Den Bossche, has claimed that the only major European success in implementing sustainable transport has been the development of Grimaldi's Euro-Med service as an alternative to long distance Pan-European trunk haulage.

An example of a successful employment of coastal RoRo services is provided by the Sunflower ships trading on the Japanese coastline. Modal shift of freight from roads to water has been a conscious policy of Japanese Governments in recent years. Shipowners and shipbuilders have received financial support from the Japanese Government for vessels capable of offering trucking firms fast coastal transits. New ferries entering into service on the Japanese Coast around the turn of the Millennium offered a time incentive for truck operators to use.[23] Two 30 knot vessels entering into service on the intensive Hokkaido 1037 km route between Tokyo and Tomakomai, *Sunflower Tomakomai* and *Hokkaido Maru,* allowed for a reduction in transits from 30 to 20 hours. The increased speeds ensured that sea transport could be utilised for fast moving perishable goods between the two trade centres. Japanese success with fast RoRo services offers an obvious model for the Green Highway

5.6 The Container Feeder Sector

Feeder shipping can be seen as a function of global container flows. The movement of containers to and from the deepsea container ports Felixstowe, Southampton, Tilbury, Thamesport and Liverpool, offers potential for smaller feeder ship linkages. Similarly, the main continental liner hubs, Antwerp,

Rotterdam and Hamburg generate container traffics for UK and Irish regions. In 2006 Southampton's shortsea feeder linkages integrated the intensive Far East deepsea services to Cork, Dublin, Belfast, Lexioes, Lisbon, Le Havre, Rotterdam and Hamburg. Coastal services extended to Manchester, Greenock and Hull. The busy ships in these trades tend to be in the 200-500 teu range which enables them to penetrate many of the smaller ports. Operating to intensive shuttle diagrams, these vessels, which normally operate under time charter arrangements and fly flags of convenience, manage up to three trips per week in the congested waters of the main line ports.

The trend in the deepsea trades for larger vessels, together with mergers and alliances of the shipping companies, is proving conducive to the feeder option in preference to road haulage. As the shift towards hub and spoke operations intensifies, the opportunities for feeder services will increase. Shipping Consultants, H.P. Drewry, detected an 800% increase in global feeder movements between 1980 and 1996.[24] Both trends lead to a concentration of container movements and allow for significant flows to the regional ports.

It is estimated that a flow of 80-150teu is needed to make feeder shipping viable. The evidence from the deepsea trades is that large post-panamax carriers with a capacity >6000teu generate in excess of a 3000teu box exchange at main line ports. This provides coastal and shortsea feeder opportunities such as Southampton to Cork, Felixstowe to Newcastle. The success of the Southampton-Manchester-Greenock feeder service ((Featured as a case study in chapter 7. See below pp.) demonstrates what is feasible given the co-ordination of the feeder ship, the port and road haulage collection/distribution of boxes with the deepsea "mother" ship service. The Southampton arrival of the twice weekly service integrates with major Far East and North Atlantic services. In particular this serves the interests of the Scottish whisky exporters. The movements of the

4646dwt Antigua and Barbuda flag, *Hajo*, are also noted in the sample survey (Appendix 1): Grangemouth-Newcastle-Rotterdam-Felixstowe-Thamesport.

On routes where an imbalance between export and import volumes prevails, the re-positioning of empty containers is particularly conducive to the shipping option. Unlike the situation with loaded containers, the time dimension is not so acute with empties. The lower tkm costs of shipping become more important than the time savings provided by land transport modes. The concentration of three major container ports in the Thames Estuary – South East regions has created a localised empty container flow. This has proved conducive to a barge shuttle between Thamesport, Tilbury and Felixstowe. The development of a fourth container port in the region at Shellhaven can only help enhance such shipping opportunities.

Imminent container port expansion developments – Antwerp, Southampton, Felixstowe/Harwich – feature feeder linkages not just as logistical extensions but also as ameliorating road haulage congestion and pollution. Planned container hubs – Scapa Flow (Orkney), Jade Port (Wilhelmshaven), introduce the concept of large scale feeder operations. Research work at Napier University has led to the conclusion that future environmental restraints on existing port developments combined with the economies of scale of a new generation of larger container ships, between 8000-15,000teu, will prove conducive to the Hubport idea.[25] Developments in deepsea container vessel size have significant impact upon feeder shipping. Technical progress has led to the design concept of the Suez Max and Malacca Max vessel size. Up until the late 1980s, vessel size had remained pegged at the Panamax size of around 4000teu. However, ship sizes in the US West Coast-Far East Transpacific and Northern Europe-Far East trades began to increase, post 1990. Having no need to limit sizes to the Panama Canal specification the economies of scale proved alluring. By the early years of the new Millennium the market leaders, were operating in the >7000teu range. By September 2006, *Lloyd's List* reported on the arrival of the >11,000teu, *Emma Maersk* on the Far East-North Europe trade lane and also that French liner company, CMA-CGM, were placing a shipbuilding order in Korea for 8 vessels in the 11,00teu range.[26] Clearly the size-race in container shipping is still active, thus enhancing the prospects for feeder shipping.

5.7 Inland Shipping

The definition of inland shipping here is defined by the UK Department for Transport (DfT):

- where a land based alternative can be made;
- where sheltered "smooth water" prevails, with wave heights normally less than two metres;
- where (according to tides) the inland water width is in the 3-5km range.[27]

Major inland locations include, the Severn, Shannon, Thames, Humber/Trent and Mersey/Manchester Ship Canal. Predominantly, UK inland traffics are bulks – coal, aggregates, oil products, grain. In Britain, this activity is restricted to principal river and canal networks – Humber/Trent/Ouse, Aire & Calder Navigation, Severn, Mersey/Weaver/ Manchester Ship Canal, Thames/Medway. Normally, the size of vessels trading under these conditions is determined by lock dimensions, low bridges and shallow water obstacles. However, it is noticeable that most of the surviving operators own vessels in excess of 250 tonnes lifting capability.

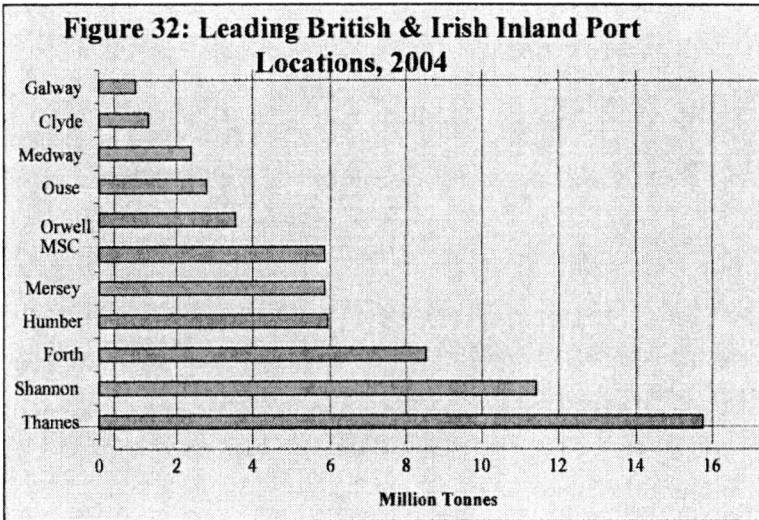

Figure 32: Leading British & Irish Inland Port Locations, 2004

Source: www.sfpc.ie, www.galwaychamber.com,
DfT *Waterborne Freight in the UK, 2004*

Whilst there has been a sharp decline in inland barge traffics in recent decades, the endurance of freight flows on the mentioned waterways is testament to the economic, environmental and logistical advantages of water transport. Oil product movements in parcels of over 500 tonnes make barging a cost competitive and environmentally acceptable alternative to road haulage. On the Humber/Trent/Ouse network oil product movements have survived mainly as a result of being able to benefit from the economies of scale of 600 tonne tanker barges. The return of barge (traffic lost to road in 1990s) petroleum movements between the Immingham refinery terminal and Leeds is partly explained by the desire to avoid congestion, both at the terminal and on the region's motorway network. Where oil products have been lost to road haulage, it is normally the case that low inventory costs associated with just-in-time truck deliveries have been seen as more economically attractive than barge costs. This was the case of the up-river movements of petroleum from the refineries of the Thames estuary to

West London. Bulk Grain movements to granaries tend to be regular flows. In this trade the low cost of bulk barging off-sets the higher speeds and j-i-t capabilities of road haulage. This appears to be the case in the grain flows between Liverpool's Seaforth grain terminal and Manchester (also Frodsham, situated on the River Weaver).

The movement of coal on the waterways of East Yorkshire has a long history starting with the revolutionary "Tom Pudding" barge trains that linked the regions coalmines with the ports. At the new Millennium the only remaining coal traffics (under threat from coal mine closures) were by barge-pushtug combinations on the Aire & Calder Navigation, linking the Ferrybridge power station with the Selby coalfield. The dumping of London's waste on coastal in-fill sites in Essex has a long tradition. However, road competition for this 1mt per annum business is acute. Containerisation of waste transportation has helped to keep river operations competitive. A unique environmentally focused aspect of the Thames services of Cory Waste and Cleanaway lies not only in the many thousands of annual road journeys that they prevent, but also in the fuel efficient utilisation of the Thames tide. By scheduling an up-river passage to coincide with the early stages of the flood tide the tug and barge combinations are virtually pushed to the heart of the capital by the powerful flood tides. Similarly, the return loaded leg benefits from the ferocious Thames ebb.

A major development in inland barge traffic was facilitated by the FFG awarded to the European aggregates leader Lafarge, for their River Trent based operations in 2000/1 (Featured as a case study in chapter 7. See below pp.). An interesting combination of inland and coastal shipping was initiated by a project commenced by the heavy haulage specialist Robert Wynn and Sons in 2002.[28] This company has a long pedigree as a national specialist in the movement of large road consignments, such as power station transformers and railway locomotives, stretching back to the times of steam traction engine haulage. The branching out from purely road operations into shipping enables the heavy freight specialist to avoid the geographic restrictions of the road system; conversely, road users are spared the heavy delays associated with slow moving heavy goods. The inland shipping part of the project involved the conversion of one 300 tonne tank barge, *Inland Navigator*, into a heavy load carrier capable of penetrating canal and river systems. The coastal aspect of the project came with the commissioning of a £7m semi-submersible vessel, designed for the shipment of heavy indivisible project cargoes, in excess of 150 tonnes. The larger coastal vessel's design specifications allow for the float on-float off (FLOFLO) carriage of the *Inland Navigator* and its freight. The system allows for the seamless carriage of large and heavy movements via inland canals and rivers and around the European coastline. The support of the project by the Government's FFG , amounting to £8.5m, is testament to commitment to policy designed at reducing the negative impact of road congestion.

5.8 The Return of LASH?

The idea of virtual floating containers as featured in the lighter aboard ship concept (LASH), also, barge aboard catamaran (BACAT), has considerable implications for inland shipping. The concept derived from the US Marines logistics of floating military hardware and supplies off the mother ship, towards the frontline. The logistics are based on FLOFLO barges which are floated on and off the mother ship. Tugs are used to push the barges up-river to discharge locations. The commercial applications of this concept were driven by its ability to avoid handling costs in the ports. For cargoes loaded in up-river locations on rivers such as the Mississippi, LASH proved a very cost effective mode for bulk and break-bulk movements to Europe. Lykes Lines Mississippi-Rhine service featured the North Atlantic transport of LASH barges between such inland ports as Cologne and New Orleans. Similar services operate between North European rivers – Weser, Rhine, Maas – and West African rivers. The LASH revolution hit the UK in the 1970s when mother ships began to make calls in the Medway and Humber estuaries.[29]

The Humber service targeted the up-stream industrial markets: on the River Trent, Nottingham, Leeds on the Aire and Calder Navigation, and Sheffield/Rotherham via the South Yorkshire Navigation. Unfortunately, the mid-river discharge in the Humber was seen as a threat to the jobs of the strongly unionised dock workers of Hull. The resulting threat of strike action led to a withdrawal of the service.[30] The return of LASH in 1998 on the Humber was very much in response to the need for efficient, low cost, bulk movement of imported rice. The importer, Westmill Foods, situated in Selby, packages around a 1000 tonnes of rice per week. This approximates to three barges each possessing a 370 tonne payload. The demand is derived from the increasing popularity of rice dishes in the UK. Loaded in Arkansas, USA, the barges are assembled in push-tug convoys which are dispatched down river to the awaiting mother ship in the Mississippi Delta. At this point the barges join Forest Line's Mississippi-Rhine service. The mother ship, *Atlantic Forest*, carries 83 barges, each with a payload of 385 tonnes. This service has calls at US ports – Charleston, Jacksonville, Pasagoula, Morehead City – and North European Ports – Rotterdam, Antwerp, Bremerhaven, Humber and Medway.

The advantages of a waterborne freight service that minimises cargo handling costs has great potential for the Green Highway. Where regular flows of products can be co-ordinated with the fixed schedules of deepsea liner services, benefits accrue to the shipper. The flow of rice from the Mississippi to North Europe and return cargoes of steel and manufactured goods has proved ideal for North Atlantic LASH operations into such European river systems – Rhine, Maas, Elbe. The link with UK rivers, Medway, Thames, Trent and Ouse offers great potential. In 2002, a similar concept to LASH was employed in the Port of Liverpool. The call of the *BACO-Liner 3* ship saw the off-loading of 6 barges laden with West African cocoa (3000 tonnes total)for tugboat dispatch in the Merseyside region.[31]

5.9 One Port Shipping

Within this sector sea dumped waste has brought the Green Highway into disrepute. Waste dumped could include household refuse, chemical residues and nuclear waste. Up until 1999 local authorities in many of the metropolitan centres, including London boroughs sent large volumes of only partly treated human waste downstream for estuarial dumping. Throughout the 1980s and up to the end of 1998 some 9mt of sewage plus industrial waste was dumped at sea. Thankfully this practice is now illegal as a result of EU legislation.[32] One port shipping is now composed of three main sectors:

- Sea Dredged Aggregates;
- Oil loaded ex off-shore installation;
- Oil rig supplies .

Sea dredged aggregates are mainly sand and gravel dredged by vessels in 1000-4000dwt category from the UK and continental coastline. Demand is primarily from the road building/maintenance and construction industry and is strongly correlated with patterns of economic growth. The surge in demand for construction materials in the early 1980s led to considerable investment in new tonnage. The stress has been on highly automated, self loading/discharging vessels. The low margins of the final product, cement, in the construction trades places emphasis on vessel loading productivity and port turnround times.[33] Since this period, the off-shore dredging sector has seen a process of mergers and consolidations; two main groupings now exist, Hanson and ARC Marine. The vessels normally have the ability to self load and, in some instances, discharge. Smaller vessels working in river and dock locations tend to have grab crane loading systems. The larger vessels tend to be suction dredgers aided by state-of-the-art sonar detection systems. Increasingly, dredging for aggregates has been

244

subject to coastline management legislation. Concerns over damage to fish habitat and coastline erosion have led to restrictions on quantities and zonal areas available for dredging. Despite the large volumes dredged – Figure 33 shows 12-15mt per annum in the early Millennium years - it was the catastrophic Thames collision between the dredger, *Bowbelle* and the pleasure vessel, *Marchioness* that brought media attention to the industry in 1989, when 51 people were drowned.[34]

Figure 33: UK Sea Dredged Aggregates, 2000-04

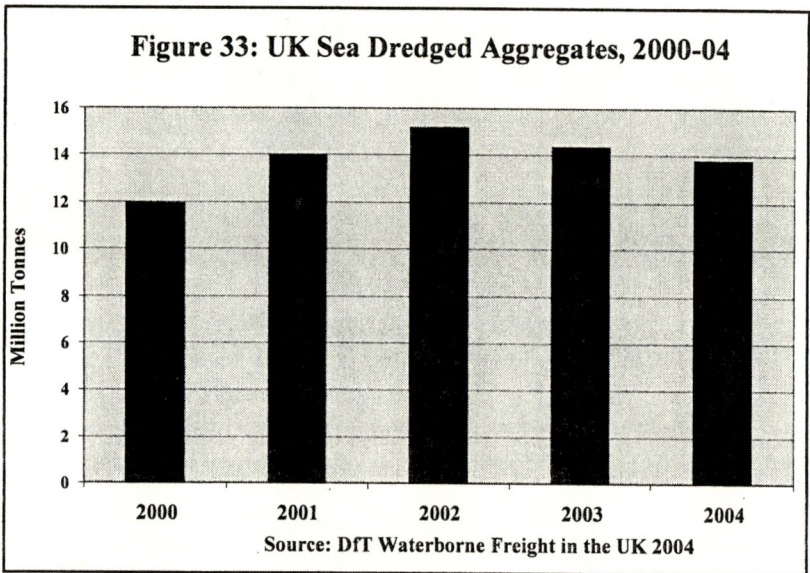

Source: DfT Waterborne Freight in the UK 2004

The sea dredged aggregates business has taken significant steps to minimise the road leg of the journey. Voyage legs can be maximised by the self discharging facilities that the modern dredger possesses. More emphasis on sea tkm (as opposed to road tkm) provides the opportunity for the aggregates companies to demonstrate their commitment to environmental sustainability.

Offshore oil rig support shipping has proved to be a specialist area of work which provided one of the few areas of opportunity for British seafarers following the UK fleet's decline which began in 1975 and continued unabated until the Tonnage Tax initiatives of 1999. Two distinct peaks in off-shore vessel buildings can be detected in the North Sea sector. Beginning in 1975, with the surge in global oil prices generating activity in the North Sea, off-shore supply vessels proved to be in great demand. This was followed in 1982 with a second wave of new buildings induced by increased activity subsequent to the 1979 oil price rise.[35]

Three distinct categories of the offshore market are: exploration, production platform support and construction. The nature of oil rig support – oil rig standby and supply vessels – is that of an essential logistics, towage, fire fighting and rescue service. The technical demands of moving and supporting oil rigs in the precarious North Sea led to the development of the anchor handling tug supply vessel (AHTS). The capabilities of these vessels and their highly skilled crews has had implications for the wider salvage and rescue sector, outside of the oil rig sector. In such cases as the salvage of the remnants of the 1999 wrecked tanker, *Erika* off the Brittany coast, these vessels have proved invaluable. The ability to maintain anchor handling, fire fighting and towage capabilities in poor weather conditions and the low afterdeck of these tugs– making for easier rescue of survivors from the sea – has led to their prominence in the increasingly important emergency towage service. Tanker accidents and resulting pollution disasters – *Braer, Sea Empress* – have led to UK Government support of four emergency towage vessels (ETVs). In 2001, the UK Government Maritime Coastguard Agency (MCA) awarded a £75m, eight year contract, to Klyne Tugs of Lowestoft. This provided for the stationing of AHTS in the Dover Straits, the Western Approaches and Northern Scotland.[36]

5.10 Chapter 5: Summary and Conclusion

This chapter has sought to outline the characteristics of the many and varied modes of shipping service within the generic heading, Green Highway. The intention has been to detail the specific business and technical nature of shipping fitting into the "coastal" category. From the perspective of roads to water it has been made apparent that some sectors are more susceptible to road competition than others. It has been shown that shipping technology and innovation has not been moribund. Although the long term trend in many of the trades has been one of decline, the ability of shipping to evolve and adapt in the deregulated marketplace has provided for an operational longevity and an ability to win new niche markets, particularly where the environmental case is paramount.

CHAPTER 5: ENDNOTES

[1] DfT, *Waterborne Freight in the UK 2004*. London: DfT.pp.7-10.

[2] *Loc.cit.*

[3] Wood, P. J. (2000) *Tanker Chartering*. London: Witherby. p. 43.

[4] BPF/DoT (1991) *Port Statistics*. London: BPF/DoT. P. 6.

[5] Tusiani, M.D. (1996) *The Petroleum Shipping Industry: A Non-Technical Overview*, Vol.1. Tulsa, OA: PennWell. p. 139.

[6] Statutory Instrument 1996 No. 2678 The Environmental Protection (Prescribed Processes and Substances Etc.) (Amendment) (Petrol Vapour Recovery) Regulations 1996.

[7] Conversation with Michael Everard CBE. Chairman F.T. Everard & Sons.

[8] "Asperity a showcase for Singapore newbuilding," *Lloyd's List*. 30.4.97. p. 7.

[9] Harris, J. & Redding, E. (1999), "Irish Firm bucks downward trend", *Lloyd's List*. 16.9.99.

[10] *Loc.cit*

[11] "Irish Fertilizer Industries" http://www.ukbusinesspark.co.uk/irs71886.htm accessed 3.4.07.

[12] Tinsley, D. (1991) *Short-Sea Shipping: A Review of the North European Coastal Bulk Trades*. London: Lloyd's of London Press. p.5.

[13] *Ibid.* p.7.

[14] Speares, S. (2001), "Shortsea operator launches takeaway service for builders", *Lloyd's List*. 2.7.01.

[15] Tinsley, D. *Op.cit.* p.141.

[16] "Ship canal sees freight lift to highest for 16 years", *Lloyd's List*. 25.6.01.

[17] Tinsley, D. *Op.cit.* pp.80-1.

[18] Cowell, R.(2000), "Localities and International Trade in Aggregates". *Geography*, Vol.85 (2). pp.134-144.

[19] *Ibid.* p.136.

[20] Zachcial, M. (1997) "Land/Sea Transport Flows in Europe." In Peeters, D & Wergeland, T. *European Shortsea Shipping: Proceedings from the Third European Research Roundtable Conference on Shortsea Shipping*. Bergen, 20-21 June 1996. Delft: Delft University Press. p.39.

[21] Packer. *Op.cit.* p.505.

[22] Zachial, M. *Op.cit.* p.40.

[23] "Sunflower Tomakomai: encouraging Japan's freight on the sea," *Significant Ships of 1999*. p.110.

[24] Drewry, H. P. (1997) *Shortsea Container Markets: the Feeder and Regional Trade Dynamo*. London: Drewry.

[25] Baird, A. (2001). "A new economic evaluation of the hubport versus multiport strategy," A Paper given to the International Association of Maritime Economists Annual Conference 2001, Hong Kong Polytechnic University, 18-20.7.01.

[26] Spurrier, A. "CMA CGM joins giant boxship race with $1.2bn surprise order," *Lloyd's List*. 11.9.06.

[27] DfT, *Waterborne Freight in the UK 2004*. *Op.cit.* Appendix One.

[28] O'Mahony, H. "UK funds pontoons to take large loads off the roads", *Lloyd's List*. 12.6.02. p. 24.

[29] Hilling, D. (1977) *Barge Carrier Systems, Inventory and Prospects*. London: Benn Publications

[30] "Going with the Grain," *Yorkshire Post*. 29.7.00. p. 15.

[31] www.baco-liner.de/dyn/press/10_2002_01.html

[32] http://www.defra.gov.uk/environment/statistics/coastwaters/cwwastes.htm#cmtb14

[33] Tinsley, D. *Op.cit.* pp. 85-6.

[34] http://www.marchioness-bowbelle.org.uk/

[35] Hartington, J. (2001) "The offshore oil sector – its impact on towage and salvage", *International Journal of Tug & Salvage*. July/August. p. 21.

[36] Gaston, J (2001) "Klyne wins £75m contract for all-year UK rescue tug cover", *Lloyd's List*. 30.8.01. p. 1.

CHAPTER 6

A Profile of Leading Operators

Having outlined the shape and composition of Green Highway trades in the previous chapter, it is next intended to detail the principal shipping owners and operators involved. The aim is to identify the key players and their market strategy and behaviour in order to develop a profile of the firms providing the Green Highway supply chain.

Gaining an appreciation of the structure and evolving nature of shortsea shipping organisation in Europe is integral to the Green Highway discussion. In this chapter, key British and Irish, as well as Dutch, German, Scandinavian and Russian operators are profiled. The shortsea, coastal and inland sectors offer considerable diversity in the types of ships, trades and their organisation and management. The geographically fragmented nature of ship ownership, management, registration and crewing is a feature of the coastal and shortsea trades. It will become apparent that a mixture of traditional owners and new entrants, family owners and public companies are trading. Additionally, the open market ethos of coastal and shortsea routes sees traditional British shipping family owners competing with (amongst others) open registry, Chinese, Russian even Cambodian flagged ships. Chinese tonnage has been used to move roadstone from Scotland to Thamesport and Russian vessels have been offered UK coastal business at freight rates well below those attainable under the UK flag. Figure 34 illustrates the participation of the four leading flags as well as the open nature of UK domestic trades. The open registry, Bahamas, is seen as the clear leader in terms of tonnes lifted, with 20.07mt (25% of the total). The UK flag comes in at second place with 13.96mt (18% of total tonnes lifted).

Other predominant flags in the UK trades, particularly the tanker trades, are the Norwegian International Registry (NIS), Liberia and Sweden. Figure 35 shows a similar pattern of flag participation. Bahamas is again the market leader with 16.97btkms (forming 31% of goods moved). The UK flag follows

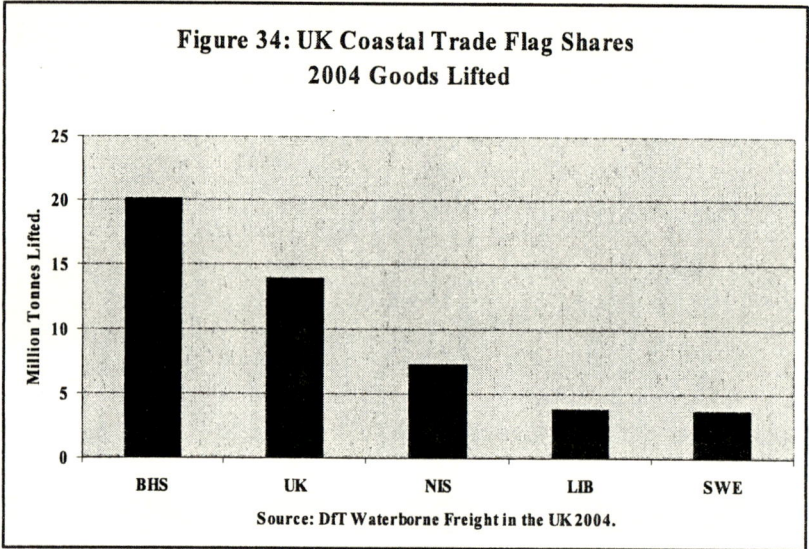

Figure 34: UK Coastal Trade Flag Shares 2004 Goods Lifted

with 8.74btkms (16% of goods moved). The participation of the high cost Norwegian and Swedish flags in the UK trades provides an interesting contrast with the involvement with the lower cost registries, Bahamas and Liberia. Later in this chapter, the strength of these flags in the tanker trades will become evident, with Norwegian owners focusing on the crude oil trades, the Swedish owners on the oil products trades. Contrasting approaches to operating, ownership and financing will be recognised. Apparent trends are the withdrawal from dry cargo operations and an increased focusing on tanker markets by three leading UK operators will be discussed. The dramatic rise of Ireland's Arklow Shipping is a feature of the dry bulk trades in the last two decades. Regional clusters of companies are identified; these will include the Kentish cluster of British firms and the German ship-owning and financing companies of Haren-Ems, Bremen and Hamburg. The predominance of German owners in the container trades and Scandinavian owners in the tanker trades is recognised. Whilst it will become evident that enterprise and diversification are inherent qualities in the shortsea sectors, it will also be seen how marginal and volatile the market can be. Shipping can be an industry where investors lose their shirt!

Figure 35: UK Coastal Trade Flag Shares 2004 Goods Moved

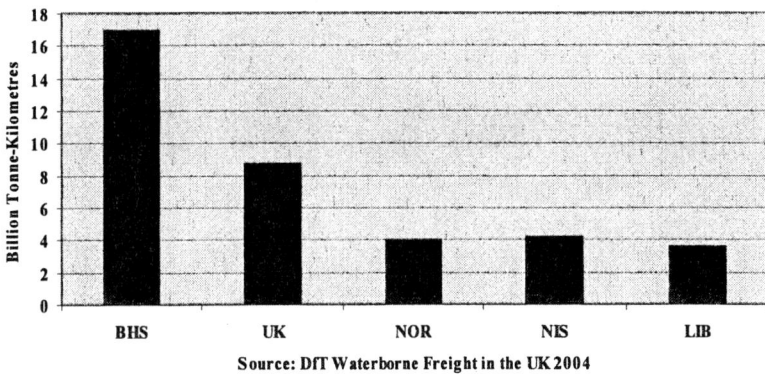

Source: DfT Waterborne Freight in the UK 2004

6.1 The Principal British Owners

The pattern of ownership has necessarily evolved in correlation with changes in industrial and agricultural demand and also as a result of increasingly globalised operations. Failure to read or respond to volatile changes in the market can have disastrous consequences. The financial fate of the Penarth shipowner, James Gould, in the inter-war years serves as a salutary lesson. Prior to WW1 the shipping magnate had over a 100 vessels trading in the South Wales coal trades. The war proved disastrous with the loss of 52 ships. Economic recession and the collapse of the coal industry in the inter-war years were to bring a torrid time for James. The loss of his business was accompanied by the loss of his South Wales mansion, plus his elegant Park Lane town house in London. During the 1930s, the entrepreneur attempted to diversify into the mobile food sector with a fleet of fish and chip vans emanating from the Billingsgate area of London. James died in 1944. It was reported that he had been living in a Council house in Coulsdon, Surrey.[1] This example shows the volatility of shipowning in the inter-war period.

6.2 The Kentish Cluster

Commencing with the Kentish owners, it will be seen how the evolving shipping firms have been influenced by changes in the market. Exampling not only these changes but also the endurance and tenacity of ownership existing in the shortsea trades in the early Millennium years are three of the leading UK operators – Crescent Shipping, F.T. Everard (became part of James Fisher plc, late 2006) and Lapthorn Shipping Ltd (became Coastal Bulk Shipping 1.11.06) These companies have their Kentish roots in the Thames sailing barge industry. As discussed in chapter 2, these two or three handed vessels served the needs of London industry and consumerism. This involved commitment to the grain, timber, brick and cement trades. The Thames-Medway estuary trading area was extended by the larger sailing barges to the Solent and the China Clay ports of South West England and the agricultural ports of East Anglia. Gradually as the trades switched to motorised vessels the prospects of trading further afield became apparent. Additionally, the growth in oil trades activity post 1930s with the development of refineries at Purfleet, Canvey Island and the Isle of Grain offered

Table 28: Leading British & Irish Fleets Owned/Managed, 1975–2005. Number of Vessels & GT

Owner/ Manager	1975		1980		1985		1990		1995		2000		2005	
	No	GT	No	GT	No	GT	No	GT	No	GT	No	GT	No	GT
Arklow Shipping	3	1735	5	3805	15	15,522	23	35,868	21	41,769	26	68,960	35	98,751
Carisbrooke Shipping	2	866	4	1475	6	3575	7	7408	11	21,497	14	28,530	20	108,289
Crescent	46	10,062	51	20,625	38	16,034	35	80,230	27	71,351	20	26,416	12	24,719
Everard	45	40950	44	45,075	47	43,043	27	28,107	28	42,795	24	31034	11	22,379
Fisher	22	43338	22	52,206	23	61,208	16	62,161	11	58,337	24	76,625	27	125,461
Lapthorn	5	1991	7	3101	10	5150	19	13,194	24	20,642	23	21,203	19	15,387
Stephenson Clarke	51	118,194	46	110,189	27	71,387	15	65288	17	72,512	12	61,092	8	44,767
Union Transport	5	2022	8	4560	14	10,690	9	12,937	9	15,224	11	17,830	13	22,072

Source: *Lloyd's Register of Shipping: List of Shipowners*

opportunities in the oil trades. Both Everard and Crescent invested heavily in tankers for the oil product trades. The proliferation of river and coastal activities in the Thames and Medway estuaries has induced entrepreneurship in the region. In many ways, the evolution of these companies from sailing and small motor barge operators, focused on the Thames estuary and agricultural trades of East Anglia to major continental traders, represents typical development of UK coastal shipping. Greenhithe's F.T. Everard and (historically) Medway's Crescent Shipping have made the transition into exclusive tankship operations. Bromley's Union Transport and Medway's Lapthorn Shipping have both focused on low air draft shipping, capable of trading in continental inland river and canal systems. The geographic position of these owners has fortuitously placed them conveniently for the growing continental trades, following European Union integration.

6.2.1 F.T. Everard & Sons Ltd

Up until late 2006, the history of F.T. Everard was very much that of a forward looking family company. A process of "going up market" is evident with the company trading its rustic river trading image for that of a highly regarded professional tanker operator in the oil product trades. Diversification has been an on-going feature of the company's progress. Ken Garrett's 1991 history, *Everard's of Greenhithe*[2] traces the company's progression from barge builder to one of the UK's leading coastal shipping specialists. The resilience of the family company was first demonstrated by the efforts of the founder, F.T. Everard, who, in the late 1800s walked the 48kms from London carrying his shipbuilders' tools on his back when setting up the Greenhithe yard.[3] In 1889, the company built its first own account sailing barge. In addition to organic growth, expansion and diversification has spread from the company's expertise. The shipbuilding tradition was further enhanced by the purchase of a Newbury engine builder, which became named Newbury Diesels in 1931 and in 1948, the controlling interest in two Great Yarmouth shipbuilders was attained. With port agency ties in such East Coast ports as Great Yarmouth and Goole, Everards could ensure reliable local representation in important shortsea ports.

Further diversification into ships' electronic services and ship-management strengthened the company's asset portfolio. Vertical integration has been an ingredient of Everard's success and longevity. The company's Greenhithe (Lower Thames) complex including oil tank storage which facilitated oil products transfer to Everard's tug and barge fleet for Thames and Medway up-river connections and even the company's road tanker fleet. The purchase of the 352 metres of Cattedown Wharves in Plymouth in 1957 proved a highly successful decision. With 70% of Plymouth's oil and dry bulk trades passing through the Wharves.[4] The purchase was particularly fortuitous in that it enabled Everards's the opportunity to offer oil storage and distribution to oil majors seeking a logistical centre in South West England.

The takeover of a number of lines, including the Glasgow based Glen & Co, brought new trading opportunities. Glen's liner linkages led to the inheritance of Scandinavian-UK/Ireland liner services. The pattern of Everard's fleet development has been one of rationalising the smaller vessels and concentrating on larger, more specialised ships. In 1956, Everard's celebrated the arrival of their 100th vessel, the 885dwt Goole built, *Century*. This traditional dry cargo coaster was to represent more the past than the future for Everard's. The labour intensive vessel would often spend several days in ports which restricted cargo work to the traditional working weekday, with no evening or weekend cargo movements. By the 1960s the company was beginning to see the benefits of tanker operations. Even with the time consuming processes of tank cleaning and ballasting, Everard's tankers were managing two trips per week in this period. The close collaboration of the company with the oil major, Shell, provides evidence of this. Recognition from the maritime community and in political circles came when Mr. Michael Everard, the last Chairman of the company, was appointed chairman of the Council for British Shipping in 1991 and in 1992 was awarded the CBE.

A significant and fairly seamless transition occurred within the Kentish cluster in 2002 when Everard's sold the remnants of their dry cargo fleet. In March 2002 *Lloyd's List* announced a joint venture of 36 small ships operating in the shortsea trades to be formed between Bromley-based Union Transport Group and the dry cargo division of F.T. Everard.[5] The joint venture saw the last two dry cargo vessels in the F.T. Everard fleet, *Seniority* and *Superiority*, sold to Union Transport, which also took on the operations of eleven managed dry cargo vessels and nine time chartered vessels. Sizes in the joint fleet were in the 800dwt to 5,000dwt range. Four chartering staff from Everard's London office and the company's Swedish representative were moved to Union Transport HQ in Bromley, Kent.

The process appears to have been achieved amiably with Michael Everard, Chairman of F.T. Everard, stating that the joint fleet would be a "substantial" influence in the market, with Union Transport, better suited to the take-over "... than any other British owner in the dry cargo sector."[6] The Chairman rationalised the divestment from the dry bulk sector as part of the increased attention to the oil products trades, stating that the arrangement more than suited his company, which wished to focus on its tanker business, "our first priority".[7]

In 2005 the company celebrated its 125th birthday by the fruition of a significant tanker fleet expansion programme. The company has distanced itself considerably from its history as a robust, cost conscious and highly combative small ship operator. The focus on quality operations in the oil products trades has been confirmed by the company's long term contracts with oil majors, Shell and

Esso. Everard's introduced their first double-hull tankers in 1979 and embodied its aggregated experience into the *Asperity*-class ships which set a new industry benchmark when they were delivered in 1997. The direction of this strategy was confirmed by the 2004-5 order of the first of four new *Speciality*-class coastal tankers from China's Qingshan shipyard. The family controlled nature of Everard's has ensured a long term approach to investment and improvement. Capt Eion Lyons, Marine Director and head of the technical department at Everard's has confirmed the commitment to developing safe and efficient designs with each new generation of tankers:

> This approach enables us to not only meet evolving business requirements and provide a competitive advantage but also, most importantly, maintain our exemplary safety record. Today's standards can always be improved upon.[8]

In January 2005, the Everard tanker fleet, owned, managed, chartered in and under construction, consisted of 15 vessels, of which 10 were double hulled, in the 3000-4600dwt range. By 2005 the company had divested much of its non-core activities in order to focus on tanker operations.

Almost as a postscript to this profile of F.T. Everard, events at the time of writing provided an unanticipated new direction for the company. In late 2006 the shortsea community was surprised to learn that the family company had been sold to one of its closest rivals, James Fisher & Sons plc.[9] Despite the divestment by the family firm, the takeover has been championed as a strengthening of British shipping, achieved by a reduction of overheads and the development of operating synergies as Everard's modern, double hulled tankers were transferred into the Fisher fleet.[10]

Company Portfolio as at 4.6.05

- Ship-owning and ship management 15 vessels;
- Marine insurance;
- The ownership and management of Plymouth's Cattedown Wharves;
- Ships' Electronic Services Ltd.

Company Status:

- Family owned limited company.

Sample Oil Products Trades:

- Immingham-Inverness;
- Fawley-Plymouth;
- Stanlow-Galway.

6.2.2 Union Transport

Closely aligned to Everard's following the transfer of the dry-cargo fleet, Union Transport has become an increasingly important member of the Kentish Cluster. The opportunities for trading within Europe to the Thames and Southern England helped to promote the development of Bromley's Union Transport. Swiss shipping agent, Hans Schenkel, together with his English partner William Roper, founded Union Transport (London) Ltd on August 14 1946. Mr. Schenkel, who had worked for the Ministry of Food during WW2, quickly became known for his expertise in arranging shipments of commodities and merchandise from the UK via the River Rhine to Switzerland.[11] The Anglo-Swiss partnership facilitated sugar flows from Tate and Lyle's Thameside refinery at Silvertown, to the heart of Swiss chocolate making on the Rhine.

The efficiency of the sea-river operation was confirmed by the retention of the sugar contract for a period of 40 years. Initially cargoes were transhipped from the chartered 400 tonne coasters in Antwerp and Rotterdam into barges for

for this and similar inland trades, eventually facilitated the evolution of the low air draft sea trader class of vessels. Continuing the Swiss connection, the appointment of the management trainee, Max Heinimann in 1961 was to prove significant to the company's development. Mr Heinimann was to become a strong proponent of not only the operations of sea-river transport but also a technical author (along with Teignmouth shipping agent, Chris Cheetham). Their joint work, *Modern Sea River Traders*[13] has proved a seminal work in the field. In 1996, *Lloyd's List* championed the MD's commitment to the sea-river concept:

> Max Heinimann is a man with a maritime mission, one of the pioneers of river sea trading and who has spent the last 20 years trying to convince a sceptical transport world, increasingly wedded to the lorry, that the low air-draft shortsea ship has very real potential as a viable alternative.[14]

A major opportunity for growth came in 2002 with the purchase of Everard's dry cargo fleet. At the time, Max Heinimann told *Lloyd's List* that the deal would help both companies to achieve improved costs. Scale economies would, he said, be available as a result of the joint venture, the Union fleet being "well-controlled" and likely to benefit from an F.T. Everard dry cargo operation that offered "no surprises."[15]

The current (2006) Union Fleet is composed of a fleet of 21 sea-river ships. Additionally, it was announced in 2005 that the company had placed an order with the Indian shipbuilder, Chowgule, for six 4450dwt multipurpose dry cargo vessels, at a cost of $46m.[16] Interestingly, the six vessels will have double the cargo carrying capacity of the average fleet size and, additionally, they will feature container carrying capacity. As well as the Bromley Head Office, the bulk logistics and project cargo specialist has a Newcastle Office and also owns the Acorn Ship repair yard in Rochester.[17] The company is proud of its independence as a wholly owned public limited company.

Company Portfolio as at 4.6.05 :

- 21 owned and managed vessels in the 1200-3000dwt range;
- Ship repairs;
- Project forwarding;
- Freight forwarding.

Company Status:

- Public limited company.

Sample Trades:

- Liege-Poole,steel;
- Szczecin-Drogheda, coal;
- Belfast-Dagenham, stone.

6.2.3. Lapthorn Shipping Ltd (Became Coastal Bulk Shipping, 1.11.06)

The story of Lapthorns exemplifies the difficulties facing operators in the dry-bulk trades. The history of the company as a shipowner began in 1951. As with Everard's early history, Lapthorn's, had their early roots in ship repair and, in particular, the conversion of sailing barges to motorisation. The company's location in the Medway estuary village of Hoo St. Wergurgh, found it well placed for the movements of construction materials to such post-war building projects as the Isle of Grain oil terminal and power station. Ken Garrett's work, *R. Lapthorn and Company: A Ships in Focus Fleet History,*[18] outlines the transition from a one barge shipowner to one of the largest operators on the UK coast. Throughout the 1990s Lapthorn's achieved growth via a number of astute fleet acquisitions. The growth in the fleet completely bucked the trend of decline in British shipping in the 1980s and early 1990s.

As coastal shipping companies left the market, Lapthorn's kept faith with the industry buying up fleets and thus becoming one of the few British shipping success stories of this period. Also, the strong collaboration between the owners and the Yorkshire Dry Docks company in Hull saw the successful introduction of an innovatory class of low air-draft box hold vessels. The attributes of these vessels, specifically designed for coastal and river trades, was low cost flexibility which enabled them to operate in marginally profitable trades and reach a number of ports restricted by water and air draft confinements. The single box hold made for easy loading and discharge and the manoeuvrability of the twin screw vessels allows for operations at minimal crew levels – four crew in certain sheltered waters. The twin screw aided manoeuvrability also makes the ships particularly well suited to the confined waters of inland ports. The point was proved by the *Hoo Marlin's* high profile delivery of aggregates to the media scrutinised construction site of the Millennium Bridge in London. The fleet is well placed to benefit from the demands created by the London Olympics construction programme.

Specialising in the stone and aggregates trades, Lapthorn's have built up a niche market which combines well with the balancing movements of steel, grain and animal feeds. Focusing primarily on coastal and shortsea trades between Cornwall and the Humber, Lapthorn's serve a number of size restricted ports, including the English Channel's, Rye and Littlehampton and the up-river ports of Cowes, Isle of Wight, and Brightlingsea, Essex. In the Wash, Sutton Bridge and Wisbech and on the Trent, Beckingham, Keadby and Flixborough, have been regular inland calls for Lapthorn vessels. The focus on smaller vessel sizes facilitates visits to size restricted ports; again Lapthorn's have bucked the trend by sticking with vessels in the 2200dwt and below tonnages. The staple fleet size remains at 1400dwt. Another niche area pioneered by Lapthorn's is in the self discharging facility. Six of the 1400dwt *Hoo Marlin* class of vessel were fitted with Samsung grab excavators in the early Millennium period. This allowed for not only the flexibility of working cargo in remote areas lacking in port facilities, but also avoids port handling costs. The limitations that some ports place on evening and weekend working by dockworkers can also be avoided, leading to greater utilisation of the fleet.

Despite the innovative stance, the competitive drive and the tangibly busy fleet, the shortsea community was somewhat rocked to hear the news in early 2003 that the Lapthorn Fleet was up for sale due to difficult trading conditions.[19] The decision taken, in co-operation with its bankers confirmed that Lapthorn's 19 small dry cargo vessels were available for sale, but the bank stressed that in the meantime the fleet was trading normally "under the owner's sole instruction". In 2003, it was estimated that Lapthorn's lost £800,000.[20] In the words of Chairman David Lapthorn, the 54 year old family company came within "inches of going out of business," before a private investor was brought in to finance a holding company. Three of the company's vessels were sold immediately. By April 2006 the fleet was reduced to 12. At the April 2004 "Why Water?" Conference in Manchester, Mr. Lapthorn outlined the company's resolve to survive the crisis, which, together with an innovative financing package, allowed for a process of re-structuring debt and the development of a new business plan.[21]

The difficulties faced by Lapthorn's in 2003, a year in which the busy fleet, averaging around two cargoes per week, carried over 2mt of dry cargoes, demonstrated the problem of depressed freight rates in the dry bulk trades. The need for a restructuring plan has forced Lapthorn's to reconsider loss making contracts of affreightment and to focus on higher earning sectors. In November 2003, the company announced a shift into the shortsea container business.[22] With vessels of a container capacity called for of at least 80teu, the implications were that Lapthorn's would charter suitable tonnage in the short-run. However, in the long-run, Lapthorn's announced the quest for returns that would prove sustainable and conducive to fleet investment programmes for the future.[23] In Summer 2006, the Lapthorn family withdrew from the business. John and Andrew Lapthorn sold their shares to Tim Lowry, the Managing Director and majority shareholder, whilst David Lapthorn's interest was acquired by Aggregate Carriers. David and John, together with David's son, Richard, left the company at the end of May 2006.[24] The house flag used by the company since formation in 1951, is owned by the family and left with them. A new green flag and funnel markings will be seen on the company's vessels. The colour change to green reflects the environmental emphasis by the new company as of 1.11.06, Coastal Bulk Shipping Ltd.[25]

Company Portfolio as at 30.4.06

- Ship-owning and ship-management – 10 vessels and 2 barges.

Company Status:

- Private limited company.

Sample Trades:

- Bremen-Grimsby, steel;
- Wash Ports-Rotterdam, wheat;
- Tees-Great Yarmouth, rock salt.

6.2.4 Crescent Tankships

The (now) Southampton based, Crescent Tankships, also have their business roots in the Kentish sailing barge trades. The evolution of the company from its sailing barge, estuarial roots, to a highly regarded coastal tank ship operator, exemplifies the challenges and opportunities that exist for British shipping expertise and enterprise. The historic parent company of Crescent Shipping, the London & Rochester Trading Company, has a very similar pedigree to Kentish arch-rivals, F.T. Everard, evolving from barge building activities to shipowning in 1928, when securing payments for newbuildings became seen as more problematic by the Gill Brothers than actually building and operating barges. With sailing barges and small motor coasters, Crescent specialised in trades in the creeks of the Thames and Medway estuaries. The geography of this region dictated small ship sizes and even as Crescent made the transition from sailing barges to motor vessels, sizes remained in the below 500dwt category. However, as the estuarial work began to erode (as outlined in chapter 2), as a result of changes in industrial location, the company did try to benefit from the economies of scale of larger vessels.[26] In 1995 four of the company's larger *Tarquence* class vessels were lengthened in order to achieve an increase in cargo capacity from 750 to 950 tonnes. Innovation and enterprise have marked the development of Crescent and this has included a focus on European inland operations, involving work on the Rhone, Rhine, Maas, Seine, Albert Canal and even the Danube. Also, the Crescent Group has diversified into Irish Sea RoRo operations.

The Hays Group takeover of the London and Rochester's Crescent's Shipping fleet, brought the unique situation of a public limited company becoming involved in dry bulk coastal operations. The purchase of Bowker and King's coastal tanker and port bunkering fleet in Southampton as well as Bristol Channel ports allowed access to the oil products sector. With the focus in the Hay's Group becoming increasingly road based logistics and business services, coastal shipping operations had become peripheral to the company. In 1997, however, a new lease of life followed Crescent's acquisition by a UK-Danish joint venture controlled by London and Wessex and Torben Jensen's Nassau based, Clipper Group. The new owners immediately set up an order for up to four clean products tankers. The £14m (US$ 22.5m) transaction gave the new venture a total of 19 vessels, nine of which were British-registered tankers plus ten dry bulkers[27]

Around the same time as Everard's divestment from dry-cargo, the withdrawal of Crescent from dry bulk operations in 2002 marked the end of a diversification and market re-focusing strategy. The company had already diversified into maritime services and ship management and also the running of the Heysham-Warrenpoint RoRo service, operating as Seatruck. In 1992,

Crescent's shortsea freight index, which had been monitored since 1981, indicated that North European dry cargo rates had sunk to a 10-year low. The continuing weakness in the market throughout the 1980s vindicated both the company's policy of developing niche business within the European trades and its conservative approach to reinvestment in its dry cargo fleet.[28] From the 1980s the focus has been on Crescent's tanker operations which have been modernised and expanded; the most recent newbuilding addition to the directly owned dry cargo sector of the fleet was in 1983.

In 2002, Crescent completed its programme to sell its nine strong dry bulk fleet having started the sell-off in 2000, Crescent Group operations director, Kevin Hobbs, defended the withdrawal: with dry bulk freight rates insufficient to cover operational costs, Crescent was "very vulnerable being in the spot market" and the overall group performance was being damaged by the weak performance of the company's dry bulk fleet.[29] The move from Crescent's historic Kentish home to new premises in Southampton marked the evolution into a forward looking company, focused on the tanker trading operations of the future and withdrawing from the dry cargo operations of the past. The move also brought Crescent closer to one of its major customers, Esso, across Southampton Water at Fawley.

By 2005, the parent Clipper group controlled some 240 vessels worldwide. The increasing involvement of the parent company has enabled Crescent Tankships to concentrate on the premium clean petroleum trades, time charter and contracts of affreightment with the oil majors which ensure long run earnings. The purchase of the Wonsild tanker fleet in 2005 has consolidated Clipper Groups involvement in tankers. Prior to the Crescent takeover, Clipper had concentrated on the dry bulk and liner trades; by 2005 the Group's fleet was comprised of 51 tankers, 10 of which were drawn from the Crescent Fleet with an order book set to increase this number to 89.[30]

Company Portfolio as at 28.1.06

- Crescent Tankships 10 vessels, 1550-2500dwt range.

Company Status:

- Wholly owned subsidiary of Danish origin, Nassau based, Clipper Group.

Sample Oil Products Trades:

- Grangemouth-Scapa Flow;
- Fawley-New Ross;
- Whitegate- Drogheda.

6.2.5 Seacon Holdings

A late arrival to the Kentish cluster is that of the vessel chartering and wharfage and distribution specialist, Seacon. The Seacon Group adds a different dimension to the cluster. Set up in 1955 the Seacon operation began essentially as an inter-European collaboration between London based charterers and freight forwarders and German shipowner-captains. The regional specialisms of both parties provided for a forward thinking, entrepreneurial linkage. The London based commercial personnel utilised their expertise in the distributing of steel and timber products in the London area; the German shipowner-captains utilised their twin skills in not only the North Sea and German river networks, but also in obtaining capital for the building of new vessels. As an example, Captain Dahl of Cuxhaven obtained his masters ticket at the age of 21. This was followed rapidly by his venture into ship-owning. The resulting contract with Seacon extended to 19 years. Seacon has traditionally specialised in the storage and distribution of quality steel products and can claim UK leadership in building the first completely undercover steel handling terminal at Millwall, Isle of Dogs. Such investments did much to placate the concerns of the steel shippers. Keeping finished steel products protected from rain is a paramount concern of the suppliers as any ingress of water can corrode the product. Providing regular quasi-liner services to inland ports in Duisburg and Goole, Seacon increased their chartering operation to

12 vessels in the 1980s. However, a downturn in the demand for European steel led to rationalisations. With 60-70% of Seacon's freight being in the steel sector, the company found itself having to scale down its chartering operations. The steel terminal at Millwall became under-utilised. This fact, coupled with the lucrative offers for land sales to the property market, led to Seacon selling the Millwall Terminal and moving downstream to the Kentish location, Northfleet. It is evident that Seacon's decision was influenced by the gentrification process, as waterside accommodation became increasingly "des-res" in Greater London. However, the company has continued to diversify. Its acquisition of Tower Wharf in Northfleet has enabled it to maintain its under-cover steel handling service. In addition, Tower Wharf is served by two other berths, one capable of accommodating 50,000dwt vessels.

In 2001 the plc Seacon Holdings became de-listed from the London Stock Exchange; and this process facilitated a re-focusing strategy, away from direct ship operations and into terminal operations. The downturn in the steel market signalled the need to diversify into new markets, including ships agency and the buy out of the specialist forestry terminal operator, Stanton Grove in 2004. This has spread the Seacon organisation to Liverpool, Tilbury, Sheerness and Newcastle.

Company Portfolio as at 4.6.05:

- Operation of 4 chartered vessels, 1800-2130dwt range;
- Operation of Tower Wharf, Northfleet – 3 berths, including covered steel terminal and deepsea berth;
- Timber and paper terminal operations – Liverpool, Newcastle, Tilbury, Sheerness.

Company Status:

- Private limited company; majority family holdings.

Sample Steel Trades:

- Duisburg-Goole;
- Dunkerque-Northfleet;
- Ijmuiden-Northfleet.

6.2.6 Scotline

With its new timber terminal in Rochester, a recent addition to the Kentish cluster is the Essex based Scotline. The company is fairly new to shortsea operations, commencing with a timber service between the Swedish port, Varberg and Inverness in 1979. Scotline proved to be an early supporter of the UK Tonnage Tax scheme; and this has facilitated modernisation and growth in the Scotline fleet. The importance of new tonnage was heralded by company MD, Peter Millatt, in 2003. On taking delivery of two new vessels, capable of 13.5 knots, as opposed to the existing fleet's 10-11 knot vessels, a step change in the efficiency of the Scotline fleet was applauded. The Inverness registered *Scot Venture* and the Rochester registered *Scot Mariner*, were at least a 1000dwt size increase on other ships in the fleet and as a consequence were better able to cope with sea conditions in the North and Irish Seas; an essential factor if the integrity of the wintertime liner schedule is to be sustained. Mr Millatt welcomed the fact that "Transit times and reliability are both much improved," particularly in the booming sawn timber trades into Northern Ireland and a new return cargo appeared to be opening up, with the back-loading sawn logs and woodchips to Scandinavia.[31]

Following the 1996 opening of its Rochester terminal, Scotline's business has soared. By 2001, the company was handling 400,000 cubic metres of timber per annum and was desperately searching for room to expand. In 2000, £500,000 was invested on two new cranes in order to speed up discharging. With the Rochester Terminal handling between three and four vessels per week, the plight of Scotline is typical of the challenges facing many British shipping and port operators. In searching for quality cargo-handling and storage space, which allows for the provision of all-weather timber and paper handling facilities, Scotline faces the problem of an encroaching property spread on the verge of the Outer London commuting zone. However, by March 2005, the company was able to announce the addition of a second berth and a new 3000 square metre storage shed at its Rochester terminal.[32]

Company Portfolio as at 2.2.06

- Operator/owner of 10 vessels (8 owned directly) in the 1700-3200dwt range;
- Timber terminals in Inverness, Goole and Rochester.

Company Status:

- Subsidiary of Intrada Ship Management, a private limited company based in Romford, Essex.

Sample Timber/PaperTrades:

- Riga–Inverness;
- Varberg-Rochester;
- Varberg-Wicklow;
- Corpach-Varberg.

6.2.7 Cory Environmental

Based on the River Thames at Charlton, Cory Environmental is one of the oldest members of the Kentish Cluster. As the principal operator of Thames waste transportation, Cory has a long history in the London lighterage trades. Cory has a rich maritime pedigree as part of one of Britain's largest shipping groupings, Ocean Transport and Trading. Within this group such world famous lines as Blue Funnel, Glen Line and Elder Dempster were key players in deepsea trades to Australia, New Zealand, the Far East and West Africa. Towage and lighterage was vertically integrated into this business network. Cory's towage and environmental operation proved to be the last survivors of this maritime empire.

Cory's London history was primarily focused on the movement of domestic coal into and around the Capital. Keenan's 1997 study of Cory's Thames operations, *The Fires of London: A History of the Thames lighterage operations of William Cory & Son Ltd*,[33] traces the history of the company from the 17th century onwards. The boom in demand for coal in the 19th century was facilitated by the growth of London and the expansion of steam power in industry and transport. In 1896 an amalgamation of seven other firms into William Cory & Son plc created one of the world's largest fuel handling firms. Cory's became a major player on the "Route One" coal trades of the East Coast.

Table 29 illustrates the extent of Cory's London and Medway cargo handling and transhipment assets at the end of the 19th century. It can be seen that the characteristics of a vertically integrated logistics provider was well developed by this period. In addition, Keenan found that the newly created plc also possessed "hordes" of railway wagons, horses and carts and a steam collier fleet which totalled 42,000 tons capacity.[34] Gradually, as the parent company diversified and divested away from deepsea shipping and eventually towage, the Thames waste operators proved to be the last area of marine related activity within the ex-Ocean Trade and Transport shipping empire.

No	Capital Assets
	Table 29: William Cory & Son Thames–Medway Assets, 1896
13	Wharves on the Thames and Medway
2	Floating coal discharging derricks
3	Tug coaling stations
2	Barge building and engineering works (Charlton and Erith)
11	Sea going lighters
21	Steam tugs
1200	Barges
42	Coal depots
25	Stables

Source: Keenan, K.E. (1997) *The Fires of London: A History of the Thames Lighterage Operations of William Cory & Son Ltd.* Keenan: Waldron, East Sussex. p.20.

As the coal trade declined, Cory's has diversified into the logistics of waste. Although the company is highly committed to the use of the Thames, its primary function has been that of a logistics provider of which the tug and barge operations are just one facet of the operation. Nevertheless, the company did invest (1998) in the first new barge handling tug on the Thames in fifty years, *Regain*. Forming a subsidiary of the third-party logistics provider, Exel Logistics, Cory Environmental became one of the UK's leading specialists in the waste trades. The £700m contract was won by Cory in 2002 to transport waste by water for the next thirty years demonstrates remarkably joined up organisational thinking from the London Boroughs, Wandsworth, Kensington & Chelsea, Lambeth, Hammersmith & Fulham. This was facilitated by the creation of the Western Riverside Waste Authority joint venture, with waste transfer sites at Wandsworth and Battersea. In April 2005, the company underwent a management buy-out with "White Knight" support of £200m from Montague Private Equity Finance Group.[35]

Despite the success of this water based logistics solution, the future was not looking secure in 2005. The threat to the waste flows by river has been the difficulty in finding a substitute for the land-fill operations at the appropriately named Mucking, Essex, some 50kms downstream from London. This 450 acre site, which has taken around 20% of the capital's waste for decades, was close to reaching its end as a reception for London's rubbish: changes in European legislation will prevent land-fill after 2007 when Mucking's planning permission is terminated.[36]..

The future of one of the last barge trades on the Thames was jeopardised by the uncertainty over building a new river-served energy-from-waste plant. traffic Cory had developed plan for the development of a multi-million pound incinerator which will process 585,000 tonnes of rubbish per year and generate 72 MW of electricity. Cory had outlined its intentions over a 10 year period but the

272

politics of incinerators do not easily lend to rapid decision making. The problem was that the site of the riverside incinerator in Belvedere, in the London Borough of Bexley, is not to everyone's liking. The Belvedere site, like another 50 such incinerator sites across Britain, was delayed awaiting a government decision. Following two lengthy public inquiries, a recommendation to accept Cory's proposals was made to the Secretary of State at the Department of Trade and Industry in June 2006.[37]

The consequences for the city are considerable. At present, Cory Environmental's six tugs and 47 barges take 440 lorry journeys off London's roads per day. The potentially damaging impact to the Mayor of London's strategy to reduce road traffic was substantial had the proposal been prevented. The continued success of this well developed example of water-based logistics – with a 100 skilled river workers futures - was secured in Summer 2006, when after 14 years and three public inquiries, Energy Minister, Malcolm Wicks gave permission for the Belvedere Energy from Waste plant to proceed.[38]

Company Portfolio as at 2.2.06 (Lighterage Division):
- six tugboats and 47 barges;
- Barge repair yard.

Company Status:
- "White Knight" supported Management Buy-Out from Exel Logistics (April 2005).

Cory Trades:
- Battersea-Mucking, Essex, containerised collection, river transportation and land-fill/incineration of London waste;
- future service of London waste transportation to Belvedere energy-from-waste station.

6.2.8 Kentish Cluster Summary

In summarising the evidence on business behaviour within the "Kentish Cluster," it is obvious that the London market has proved instrumental to shaping shipping activation in this vicinity. The demise of the river and creek trades has forced the traditional owners to diversify into more distant trades. Pressure on riverside land-space has increasingly registered as a problem for operators.

Whilst Scotline have increased their activities in the Medway area with the expansion of their timber wharfage at Rochester, old established shortsea operators from the same port, Thomas Watson Shipping, withdrew from shipping activities in the early 2000s, citing falling earnings.[39] The fate of Lapthorn's was almost identical.

6.3 Profiling Irish Shipping

The importance of shipping to Ireland has been endorsed by the growing maritime lobby in Ireland. Irish companies have always participated in the Anglo-Irish trades, however these were somewhat controlled by British shipping lines. The increased participation of Ireland within the European Union has presented opportunities for direct services to the Continent as well as the traditional trades with Britain. Two major fleets dominate the Irish Register; Irish Ferries with its subsidiaries in the container trades – Eucon Shipping & Transport Ltd, Eurofeeders and Feederlink – and Arklow Shipping.

In addition to these leading operators, the salutary case of the dramatic rise and fall of the Netherlands-Irish company, Bell Lines, is considered.

6.3.1 The Bell Lines Debacle

The initial objective for this chapter was to profile existing carriers. However, as more information on the history of Bell Lines was uncovered the more it became evident that this company's experience had significant implications for the Green Highway. It is difficult now to envisage that the early convert to containerisation, Ireland's Bell Line, along with the Port of Waterford, set the pace in European shortsea shipping for several years. One *Lloyd's List* heading rather sums up the roller-coaster experience of the company: "From triumph to disaster, a story of a line that led the field but lost its way"[40] At the very out-set of containerisation in 1963, Bell Lines opened its first office in Waterford and began trading to Liverpool and Preston. In those days container capacity was quite modest with the 22teu *Astarte* chartered in to operate the service. By 1990, the pace of design and technology had moved on considerably and Bell Lines were to consolidate their reputation as market leader in the European shortsea trades with the delivery of the world's first hatchless container ship, the 300 teu, *Bell Pioneer*. Shortsea correspondent, David Tinsley, acknowledged the innovatory leadership that this ship gave the company:

> Bell Lines, one of the pioneers of containerisation in the shortsea trades, has phased a highly advanced, unconventional design of box vessel into its North European service framework.[41]

The revolutionary, Japanese built vessel maintained a normal service speed of 14.5 knots and a 15-20% reduction in port turnround time (as a result of the hatchless arrangement) gave Bell Lines the edge in an intensively competitive market. Trade on the Irish-continental route had been growing and the company's investment programme in its Netherlands Terminal was to further enhance the quality of the express Waterford-Rotterdam service.[42] What was to become a pan-European Freight transport group, Bell Lines confirmed its long association with Waterford and operated from the port's Belview Terminal. In 1996 Bell

Lines offered a seven-days-a-week, door-to-door service to the UK and continental Europe made up of 13 sailings per week: 4 to Bristol, 2 to Belfast/Greenock, 2 to France (Radicatel), 2 to Spain (Bilbao) and 3 to Rotterdam. Bell Lines Director, Pat Hayden praised Waterford's port's labour force, acknowledging the efficiencies of handling the 13 weekly sailings with just two cranes and a five-man shift team. [43]

Prior to reforms within the Port of Dublin, the Waterford option was seen as an attractive way of avoiding the delays and cost associated with labour disputes. The Port enjoyed a "Felixstowe of the Irish Sea" status in that it was not shackled by any of the management-union entrenchment of the more established ports. The use of rail express inter-modal container services to Dublin gave Bell Lines and the Port of Waterford a competitive edge. This inter-modal operation provided a clear leadership in sustainable logistics, minimising road tkm and maximising rail and sea transport. In retrospect, it is evident that the collapse of the service has had a damaging impact on Irish Rail's freight network.

The year 1996 started promisingly; however, a series of un-foreseeable misfortunes were to bring down the company. In late October a gust of wind forced two unsecured container cranes together, causing catastrophic damage and, ergo, the costly diversion of ships to Cork and Dublin.[44] The impact of the Channel Tunnel was to have mixed blessings. Bell Lines were involved in inter-modal operations from day one of the Tunnel opening and were quick to develop the "Bell Express" service between Manchester and Milan.[45] However, the pressure on North Sea rates, where Bell Lines were also heavily committed, brought about by the alternative route to Europe via the Tunnel caused the company cash flow problems. Intense competitive pressure on the Irish Sea routes did not help Bell's plight. The demise of Bell Lines had the immediate effect of stranding over a 1000 containers in transit, 600 direct jobs were lost, over a 100 Waterford truckers – many of whom were totally committed to Bell Lines

276

contracts – were seriously damaged financially and Irish rail lost a major customer and the future of rail-freight services to Waterford were jeopardised.[46]

As a post-script, the collapse of Bell Lines, which, in the words of *Lloyd's List* Port's correspondent, Tom MacSweeney, had shaken "…the operation of Waterford Harbour to its foundations"[47] took almost eight years to recover from. Benefiting from the Irish Government's assistance - guaranteeing of accumulated debts – the port was well on the way to revival by the early years of the Millennium. Shipping lines such as Seawheel and Maersk subsidiary, Norfolk Line, have committed themselves to Waterford. In 2003 Norfolk Line, which operates a thrice weekly service to Rotterdam, consolidated its commitment with the naming of the 600teu new container vessel, *Maersk Waterford,* and in 2004 it was reported that container liftings were up to 180,000teu, surpassing the performance pre-Bell collapse.[48]

The evidence from what was referred to in the Irish Parliament as, the "Bell Lines debacle,"[49] shows how even in busy times the best of shipping companies can be vulnerable to market pressures, cash flow slippages and operational accidents. The Bell Lines connection provided the Port of Wexford with 40% of Irish container trades and was of strategic importance to the South East region and proved a Green Highway alternative to the RoRo ferry services of the more central routes.

6.3.2 The Irish Continental Group

The Irish Continental Group (ICG) has its roots in the now defunct, national Irish company, Irish Shipping Ltd. Prior to 1942, Ireland had lacked a major flag line, particularly in deepsea shipping. The political and logistical exigencies of WW2 forced the Irish Government to act on the creation of a national fleet. As a result of the German submarine and aircraft blockade of British coastal waters and the Anglo-Irish dispute over Ireland's strictly neutral status, British ships were ordered to withdraw from Irish trades.[50] The shortage of coal for Irish Railways, shipping and industry was an immediate result of the trade embargo. The conditions were ripe for the development of a national shipping line, the Irish Shipping Line resulted. A sizeable, modern and well found fleet was built up in the post WW2 period. It was to be the cash flow crisis of the 1980s, however, that brought the downfall of Irish Shipping Ltd. The national line had built up a modern fleet of bulk carriers and tankers in the 1960-70s period, however the collapse in freight rates in the early 1980s led to a financial crisis at a time when the line was committed to a new building programme.[51] As a survivor of its parent company's collapse, ICG was able to focus on RoRo passenger and freight services offering Irish shippers direct access to the European Mainland but

also via the UK landbridge. In 2005, Irish Ferries offered direct services to France and intensive services to the UK. The Irish Ferries timetable consisted of:

- Cherbourg 3 x Weekly
- Rosslare – Pembroke 2 x Daily
- Rosslare – Roscoff 2 x Weekly
- Dublin – Holyhead 6 x Daily

The RoRo services offer freight shippers direct access to the European Mainland but also via the UK landbridge. The ICG group suffered a 42% first half fall in pre-tax profits in 2003 as fewer passengers booked services. Irish Ferries saw annual passenger numbers falling by 5.1% to 750,000 in 2003, although this was partly compensated by a 5% rise in RoRo freight loadings, further evidence of the endurance of the road-ferry shortsea option.[52] The economic problems of operating a relatively high cost, Irish flagged, Irish crewed, ferry operation became apparent in the company's 2004 Annual Report, which outlined a 48% fall in profits. Interestingly, whilst passenger numbers fell by 7.4% and cars by 5.7%, the freight market went up by 1.5%, with a record number of trucks, 204,000 carried.[53] The events of late 2005 provided further evidence of the difficulties facing the operator. When management attempted to replace Irish national seafarers with lower cost East Europeans, all sailings were halted. The incumbent Irish crews occupied strategic parts of their vessels and embarked on a lengthy strike. This resulted in the suspension of sailings for a period of over two weeks and the company losing an estimated €11m.[54]

Intense competitive trading conditions persisting on the Irish Sea may also be seen to have influenced the market behaviour of ICG's shortsea container shipping subsidiary lines, Eucon Shipping & Transport and Eurofeeders. Both lines aligned themselves in a vessel sharing agreement (VSA) with Mersey Dock and Harbour Company's (now Mersey Ports) subsidiary, BG Freight Line. Pooling capacity was seen as the rationale for this alignment and the two parties were able to claim this would offer only benefits for shippers. The new partners agreed to share routes linking North West Mainland Europe, Ireland and Great Britain and, according to Liam Lacey, ICG's Managing Director, Container Division, the new arrangement increased efficiency, reduced costs and improved services.[55] Mr. Lacey claimed that, "From a customer perspective, there has been an improvement in both schedule and level of service, with more reliability and more frequency," adding the arrangement would "inevitably squeeze costs out of the system".[56]

The new agreement was immediately consolidated by the addition of two new vessels – *BG Ireland* and *Eucon Progress* to the Ireland-continental trades. The VSA provided a Green Highway linkage to the UK and Continental Europe via the co-ordination of 13 vessels. These connect the ports of Dublin, Cork and Belfast to Southampton, Felixstowe, Le Havre, Antwerp and Rotterdam. The core of the service is based around six sailings a week in each direction between Dublin and Rotterdam, plus increased peak capacity on all routes linking Dublin, Cork and Belfast to the continental ports of Antwerp and Le Havre. Given the difficulties in the passenger/RoRo trades, the LoLo business has looked increasingly attractive to ICG.

VSA Company Portfolio as at 1.2.06:

- 13 Shortsea Container Ships.

VSA Company Status:

- ICG, Listed Dublin Stock Exchange; MDHC London Stock Exchange.

Sample Container Trades:

- Rotterdam-Cork-Dublin;
- Rotterdam-Felixstowe-Belfast;
- Rotterdam-Dublin-Warrenpoint;
- Antwerp-Cork-Dublin.

6.3.3 Arklow Shipping

In chapter 3 the importance of the Arklow fleet to the Irish Register was stressed. Arklow Shipping, can claim a truly European success in the dry bulk trades and also as the premier fleet sailing under the Irish flag. The Irish East Coast Port of Arklow has a long history of Irish Sea operations. Historically, Arklow's position as a major fishing port was supplemented by merchant shipping following the discovery and exploitation of copper 10kms up-stream on the River Avoca. The merchants of the area were quick to promote the Port of Arklow plus a shipping community under the traditional 1/64th share system.[57] By the end of the 19th century some 80 trading vessels were based in the port.[58] Arklow schooners provided an important link between the region's pyrites supplies and the major chemical installations of Merseyside and Mid-Cheshire.[59] The eventual decline of this trade brought the need to rationalise fleets.

This became apparent in the 1960s as new tonnage replaced motorised schooners and steamships. The established Arklow shipowning family, Tyrrell, promoted the idea of an umbrella management organisation for the co-ordination of the Arklow fleets in 1966.[60]

The growth in ownership and management of the Arklow fleet has projected the Irish company into the major league of North European dry bulk shipping. The 2003-4 delivery of three new builds from Japan in the 13,800-14,000dwt category has allowed for Arklow to compete in a larger ship sector in European markets. The three 13.3 knot vessels, *Arklow Wave, Arklow Wind* and *Arklow Willow,* possess a 2 knot speed advantage over the rest of the Arklow fleet, which tends to be much smaller, in the 3000-4000dwt range.

Arklow's trading pattern typically lies in the Amsterdam-English Channel-Irish Sea-Shannon Estuary arc. Alumina flows from the Shannon port, Auginish to the Alcan Alumina Plant in Blyth provide regular bulk cargoes for the three larger vessels. Additionally, the grain flows from Western France to the Cerestar Mill in Manchester supports a regular and intensive service, often balanced by scrap loadings from Manchester to the Spanish port of Pasajes. In the February 2002 survey of British and Irish traffics (Appendix 1), Arklow ships were noted on the following trades, Llanddulas-Newhaven (stone) and Workington-Limerick (steel).

This short profile of Arklow Shipping serves to illustrate the symbiotic effect of traditional shipping expertise and enterprise, a supportive investment community and a favourable maritime policy.

Company Portfolio as at 2.2.06:

- 37 owned and managed Irish and Netherlands flag vessels in the 3000-13000dwt range;
- Operating and chartering offices in Arklow and Rotterdam.

Company Status:

- Private limited company.

Sample Trades:

- Bordeaux-Tilbury, grain;
- Drogheda-Sharpness, cement;
- Briton Ferry-Drogheda, crushed slag.[61]

6.4 Carisbrooke Shipping

The Isle of Wight based Carisbrooke Shipping has achieved a rapid growth history recently. Following the founding of the company in 1969 by the late Mark Croucher with the purchase of the 30-year-old, 250dwt general/bulk carrier *Vectis Isle*, the Roman name for the Isle of Wight, the company has enjoyed a rare growth profile in British shipping. In the same year as Mark Croucher's purchase, Dutch Captain Willem Wester, having gained his master's ticket in 1968 at the age of 25, bought a ship, the 330 dwt *Anja*. Working as 'owner-driver', he fixed the ship into time charter and within two years paid off all the debts incurred in buying and refurbishing the vessel. Isle of Wight trading connections brought the two men together. In 1972, Captain Wester sold *Anja* and joined forces with Mr Croucher, who had become by this time Managing Director of an expanding Carisbrooke Shipping. Another ship was purchased, Captain Wester became a shareholder and continued to sail as master.[62] The partnership of business and operational skills provided a strong foundation for growth.

In the 1980s, Carisbrooke became a leading shipping proponent of the Business Expansion Scheme (BES) and following this in 1996 Carisbrooke Shipping plc became the first pure shipping company entrance into the London Stock Exchange's Alternative Investment Market (AIM). In 1996, *Lloyd's Shipping Economist* offered the opinion that the AIM listing gave previous BES investors, plus new investors, a stake in one of Europe's leading mini-bulker fleets. The intention was to induce up to £2m in investment funds.[63] By 1999, however, the company was returned to private ownership with a £5m management buy out.[64] In several ways the company has a continental organisational profile in that it combines localised trading expertise with an entrepreneurial Captain-shipowner fleet. Many of the vessels in the 29 strong fleet are owned by single or two ship companies. Flags flown by the Carisbrooke fleet include British, Isle of Man, Swiss and the Netherlands. In addition to the existing fleet, Carisbrooke's website in 2005 showed an expansion of seven new builds in the 10,500-13,400 range.[65] The size of this new wave of tonnage makes it clearly evident that the company is intent on spreading its risk by venturing into deepsea markets. Diversification into larger bulk carriers up to 19,000dwt has enabled worldwide trading patterns.

Carisbrooke has earned a preferred carrier status in the steel trades, including steel coil exports from the Corus plants of South Wales. The history of the company exudes a willingness to creatively innovate. In October 2005, Captain Wester outlined the target market of the new buildings which: "will be used on the marine highways of the European coast to move steel products, paper and other cargo." In August 2006 it was reported in *Tradewinds* that Carisbrooke had some 13 vessels on order in Chinese shipyards.[66]

Company Portfolio as at 2.2.06:
- 36 owned/managed bulk carriers, 3,300-19,465dwt range.

Company Status:
- Private limited company, based in Cowes, Isle of Wight

Sample Shortsea Trades:
- Liege-Poole, steel;
- Teignmouth-Leixoes; china clay;
- Llanddulas-Dagenham, stone.

6.5 James Fisher & Sons PLC

The history of Fisher's is very much an integral part of the industrial development of the Barrow in Furness region. Just as the collier companies had their roots in the North East-Thames coal trade and the Kentish owners were instrumental in London's foodstuffs, beer and materials supply chain, Fisher's were to become synonymous with the industrial demands of the Furness Peninsula. Nigel Watson's definitive history of the company, *Around the Coast and Across the Seas: The Story of James Fisher and Sons,*[67] traces the transition of the traditional farming family into successful ship owners. The rapid development of the Barrow region in the early days of the railway led Industrial Revolution also provided opportunities for shipping. The area's rich deposits of haematite ore became intensively mined in order to serve the burgeoning iron and steel trades. In 1800 only 11,000 tons of ore were mined; by 1867 this had grown to 670,000 tons and therefore the conditions proved conducive for the Fisher family's move into the booming shipping industry.[68] The railway and shipping linkages to the hitherto isolated mineral riches of the Furness Peninsula also promoted a dramatic population influx into Barrow, a town which was to become known as the "English Chicago" as a result of its wild, reckless, laissez-faire nature. In this "Klondyke" environment, the mixture of farming community resilience, entrepreneurial dynamism and acquired financial acumen in shipping led to Fisher's undergoing a rapid fleet development in the late 19th century.

The nature of the ore and steel trades meant that Fisher traditionally maintained a strong presence in the dry cargo trades. However, diversification and a capital deepening of the shipping fleet were to point the way to survival. In 1948 the Fisher steamer, *Pool Fisher,* was involved in such trades as sugar, Grimsby-London, barley, Plymouth-Belfast, coal, Swansea-Amsterdam, fertiliser, Ghent-Southampton, cement, London-Kircaldy. However, the vessel's earnings amounted to just £4500.[69] By way of contrast, the specialist ships *Sea Fisher* and

Race Fisher earned more than £52,000 between them in the same year. It is also of interest to note that the *Sea Fisher* was an early proponent of inter-modalism and the containerisation process, servicing a British Rail charter to ship containers across the Irish Sea between Heysham and Belfast.[70] The company went public in 1952 in order to avoid the financial burden of death duties and as a way of securing the future of the diversifying company.[71] The specialisation process was enhanced by the group's takeover of the Liverpool based Coe-Metcalfe tanker fleet in 1984 and the P&O Tankship fleet in 1996. The inherited fleet had a long pedigree in the tanker trades. Having bought into the Rowbotham tanker fleet, P&O and later Fisher's, were to benefit from the takeover of one of the early market leaders in UK and Irish tanker trades.[72] Diversification has been a major strength in Fisher's investment strategy, contributing to longevity in shipping. The current fleet is comprised of highly specialised sectors – nuclear reactor carriers, cable ships – as well as oil products tankers.

It is of interest to note that Fisher's, along with Everard's and Crescent, announced their withdrawal from the dry cargo trades in 2002. The emphasis appears to be on the stable earnings of the clean petroleum market and high value added activities. These are composed of cable laying activities and marine support services. Both mark a conscious diversification strategy away from low value dry bulk shipping. The cable laying activities are linked to the global telecoms market. Figure 36 illustrates (and vindicates) the diversification strategy, with marine services managing over 40% return on capital employed, cableships over 15% and tankships in the 11% region. The marine services sector provides specialist services, including the management of the UK Ministry of Defence's Strategic Sealift Service. Strong local ties can be detected in Fisher's collaboration with the North West England based British Nuclear Fuels Limited(BNFL). The 1997 product tanker new buildings, *Thames Fisher* and *Mersey Fisher* were both constructed at the local shipyard, Vickers of Barrow-in-Furness. In 2002, it was reported that 80% of Fisher's 23 strong tanker fleet was operating under Contract of Affreightment arrangements with oil majors, including Chevron and Shell. This amounts to some 30% of all clean oil movements around the UK coastline.[73]

Figure 36: Fisher's Segmented return on Capital Employed. (Jan-June 2002)

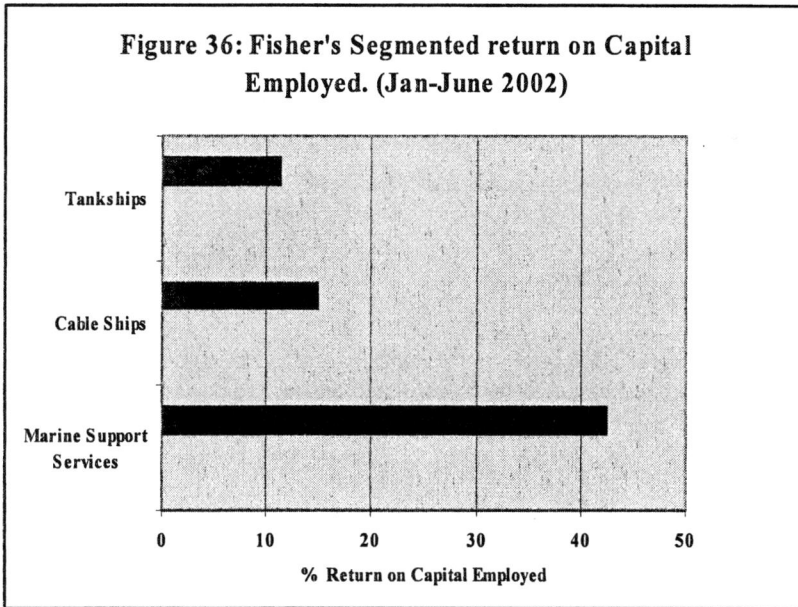

Source: *Lloyd's Shipping Economist,* Vol.24. November 2002. p. 36

Fisher's have been a major supporter of the UK Tonnage Tax and this has allowed them to long-term charter the 1997 built, 14,122dwt *Pembroke Fisher*, thus providing for a major contribution to the tanker fleet. This increase in vessel size (Fisher's tankship fleet averages around 4500dwt) gives Fisher's the ability to compete in a larger tonnage range, particularly against Scandinavian operators. At the time of writing, the takeover of F.T. Everard (see above p. 254) has led to an 11 vessel increase in the Fisher fleet. This can only enhance the market strength and performance of the company. In December 2006, reporting on the £23.7m takeover, *Tradewinds* offered the opinion that:

> The deal will give Fisher a predominantly modern double-hull fleet to add to its own fleet of products tankers, and perhaps more importantly provide cash flow with which to expand its marine support services.[74]

Company Portfolio as at 6.12.06:

- Tankships: 27 vessels, 2000-14,000dwt range;
- Marine support services: Ship management, Underwater services;
- Heavy- Lift operations;
- Cableships: three ships.

Company Status:

- Barrow in Furness based, Plc listed London Stock Exchange.

Sample Oil Products Trades:

- Whitegate–Eastham;
- Stanlow–Derry;
- Pembroke–Cardiff.

6.6 Stephenson Clarke

This Newcastle based bulk carrier owner has strong roots in the North Sea collier trades. The company has claims to being the UK's oldest shipping firm[75] and at one stage in the 19th century operated 120 ships on East Coast collier routes. As a consequence, the demise of this market was bound to have serious repercussions and it will be seen tough business decisions have been forced on the company. The disappearance of the coal trades out of North East ports has necessitated diversification into new markets. In the 1960s, the company operated around 40 vessels, primarily in the East Coast, Route One, coal trades. Stephenson Clarke was one of the first of the UK coastal operators to invest in vessels over 3500dwt. The resulting economies of scale of vessels in the

12,000dwt range has allowed for entrance into the Polish coal markets, as well as stone and cement clinker movements in the Baltic and Mediterranean and Black Sea. The 12,000dwt vessels, *Donnington* and *Durrington* were both observed in the sample survey (Appendix 1), operating in the Aughinish-Blyth alumina trade.

The company became a subsidiary of bulk terminals operator, Powell Duffryn, in 1928 and in 1992 a controlling interest was sold to Anchorjade, an investment group based in the Channel Islands. The remaining interest was sold to the group in July 1994. In 1997 the company was responsible for some 160 sea-going personnel. On the 1997 takeover of Stephenson Clarke by the Southampton based International Maritime Group (IMG), a healthy five years profit record was reported, despite the slump in North Sea freight rates. At the time of the takeover Stephenson Clarke's Managing Director David Watkins said his company, under IMG ownership, would be in a position to offer turnkey solutions in partnership with other IMG companies. It would be able to provide both shipment of bulk products and the infrastructure to handle the goods on site.[76] The takeover brought together an interesting combination of traditional shipowning with a fast growing services provider with a desire to enter into freight logistics. Since IMG's 1992 creation, the company has achieved rapid growth through acquisition of consultancy and advisory businesses in the marine and civil engineering fields. At the time of the takeover, maritime services entrepreneur and founder of IMG, Barrie Gilmour, demonstrated a strong belief in the potential of intra-regional traffic in Europe. This was reflected in the takeover of Stephenson Clarke's fleet of bulkers, accompanied by a projected move into shortsea terminal and port operations on a direct ownership basis. Bringing Stephenson Clarke and its associated companies into the IMG fold was seen as an ideal strategic fit by executive chairman, Mr. Gilmour:

> It provides a useful vehicle for the release of synergy throughout the group in relation to ship and maritime operations and creates opportunities for new routes and services.[77]

The buy out of Stephenson Clarke was at the time seen as a manifestation of optimism, commitment and belief in the expertise inherent in the UK shortsea sector. In the article "Stephenson Clarke purchase fulfils IMG founders dream", *Lloyd's List* shortsea correspondent David Tinsley saw that IMG were intent on achieving competitive advantage via the utilisation of the rich vein of maritime expertise that prevailed in traditional British companies.[78]

Despite this avowal of faith in British shipping, by 1999 economic necessities had led to Stephenson Clarke having to "flag out" their vessels to flags of convenience, with British national officer and ratings replaced by lower labour cost, East European crews. The loss of contract, as a result of open registry competition, to move coal between the Clyde Estuary port, Hunterston, to Northern Ireland ports was to force a re-think by management. A process of flagging out of ships and replacing British crews with Polish nationals was seen as a way of reducing labour costs by 30%.[79] The seafarers' union, Railway and Maritime Workers Union (RMT), was particularly scathing in its criticism of the "crewing out" process, accusing the Isle of Man registry of allowing "flag of convenience" standards.[80] The company pointed to the inevitability that such changes were a reality of the globalised market and the tough competitive conditions in existence in the coastal and shortsea trades, admitting that reluctantly:

> We have always been very keen to support the British registry...We have no alternative but to pursue this route...We are very disappointed, but we all live in a commercial world.[81]

Again this shows the extent of the intense competition in the dry-bulk trades, illustrating the difficulties facing UK operators. The survival of "Britain's oldest shipping line," demonstrates the tenacity of the coasting tradition. However, it most also be noted that sustaining the hitherto domestically focused firm has required a break from tradition. The moves to larger ships enabled an extended international trade range and switches in flag and crew supplies has been seen as a necessity in order to survive in dry-bulk trades.

Company Portfolio as at 11.11.06

- 13 owned/managed bulk carrier vessels;
- Ship's agency and freight forwarding in North East ports.

Company Status

- Private limited company.

Sample Trades:

- Auginish-Blyth, alumina;
- Narvik-Dunkerque; iron ore;
- Antwerp–Medway, coal.

6.7 Borchard Lines

With 13 container vessels, Borchard Lines has become a major player in the North European shortsea and Mediterranean container trades. Based in London, this company has had a turbulent history. The Borchard family have strong origins in the Hamburg shipping community and are still operating the renowned Hamburg and Rotterdam tug operator, Fairplay Towage. The family's emigration to the UK in the 1930s. along with their fleet of steam tugs, initiated a British based shortsea enterprise. As a consequence, a valuable contribution to the allied cause was made in terms of both capital and maritime expertise. In the post 1945 period, the family were able to concentrate their business skills in the shortsea trades. Borchard Lines has become a leading UK based company, with the focus on weekly liner sailings in the London-Hamburg-Rotterdam-Antwerp-Gibraltar-Mediterranean ranges.

Growth and capital investment have become features of Borchard's strategy. Expansion came in 1989 when the company took over the ownership and services of Liverpool based Gracechurch Container Line Ltd, with its 5/6 day frequency container service linking Liverpool-Cardiff-Dublin-Belfast to Mediterranean Ports. In addition, Borchard operate Bosphorus and Western Mediterranean services. The company has concentrated on integration with numerous agents, a number of its own overseas offices and has specialised in through transport of containers from door to door. An increasing number of the containers and road transport vehicles used are fully owned by the Borchard Group of Companies. The age and performance profile of the Borchard Fleet was enhanced in 2001-2 with the fleet bolstered by 9 vessels offering speeds in the 18-20knot range.[82]

The firm has developed a niche shortsea and medium sea liner service. Integration with port agencies, freight forwarders and truck operators is obviously a strength of the family oriented company. Consistent investment in new tonnage has reaped benefits in terms of transit speed and the economies of scale accruing from larger vessels. The liner services provided by Borchard Lines offer a reliable, competitive, Green Highway alternative to long distance continental and inter-continental road haulage.

Company Portfolio as at 2.2.06

- 13 owned and managed vessels. 20,000 Containers. Road haulage fleet;
- Agencies in key North and South European;
- Ship management services.

Company Status:

- Family centred private limited company.

Sample Liner Trades:

- Gracechurch Lines West Mediterranean Service: Cardiff-Dublin-Liverpool-Leixoes-Piraeus-Limassol-Ashdod-Haifa-Salerno-Mersin.

6.8 Seawheel Limited

Ipswich based Seawheel has become a major provider of intermodal door-to-door logistics services throughout continental Europe. The company has a long and eventful history in the shortsea container business. This includes an attempted radical diversification into RoRo shipping and hasty return to its core LoLo traditions. The experience has provided a valuable insight into business behaviour in the shortsea industry. Further changes were set to occur when in 2005 the company was taken over by the expanding Icelandic Samskip Group. The investment focus at Seawheel has been on remaining "asset lite", chartering in rather than owning its 15 vessel fleet and co-ordinating haulage and stevedoring activities which are also contracted out to third party operators. Seawheel has focused its core business activities in the consolidation of container flows and is supported by offices in Dublin, Rotterdam, Duisburg, Hamburg and Antwerp. In addition, Seawheel operated a European agency network. The company owned and controlled its fleet of containers and flatracks and its dedicated IT system.

In March 2002 Seawheel acquired the Forthline LoLo service, operating between Grangemouth and Rotterdam, from Forth Ports Plc. This service completed Seawheel's network by adding this East Coast of Scotland route to Seawheel's European network. The future of Seawheel appeared to be taking a new direction when it was bought out by the port operator, Simon Group in 1998. The Simon Group had developed terminals in The Humber and in the East Coast port, Sutton Bridge. However, the results were not as anticipated and large losses were incurred. One particularly radical move following the take-over was the switch of Seawheel's LoLo Goole-Duisburg service to a RoRo Humber-Hamburg service. Such a shift was to have interesting ramifications for the Green Highway. The loss of traffic from the up-river ports of Goole and Duisburg meant increased road tkm. However, the switch had initially looked rather irresistible in terms of business synergy, economics and logistics – a seeming victory for economic rationality at the expense of environmental integrity. The reverse, however, turned out to be the case. In June 2000, Seawheel acquired the business of Cargo-Connect Transport Logistics GmbH (CCTL), a Hamburg-based operator of a door-to-door freight service using two chartered RoRo vessels between Rotterdam and the Humber. The CCTL business was focused on the Killingholme Humber Sea Terminal, a fully owned Simon Group terminal. The move was obviously attractive as it allowed for organizational synergy between Seawheel and the parent company, resulting in terminal cost savings. The move was also heralded as a way of saving vessel time and costs as the inland Port of Goole is some five hours up-stream from the Humber estuary. Given the additional voyage times, plus tidal window and size restrictions, the move towards the estuary was seen as a cost saving and efficiency exercise. Large RoRo ferries could be employed and tidal and draft restrictions avoided. The 18 knot, 7400dwt vessel, *Cupria*, which could achieve a 14 hour passage between the Humber and Rotterdam was seen as a more cost effective option; previously the Goole-Duisburg service had been undertaken by 13 knot, 2500dwt sea-river ships.

The switch from LoLo services signalled an emphasis on road haulage movements with RoRo operations minimizing the sea leg at both ends of the journey. Despite the apparent economic rationale for the switch, the optimism shown in 2002 by Seawheel executives notwithstanding, within less than twelve months the RoRo service was withdrawn and the up-river LoLo service re-instated back to Goole. The reality was that Seawheel suffered from increased charter rates, fuel consumption and port costs without a corresponding rise in revenue. As a consequence, the RoRo service contributed to Seawheel losses of £13.5m in 2002 and £10.0m in 2003.[83]

The losses that the Simon Group suffered in the 1998-2003 period were partly attributed to the Seawheel takeover and facilitated a £1 giveaway management buy out, which was seen as the best debt crisis solution in the interests of shareholders, whilst the re-structured Simon Group returned the focus to port terminals operations.[84] The return to Goole was welcomed by Seawheel MD, Alan Jones, as a re-affirmation of sea-river shipping's competitiveness, given the opportunities that exist in the LoLo market. In particular, Mr Jones has concentrated on the difficulties faced by hauliers and the rising costs they face: "at a time of truck driver shortages we have both the working time directive and European road tolls coming along."[85] With road haulage costs rising, Mr. Jones has proclaimed the economic and environmental benefits of sea-river shipping logistics such as the Goole-Duisburg route:

> In order to reduce that (road haulage) cost vessel operators will need to go further inland so that they can shuttle the goods between the ship and the customer. It is better for the environment and also makes economic sense. [86]

The return to Goole was also welcomed by the MD as its central inland location allowed for Seawheel's contracted hauliers to complete two round trips per day.[87] The Port of Goole is one of the UK's few genuinely inland nodes and is well placed for rail and road deliveries to the industrial Northern and Central England regions. Similarly, the Rhine port, as was demonstrated in chapter 3 (see above pp.115-9) shown Duisburg, offers a comprehensive inland logistics hub, based around river shipping and inter-modal operations situated in the heartlands of Germany's premier industrial region.

The financial difficulties facing Seawheel were ameliorated to some extent by the enhanced container carriage contract with the American owned medical supplies producer, Tyco Healthcare, which runs four plants in Ireland – Tullamore, Ballymoney, Athlone and Galway. The 1000 containers per year, door-to-door contract, to chemical plants in Belgium and Germany has significantly contributed towards reducing Ireland's heavy import-export container trade imbalance with continental Europe. Moreover, the export business helped to provide a two-way load revenue for Seawheel. As with the restoration of Goole services, the Irish business, facilitated by an intensive seven sailings per week schedule, has made a positive contribution to the Green Highway, by diverting container traffics away from truck-RoRo logistics. Despite the longer journey times, cost savings and service reliability were thought to be major considerations in Seawheel winning the contract.[88]

As verification of Seawheel's recovery, the company gained the prestigious *Lloyd's List* Shipping Line of the Year Award (shortsea sector) in 2005.[89] In 2005, Seawheel operated approximately 50 shortsea sailings per week with 14 vessels on charter. The 2005 takeover of Seawheel by Icelandic shipping and logistics conglomerate, Samskip, was welcomed in the sense that it helped alleviate the financial problems facing the company.[90] The takeover followed close on the heel of the same company's purchase of the Dutch door-to-door market leader, Geest Line-North Sea (to be discussed see below pp.). As a consequence, two major shortsea competitors were amalgamated into the Samskip organisation, offering an opportunity for consolidation and scale economies.[91]

The turbulent history of Seawheel and the company's trade success illustrates the resilience of the shortsea sector; it also demonstrates the vulnerability of firms to the financial risks inherent in highly competitive markets. From this perspective, the trends towards market consolidation should bring some degree of market stability. Furthermore, the return to the LoLo Goole-Duisburg route represents a tangible victory for the Green Highway as it results in a significant saving in lorry tkm.

Company Portfolio as at June 2005:

- 14 vessels in the 2200-3250dwt range.

Company Status:

- Subsidiary of Icelandic owned private limited company, Samskip.

Sample ContainerTrades:

- Rotterdam-Belfast   x3 per week;
- Greenock-Bilbao   x1;
- Tilbury-Rotterdam   x4.

6.9 Charles M. Willie & Co (Shipping) Ltd

The Cardiff shipowner, ship manager and terminals operator, Charles M. Willie has a coal trades and railfreight history. The business commenced in 1912 with the emphasis on coal exporting and timber (pit prop) imports. As a consequence, the future of Willie was linked to the survival of the South Wales coal industry. The demise of King Coal has necessitated an astute diversification into new markets. The company has been highly successful in niche areas – containers, steel and timber. The focus on Iberian and Baltic liner trades has provided Willie with growth opportunities in steel and timber transportation, storage and distribution. With in-house terminals in Cardiff and Howdendyke (River Ouse) and offices in several UK, Spanish, Portuguese and Baltic ports, Willie is able to offer integrated logistics packages with a mixture of owned, chartered and managed vessels. In addition to the fortnightly Cardiff and (less frequently Howdendyke) calls for the Spanish service, Willie's intensive Baltic timber service takes in Warrenpoint, Belfast, Wicklow Barry and Sharpness, as well as Cardiff. The Portuguese service includes calls at Mistley and Bromborough.

The involvement in terminals and the provision of ship management services, including the management of several ships of the Borchard Line, allows Willie to spread risks. The company employs and manages a mixture of British, Russian and Polish crews. Flags used are UK, Bahamas, Antigua and Barbuda. With services concentrated on a number of the smaller regional ports, including the up-river calls, Mistley and Howdendyke, Willie's provide shipping connections close to the final customer. As a consequence, sea-leg distances are maximised and road-leg distances minimised. Thus Green Highway benefits are secured. In May 2006 the Willie Group announced the addition of 5 new dry cargo vessels in the 2950-3400gt range, thus demonstrating commitment to the European, Scandinavian and Baltic trades.[92]

Company Portfolio as at 3.2.06:

- 16 owned/managed/chartered dry cargo vessels in 2300-5700dwt range;
- Terminal ownership and management; ship management;
- Port freight forwarding office and agency offices - Cardiff, Sharpness, Mistley, Bilbao, Leixoes, Lisbon, Riga.

Company Status:

- Private limited company.

Sample Liner Trades (general cargo):

- Riga-Barry;
- Bekkeri-Warrenpoint;
- Mistley-Leixoes.

6.10 Principal Continental Operators

The open market condition existing in British and Irish coastal and shortsea markets has proved conducive to competitive assault from niche continental and Scandinavian fleets. In the dry bulk and break-bulk sectors, German and Dutch operators have long enjoyed a strong competitive position in the British and Irish trades. This is explained by a number of factors: (1) the

German and Dutch shipbuilders and owners were generally more advanced in their switch from steam to diesel power – thus enjoying technological leadership over many British owners; (2) important shortsea shipping clusters – Duisburg, Bremen, Haren-Ems in Germany; Delfzijl, Groningen, Dordrecht, in the Netherlands – provide a conducive blend of shortsea shipping skills, enterprise and finance; (3) the KG system of raising capital from the small investor community, coupled with a supportive banking system ensures investment. In 1984, shortsea specialist David Tinsley, commenting on the doubling of shortsea capacity in Germany in a six year period, referred to how this:

> vivacious approach to small-ship trading encapsulates... a special kind of commercial and technical prowess in the shipping and shipbuilding communities and the shipping infrastructure.[93]

Two leading companies have been selected from the large German and Dutch shortsea fleets, Rhein Maas See (RMS) of Duisburg and Geest Line-North Sea of Rotterdam.

6.10.1 Rhein Maas und See Schifffahrtskontor GmbH (RMS)

RMS is a well known operator in many British and Irish ports. But, despite its size and renown, the company has experienced the usual ups and downs of the shortsea sector. In 1995, RMS' moves into container operations were abandoned in order to off-set heavy losses. The company has had a long association with Duisburg but this did not prevent the company being taken over by, firstly, the French logistics provider, Sanara, followed by the Goole based company, Alexglade in 1995, which attained 74.9% of RMS shares, the remainder being held by RMS managers. The purchase by Alexglade followed Sanara's financial difficulties caused by the collapse of Italian parent company, Tripcovich in 1994.[94] The link between RMS and Seawheel commenced in this period when RMS sold its container activities for DM5.1m ($3.57m) to United Transport

Container Holdings of Ipswich, the parent company of Seawheel. Identifying RMS's container services as the principal source of loss-making, their sell-off became an inevitable aspect of the company's survival strategy. The link with Seawheel was further reinforced in early 2005 when the former signed a long term deal to use the latter's Goole terminal for its Duisburg service.

Following the demise of RMS's container sector in 1995, it was announced that growth in the 114 strong fleet would be boosted by seven new buildings in the dry cargo sector.[95] However, the long term trend has been for fewer but larger ships. By 2005, the RMS fleet was made up of 75 ships, 29 of which are directly owned by RMS. The parent company is based in Duisburg, whilst RMS Europe is based in Goole. The inland terminal at Goole features under-cover steel handling facilities which underwent a 2005 £8m up-grade in partnership with port owner, ABP.[96]

The RMS group works as a loose federation of European operating, managing and port agency and port operation companies. David Tinsley has attributed the group's success to its focus on the key specifics of shortsea demand and supply. RMS' Duisburg pedigree facilitated access to the local Ruhr steel trades, achieving a "continuous dialogue with shippers." On the supply-side RMS has developed links with the family shipping businesses, investors and owner-masters of the Ems, Weser and Rhine.[97] Serving as an umbrella company for many small fleet and one ship companies operating under the KG system, the RMS banner provides cargo consolidation, operational efficiency and a sense of financial security. Additionally, many of the RMS ships feature dual registry and a complex investor-owner-manager organisational structure. As an example, the 1350dwt *RMS Homberg* has the following ownership and management aspects:

- Home port: Duisburg;
- Flag: Antigua and Barbuda;
- Owner: BWK Schiffsinvest GmbH & Co;
- Managing Owner: KG MS *RMS Homberg*, Duisburg.[98]

Company Portfolio as at 5.2.06:

- 75 ships, 42 of which sea-river ships in the 1500-3500dwt category.

Company Status:

- Holding Company for shipowners and investors.

Sample Trades:

- Duisburg-Goole, liner service;
- Hamburg-Drogheda, steel;
- Cork-Lubeck, shredded plastics.

6.10.2 Geest North Sea Line

Geest North Sea Line, with six vessels operating in the North Sea, plus three operating a Rotterdam-Ireland service, is a long way from being the Netherland's largest shortsea fleet. However, in terms of innovation and entrepreneurial drive Geest can truly claim to be a market leader within its field.

The North Sea venture grew from the Geest family's Caribbean reefer trades which emerged post 1953. The emphasis on fruit carriage in the shortsea trades proved conducive to Geest's entrance into incipient containerisation, late 1960s. Two areas where Geest have been particularly innovatory are: (1) container design; (2) promoting inter-modalism. Geest have pioneered the 45ft container in the shortsea trades. As opposed to the standard deepsea 40ft container, Geest pursued the 45ft container as a means to provide competitive advantage against Intra-European truck – RoRo ferry combinations. In 1966, Geest's first ship in the North Sea trades was the 10knot, 425dwt, *Geestdiep,* which moved 40 8x8x8ft fruit containers from Rotterdam to Ipswich.[99] In order to remain competitive, both containers and ships have increased in size, the latter have also increased in terms of speed. The two new additions to the fleet in 2004-5, *Geestroom* and *Geestdjik* are 18.5 knot, > 800teu vessels.

The family oriented firm has retained a sharp focus on technical development and the introduction of the 45ft pallet wide, container has helped to maintain leadership. The 2.5metre (pallet wide) container is able to accommodate two rows of the 1.2metre width Europallets, as opposed to the standard deepsea 2.3metre wide deepsea container which is, therefore, limited to one row. Additionally, the 45ft pallet wide container provides for three more pallets than the standard deepsea 40ft container and an extra 10 cubic metres of space. The 45ft container (13.5metres) also closely matches the length of the 13.6 metre road trailer. In order for the 45ft container to conform to European road legislation, certain adaptations had to be made to container truck cornering. Geest demonstrated their innovatory skills by developing and patenting a container specification which was compatible with European rules on road haulage articulated unit turning circles.

The second area of leadership exuding from Geest is the championing of inter-modalism. In addition to its own road fleet, the company has diversified into Rhine barge services and has initiated intra-European and, latterly, domestic railway services in the UK. The inter-modal strategy was outlined in 1998 by Geest Sales Director, Perry Glading, not only as a way of attaining modal integration but also as a hedge against third party cost escalations:

> We do not see competition from road or rail as we use both. A seamless transport chain is an essential, but also an effective cost control in order that we can maintain a level of profitability for further investment.[100]

In 2003, Geest moved 210,000 boxes internally in Europe – an 18.6% increase on 2001 volumes. Figure 37 illustrates the increasing percentage share of rail and barge in these volumes. The increased road costs associated with the German "green road tax," LKW-Maut, has proved a financial spur to this modal shift. The dedicated Geest rail service initiated between Rotterdam and the German industrial town, Worms, signals the determination of the company to switch to more sustainable transport modes.

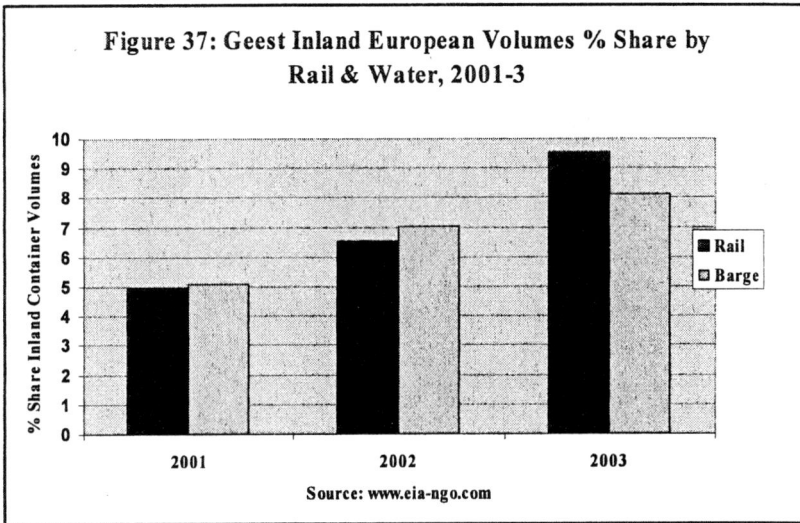

Figure 37: Geest Inland European Volumes % Share by Rail & Water, 2001-3

Source: www.eia-ngo.com

The 450 km rail link was given a target of reducing annual road journeys by 250,000 and, moreover, €1.5m savings on LKW-Maut were predicted.[101]

A strength of the company has been its ability to retain a strong commitment to in-house logistical operations. Developments in the design of the 45ft container were attributable to the company's technical manager (the late) Peter Van Dijikin in particular.[102] The response to 60-72 hour barge delays in the ports of Rotterdam and Antwerp prompted Geest to develop their own in-house service.[103]

The 2005 takeover of Geest by the Icelandic shipping group, Samskip, has led to a merger with Seawheel. This consolidation brings together two major North Sea/Irish Sea players. Seawheel's expertise in sea-river shipping and

Geest's proficiency in inter-modal integration offers significant opportunities for Green Highway development.[104]

Company Portfolio as at 2.2.06:

- Intermodal door-to-door operator. Samskip takeover in 2005 creates a fleet of 20 vessels in the 340-1000teu range;
- Merger with Seawheel potentially adds a further 14 vessels.

Company Status:

- Dutch subsidiary of Iceland public company, Samskip.

Sample Container Trades:

- Rotterdam- Tilbury;
- Rotterdam-Hull;
- Rotterdam-Drogheda.

6.11 Scandinavian Tanker Operators

A feature of the oil and gas movements around the British and Irish coasts is the high level of participation of Scandinavian operators. In the crude oil trades, Norwegian tankers from the Knutsen and Navion fleets benefit from the flag protection afforded to cargoes from the Norwegian sector oil fields and terminals. These tankers, in the 100,000-120,000dwt category, tend to be operating a shuttle service to UK refineries as well as Cork's Whitegate Refinery. As an example of Norwegian flag participation in UK oil imports, the 126,741dwt *Navion Scandia,* was noted on the crude oil supply chain between the Norwegian off-shore, Njord Field and both Coryton (Thames) and Tranmere (Mersey) in the sample survey (Appendix One). The Norwegian operators have established an expertise as well as a highly regarded quality status in the oil trades. The Bergesen Fleet has strengths in crude oil movements, but in recent years has pursued a diversification strategy into the more value-added LPG and LNG sectors. The high environmental standards employed by the Norwegian operators come at a high cost. The Norwegian flag has some of the highest costs in the world maritime taxonomy. However, national flag preference in the Norwegian oil export trades does help support some 2.3mdwt of Norwegian flagged and crewed vessels.[105] Norway has some claims to owning one of the largest tanker fleets in the world. In July 2005, Norwegian owners accounted for some 23.4mdwt of tankers, including 6.4mdwt storage and shuttle tankers employed in the Norwegian Fields-North Europe oil supply chain.[106]

In the LPG trades, the Danish operator Kosan has leadership in the niche area of LPG distribution. With its roots in the innovatory gas tanker shipping and distribution of LPG supplies, the well maintained, yellow hulled ships of the Kosan fleet, are well known in many British coaster ports. The demand for LPG in the remote island communities of Denmark was initially met by the 127m³, *Kosangas*, in 1951. With the vertical integration of sea and road transport, the company was able to supply a healthy market. Kosan's road tanker lorries featured the slogan headboard: "Kosangas: The housewives burning desire".[107] By 1960 the expertise in compressing, bottling and transporting coal gasses had led to increased industrial demand served by a fleet of ten vessels in the 500m³ category.[108]

6.11.1 Broström Tankers (BTAB)

In the oil products sector, the Swedish group, A.B. Broström (BTAB) is a market leader servicing several contracts of affreightment with oil majors. With vessels in the 8000-22,000 dwt range, the "Bro Tankers" are well suited to linking the main UK refineries plus Ireland's Whitegate Terminal with regional oil depots. The vessels are regular traders to Fawley, Stanlow on the Manchester Ship Canal, Plymouth, Belfast and also trade to Irish ports, Waterford and Dublin.

The history of Broström is very much one of growth via consolidation, accompanied by a well established reputation with leading oil majors. The

304

company has provided an umbrella organisation for a number of European and Scandinavian shipowners, including Rigel Schiffahrts of Hamburg and Swedish companies, Rederi AB Donsötank and Erik Thun AB. However, in early 2005 it was decided that improved transparency and increased focus on fleet development would be facilitated by full ownership of the fleet and all three strategic partners were bought out by BTAB.[109]

BTAB has fostered a strategy of close working relationships with its customers in the oil and chemical sectors. This extends to vessel officers becoming involved in commercial information and the importance of customer relations at all levels. The emphasis on professional, informed, working relationships underpins the desire to maintain long-term working partnerships with the oil and chemical companies, culminating in the market stability attained by contracts of affreightment. The desire to constantly improve the environmental and safety quality of the tanker fleet was rewarded by the 2006 accomplishment of winning the *Lloyd's List* "ship of the year award". This was awarded for the Broström designed products tanker, *Bro Deliverer*. In 2003, BTAB MD, Tore Angervall, outlined the importance of building and nurturing sound customer relations:

> ...It is our specialists onboard who present a public face on behalf of the company and who deliver the service ...It is our officers and crew onboard who regularly meet customer representatives...It is imperative that our shipboard people are fully aware of our company's way of doing business and of its outlook.[110]

Company Portfolio as at 2.2.06:

- Shipowning/managing/chartering company. 31 vessels in the products trades.

Company Status:

- Public listed company – Swedish Stock Exchange.

Sample Trades:

- Pembroke–Plymouth, oil products;
- Braefoot Bay–Fawley,oil products;
- Finnart–Plymouth, kerosene.

6.12 Former USSR Shortsea Shipping

An unexpected result of the liberalisation and subsequent collapse of the Soviet Union has been the re-deployment of shortsea and river shipping into Northern European, Iberian and Mediterranean trades. The lack of industrial activity on the River Volga and the Ladoga and Neva Lakes has brought the former river-lake ships into shortsea trading. This factor has placed additional competitive pressures on North European owners. Cost competition is paramount here with Russian crew costs much lower than North European. Many of the vessels are ageing and as a consequence have low capital costs. A number of Russian operators have flagged out their vessels in order to avoid what are seen as swingeing taxes.

6.12.1 North-Western Shipping

One of the major Russian fleets is that of St. Petersburg's North-Western Shipping Company. This holding company for 14 subsidiaries lists 500 ships in its fleet, including 250 sea-river ships, 130 trading internationally.[111] With 15,000 employees the company is of strategic importance to the Russian economy. The company was privatised in 1992 with 51% of company shares distributed to employees. In 1995, modernisation was facilitated by a DM51m loan from the European Bank of Reconstruction and Development (EBRD).[112] In 2004, the company operated 15 Ladoga class vessels on European coastlines and waterways. These vessels are built to the specifications of Finland's Saimaa Canal network, thus linking forestry regions with the Baltic. In April 2004, Ladoga vessel movements included:

- Riga–Wisbech;
- New Holland–London;
- Southampton–Rostock;
- Peterhead–Wicklow
- Bayonne–Flixborough.[113]

The company appears to have targeted grain, scrap, aggregates and animal feedstuffs as a counter-balance to its timber loadings from Russian ports. In October 2004, it was reported that Russian cargo timbers to British West coast and Irish ports were balanced by aggregates loadings at Falmouth's Dean Quarry for RMC, Dagenham. This development was at the expense of Lapthorn's British flagged vessels.[114] North-Western Shipping has bucked the flagging out trend in that they have remained with the Russian flag. Also, in 2002, they were the first Russian company to order new tonnage from Russian shipyards since the collapse of the USSR. The order of ten 5100dwt mini bulkers will allow the line to become quality competitors in the European mini-bulker trades.[115]

Company Portfolio as at 2.2.06:
- Major shortsea operator with 130 vessels trading in Baltic;
- North Sea, Iberia, Mediterranean and Black Sea regions.

Company Status:
- ex Soviet company formed in 1923;
- St. Petersburg based joint-stock company;
- Holding company specialised in bare-boat chartering of sea-river vessels.

Sample Trades:
- Falmouth–Dagenham, stone;
- Bideford–Naantali (Finland), brick clay;
- Riga–Shoreham, timber.

6.13 New Entrants to the Green Highway.

A number of companies have now been identified at work in the Green Highway. It has been made evident that many of these companies have well established origins. However, it is also noticeable that several new entrants have contributed to the shipping supply chain. The 1990s re-emergence of entrepreneurialism and deregulation has facilitated new shipping ventures. The privatised ports were quick to realise the potential of shipping integration (see above pp.131-32) The Mersey Docks and Harbour Company (now part of Peel Ports) became a leader of diversification into container services, with three subsidiaries – Coastal Container Lines, BG Freight and Concorde Container Lines.

The move of Clydeport into shipping operations stems from an astute re-activation of an under utilised port assets and staff expertise. The closure of the Clyde Valley Ravenscraig Steel Plant in 1992 led to the premature redundancy of the deepwater, Clyde estuary, Hunterston Bulk Terminal, where large capesize bulk carriers had discharged iron ore. The terminal has proved well placed for the transition to a deepsea coal importing hub – spawning intensive bulk-rail services and also Clydeport's coastal and shortsea coal trans-shipment flows to Warrenpoint, Ellesmere Port and Northfleet, for around 3mt of imported coal per year.

In addition, Clydeport have revived the under-utilised Greenock Container Terminal by operating container feeder services to Southampton, with calls at Belfast and Manchester (this service is considered more closely in chapter 7, see below). The announcement by Clydeport of a £200m investment in a new container terminal at Hunterston offers additional scope for coastal and shortsea feeder services. These would logistically link the deepsea traffics sought by Clydeport.[116]   The consolidation of the Mersey and Clyde port and shipping operations under Peel Ports ownership in 2005-6 further strengthened port-shipping line integration.

In the dry-cargo trades, divestment of tonnage by such companies as Everard's and Crescent has provided opportunities for entrepreneurial new entrants. Faversham Ships Ltd has developed its fleet by a series of sale and purchase activities. Captain Heather Chaplin has developed her River-Sea Trading company with vessels under 1000dwt, trading in the Mersey-Manchester Ship Canal and also in Scottish Island trades. The company was awarded a Freight Facility Grant (FFG) in 2002 to move salt down the River Weaver. The 825dwt vessel, *River Dart*, was purchased for this trade. However, British Waterways deliberations have postponed the implementation of this trade. By March 2006 there were still no signs that the trade was starting.[117] Another FFG supported new entrant in the Mersey-Manchester Ship Canal is that of KD Marine, whose inland grain shuttle service is discussed further in chapter 7 (See below). The emergence of new entry shipping companies onto the Green Highway can be welcomed as an injection of innovation and enterprise and seen as an indicator of opportunities for growth.

6.14 Summary & Conclusion

This review of selected operators to be found participating in the Green Highway has revealed a number of trends and determining factors. For three of the leading UK operators – Crescent, Everard's, Fisher's – the divestment of dry cargo ships and concentration on product tankers is a seemingly irreversible strategy. This can be explained as a move towards higher value, more secure business. The need for oil and chemical shippers to access high quality environmentally sensitive shipping, explains why the relatively high cost British and Scandinavian fleets can survive. Conversely, the hard economic decisions faced by such well established dry cargo operators – Lapthorn, Stephenson

Clarke – points to the major economic pressures facing fleets in this low value, highly competitive sector, with cost competition from flag of convenience and East European operators. Likewise, the recent history of the RMS Line has highlighted the financial pressures on operators. In the container sector, the demise of Bell Lines and the precarious finances of Seawheel also show the difficulties facing operators in highly competitive markets. These examples demonstrate the harsh fact that the attainment of a hard working fleet is no guarantor of economic stability.

Various types of integration have been noted as a positive factor in shipping logistics. Both Seacon and Scotline have supporting cargo handling and warehousing systems for their break-bulk liner services. Geest Line-North Sea's logistics strategy is based around inter-modal integration, including barges and rail services. Extending the supply chain helps to achieve a direct door-to-door freight flow. Borchard Line's integration with port agencies, freight forwarders and trucking providers obviously helps to deliver a seamless supply chain.

Two clear trends are evident. Firstly, dry cargo trades vessel sizes are increasing, allowing such companies as Arklow Shipping, Carisbrooke Shipping and Stephenson Clarke Bulk Shipping to benefit from the economies of scale and to enter into new markets for 12,000-15,000dwt ships. Secondly, a movement towards market concentration can be detected, particularly in the container trades. The vessel sharing agreement between Irish Continental Group's container subsidiaries, Eucon and Eurofeeders and Mersey Docks and Harbour Company's, BG Freight subsidiary, points to route rationalisation in the Ireland-Continental trades. The Samskip takeover of both Seawheel and Geest Line North Sea is a significant move towards market concentration in North Sea and Irish Sea trades. The convergence of the Everard and Fisher tanker fleets is further evidence of the concentration process.

310

Finally, the general picture is one of leading companies embarking on ambitious investment programmes. This reflects the market highs of the early Millennium. Innovative funding methods and collaborations with shipbuilders have been employed. The British and Irish Tonnage tax schemes have also facilitated new tonnage. The following chapter will consider how these various components of shipping supply in the Green Highway will match the economic and logistical demands of the market in Britain and Ireland.

CHAPTER 6: ENDNOTES

[1] Thorne, A. "Penarth's Maritime History," *Marine Information Association News.* Spring/Summer 2004.

[2] Garrett, K. S. (1991) *Everards of Greenhithe* Kendal: World Ship Society.

[3] Garrett, *Op. cit.* p. 11.

[4] www.ft-everard.co.uk 4.6.05.

[5] Grey, M. (2002) "Union Transport and F.T. Everard link dry bulk fleets," *Lloyd's List.* 13.3.02.

[6] *Loc.cit*

[7] *Loc. cit.*

[8] "Everard maintains its innovative edge with new delivery from Qingshan," *Lloyd's List.* 20.5.05.

[9] "James Fisher buys FT Everard," *Fairplay International Shipping Weekly.* 6.12.06.

[10] *Loc.cit*

[11] "Pioneer of the river sea trades," *Lloyd's List.* 13.8.96.

[12] *Loc. cit.*

[13] Cheetham, C. Heinimann, M.(1993) *Modern Sea River Traders.* Teignmouth: Cheetham.

[14] "Max Heinimann in the news," *Lloyd's List.* 13.8.96.

[15] Grey, M. Union Transport and F.T. Everard link dry-bulk fleet," *Lloyd's List.* 13.3.02

[16] "Union Transport turns to Chowgule for multipurpose sextet," *Lloyds List.* 28.6.05.

[17] www.uniontransport.co.uk. Accessed 6.5.05

[18] Garrett, K. (2001) *R. Lapthorn and Company: A Ships in Focus Fleet History.* Preston: Ships in Focus.

[19] Gray, T. (2003) "Lloyds TSB confirm that Lapthorn fleet is for sale," *Lloyd's List.* 28.1.03.

[20] Osler, D. "Corus accused in row over Ukranian seafarers pay," *Lloyd's List.* 20.9.04.

[21] www.lapthorn.co.uk accessed 4.6.05.

[22] Grey, M. (2003) "Lapthorn targets container feeder trades," *Lloyd's List.* 21.11.03.

[23] *Loc. cit.*

[24] www.lapthorn.co.uk accessed 31.10.06.

[25] http://www.coastalbulkshipping.co.uk/index.asp?news accessed 9.11.06.

[26] www.thamesbarge.org.uk

[27] Gray, T. "New crescent owners consider orders," *Lloyd's List.* 4.11.97.

[28] Tinsley, D. (1992) "Special report on European shortsea trades index show 10 year low in dry cargo." *Lloyd's List.* 13.5.92.

[29] Speares, S. "Crescent exits dry bulk for expansion," *Lloyd's List.* 11.2.02.

[30] www.clipper-wonsild.com accessed 29.1.06.

[31] "Tonnage move pays dividends to Scotline capability," *Lloyd's List.* 11.11.03.

[32] Landon, F. (2005) "Business Briefing: Scotline expands" *Lloyd's List.* 11.3.05.

[33] Keenan, K. E. (1997) *The Fires of London: A History of the Thames lighterage operations of William Cory & Son Ltd.* Waldron, East Sussex: Keenan.

[34] *Ibid.* p. 20.

[35] Rowlinson, M. "How London was shaped by its 'tidal highway' and the skilled operators that work it." *Lloyd's List.* 25.9.05.

[36] *Loc. cit.*

[37] Port of London Press Release,: "Cory Environmental – London's green electricity boost." 15.6.06.

[38] "Cory gets go ahead for an energy from waste power station at Belvedere," *Cory Extra* Summer 2006. www.coryenvironmental.co.uk accessed 6.4.07

[39] Grey, M. (2002) "End of an era in the shortsea trades on the Medway," *Lloyd's List.* 1.11.02.

[40] "From triumph to disaster, a story of a line that led the field but lost its way," *Lloyd's List.* 7.7.97.

[41] Tinsley, D. (1990) "Special Report on Shortsea Europe: Hi-Tech box ship for Bell." *Lloyd's List.* 8.10.90.

312

[42] *Loc: cit.*

[43] "Rapid growth curve at Waterford," *Lloyd's List.* 20.6.96.

[44] "Storm puts bell box terminal out of action," *Lloyd's List.* 29.10.96.

[45] "Pace setter Bell enjoys growth," *Lloyd's List.* 21.8.95.

[46] Special report on Ireland: Industry gets to grips with Bell Lines crash." *Lloyd's List.* 29.7.97.

[47] MacSweeney, T. (1998). "Irish Eye: Waterford Port leaves Bell behind," *Lloyd's List.* 15.6.98.

[48] www.portofwaterford.com 7.6.05.

[49] "Bell Lines debacle: serious repercussions for the South East," Adjournment Debate. Tithe Oireachtais. www.gov.ie/debate 9.7.97.

[50] Spong, H. S. (1983) *Irish Shipping Ltd. 1941-1982.* Kendal: WSS. pp. 7-8.

[51] Higgins, J. "Irish Shipping Ltd – The Economic Reality," *Maritime Journal of Ireland.* Summer 1991 No. 2.

[52] "Flagging economy drags down Irish Continental," *Lloyd's List.* 15.9.03.

[53] www.finfacts.com 7.3.05.

[54] Osler, D. "Irish Ferries issues ultimatum to strikers," *Lloyd's List.* 14.12.05.

[55] "Vessel-sharing pact bears fruit for partners," *Lloyd's List.* 11.11.03.

[56] *Loc. cit.*

[57] The process of offering 1/64th in a ship allowed for small, local port community investors to participate in the shipping business

[58] Harvey, W. J. (2004) *Arklow Shipping: A Group Fleet History.* Bristol: McCall. p.4.

[59] Starkey, F. (1998) *Schooner Port: Two Centuries of Upper Mersey Sail.* Bebbington,: Wirral: Garth Boulevard. p. 62.

[60] Harvey, *op. cit.* p. 8.

[61] Harvey, W. J. (2004) *Ibid.* p.4.

[62] Clegg, P.(1998) "Carisbrooke maps route to expansion," *Lloyd's List.* 28.11.98.

[63] www.ukbusiness.co.uk 29.4.96.

[64] www.ukbusiness.co.uk 24.6.99.

[65] www.carisbrookeshipping.net. 23.6.05.

[66] "Carisbrooke orderd four more MPPs," *Tradewinds.* 18.8.06

[67] Watson, N. (2000) *Around the Coast and Across the Seas: The Story of James Fisher and Sons.* Leyburn, N.Yorks: St.Matthews Press.

[68] *Ibid.* pp. 1-28.

[69] *Ibid.* p.77.

[70] *Loc.cit.*

[71] *Ibid.* p. 82.

[72] Huckett, A. (2002) *Rowbotham.* Gravesend: WSS.

[73] "Out with old, in with the new," *Lloyd's Shipping Economist,* November 2002. p. 33.

[74] "Fisher swallows Everard," *Tradewinds.* 6.12.06.

[75] http://www.scsbulk.com/home.htm accessed 6.4.07

[76] "Origins in the Coal Trade," *Lloyd's List.* 18.9.97.

[77] Tinsley, D. "Stephenson Clarke purchase fulfils IMG founders dream," *Lloyd's List.* 28.11.97.

[78] *Loc. cit.*

[79] Select Committee on the Environment, Transport and Regional Affairs (2004). Appendices to Minutes of Evidence. Supplementary Memorandum by NUMAST (FUS1A) The Future of the UK Shipping Industry. www.parliament.thestationeryoffice.co.uk

[80] www.rmt.org.uk Submission to the ITF on the Isle of Man Flag – 2000.

[81] Osler, D. (1999) "Stephenson Clarke in European crew move," *Lloyd's List.* 29.1.99.

[82] www.borlines.com/history

[83] "Full circle for loss making Seawheel MBO team," *Lloyd's List.* 14.2.05.

[84] "Seawheel swaps ro-ro with popular lo-lo." *Lloyd's List.* 20.12.04.

[85] "Seawheel heads back for profit under new owner,." *Lloyd's List.* 16.2.04.

[86] *Loc. cit.*

[87] "New European Link for Seawheel," *Containerisation International,* January 2004, p. 23.

[88] www.seawheel.com 27.6.05. Tyco case study.

[89] "Company News: A fair cop," *Lloyd's List*. 22.6.05.

[90] Porter, J. "Buyers line up to bid for Seawheel." *Lloyd's List*. 17.6.05.

[91] Porter, J. "Samskip confirms acquisition of shortsea operator, Seawheel." *Lloyd's List*. 5.8.05.

[92] http://www.williegroup.co.uk/home/Newsstory.asp?news=33 accessed 7.4.07.

[93] Tinsley, D. (1984) *Short-Sea Bulk Trades: Dry Cargo Shipping in European Waters*. London: Fairplay. p. 38.

[94] Fromme, H. (1995) "RMS sees return to profitability," *Lloyd's List*. 21.10.95.

[95] *Loc. cit.*

[96] www.rms-europe.co.uk/stevedoring 30.6.05.

[97] Tinsley, D. *op.cit.* p. 40.

[98] Detlefsen, V. G. U. (2004) *Detlefsens Illustries Schiffsregister, 2004-5*.

[99] www.zeevaart.web-log.nl 16.1.05.

[100] "Shortsea shipping – the seamless chain," *Lloyd's Shipping Economist*. ShipEcon.com. 1.3.98.

[101] www.eia-ngo.com accessed 6.2.06.

[102] It was sadly reported that Peter died at the age of 43 on 10.8.04. www.worldcargonews.com Obituary, October 2004.

[103] "Geest does its own thing," www.worldcargonews.com August, 2004.

[104] Wainwright, D. "Samskip acquires Seawheel," *Tradewinds*. 7.7.05

[105] www.rederi.no/file.asp accessed 6.2.06.

[106] *Loc. cit*

[107] Gray, R. (2004) *Bulk liquid cargoes by sea: the early years*, London: Siggto.

[108] Hornsby, D. (1996) "From Tholstrup to Kosan," *Black Jack: The Quarterly Magazine of the Southampton Branch of the World Ship Society*, Spring 1996, pp. 4-6.

[109] "Bröstrum buy-out." *www.lloydsshipmanager.com* 1.1.05.

[110] "Bröstrum refines its 'fleet for Europe'." *Lloyd's List*. 26.8.03.

[111] www.ceebd/ceebd.nwshipco.htm

[112] "EBRD signs Russian North-West Shipping Company loan" www.ebrd.com press release 1.3.95.

[113] *Lloyd's Shipping Index*, 12.4.04.

[114] "Bits 'N' Pieces," *Coastal Shipping*. Vol. 11. No. 5. October 2004. p.167.

[115] "Russian shipbuilding: A Sleeping Giant Awakes," *Naval Architect*. September 2002.

[116] www.clydeport.co.uk accessed 1.3.06.

[117] Hilling, D. "Inland Shipping" www.waterways.org.uk accessed 1.3.06

CHAPTER 7

The Economics and Logistics of the Green Highway

This chapter will discuss the role and prospects of the Green Highway in the UK and Irish supply chain. First, the competitive aspects of shipping *vis-à-vis* road haulage and to a lesser extent, rail freight are considered. Secondly, it is proposed to consider the main determinants of vessel costs. Thirdly, some discussion will be made on the issues of investment in shipping. The overall objective is to investigate the demand and supply factors pertinent to the Green Highway. This approach aids the exploration of the Green Highway's prospects within the context of modern business location, storage, distribution and transport trends. Essentially, the Green Highway must recognise and respond to the needs of the market. Modern just-in-time logistics, with its reduced stock levels and lean manufacturing, poses difficult challenges for shipping. Achieving increased participation in the supply chain will not be easy; it is vital, therefore, to critically assess the barriers to attaining modal-shift from roads to water. Finally, nine short case studies will be discussed. Particular attention will be given to the logistical factors that have proved conducive to the integration of shipping in the supply chain.

In order to examine both the performance and potential for shipping-based logistics in the supply chain, it is necessary to identify the key determinants of modal choice. The logistics concept has held much sway in transport and distribution in recent decades. The concept helps to place transport into the framework of supply chain linkages. From this perspective the whole process of production, packaging, storage and transport and distribution is considered. Over short distances, the orthodox perception is normally that of the road haulage mode fulfilling the transport function in the supply chain. Road haulage fits well into a supply chain pattern that demands flexibility, reliability and just-in-time deliveries. However, in select cases where distances, volumes and frequencies are favourable, water transport can provide efficient, reliable, supply chain transport. The economies of scale inherent in shipping can prove attractive if these are not negated by handling and storage costs. Where shipment volumes are significant and fast transits are not paramount, shipping can prove a viable alternative to road haulage. However, this message may not get to transport decision makers. It has been estimated that some 90% of modal and 75% of transport chain organisation is managed by dispatching and receiving companies.[1] This means that the Green Highway needs to fit into the demands of the supply chain. This chapter, therefore, provides a critical assessment of the Green Highway within this logistical context.

7.1 Fitting the Supply Chain?

The shift in the industrial base brought about by the de-industrialisation process has forced critical changes in the demand and supply of transport. Road haulage has become integral to the spread of industry and has been a major contributor to the lean supply chain. Historically, the idea of supply chain management was very much an alien concept to the traditional ship operator. When industrial location was closely aligned within the port infrastructure, the transhipping process to road, barge or rail was not such a major cost in-put.[2] The final destination of much of Route One's, North East-Thames/Medway coastal coal flow was directly into the bunkers of riverside power stations. As a consequence, this route facilitated the economies of direct A-to-B shipping whilst minimising inland transport costs. As industry has become aligned to the motorway network, often located significant distances from the port hinterland, more attention has been given to the inland linkages. Developments in the logistics concept have necessitated focus on the whole package of production, storage and distribution. The modern transport operator is now seen as an integral part of the supply chain. Within this context, the growth and dominance of road haulage has appeared unassailable.

Road haulage's development has enabled industry and distribution hubs to locate at the optimum point for motorway links with population and industrial centres. Under these conditions, haulage has consistently increased the average length of haul (ALH) in the decades up to the Millennium. Three explanations have been offered by Herriot-Watt logistics Professor, Alan McKinnon, for the spatial and productivity changes that have induced increases in the ALH:

> (1) the expansion of the firm's market area;
> (2) the spatial concentration of the production and stockholding;
> (3) the relocation of production.[3]

Such major industries as steel, automobiles, chemicals, brewing and foodstuffs have rationalised production and distribution, thus contributing to the increased ALH. The moves towards just-in-time operations brought significant implications for shipping. Just-in-time (JIT) methods may be defined as the organisation of all operations so they occur at exactly the time they are needed. Unnecessary stocks of materials are eliminated and inventory costs are minimised. The concept was developed and popularised by leading Japanese manufacturers such as Toyota in the 1970s, although there are earlier examples: Ford pioneered the focus on supply chain logistics in the 1920s when it achieved a flow of iron ore shipments to its Detroit steel furnaces.[4] The road haulage sector has embraced the marketability of the logistics concept. A number of logistics managers interviewed in the course of this work have remarked upon this trend: "yesterday's haulage owner-driver is today's mobile phone clutching logistics consultant". The competitive impact of haulage has become manifest in a number of areas. Increases in the size of haulage vehicles have brought about economies of scale and this has led to an ever reducing cost per tkm. In chapter 2, the historic decline of domestic shipping was linked to developments

Figure 38: Transport & Inventory Costs

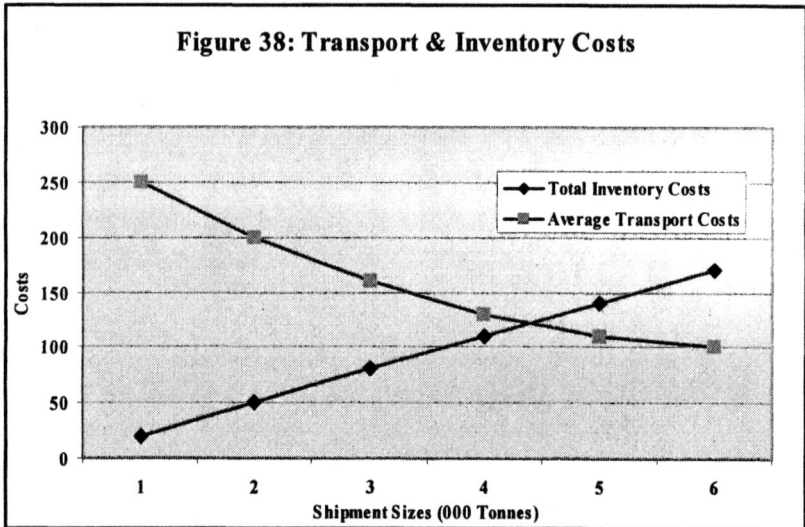

in road haulage efficiencies, particularly in scale and speed. For shipping to compete successfully against road haulage it needs to match not only low tkm costs but also must provide high quality services.[5] This, however, is not a completely new phenomena; as early as 1844 the relative transport and inventory costs of road and canal modes were contemplated by transport users, with journey timings and warehousing aspects compared and contrasted:

> The fact is that carriage by road being quicker, more reliable and less subject to loss or damage, it possesses advantage to which business men often attach a considerable value. However, it may well be that the saving of 0.87fr induces the merchant to use the canal; he can buy warehouses and increase his floating capital in order to have a sufficient supply of goods at hand to protect himself against slowness and irregularity of the canal, and if all told the saving of 0.87fr in transport gives him an advantage of a few centimes, he will decide in favour of the new route.[6]

The focus on inventory in the supply chain can be seen as an integral consideration in modal choice. Essentially, road haulage has the capability to deal with small consignments, proving highly competitive *vis-à-vis* shipping. Whereas a road haulage journey may be viable with a 5 tonne payload, a barge may need 250 tonnes! Additionally, the consolidation of this 250 tonnes of cargo may need storage over a number of days. As a consequence, inventory costs are incurred. The position is reflected in Figure 38 which shows the inverse relationship between transport costs and inventory costs. It can be seen that as the shipment size increases, average transport costs fall. In terms of tkm costs the average will normally fall in accordance with the economies of scale. The rise in shortsea vessel sizes (identified in chapter 6) may be explained by the shipowners desire to benefit from the competitive advantages of larger vessels. Figure 38 also shows the rise in inventory costs as shipment sizes increase. It follows that high value goods will quickly build up inventory costs and are more likely to be distributed on a just-in-time basis – most conducive to high frequency, smaller shipment sizes of road haulage, than the low frequency, large shipment sizes by ship. Between the juxtapositions of transport and inventory costs, therefore, the supply chain manager makes decisions based on the perceived optimum mix of transport and inventory costs.

Despite these logistical barriers to shipping it is now apparent that the once accepted view of an unassailable road haulage industry is becoming challenged. At this stage it is timely to endorse the impact of the growing problems of road haulage, considering how this can alter the balance between transport and inventory.

7.1.1 Road Haulage Problems?

The trend towards JIT logistics has proved conducive to road haulage which has maintained consistent growth post WW1, although a number of restraining factors are now beginning to impede the hitherto unbridled dominance of the lorry on European roads. At the turn of the Millennium, the UK road haulage industry was seen to be in something of a crisis. A 2001 KMPG survey found that profit margins were slim, as low as 3%.[7] The industry faced the highest fuel duty in Europe; driver shortages were being exacerbated by wage cuts. It was also found that 50,000 UK jobs had been lost in the industry due to either European competition or UK firms relocating to continental Europe. Many of the

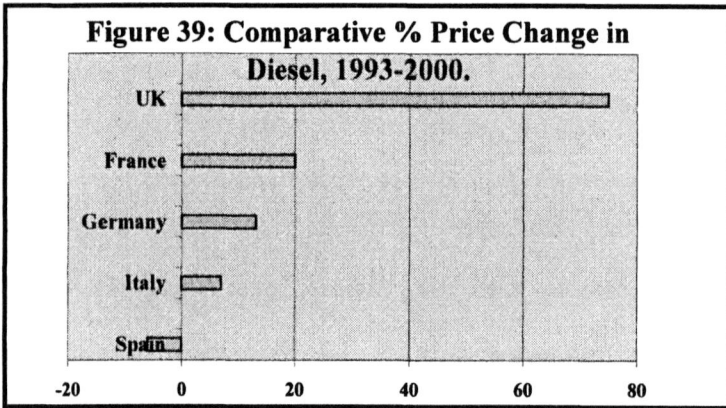

Figure 39: Comparative % Price Change in Diesel, 1993-2000.

Source: *EC Oil Bulletin*

owner-drivers in particular, were finding things difficult by the Millennium. In the first quarter of 2001, 54 UK hauliers announced significant business problems, compared with 18 in the corresponding period one year earlier; and, additionally, more haulage businesses failed in the 1998-2000 period than in the eight preceding years.[8] The issue of the comparative cost of fuel came to a head in Autumn 2000 when a combination of farmers and lorry drivers concerted to block the movement of fuel ex oil refineries. In 2000 it was estimated that a 1000 litre tank of diesel would cost £833 in the UK and between £527 and £557 in France, Germany and Italy. The price impact of the fuel tax escalator policy is demonstrated by Figure 39. Both London and Edinburgh suffered road blockades from convoys of tractors and HGV's. The outcome revealed a political sensitivity to the fuel tax issue bringing a reversal of policy towards tax rates.[9]

The fuel tax escalator was a short-lived directive that set out to increase fuel duties by six percentage points above inflation per annum. The intention was both to limit the growth in UK haulage – facilitating a switch to alternative greener modes such as rail and shipping – and encouraging hauliers to switch to greener fuels such as LPG (which was exempt from the tax escalation). Things came to a head in 1999 when the escalator increase led to UK diesel prices rising by 11.6%. The resulting protests by hauliers and farmers led to a review of this policy. The problems of the industry were further deepened by the imposition of EU Working Time Directive in 2004. This resulted in the drivers' working week maximum hours being reduced from 55 to 48. Long distance operations in particular were threatened by the reduction of the night time maximum working hours of ten hours (9 hours driving max + 1 hour attendance).[10] It was estimated that an additional 80,000 drivers were required to fill the gap that this created.[11]

In addition to the fuel cost and driver shortage crisis the industry is also feeling the negative impact of congestion. The Freight Transport Association (FTA) has expressed its concern:

> Congestion is bad for everybody and has high costs for vehicles caught in it – a lorry standing idle in traffic costs GBP 25 in operating costs alone, apart from the cost of missed deliveries.[12]

The problems of road haulage were highlighted by the major Hong Kong container ship operator, Overseas Orient Container Line (OOCL) in 2001.[13] Mr. Ted Wang, of the OOCL Board, announced that the company was switching to rail from road for the trunk route, Southampton-Manchester. The 10 year deal providing for a dedicated OOCL Freightliner service would help boost rail's share of OOCL's UK box movements from 25% towards 50%. Mr. Wang identified three problem areas of road haulage in the UK:

- Motorway congestion, particularly on the M6 approach to Manchester;
- Driver shortages (47,000 vacancies);
- The looming impact of the EU Working Time Directive.[14]

The initiative was also welcomed by Southampton Container Terminals, particularly the positive impact the rail mode would have on reducing road congestion in the port area.[15] The difficulties facing hauliers in the early years of the Millennium may not have suppressed the dominant position of the road mode in British and Irish supply chains. It has become evident, however, that the consideration of alternative modes is becoming prevalent. The combination of high fuel costs, congestion and driver shortages can only increase the attraction of the Green Highway.

7.1.2 The Hinterland Obstacle

Despite the many apparent and looming problems facing road haulage across Europe it is still most evident that significant barriers to modal transfer of traffics from road exist. A principal obstacle to be overcome lies in the hinterland linkages between the port and the final inland destination. The cost and time barrier of transhipping cargo from inland transport to ship can be prohibitive. At the 2000, 6th Shortsea Europe conference held in Duisburg, the modal-transhipment barrier was clearly outlined by the representative of Dutch brewer

Bavaria, who reported difficulties in attempting to move its South European exports by sea. Three obstacles were identified by the brewer:

> (1)   trucks returning from Northern Germany after delivering fruit offered highly competitive rates for backhauls into Southern Europe;

> (2)   the cost of road carriage between the brewery and the container terminal – a distance of only 15kms – contributed to 20% of total carriage costs;

> (3)   the considerably longer lead times and comparative inflexibility associated with shortsea shipping deliveries *vis-à-vis* road haulage.[16]

The obstacles faced by the brewer in attempting to utilise the Green Highway clearly illustrate the problem of cargo double handling. This evidence fits with the pessimistic findings of the 1994 study *Roads to Water*[17] (see above p.23) which questioned the viability of shipping over short distance, when the port (interface) costs – cargo handling, stevedoring, wharfage can account for up to 80% of a coastal voyage costs. *The Roads to Water* study concluded that only over long distances could shipping prove competitive. This is summarised in Table 30.

Table 30: Roads to Water Report: UK Shipping Viability Distances	
Direct Shipping Collection & Delivery	Shipping + Road Collection & Delivery
400km Viability	560-640km
Source: Packer, J. (1994) *Roads to Water: Overview of Coastal and Short Sea Shipping*. London: HMSO.	

Research conducted for the European Conference of Ministers of Transport (ECMT) in 2001 has identified the importance of two factors in determining intra-European modal choice: time and cost.[18] Table 31 displays time and cost ratios for selected European freight flows. Distances have been added to the ECMT

324

research in order to gain perspective. It can be seen that the comparatively long sea-leg from Hamburg to Venice has relatively high sea costs *vis-à-vis* road. This is explained by the sea-leg (via the Iberian Peninsula and Gibraltar Straits) being 4.5 times that of the road leg. Where the disparity in distances is not so pronounced, the cost advantages of sea transport become more evident; the time disadvantages less pronounced! Sawn timber between Sweden and both Rouen and Bilbao has road cost ratios 3.00 and 3.71 respectively higher than sea costs. Additionally, on this difficult intra-European road route, road only has 3.31 and 2.51 time advantages over sea.

Table 31: Relative Road and Sea Cost/Time Ratios					
Cargo/Routes	Price Ratio Road : Ship (1)	Time Ratio Road : Ship (2)	Distance Kms		Price/Time Ratio(1)/(2)
General Cargo Hamburg to:			Road	Sea	
Venice	1.27	7.26	1300	5926	0.17
Piraeus	2.55	4.51	2700	5556	0.57
Sawn Timber Sweden to:					
Rouen	3.00	3.31	1900	2400	0.91
Bilbao	3.71	2.51	2600	3229	1.48
Containers Bremerhaven to:					
Marseilles	1.58	4.59	1550	4178	0.34
Cadiz	3.24	1.30	2800	2798	2.49

Source: Derived from ECMT (2001) *Short Sea Shipping in Europe.* Paris: OECD. p.11

The outcome of these price-time ratios is that shipping normally competes on the lower cost, slow moving cargoes. In the case of low value bulks such as aggregates the emphasis is on finding the lowest cost form of transport – bulk shipping.[19] However, it is timely to recall that the historic time advantage that road haulage has held over shipping is beginning to narrow, as a result of congestion. Also it was made apparent in chapter 5 that new vessel speeds are increasing, thus further reducing the margin. For shipping to become a successful link in the supply chain it is apparent that it will have to take cognisance of the trends in modern logistics. Intermodal specialist, Zachcial, has outlined the need for land/sea integration to achieve the following four points:(1) maintain control over the complete chain from dispatching to receiving;(2) guarantee delivery times;(3) minimise delays in ports;(4) offer maximum service frequency.[20] A 2002, *Lloyd's Shipping Economist* study into the prospects for intra-European shipping outlined the following key reasons why shippers preferred road to water transport:

- Lack of information about maritime alternatives;
- perception of insufficient volume to consider shipping;
- shippers consign goods to forwarders or logistics providers without specifying transport mode;
- flexibility allowing door-to-door services;
- just-in-time deliveries;
- low prices with no extra handling costs;
- no additional charges for port and cargo dues;
- avoidance of delays due to weather;
- no delays due to intermodal transfers.[21]

7.1.3 The Distance-Cost Factor

Over short distances the almost automatic choice by transport decision makers is that of the road haulage mode. It has been made evident that road haulage is highly compatible with high frequency JIT. However, the inherent cost advantages that shipping enjoys are drawn from its ability to achieve relatively low tkm costs between two geographic points. Measured in terms of both capital and operational costs per tkm, shipping enjoys competitive advantage over road. However, when such additional outlay as port costs, transhipment and storage costs are considered, the advantage diminishes, possibly disappears! Figure 40 outlines comparative road, rail and sea costs over distances up to 600km. The graph is derived from research conducted by the inter-modal specialist consultant, MDS-Transmodal and the sea and rail legs also include the estimated costs of road collection and delivery. It can be seen that over short distances, container

Figure 40: Comparative Modal Costs per Container over Distance.

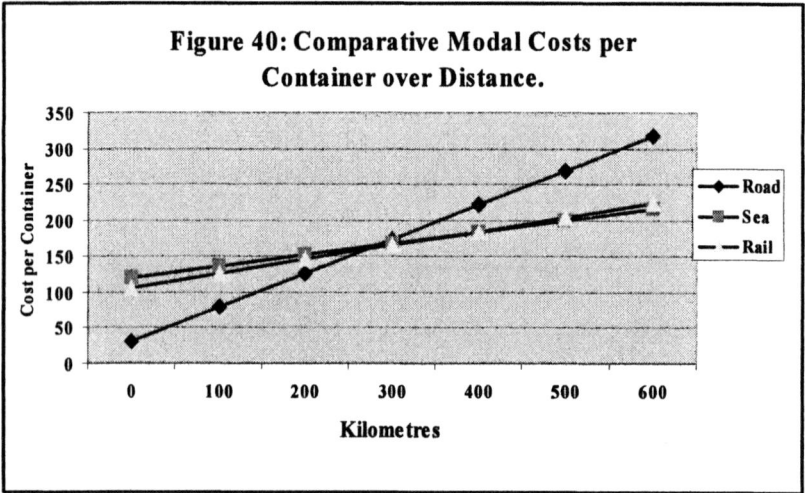

Source: Derived from Garratt, M. (2004) Sea and Water Conference, Why Water? Manchester 6.4.06

movements by road have a clear cost competitive edge over both sea and rail. This may be explained by the comparatively high infrastructure charges incurred by rail and sea. Towards 250km this road cost advantage disappears. Beyond 400km, the low, marginal, tkm costs of both sea and rail modes *vis-à-vis* road haulage become evident. EU supported research group, Regional Action for Logistical Integration of Shipping Across Europe (Realise), found that 400km was a cost threshold for the use of shipping, but as a proviso, where volumes achieved a high level of density, 100km could be feasible. [22]

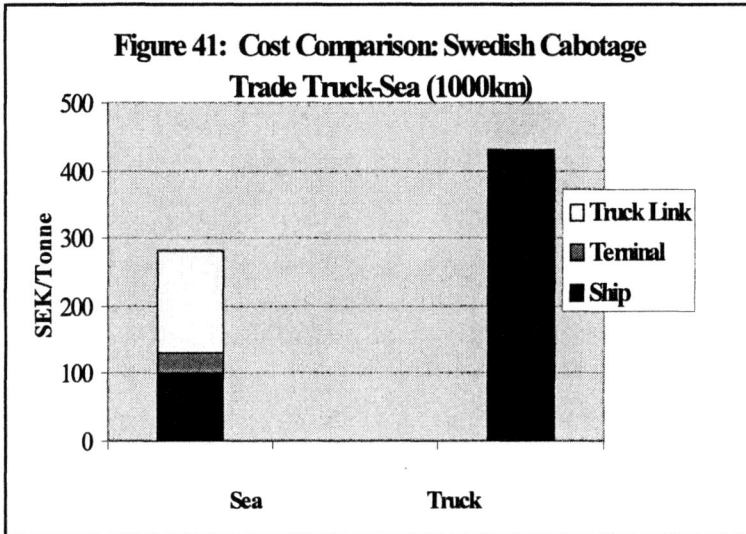

Figure 41: Cost Comparison: Swedish Cabotage Trade Truck-Sea (1000km)

Source: MariTerm AB. (1993) *Coastal and Shortsea Shipping: Technical Feasibility Study*. Göteburg: Swedish Transport Research Board. p.3.

The Swedish Transport Research Board's 1993, *Coastal and Shortsea Shipping: Technical Feasibility Study*,[23] contrasted the costs of road haulage and a technically advanced coastal liner service. Despite the high capital costs of the perceived daily 14 port call, 1000km liner service, it was calculated that the sea option would have costs around SEK 120 per tonne lower than the road alternative, with one daily sailing replacing a 100 daily heavy lorry journeys between Northern Sweden and Stockholm. From Figure 41 it can be seen that the truck linkage between the ship and the delivery point is a higher component of transport costs than the sea leg of the journey. This also reflects the high modal transhipment cost findings of the Bavaria brewers. Figure 42 illustrates the relatively high cost of trucking in the supply chain. The 49% of transport costs allocated to port-hinterland movements by road contrasts with the 39% of port to port costs by ship.

Figure 42: Cost Split for Coastal Shipping (1000kms)

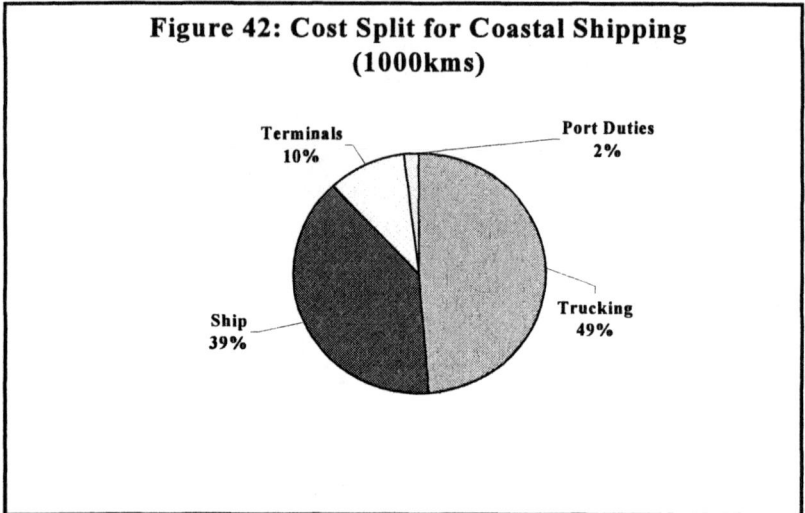

Source: MariTerm AB. (1993) *Coastal and Shortsea Shipping: Technical Feasibility Study.* Göteburg: Swedish Transport Research Board. p.3.

In addition to the Swedish findings, postgraduate research at Southampton Institute (now Solent University) has also revealed the problem of additional costs generated by port and transhipment costs. Evidence of the economics modal transfer from roads to water reveals the problem of handling and distribution costs involved. The short inland movement by road to and from the ports involved proves a difficult cost obstacle. Figure 43 details the comparative costs of a North-South England break-bulk traffic. The road haulage figure of £19.00 per tonne initially compares unfavourably to sea transport's £8.00 per tonne. However when the collection(C) and delivery (D)of the freight by road (distances of 16km and 7km respectively) are added, the transport costs rise to £15.00 per tonne. With additional handling and other associated port costs, the sea option quickly becomes uncompetitive. The burden of port cost is a recurring criticism made by shipowners. In 1995, F.T. Everard Chairman, Mr. Michael Everard, calling for a reduction in port costs for small coasting vessels, drew attention to the high proportion of voyage costs allocated to port disbursements.[24] A similar concern was expressed by Lapthorn Shipping's Chairman, Mr. David Lapthorn in

2004, arguing that his fleet was in acute competition with a road haulage industry which does not face port charges. Conversely, coastal and shortsea faced port disbursements equal to around 30% of vessel earnings.[25]

Figure 43: Comparative North-South England Modal Per-Tonne Costs, Break-Bulk.

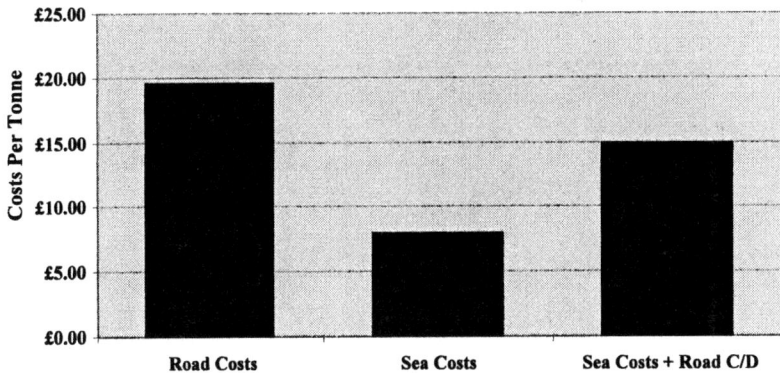

Source: McNamara, T. (2005), British Waterborne Freight: The Waterborne Alternative to Road Transport in the UK. Southampton Solent University.

Belgian shortsea specialist, Professor Marchal, has modelled a number of modal cost comparisons which demonstrate the impact of distance and cargo transhipment on total costs. Distances have been added to Marchal's calculations. The following routes are:

- Route A Truck Liege-Zeebrugge, Container Ship, Zeebrugge-Harwich, Truck London/Liverpool, Container Ship Liverpool-Dublin;

- Route B Truck Liege-Calais, RoRo Ferry Calais-Dover, Truck Dover-London/Liverpool, RoRo Ferry Liverpool-Dublin;

- Route C Sea-River Ship Liege-London/Liverpool/Dublin direct.

In comparing these freight flows from the inland Port of Liege to London, Liverpool and Dublin it is made evident (Table 32) that Route A & B ship-truck combinations utilising the "UK Landbridge" can provide a shorter more direct route to Liverpool and Dublin. However, whilst Routes A and B have a distance-cost advantage in its Liege-Liverpool service, the additional handling and transhipment costs for the Liverpool-Dublin leg force the cost ratio above direct sea-river linkages, despite the extra distances involved.

Table 32 Index Ratio of Comparative Modal Costs ex Liege

Route	Truck-SS Container Ship-Truck) (A) =100	Truck-RoRo-Ferry-Truck (B)	Sea-River Ship (C)	Distances (Km)		
				(A)	(B)	(C)
Liege-London	100	84	68	500	467	482
Liege-Liverpool	100	125	127	780	816	1412
Liege-Dublin	100	119	95	999	1036	1292

Source: Derived from Marchal, J.L.J. "Shortsea Shipping from Hinterland Ports by Sea-River Going Vessels: Study of the Influence of a Free Cabotage Policy," in Wiljnolst, I.N. & Peeters, C.(1995) *European Shortsea Shipping: Strategies for Achieving Cohesion in Europe through Shortsea Shipping.* Delft/London: LLP

The focus in this chapter thus far has been upon the Green Highway competing with road haulage. It has been noted that the modern supply chain places stringent demands upon the transport mode. However, the problems faced by road haulage in the early years of the Millennium, does serve to encourage alternative modes, rail and water. Figure 40 demonstrated the close cost-distance profile of rail and water transport. It next remains to consider the relationship between the water and rail modes.

7.2 Railway Competition or Co-operation?

The economic situation faced by railways *vis-à-vis* road haulage is rather similar to the position of shipping. Rail costs tend to be high over short distances and with low volumes; as distance and/or volume increases rail freight becomes more competitive. In some markets this can lead to competition with shipping. Rail is well suited, like shipping, to the movement of low value, bulk volumes – iron ore, coal, cement. Whilst rail networks have increased flexibility in reaching towards final transport destinations over water, they still normally need road connections from the railhead. Rail, like shipping, can claim environmental integrity in that freight transfer from road to rail has the capability to reduce congestion, pollution and fuel consumption. The privatisation process in the UK has wrought radical changes in the way the rail system operates. The impact on the rail freight sector has been noticeable in its revitalised response towards quality services and competitiveness.

The rail system is heavily concentrated on main lines to London. Paralleling the Route One sea route down the East Coast of Britain, rail and road links have achieved major national importance. The East Coast Main Line (ECML) running between Edinburgh via Newcastle and York to London's Kings Cross is a major passenger trunk route. It was electrified in 1991 and the main line train operating company (TOC) Great North Eastern Railway (GNER), which is owned by the Bermuda shipping group, Sea Containers, has enjoyed high growth since privatisation in 1996. Between 1996 and 2003 the number of daily express passenger trains on the route increased from 100 to 122, passenger numbers increased by 26.8% from 11.9 to 15.1 million.[26] The success of GNER on this premier route, however, has been achieved because passenger services have achieved dominance. Anglo-Scottish freight is primarily diverted to the West Coast rail route. This has freed up valuable track space for high speed passenger movements on the ECML.

The West Coast Main Line (WCML) route running north from London Euston attracts a high share of freight traffics, including container traffics from the Southern England ports, Southampton, Felixstowe, Tilbury and Thamesport. In 2006 it was reported that 43% of UK railfreight used the WCML and that a £37.6b budget was allocated to boosting line speeds and capacity, including a 60-70% increase in freight.[27]

Figure 44: UK Railfreight Tonne-Kilometres 1993-2005 (billions)

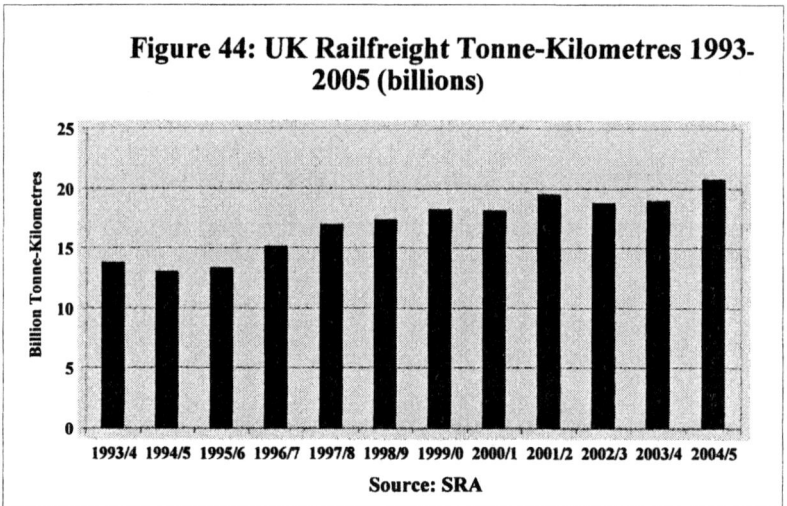

Source: SRA

To the credit of the railfreight operators, the pessimistic outlook for the UK railfreight system, as envisaged by the John Major Government in 1994, has not occurred.[28] Conversely, growth in tkm has been achieved. Figure 44 illustrates the 50% increase in rail freight tkm, from the pre-privatisation level of 13.8.btkm a decade earlier. The movement of coal to the Forthside Longannet power station, one of Europe's largest coal burning facilities, is one example where rail and water have been assessed as potential competitors. The closure of local coal mines in recent decades has necessitated a much increased dependence on imported coal. The choices facing Longannet's owners, Scottish Power, to move its coal imports from the selected deepsea terminal to the power station were:

(1) to tranship to rail from the Clyde estuary port, Hunterston;

(2) to tranship to barge from the Forth port, Burntisland.

The decision to use the Clyde option was obviously part of the overall logistics of the two choices. But the ability of the rail operator, EWS, to increase 75mph merry-go-round train payloads, from 1000 to 1500 tonnes was integral to the decision.[29] By way of contrast, imported coal movements to the Merseyside, Fiddlers Ferry Power Station from Hunterston is via double transhipment: to coastal shipping into the Manchester Ship Canal port, Ellesmere Port and by rail onto Fiddlers Ferry. Oil products move from Southampton's Esso Fawley Refinery to Plymouth by both rail and coastal shipping. The railway dislocations brought about by the Hatfield Disaster aided coastal shipping competition, particularly in grain and container movements. The 2002 start up of the Southampton-Manchester-Greenock feeder service was timely in that it corresponded with the post-Hatfield 2000-03 "melt down", when rail schedules were severely disrupted by the sudden surge of emergency speed restrictions imposed on the network.[30] Railborne malt barley flows from East Anglia and Southern England were lost to sea and road competition in this period. Conversely, the tanker chaos caused by the *Erika* and *Prestige* disasters, rendered older, single hull tankers inoperative, bringing a tanker shortage, thus boosting rail freight movement of oil products. This shows the flexibility that bulk flow shippers have between rail and water modes.

It is evident there are areas of competition between the two modes. However, it also follows that geographic characteristics tend to pre-select the mode. The coal flow to Fiddlers Ferry power station demonstrates the potential for modal-integration between the Green Highway and rail.

The evidence of Irish rail freight strategy by the operator Ianŕod Éireann in the early years of the Millennium suggests an industry that is heading in a different direction to UK rail-freight. Increased freight charges and rationalisation of services have been criticised by customers, including the Irish Exporters Association.[31] The Shannon Foynes Port company has also been critical of poor port-rail linkages, hampering expansion plans.[32] In October 2005, *The Irish Times* reported that a private European logistics operator was attempting to enter into the Irish rail freight market.[33] It is evident that unless a dramatic competitive reversal of rail-freight occurs then the Green Highway will be the only sustainable alternative for Irish goods traffics.

The analysis so far in this chapter has considered the factors determining shipping's prospects in the supply chain *vis-à-vis* modal competition. It next remains to consider just how the industry responds to the demands of the supply chain – the dynamics of shipping supply.

7.3 Shipping Supply Issues

In order that shipping fulfils its potential the supply question begs some consideration. The supply of shipping is integral to the development of the Green Highway. In meeting increased demand it is vital that investment in new tonnage is accelerated. The issues of investment, costs and how these are allocated in the charter market are now considered.

7.3.1 Investment Issues

Thus far this chapter has concentrated upon the competitive aspects within the logistics chain. It is also pertinent to discuss the issues of shipping investment in order to participate in this chain. The problem facing shipowners in a volatile market is how to invest with confidence. This is particularly the case when, as reported in chapter 6, a number of companies had experienced trading difficulties in the early Millennium period.

Variation in the capital costs of new buildings is a function of supply and demand. The supply of shipbuilding capacity is an obvious determinant of new building costs. Also, raw materials – principally the costs of steel per tonne - and labour costs will have a major influence. It is apparent that these factors have favoured lower new build costs. Traditionally the enduring over-capacity of world shipbuilding has exerted a downward pressure on rates. Similarly, over-capacity in global steel production has depressed steel prices. Under these conditions shipbuilding labour needs to achieve a high level of production efficiency in the market. The globalisation impact has registered even on European based shipping. Examples in the 1990s include the building order package of $23.5m by the Kentish operator, F.T. Everard for two products tankers, *Asperity* and *Audacity* in Singapore. Several of the Netherlands yards have taken advantage of the lower labour costs of Eastern Europe by ordering the basic hull structure from Bulgarian shipbuilders. In addition to the cost impact of globalisation, the economics of newbuildings are often distorted by state intervention in the shape of subsidies and easy credit terms. The construction of the sister ship product tankers, *Mersey Fisher* and *Thames Fisher* at the Barrow in Furness yard, Vickers Shipbuilding and Engineering Ltd, was carried out at highly competitive rates. The rationale of this is the desire to achieve a diversification from warship to merchant shipbuilding, with the new *state-of-the-art* tankers serving as a shop window role for the builders.[34] Another example of the globalised spread of shipbuilding, plus the options this makes available to owners, was provided by the 2001 new buildings, *Crescent Rhine* and *Crescent Seine*. The new sea-river bulkers were completed for long term charter to Crescent Shipping of Southampton by the Netherlands shipbuilder, Volharding. However, this was not a simple Netherlands-UK collaboration. The hulls of the two vessels were constructed by Daewoo Mangalia in Romania. The vessels were built for the account of the German shipping operator, Reederei Shipcom, who then chartered them out the to Crescent Shipping for a ten year period, accompanied by an option to buy.[35] Although the hull construction in Romania necessitated the long towage to the Netherlands, economic gains were attained. Volharding's Director of Engineering and Design, Hans Suurmeijer, has outlined the advantages of the Romanian tie up. The synergy of the link allowed Volharding to complete seventeen of its innovative sea-river buildings in 2000. With the Netherlands yard working at full capacity, output would have been limited to seven or eight without the Romanian venture. Mr. Suurmeijer heralded the benefits of "intensive" co-operation as providing customers with low cost, high quality fabrication; a major cost component in the final delivery price.[36] Table 33 provides information on newbuildings for British and Irish owners. Throughout the 1990s it was rare for British owners to commit themselves to new tonnage, particularly vessels below 3000dwt in the dry-cargo sector. This points to the difficult trading conditions that persist in dry trades. At the start of his career, sea-river entrepreneur Max Heinimann was warned to expect 3 good years and 7 bad ones![37] The difficulties facing even the most adventurous operators such as Carisbrooke Shipping, was exampled by the company's withdrawal from the London Stock Exchange's Alternative Investment Market (AIM).

Vessel	Owner/ Operator	Builder	Date	Type	Size dwt	Cost ($m)
Table 33: Information on Selected Newbuildings for European Trades						
Arklow Sky	Arklow Shipping, Arklow	Barkmeijer Stroobos	2000	General Cargo	3200	$7.1
Asperity	Everard, Kent	Singmarine, Singapore	1997	Products Tanker	3778	$11.75
Crescent Seine	Crescent Shipping, Southampton	Volharding, Netherlands	2001	Sea/River Bulker	2770	$5.5 est
Navion Britannia	Statoil, Stavanger Norway	AESA Bilbao	1998	Crude Oil Shuttle Tanker	124 821	$90.00
Jaynee W	Whitaker Holdings,Hu ll	Yorkshire Drydocks, Hull	1996	Coastal Bunkering Barge	2850	$7.10
Johanna C	Carisbrooke Shipping, Cowes	Damen, Netherlands	1998	General Cargo	4290	$6.50
Rix Owl	J.R. Rix & Sons	Hepworth East Yorkshire	2003	Products Tankbarge	650	$1.6
Speciality	Everard, Kent	Qingshan, China	2005	Products Tanker	3780	$13.50
Shannon Fisher	Fisher Tankships, Barrow	Damen, Galati Romania	2006	Products Tanker	5000	$11.60
Thames Fisher	Fisher Tankships, Barrow	VSEL, Barrow	1997	Products Tanker	4765	$11.25

Source: *Lloyd's List. Fairplay*, Rina, *Significant Ships.*

In July 1999 *Lloyd's List* reported that

> Like many small shipping companies Carisbrooke has been prevented from raising further equity capital with its shares languishing at a fraction of the offering price.[38]

These conditions place great emphasis on the economics of operation, where costs are made up of crew, maintenance and stores outlays. These are the inescapable costs of keeping a vessel in service. Voyage costs are primarily made up of fuel and port costs. The emphasis on cost competition has invariably pressurised crew supplies. This has become manifest in two ways: (a) the reduction of crew numbers; (b) the replacement of North European crews by lower cost labour drawn from such sources as Eastern Europe, the Cape Verde Islands and the Philippines. Labour saving technology such as automated hatch covers, tank cleaning devices and One Man Bridge Operation (OMBO) have reduced crew levels and thus costs. The International Convention on Standards of Training and Certification of Watchkeepers (STCW) stipulate that two watchkeepers are on bridge/look-out duties during the hours of darkness or restricted visibility; OMBO seeks to reduce the costs of any extra seaman on look-out duties by providing technical back-up to the sole navigational watchkeeper.[39]

Given the changes in the global sourcing of capital and labour markets that have occurred in deep-sea shipping post 1960s, it was inevitable that small shipowners would belatedly pursue a similar strategy. This has meant the steady erosion of North European crews with lower wage third world nationals. Often this process has been accompanied by the flagging out of vessels to registries specialising in small ships – Gibraltar, Cyprus, St. Vincent and the Grenadines, Antigua and Barbuda. The imperative of achieving economies in the small ship market is to minimise empty running. This is particularly the case in the low value dry bulk trades, where freight rates are insufficient to sustain long, nil revenue, return voyages. The art of survival in the scrap, grain, salt, aggregates, timber and china clay trades is to seek return cargoes from closely located loading ports, thus minimising empty voyage legs. Grain imports and scrap exports can be observed in such ports as Southampton, Newport and Manchester. Regular steel import flows into the Dorset port of Poole from Belgium, France and Germany are balanced by return loads of grain ex Poole or china/ball clay from the nearby Devon port, Teignmouth.

An interesting angle on the economics of shipping has been raised by the European Short-Sea Shipping Roundtable Forum. The Delft Paradox (1994) and the Vouliagemeni Paradox (1996) was acknowledged in chapter 1 as defining the parameters of vessel size and the extent of government support. The 1994 Conference led to the creation of the "Delft Paradox." The ideas raised in this forum have implications for the investment question. Essentially this asked what the limits would be in the trade off between the economies of scale of larger coastal vessels and the ability of smaller vessels to visit smaller ports and to penetrate inland waterway systems. In order that vessels realise their full competitive advantage against road haulage, it is apparent that a certain critical size level needs to be attained. At its most extreme point this means the low tkm costs of large vessels and large ports. This, however, needs to be weighed against the environmental advantages of the smaller vessels ability to reach closer to the point of final destination. The intention here is to assess the "Delft Paradox" within the British Isles context, with particular emphasis on inland trading on such rivers as the Severn, Trent and Weaver. A number of key factors will be considered here – distance, volume and transhipment costs. It is apparent that the average size of coastal vessels has grown in recent decades, with the 3000dwt tonne vessel becoming more in evidence than the 750dwt vessel.

Figure 45 clearly displays the decline in small ship investment in the UK dry-cargo post 1985, when new orders peaked at 20 vessels. [40] By the new Millennium Orders were down to an average of two per year. Adding to the problem of new tonnage shortages in the <2500dwt dry cargo sector, container feeder supply levels have been a cause for concern.

In particular, an incipient imbalance between surging orders for deepsea tonnage and a dearth in the feeder sector has been identified.[41] In 2005 it was estimated that the deepsea container vessel fleet was growing at 20%, whilst the feeder/shortsea fleet was only achieving a 9% annual growth. Given the need for

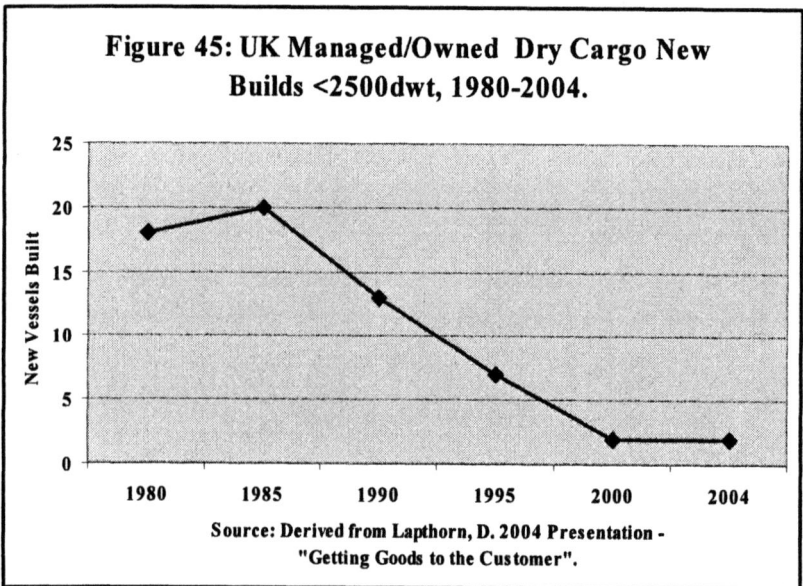

Figure 45: UK Managed/Owned Dry Cargo New Builds <2500dwt, 1980-2004.

Source: Derived from Lapthorn, D. 2004 Presentation - "Getting Goods to the Customer".

feeder ships to connect with their deepsea "mother" ships in the supply chain, Lloyd's Register has estimated that in order to meet the demand for feeder tonnage, up to 2,000 new vessels were needed by the end of the decade, requiring a building rate far in excess of the actual contemporary level. Furthermore, the reality of an ageing feeder fleet, with some 40% of tonnage exceeding 15 years old could only serve to exacerbate the problems of supply In the tanker sector size increases are evident. The 1997 addition of the *Asperity* and *Audacity* to the Everard coastal tanker fleet saw a 30% increase in tonnage over the company's 1990 newbuilding tankers.[42] The addition of the *Speciality* class of tanker in 2006 brought a further 17% increase in tanker size.

The second paradox emanates from the Shortsea Shipping's Roundtable Conference in Greece, 1996, the Vouliagmeni Paradox. This was derived from the complex issues of state involvement in transport operations. It has been made apparent that some shipping services will struggle to remain competitive with road haulage whilst still providing the shipowner with a modest rate of return. The problem can be particularly acute during the early days of a new shipping venture. Support from freight forwarders is traditionally slow to build up as the new service remains untested and road haulage competition turns particularly predatory in the bid to stifle the new challenger. Given the paradox of the desire of European governments to achieve a more effective use of water transport and the inability of the free market to achieve this objective, the role of the state becomes paramount. On one hand it can be seen that the some degree of state support is necessary to supplement entrepreneurial risk, on the other this prejudices the Community's commitment to free and unhindered markets. Such state encouragement as the Freight Facilities Grant supplied by government is obviously integral to this debate. In order to provide some context on the economics of the Green Highway, attention to vessel cost structures is now provided.

7.3.2 The Cost Structure

The economics of ship ownership can be divided between the fixed costs of purchasing the vessel and the costs of maintaining, crewing and operating. Voyage costs are the variable costs incurred by the trip. Chartering the vessel is a way of avoiding the capital costs and, in some instances, the operating costs, depending on the terms of charter. Whatever the financing arrangements, for the shipping option to be successful it must attract significant investment and be managed effectively. The vessels cost structure can be divided into three main categories: (1) capital costs; (2) operating costs;(3) voyage costs.

7.3.3 Capital Costs

The capital costs are fixed in that they represent the annual cost allocated to the buying of the vessel, including mortgage and interest repayments. The initial builder's price is likely to be depreciated over a fifteen or twenty year period. From the data of Table 33 above it can be seen that these costs vary from the $90m, 124,821dwt specialist shuttle tanker *Navion Brittania,* to the $1.6m tank-barge, *Rix Owl.* It can be seen how capital costs are a function of both size and the amount of on-board technological sophistication. Dry bulk vessels are most likely to have lower costs than product tankers.

7.3.4 Operating Costs

Operating costs are allocated to the vessel technically ready and crewed for service. Crew costs tend to be the largest element in this account; and this helps explain the attention that owners and ship managers pay to attaining lower cost crew supplies. Table 34 is derived from Moore and Stephens study of 2001 operating costs from a sample of 55 coastal vessels, averaging 3,349dwt. It shows a total annual crew cost of $446,375; half of total operating costs. This provides explanation for the concentration on crewing cost, particularly the replacement of North European and Scandinavian crews with lower wage East European and developing nation crews. Other operating costs are allocated to spares, stores, lubricants, maintenance and dry-docking.

7.3.5 Voyage Costs

The major element in voyage costs is bunkers, which is the fuel oil and/or diesel oil consumed on the voyage. Other voyage costs include port entry dues,

Table 34: Coastal Vessel Operating Costs, 2001 (3349 dwt)		
Cost Item	**US$ (Per Year)**	**US$ (Per Day)**
Crew Wages	376,486	1,031
Provisions	26,290	73
Crew Other	43,599	119
Crew Costs Total	*446,375*	*1,223*
Lubricants	15,626	43
Stores Other	44,035	121
Stores Total	*59,661*	*164*
Spares	110,999	304
Repairs & Maintenance	56,580	155
Repairs & Maintenance Total	*167,579*	*459*
P&I Insurance	20,674	57
Insurance	29,576	81
Insurance Total	*50,250*	*138*
Registration Costs	3,564	10
Management Fees	60,657	166
Sundries	91,053	249
Administration Total	*155,274*	*425*
Total Operating Costs	US$ 879,139	US$ 2,409
Source: Moore Stephens: *OpCost 2002: Benchmarking Vessel Running Costs*		

canal dues, hold and tank cleaning and surveying. The impact of rising fuel costs can bear heavily on the operator, particularly for faster vessels with high tonnes per day consumption. Fuel costs were a major ingredient in the painful restructuring of Irish Ferries crewing arrangements, late 2005. The switch from Irish to Latvian seafarers was rationalised by management as a cost saving imperative, following a predicted doubling of fuel costs, 2004-6.[43] In early 2006, the future of Stena Line's high speed Irish Sea and North Sea services was reported to be in jeopardy because of declining passenger revenues and rising fuel costs.[44] Determining the appropriation of costs is defined by the terms of the vessels charter party.

7.4 The Charter Market

The investment issue is also influenced by the nature of the charter market. A number of options exist in the supplying of vessels. The type of charter has implications for the economics of the specific trades. The charter party is the contractual document between the shipowner and the charterer. This document has a long lineage as an agent of accord between the two parties. In Roman times, the absence of such administrative aids as carbon copy paper and photocopiers necessitated the *Charta Partita* to be written out twice with each party retaining a copy in case of a dispute.[45] Four principal types of vessel charter may be utilised in the coastal trades:

      (1)   Voyage Charter;
      (2)   Time Charter;
      (3)   Bareboat or Demise Charter;
      (4)   Contract of Affreightment.

7.4.1 The Voyage Charter

The voyage charter is the most common use of contract between the shipper and the carrier. In the bulk and break-bulk trades the voyage charter provides a spot market arrangement for such staple cargoes as grain, coal, cement, timber and steel. Under the arrangements of the voyage charter, the ship-owner is paid a per tonne rate. This is referred to as "the freight rate". The shipowner is therefore accountable for all operating and voyage expenses, with the exception of cargo handling costs. Although the short term nature of coastal voyages suggests that the voyage charter fails to provide long term security, it does complement the pattern of trades. Under these conditions each cargo working in port will be allotted a certain amount of laytime for cargo operations. If this time is exceeded then the shipowner is entitled to compensation in the form of demurrage; conversely, if not all the laytime is used the shipowner is liable to pay compensation to the charterer in terms of despatch monies.[46]

In particular, the voyage charter provides flexibility when seeking out "backhaul" cargoes. For instance a regular "backhaul" balance is imported animal feeds into the Belfast ex Benelux countries and return cargoes of stone to London. As a consequence, empty running is minimised and the shipowner benefits from maximising the earning potential of the vessel. Also, the shipper benefits from the lower freight rates that the "backhaul" facilitates. In addition, the erratic nature of the bulk trades promotes a short-term strategy which is conducive to the voyage "spot" market. The seasonal and weather dependent character of the grain trades, in particular, can lead to a surge or a slump in demand.

The voyage charter is favoured by shippers with either a one-off cargo or with a need to supplement existing shipping arrangements. They are also employed by traders wishing to speculate by loading a cargo not for a specific port but for a geographic range such as Antwerp-Hamburg. The cargo is sold whilst the vessel is on passage and a specific port is nominated.[47] Although freight rate information is not so readily available as in the deep-sea trades with their Baltic Freight Indices, it is evident that the two parties and their shipbrokers and freight forwarders are acutely aware of the market price of each trade. The open access characteristics of the market, however, make it easier for new market entrants. This makes for acute competition and falling freight rates. As a result, British firms like Lapthorn's have faced difficulties in achieving sustainable revenues, despite their fleet working at full capacity. The dry cargo voyage market has been attacked by flag of convenience and East European tonnage (often flying flags of convenience). The intense cost competition has resulted in the economic phenomena of negative cash flow. The "mass retreat" from the dry cargo market in 2002 by three of the UK's leading operators – Crescent, Everard and Fisher – can be linked to this seemingly entrenched problem.

7.4.2 The Time Charter

The concentration by these three aforementioned companies on the product tanker sector can be explained by the prevailing stable charter market. The time charter can be attractive to both shippers and shipowners confident in future freight flow levels. The time charter can be agreed for any time span between a few weeks and more than a decade. The shipowner is still responsible for operating the ship but instead of the vessel earning on a per tonne basis, freight earnings are paid as an agreed amount per day/month. Under these conditions costs are shared between the shipowner and the charterer. Basically, the charterer is responsible for finding the cargo and covering the vessel's voyage costs – fuel, port, cargo handling, canal, tank/hold cleaning.

A feature of coastal oil products distribution in recent years has been for the oil majors to divest from own-account vessel owning and the engagement of third party tanker operators on long term time charters. Traditional British operators, Crescent Tankships, Everard and Fisher have benefited from time charters from such oil majors as Shell, Chevron and Exxon.

In the container shortsea and feeder trades, time charters are offered to shipowners (predominantly German KG) by specialist operators. Companies such as Seawheel, Concorde and Clydeport have all chartered in German owned, open registry tonnage.

7.4.3 Contracts of Affreightment (COA)

Also providing for the long-term market, thus earnings stability, the contract of affreightment provides for agreement between the shipowner and charterer over the amount of tonnage to be moved in a fixed period of time. The shipowner may wish to allocate any number of ships to the ensuing freight flow. This provides for an operational flexbility in matching voyages to potential backhauls of cargo. In addition, the shipowner is able to boost capacity by chartering in tonnage to prevent any shortages of his/her own tonnage. Where large volumes are moved over relatively short voyages, the COA has considerable advantages. It reduces the administrative task of completing numerous voyage charters and it allows shipowners the flexibility to keep the vessel operating in revenue (loaded). For example, voyages in the stone trade from Glensanda to the Baltic can be balanced with return cargoes of Polish coal to the Humber. The emphasis on time charters and contracts of affreightment by leading owners, points to a schism occurring in the market, with quality owners attempting to balance their relatively high costs against the more secure earnings achieved.

7.4.4 Bareboat or Demise Charter

This document allows the charterer to manage and operate the ship, covering all costs with the exception of capital cost and interest repayments. The charterer becomes the disponent owner and is responsible for crewing, managing and employing the vessel. The owner will receive a fixed rate of hire at regular intervals. In the coastal trades, this type of charter allows financial concerns to own vessels in order to benefit from fiscal allowances and earnings potential, whilst delegating the task of managing the vessel to shipping specialists. Traditional companies such as Arklow Shipping, Stephenson Clarke and James Fisher and Sons have been able to access new tonnage without facing the burden of capital outlay. A relatively new pattern of ownership and operation is provided by the ship management concept. Under these conditions a split occurs between the actual owners of the vessel and the operators.

7.5 Vertical Integration

The Green Highway supply chain in terms of vessel investment takes on a different perspective when shipping becomes vertically integrated into the core business. For firms vertically integrating transport into their strategic supply chain, costs may be less important than qualitative factors such as reliability, safety and environmental integrity. A trend towards integration in specialist, niche markets can be detected. Three short examples of unlikely shipping operators are now considered: (1) the aerospace industry, (2) the heavy haulage industry, (3) the sand quarry industry.

The long term charters given by Airbus Industries for specially designed craft capable of moving aircraft parts from European production sites provides a clear example of this logistics perspective. The assembly of the giant Airbus passenger jet at Toulouse has presented many opportunities for shortsea logistics. The barge, *Afon Dyfrdwy,* designed for the River Dee leg of the journey from the aircraft plant to the transhipment wharf, demonstrates the capability of inland shipping in the supply chain. The linkage with purpose built vessels at the North Wales port, Mostyn, provides for an almost all-water supply chain to the Toulouse assembly plant.[48]

A revolutionary development in the logistics of heavy indivisible loads was achieved in 2002-4 when the specialist heavy haulier Robert Wynn & Sons Ltd, with a road transport history stretching from 1863,[49] extended its supply chain to inland and coastal shipping. The rationale of the project, which was supported by a £8.5m FFG, was to remove slow moving heavy goods movements from UK roads. Wynn's had estimated that up to 1500 "superloads" in excess of 150 tonnes disrupt UK traffic flows per year.[50] The conversion of the inland barge *Inland Navigator* and the construction of the purpose built *Terra Marique,* enabled Wynn's to integrate heavy goods movement of such indivisible cargoes as power station transformers, maximising the water-leg of the journey around the UK and European coastline and inland waterway systems, including the River Trent and Manchester Ship Canal.

The development of sand and gravel deposits in rural Essex has provided a sustainable logistics challenge for the Fingringhoe (Near Colchester) based quarry owners, Prior. The Prior family have a barging history stretching back to the late 1800s. In the inter-war period, they built up a fleet of motor barges in order to service heavy demand for construction materials in London.[51] Water transport is seen by the company as an extension of its environmental commitment to responsible minerals extraction, which provides for quarry sites to be restored to agricultural land on completion of extraction activities. Prior's are proud to claim that 30,000 lorry journeys per year are kept off the Essex/London regions roads per annum.[52] The company has been supported by the FFG for the up-grading of its fleet of eight vessels. The ownership of the fleet bestows on Prior's the ability to meet supply chain demands in central London, providing a 24 hours service to Thames terminals. By planning sailing schedules, utilising the strong tides of the Thames estuary, optimum efficiency can be attained by minimising fuel consumption.

The inclusion of a directly owned, vertically integrated, shipping fleet into the firm's supply chain provides a number of advantages. Complementary to the dedication of the fleet to the firm's production stream, vessel ownership provides a handle on costs and operational expertise. Moreover, the firm can claim commitment to environmental integrity.

7.6 Case Studies in Green Highway Logistics

Having considered demand and supply factors of the supply chain, it is now felt timely to appraise existing supply chains involving the Green Highway. Nine short case studies are provided here under conditions where shipping is attempting to fulfil the logistical demands of the market. The essential elements determining success (or failure) in these supply chains will be identified in order to consider what lessons can be learned – essentially determining the bench mark conditions for a vibrant Green Highway?

7.6.1 Case Study 1: Foster Yeoman's Quarry Stone Flows

Breaking the mould somewhat in the world of commodity trading is the strategy of stone quarry owners, Foster Yeoman. The Somerset based company has extended its participation in the supply chain by diversification into shipping and rail operations. This includes increased involvement in the chartering and operating of bulk carriers and, additionally, ownership of a fleet of tugs and barges, thus providing for an integrated sea-river transhipment logistics chain. Also, the company operates a rail-fleet of 59 locomotives and 400 hopper trucks.[53]

The history of the quarrying company has long been focused on the stone quarrying areas of the Wiltshire and Somerset area. Essentially these quarries are rail served for bulk haulage of stone. However, the desire to exploit new stone supplies away from environmentally and politically sensitive English rural regions has led to concentration on new quarrying opportunities. The North European flow of stone from quarries in Eire (Bantry Bay), Scotland (Glensanda) and Norway (Espevaer) accounts for around 6.5mt of coastal and shortsea trade for the Foster Yeoman Group.

Part of the group's success story is explained by its advanced quarrying, rock processing and cargo handling methods, particularly at the coastal super-quarry, Glensanda.[54] The company bareboat chartered three large self-discharging bulk vessels in the early Millennium years - *Yeoman Brook* (75,000dwt), *Yeoman Bank* (37,000dwt), *Yeoman Bontrup* (97,000dwt). Of particular note is the role of the subsidiary management company, World Self-Unloaders (WSU). The three large bulkers are managed by WSU, who place great emphasis on achieving the maximum utilisation of the capital-intensive self-discharging vessels. When the self-discharger vessels were added to the fleet, Foster Yeoman heralded the long term security and stability that operating these highly flexible vessels gave within the vertical integration of the stone supply chain.[55] In addition, some 300 smaller coastal vessels are chartered per year.[56] Surprisingly, Foster Yeoman's Shipping Division is located in Frome in rural Somerset. This is a result of the group's intense activity in the Somerset/Wiltshire quarry region, which is primarily rail-borne bulk traffic carried by Britain's heaviest freight trains (12,000 tonnes). However, modern communications methods ensure that the shipping link is maintained; the process of vessel chartering and logistics co-ordination is conducted remotely from the coast. Figure 46 illustrates principal port calls linking the quarries in Bantry Bay and Glensanda with Glasgow, Liverpool, Southampton and the Isle of Grain.

The self-discharge facility on the three large vessels is an expensive addition to capital overheads, apportioning around 50% of the vessels' new building cost. Conversely, this facility does provide for both the flexibility of being able to discharge in ports lacking handling infrastructure and for much reduced stevedoring charges. Foster Yeoman have estimated that the vessels, which move around 5mt annually from Glensanda, achieve a per-km cost 200 times lower than road costs.[57] Furthermore, the self-discharging vessels are also available for non-stone charters outside of the Foster Yeoman ambit. A typical voyage pattern could be Glensanda-Southampton (loaded stone), Southampton-Zeebrugge (empty in ballast), Zeebrugge-Port Talbot (coal) and back up the West Coast to load again at Glensanda. The re-deployment of the ex-oil jetties at the Isle of Grain as a "virtual quarry" storage/transhipment facility provides opportunities for movement to the Inner and Greater London area by barge and rail. The logistical link between coastal and river movements of stone was further strengthened in 2002, when Foster Yeoman took a controlling interest in their Thames estuary business partner, A.C. Bennett, who had built up a tug and barge fleet in the region. The partnership between the two family businesses was consolidated as a joint application for a FFG was made in order to assist funding of new river craft.[58]

The assimilation of the Bennett fleet into Foster Yeoman's operations allows for vertical integration of the supply chain, from the quarry to up-river wharfs. These Thames wharfs can now be seen as strategically well placed to serve the construction industry's demands, particularly given the surge in East London building activity facilitated by the 2012 London Olympics. The integration between large bulk carriers and tug and barge combinations, also railfreight, allows for a seamless in-house logistics movement from the super quarry via the virtual quarry stockpiles to inner-city distribution hubs. At the time of writing, the 83 year lineage of the family controlled firm was undergoing a significant ownership change in the shape of a £300m takeover by a leading global supplier of aggregates, Holcim.[59]

Figure 46: Foster Yeoman Stone Flows

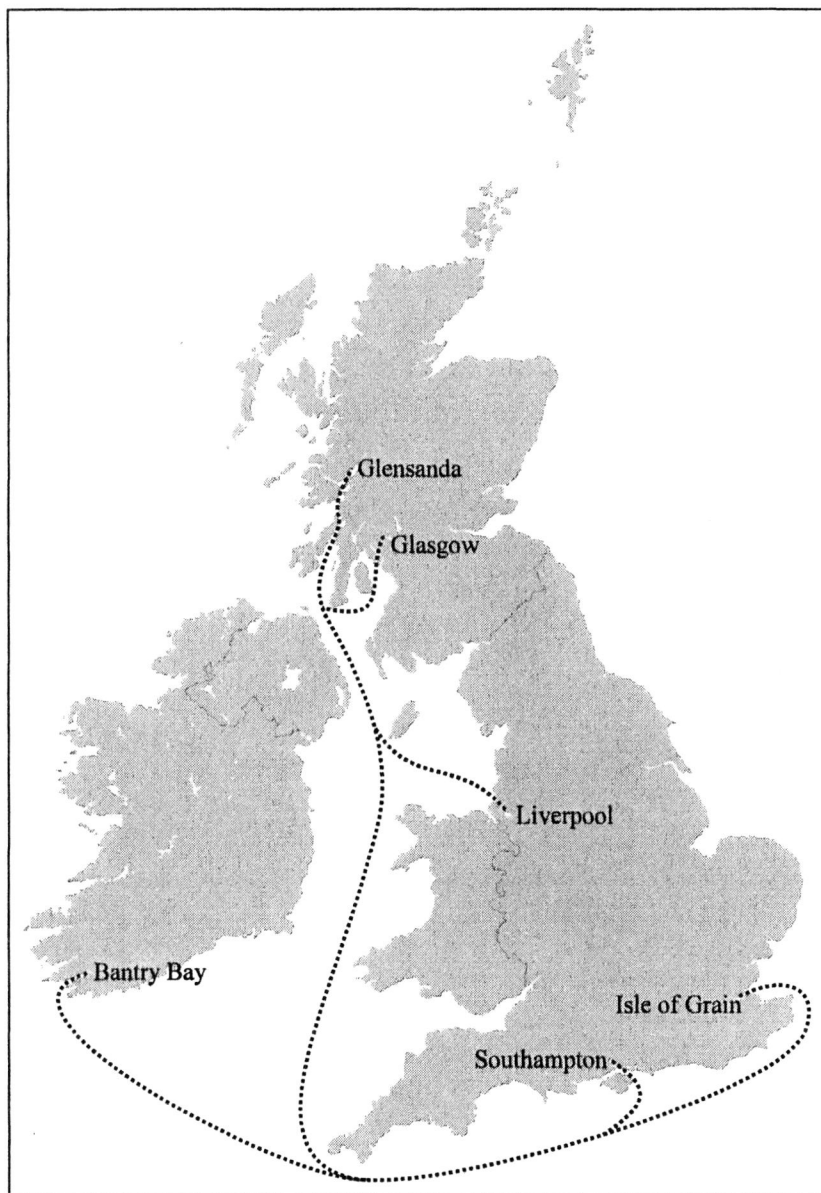

7.6.2. Case Study 2:Intermodal Services: The Road to Widnes!

A benefit of freight transport de-regulation has been the involvement of road hauliers in inter-modal operations. The Scottish haulier, Malcolm Group, has become a leading advocate of rail integration, running up to 85 freight trains per week.[60] The Merseyside haulier, O'Connor Group, has achieved inter-modalism using sea, rail and road, based around the company's Widnes Inter-Modal Rail Terminal. The Upper-Mersey town of Widnes lost its own up-river port in the 1970s, however, the Green Highway linkage is maintained by integration between shortsea, rail and road. The de-regulation and privatisation of ports and rail networks has provided some opportunities for inter-modal integration. The European Commission sponsored network study, Regional Action for Logistical Integration of Shipping across Europe (REALISE)[61] has examined the prospects for European short-sea shipping within the context of modal integration. One potential freight flow considered was between the Southern Italy container hub, Gioia Tauro and the Lancashire city, Preston, illustrated in Figure 47.

Two modal options were compared in terms of transport costs; a direct road option, via the North Sea crossing and a truly multi-modal option, involving shortsea, rail, barge (Basel-Rotterdam), shortsea, rail, and finally road delivery for the remaining 75km journey leg, Widnes-Preston.. Figure 48 shows the cost advantages of the inter-modal choice *vis-à-vis* the all- road option. Despite the high level of cargo handling and its associated costs, the multi-modal option came out at a total cost of €1949.54, some 68% of the direct road costs of €2879.71. Such examples highlight the economic possibilities of the Green Highway integrated into the supply chain. Whilst it is evident that such a multi-modal approach would face significantly longer transit times, the cost saving plus

Figure 47: Gioia Tauro – Preston Inter-Modal Route

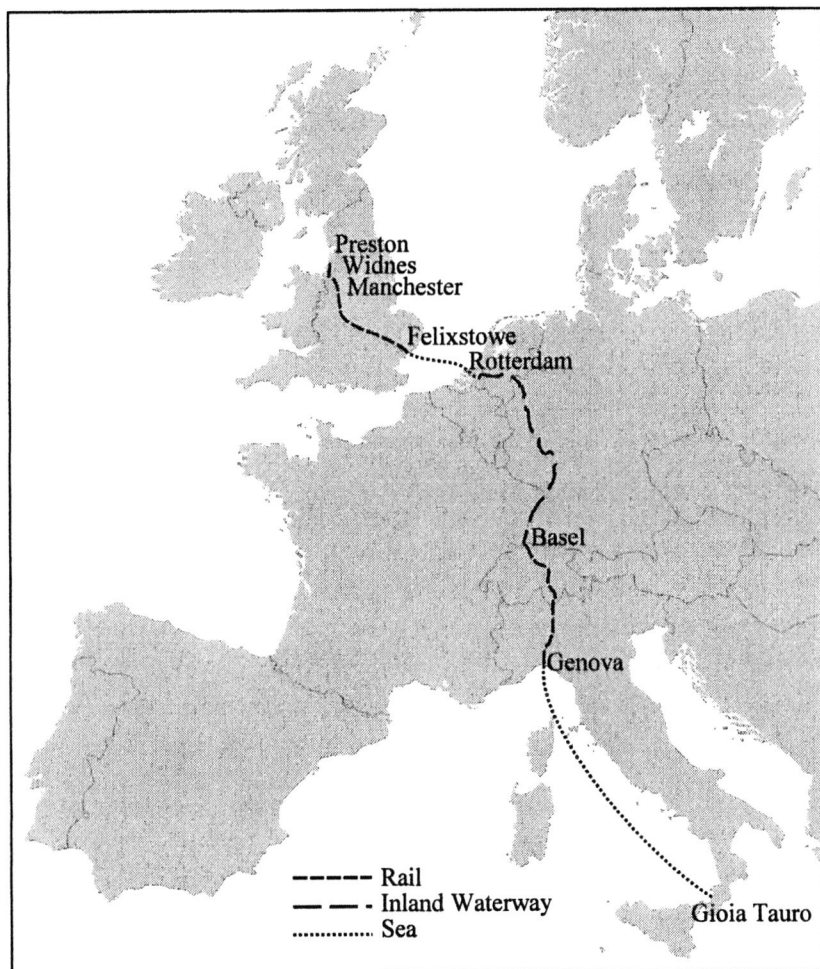

356

environmental gains of utilising existing sustainable transport services make for an attractive alternative to road haulage in both business and political terms.

Figure 48: Modal Cost Comparison, Container Movement, Gioia Tauro-Preston.

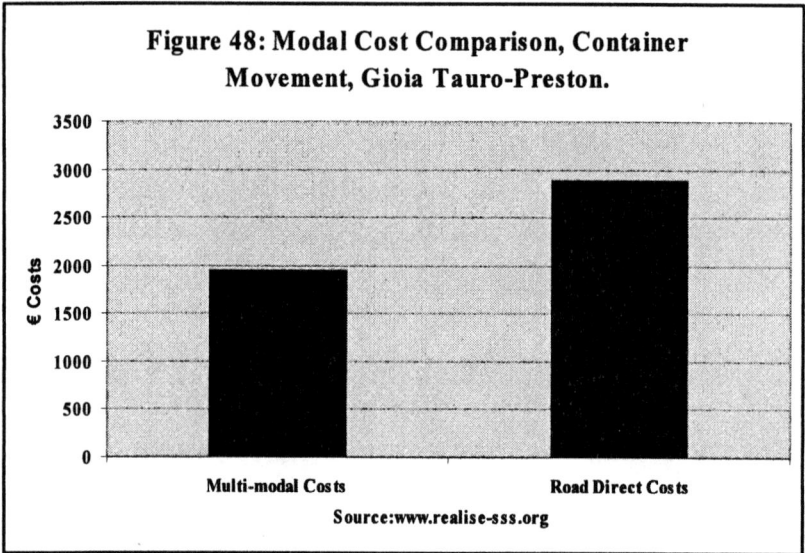

Source:www.realise-sss.org

The inter-modal linkage to Widnes has been facilitated historically by rail links with the Port of Harwich. Harwich's history is very much that of a railway port. As the ferry terminal for the Great Eastern Railway's passenger and freight services to the Benelux countries, the port's fate has invariably intertwined with the rail interest. British Rail's innovatory Freightliner intermodal service in 1968 proved to be an early example of rail-sea logistics in the shortsea trades. As the service provider between Ford's Dagenham and mainland European plants, British Rail achieved a market leader status in fully cellular container shipping in the shortsea trades. Unfortunately, for the port, the trade easily lent itself to transfer to the Channel Tunnel; as a consequence, railfreight services were withdrawn in 1994.

The return to rail operations in 1997 was something of a reversal in trends in that it offered a Lo-Lo route to Zeebrugge as an alternative to Channel Tunnel intermodal services. The dynamics of rail's return to Harwich can be seen as the result of five factors: (1) the desire of shippers to link UK freight flows with continental services from Zeebrugge to Central and Southern Europe; (2) the quest by shippers for both a quality and a cost competitive alternative to the premium tariffs of the Channel Tunnel; (3) the participation of road hauliers in the service; (4) the considerable intermodal expertise that the port has accumulated, providing for optimum efficiency in rail-sea integration, (5) finally, the willingness of EWS to invest in new traction and rolling stock on the Widnes-Harwich routes. UK Rail Haulage distances from Harwich are in the 200-600 km range.

The North Sea LoLo schedules linked with daily rail-freight services ex-Harwich. These included trains to Doncaster combining with EWS services to Teesport, an important source of chemical traffics. Harwich-Wembley, offered connections to Newport and Widnes as well as the Seaforth container terminal in Liverpool. The Widnes link is notable in that it features collaboration with a local haulier and has led to the opening of an international terminal, supported by a Freight Facility Grant. The 44 tonne dispensation for road-rail interchange, which existed between 1991 and 2001 and the strategy to minimise the road trunking of hazardous goods had proved attractive to chemical shippers in the Widnes-Runcorn industrial region. The new arrival of EWS' low platform megafret wagons helped boost services by allowing for the unhindered carriage of 9ft 6in containers through the restricted tunnel and bridge gauges of the British rail system.. By 2006 the growing inter-modal traffics had moved away from Harwich, becoming focused on the deepsea ports of Southampton and Felixstowe, as well as the Thames shortsea port, Purfleet.

The regular flow of LoLo traffics is balanced by foodstuffs moving north from Milan with chemicals moving south from the UK's Merseyside and Teeside

358

industrial regions. Initially, the intermodal operation was the result of the astute combination of regular traffic flows and the highly efficient Stena Line's nightly container service, carried out by the 200teu sister vessels, *Hera* and *Apus*. The integration with road haulage operations in the Widnes area and the custom generated by P&O Ferrymasters has enhanced co-operation rather than competition with hauliers, in particular, the diversification of the O'Connor Group into inter-modal and terminal operations. The environmental benefits of using rail trunk-haul links to serve the Widnes Inter-Modal Rail Terminal became apparent in 2005 when the O'Connor Group moved 40,000 units by rail, approximating to 16m lorry kms.[62]

The evidence from this example of inter-modal enterprise demonstrates the opportunities available in achieving integration in supply chains, with each particular journey leg maximising the economic and environmental benefits of the selected mode.

7.6.3 Case Study 3:Boston's Steel Trade

European integration in the steel trades has provided further opportunities for sustainable modal integration. The Lincolnshire up-river port, Boston, markets itself as the provider of the nearest East Coast ship discharge to the Birmingham and West Midlands industrial region. Primarily, the port's trade is European short-sea and reflects East Anglia's agricultural base. The steel business passing through the port can be seen resulting from the re-organisation, integration and rationalisation of European production sites. The selective run down of UK steel production from the 1980s onwards placed emphasis on imports from Belgium, the Netherlands and Germany. Competition for the handling of steel coils – bound for the automotive and metal fabrication industries of the West Midlands – is considerable, totalling at least ten ports. Included are the Humber and Trent ports, the East Anglia ports, Kings Lynn, Ipswich and even the South

Coast ports, Shoreham and Poole, all vying for the business. Although cost competition is at a premium in the steel trade, quality factors are also paramount in the handling, transportation and storage. Figure 49 illustrates the steel supply chain from the Belgium producer in Liege – accessed by sea-river shipping via the Albert Canal – and the West Midlands distribution hub.

The withdrawal of railfreight facilities in 1993 can now be seen as a result of the uncertainties of the privatisation period. However, a number of demand and supply factors in favour of rail's return in the mid 1990s converged. These included (1) the preference of the West Midland's steel stockists for trainload deliveries of steel, approximating 1000 tonnes net; (2) the enduring energy of the port management in traversing the prolonged, complex and cumbersome planning processes, in order to attain the logistical and environmental benefits of sea-rail integration; (3) the emergence of a business led culture in railfreight following the US railroad corporation, Wisconsin Central setting up EWS in order to take over British Rail's railfreight companies; (4) finally, the provision of Freight Facilities Grants (FFG) to assist with the specialist handling and storage equipment at both ends of the rail journey and a Track Access Grant, proved an inducement to freight transfer to rail. Despite the considerable pressure exerted by these forces for a return to rail in the port it took over three years to get the trains running! Additionally, during this prolonged planning period, it was necessary for the local council to act rapidly to prohibit the selling off by Railtrack of an essential component of the rail linkage to a supermarket chain! The distances involved are on the low side of orthodox rail threshold being in the 140-170km range. The up-river bulk flows, however, compensate somewhat: vessels arrive with between 2000 and 4000 tonnes of steel. The sea-river journey component features services

Figure 49: Liege-Wolverhampton Inter-modal Steel Flows

from Liege (MaasRiver) and Bremen (Weser River). The frequency and volumes involved have proved conducive to an integration of river-sea-rail transport, providing for up to five rail services per week between Boston and the West Midlands.

The early experience of Boston's sea-rail mission was marred somewhat by intensive road competition, with haulage rates reported to be falling by up to £1.50 per tonne. However, local haulage rates fluctuate in accordance with the seasonal demands of the region's agricultural trades. This provides some advantage to the rail carrier, EWS, given their ability to offer a more stable rate over longer periods of time. In 1997, Boston Port Manager, Mr. John Healy, outlined the obstacles to modal-shift:

> Eighteen months ago the grant we applied for was enough but the goalposts have moved. The road haulage rates have dropped by around £1.50 a tonne for door to door traffic. Everybody has dug deeper into their pockets but the steel import market has dropped, so the customer does not want to pay. [63]

This evidence displays the predatory behaviour of hauliers intent on "seeing off" the modal competition. Despite the competitive pressures faced from road haulage it has become evident that the integration of rail and short-sea shipping services has provided the Port of Boston with considerable market advantage in the highly price sensitive steel trades. Furthermore, the use of sea-river ships has allowed for the Green Highway to extend from up-stream Liege, via the Albert Canal, to up-stream Boston, via the River Witham. The sea-river integration with rail freight ensures a sustainable transport link to Central England.

7.6.4 Case Study 4: The North-South Coastal Highway?

It was seen in chapter 2 that a history of coastal liner services operating between the Tay, Forth, Clyde, Tyne and the Thames and South Coast ports exists. These had operated from the early days of steam. Companies such as Coast Lines and the Dundee, Perth and London Shipping Line ran regular, tightly scheduled coastal services up until the 1960s. The idea of coastal services was renewed with the 1983 University of Newcastle's study, *The use of Roll-on Roll-off Vessels for Moving Domestic Freight between the Tees and the Thames.*[64] The 2000-2 "Marine Motorways" research programme financed by the EPSCR and managed by the Edinburgh Universities, Herriot Watt and Napier, has explored the possibility of fast freight ferries on the UK coast. The rational here was to provide a fast, cost competitive, alternative to long distance road haulage on the London/South East-Scotland corridor.

A European precedent exists with the "Autostrade del Mare" project. The Italian idea is to run fast RoRo services between such Northern ports as La Spezia, Genoa and Venice to the Southern ports of Brindisi, Bari, Naples and Palermo. With distances in the 500-700 kilometre range – similar to a Forth to Thames leg – the ferries offer combined passenger and freight services that feature timings compatible with the road leg, taking congestion and driver's hours' legislation into consideration.

Another possible source of inspiration is provided by the coastal shipping fleets of Japan. Operating over similar distances as Forth-Medway, the Japanese

RoRo fleets provide intensive coastal services. Logistics and Ports specialist, Dr. Alf Baird has contended that the Japanese coastal trades are exemplary:

> Any country with a long coastline, and which suffers from acute road congestion plus continual road traffic growth, should ensure that planners investigate the potential for fast ferry services along similar lines to the Japanese model.[65]

A variation of the marine motorway was implemented in 2002 when a RoRo passenger and freight ferry service was instigated between the Forth Port, Rosyth and the Belgian port, Zeebrugge. Figure 50 illustrates the 405nm route. The Port of Rosyth was awarded a £10.96m FFG in order to develop RoRo loading facilities. The target was to save 2.000b UK lorry kms. The Superfast sailing schedule brought state-of-the-art, 30 knot tonnage to the North Sea. The service has been simultaneously heralded as a major contribution to sustainable transport and criticised as both costly and unfairly subsidised. In 2002, Scottish Enterprise praised the service as a sustainable alternative to the long drive south to English ports: By reducing sea-transit time to around 17.5 hours with an overnight crossing, Superfast Ferries set about revolutionising transport and trade between Scotland and Europe.[66]

The service operator, Superfast Ferries, did not endear itself to European and Scandinavian hauliers when in 2002 it rationalised its commitment to Germany-Sweden services, in order to concentrate on the Rosyth-Zeebrugge route.[67] The FFG award caused some chagrin with operators on the shorter North Sea routes, feeling that Government was unfairly subsidising the Rosyth route. In the first year of operation, it was suggested that freight rates were too high. Critics suggested that truckers driving south for ferry crossings could save £100 each way by using Newcastle, or could reduce ferry costs by up to 40% by crossing the English Channel at Dover.[68]

Figure 50: Zeebrugge-Rosyth RoRo Service

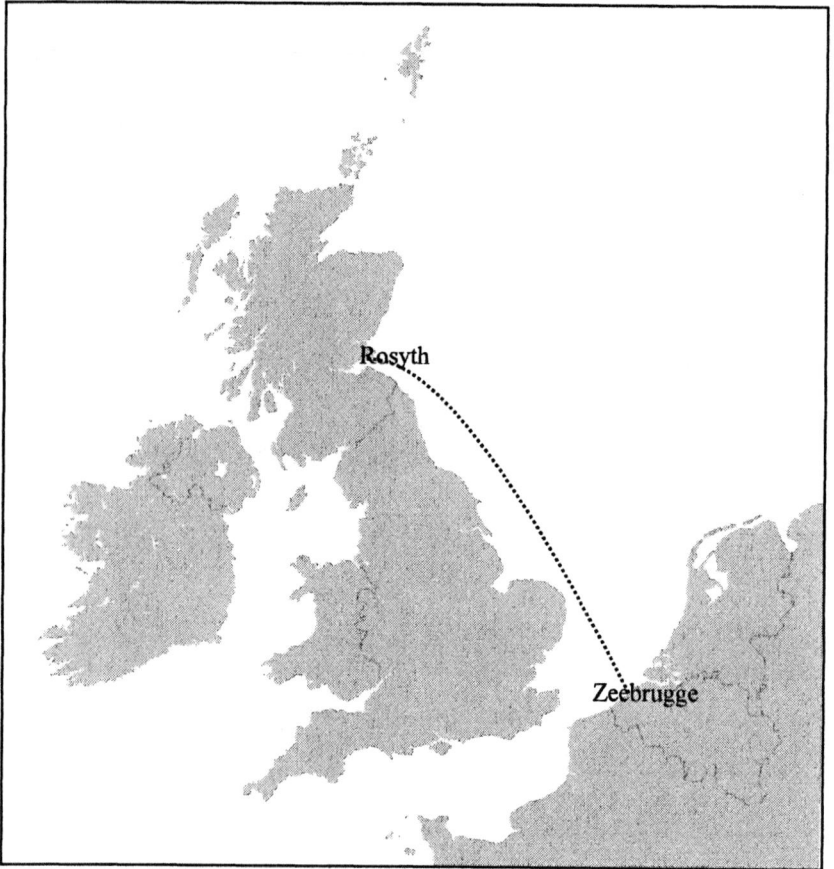

In direct contradiction to these charges came the testament of Kircaldy based European haulier, Andrew Wishart, who has argued that the costs of sailing from Rosyth must be compared to the lorry kms, fuel and drivers hours saved, particularly given the probability of Forth-Dover driving time exceeding the normal 9 hours legal limit. By using Rosyth, Mr Wishart claimed his drivers could do a day's work before taking rest-breaks on the overnight service to Zeebrugge, arriving in Belgium at 10.30 in the morning.[69] The Wishart road fleet is committed to the just-in-time demands of the foodstuffs distribution sector.

An additional advantage of using the route – as opposed to the shorter crossings - is the access to the lower cost diesel fuel supplies *vis-à-vis* UK diesel prices available in Belgium. The attraction of fuel cost savings has led to Wishart's diverting Spanish traffics to the Rosyth route, as opposed to driving through the congested North-South motorway network to Portsmouth. Such examples demonstrate the road tkm savings capability of the longer distance ferry crossing.

In 2003, 32,500 freight units and 200,000 passengers used the route and a healthy growth was reported. Freight grew by 24% in 2004 to 40,300 units.[70] Despite this early optimism and a £520,000 operating subsidy paid to Superfast, disappointment could not be denied in 2005 when the Superfast management rationalised the service by 50%, deploying one of the vessels to a more profitable Baltic service.[71] Superfast's first half results for 2005 reported a 27% increase in freight carried by its two vessels on the Rostock-Hanko routes - 30,828 freight units in the six months. As this was double the volumes moved on the Rosyth-Zeebrugge service, the re-deployment of the *Superfast IV* was seen as optimising the fleet's earnings potential.[72] The impact of this service reduction was felt in February 2006, when P&O Ferries reported increased freight volumes on its Teesport-Zeebrugge route. This was partly explained by the diversion of Scottish traffics from the rationalised Rosyth route.[73]

The evidence from this service does demonstrate the difficulties faced by operators attempting to build up traffics in a highly competitive market. Whilst volumes had achieved a steady growth, the opportunity costs of the route, given the more lucrative earnings of the Baltic services, were obviously too high for an organisation intent on maximising earning potential for its high capital cost assets. A second lesson that can be learned from this enterprise is the political issues of government selecting and supporting one particular route. Operators on rival routes will inevitably feel aggrieved at the economic support funnelled to their competitors.

7.6.5 Case Study 5: Clydeport Feeder Service.

The growth in deepsea container traffics has provided some opportunities for coastal transhipment. Particularly heavy demand for container space in the ports of Felixstowe and Southampton has placed some emphasis on the alternatives to road haulage. This has provided opportunities for the Green Highway, which took a significant step forward in 2000 with the inception of the Southampton-Liverpool-Greenock service. The new entry feeder service, illustrated in Figure 51, initially provided a weekly container service. The vessel *Nordsee* was chartered by Greenock's owners, Clydeport plc, to link with North Atlantic services ex-Liverpool and South Atlantic and Far East services ex-Southampton. The success of this service was confirmed by the introduction of an additional vessel, *Tinka*, in Summer 2001. The staple traffics identified between the Clyde and Southampton were Scottish whisky exports and electronic and consumer exports and imports. This, in a way, was a revival of the pre containerisation, whisky feeder service that had been provided by the Dundee, Perth and London Shipping Line in the inter-war years.[74]

Figure 51: Southampton-Greenock Feeder Service

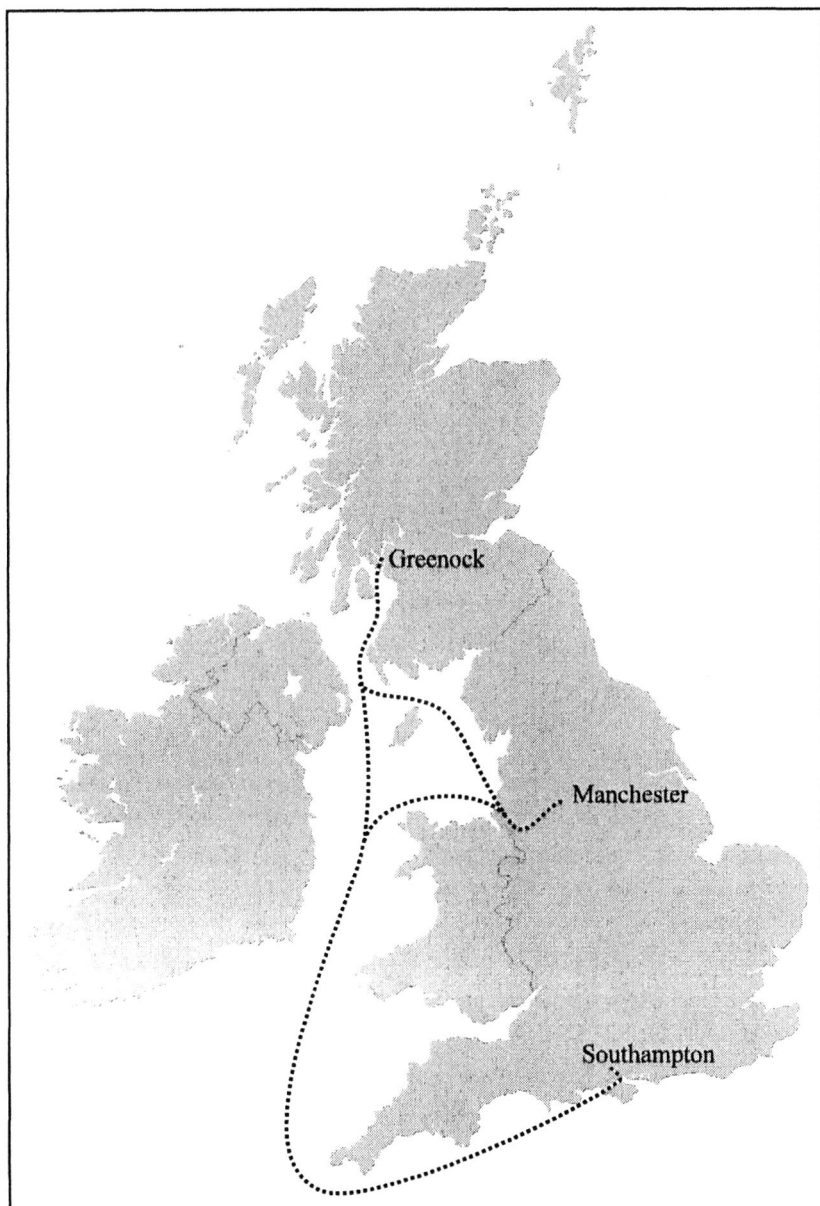

By late 2001, the Clydeport service was able to benefit from Channel Tunnel freight services disruption. The security problems associated with illegal immigration stowaways on freight services caused a serious delays to the freight timetable and whisky exports to continental Europe were affected. The feeder option proved to be a viable alternative to rail.[75] This rail dislocation led, in April 2002, to Clydeport adding a third ship to the route with an additional call into Le Havre. Moreover, the service can be seen as an antidote to the "southern discomfort" phenomena of port, rail and road congestion in Southern England, offering a viable alternative to North Sea feeder services between the Scottish East Coast and Rotterdam.

In 2002, Clydeport's Commercial director, Peter Lawwell, expressed the view that the West Coast feeder route would gain increased amounts of Scottish traffics, connecting, via hub ports, to the Far East and the USA.[76] Although the Le Havre service proved difficult to sustain, the 2002 buy out of Clydeport by the property owning Peel Holdings Group, has provided for an interesting new development of this service. Having already taken over ownership of the Manchester Ship Canal, which included custodianship of the 36 mile waterway, as well as its considerable property assets, Peel Holdings were able to combine their inland shipping expertise with Clydeport's container service management. This led to the diversion of the Liverpool call of the Greenock-Southampton service to a restored berth on the canal, at Irlam.[77] The service now finds itself well placed to service the multi-million pound "tri-modal" freight village to be built at Barton, close to Manchester's large industrial estate, Trafford Park. With a capacity of 300,000teu this inland shipping development will prove a major turning point in the Canal's history.[78]

The service not only marks the first container shipping service on the upper reaches of the Canal since the 1970s withdrawal of Manchester Liner's North Atlantic and Mediterranean services, but also a remarkable restoration of faith in the ability of coastal/inland shipping to serve the modern global supply chain. By providing reliable linkages with deepsea "mother ship" services out of Southampton, the Peel Holdings ports are able to gain linkages to major world trade lanes. The success of this feeder service can be seen as a result of Clydeport's willingness to take a long-term risk calculation. With shippers initially proving averse to committing themselves to the 550nm (1020km) route from the Clyde, via Land's End, to the Solent, Clydeport had the confidence to support the service. This is particularly so following the inauspicious start of the inaugural voyage when only one loaded container was carried! Only by the end of the first year of the operation was the break-even point reached. In addition to Clydeport's persistent support, the service has attained a remarkable utilisation of hitherto under-employed port assets at Greenock, as well as the under-used Manchester Ship Canal. Clearly the link between port ownership and feeder service provision has been a key aspect in attaining viability. By 2004, the two ships on the run were reporting full loadings.

7.6.6 Case Study 6: Barging around the Ports

The concentration of logistics activities around ports provides some opportunities for barge movements for distances well below the limitations stipulated by the Roads to Water study. Although UK ports lag a long way behind such ports as Rotterdam, Hamburg and Antwerp, some prospects have been realised. It is in the clustering of logistics activities around ports that provides for barging opportunities, combining a range of cargo activities. In short, the capital equipment of barges and tugs exists, as does the logistical expertise of personnel. It makes good economic sense to extend the employment of these assets to the Green Highway. Evidence is now discussed from the Thames, Mersey, Humber and Solent.

It was demonstrated in chapter 2 how the demise of the London dock system post-1970s all but decimated the Thames lighterage trades. However, it is also evident that the logistical and environmental challenges now facing ports is forcing a rethink of barge connections. One innovatory attempt at reviving barge traffics occurred downstream towards the Thames estuary. Container re-positioning movements between the Essex Port of Tilbury and the Kentish Port of Sheerness has featured barge operations. Sheerness has become a major import destination for fruit cargoes. The port is served directly by specialist refrigerated (reefer) ships, but in addition the rise in containerised refrigerated trade has induced traffics via Tilbury and Thamesport – the two principal container ports in the Thames and Medway regions. Also, an opportunity for transhipping South American export containers at Tilbury for returning reefer services ex-Sheerness was identified. This early Millennium collaboration between Tilbury Container Services (TCS), the principal terminal container operator at Tilbury and barge operator, Victory Marine Ltd, successfully targeted 4300 lorry movements between the two ports.[79] The road distance of 80km and river distance of 43km is well below the Roads to Water[80] distance threshold, but can be seen as a result of co-ordinated determination to use the Green Highway option.

It has already been shown (see above pp.347-50) how the take-over of the Bennett tug and barge fleet by Foster Yeoman has facilitated up-river traffics. The Bennett fleet has also been successful in distributing Lighter Aboard Ship (LASH) traffics in the Thames and Medway. Rice traffics loaded into LASH barges in the Mississippi are delivered by Bennett's tugs at the Ventee Flour Mill in Rochester.[81] In chapter 5 the return of LASH services to the UK was examined It was shown how on the Humber, linkages between the North American Lash services and the tug and barge operator, John Deane, have culminated in regular barge shuttles of rice up-stream to Selby. Again, the operator is able to combine this work with a range of barging activities in the Humber and Trent regions.

In the Port of Liverpool, barge activity has been re-activated with the assistance of a £389,000 FFG. Bagged West African cocoa movements from the Barge-Container (BACO) liner service have been moved to storage using barges and tugboats (See above pp..). The successful application of a FFG has enabled the cargo-handlers to develop warehousing facilities, thus securing an all water supply chain from inland river locations in West Africa, integrating deepsea and dockside logistics. As a result, an estimated 5.34m UK lorry kms are saved in the Merseyside region.[82]

A second FFG awarded to Liverpool operators of £926,000 went to the ships' bunker specialist, Henty Oil. This has led to vessels in the Port of Liverpool and Irish Sea Ferries at Holyhead being supplied with fuel oil "bunkered" by sea rather than road, thus saving an annual 8.12m UK lorry tkms in the Liverpool and North Wales region.[83] Henty's MD, Paul Henty, has estimated that the companies £1.5m investment in dockside fuel oil storage has eliminated around 22 road tanker deliveries per-day[84]

Although the Port of Southampton is better known globally as the home of such high profile passenger ships – *Aurora, Oriana, and Queen Elizabeth 2* - as well as the new Cunard flag ship *Queen Mary 2*, barge traffic around the port is significant. Fuel oil and waste collection services for the port's large passenger, dry cargo and tanker vessels form a major component of waterborne trades. In addition, sewage waste is moved from the upper reaches of the River Itchen to down stream treatment plants and deep-sea vessels are loaded by lighters transhipping a range of project cargoes, including military hardware, civil aircraft components and – a major Isle of Wight export – windsails. Petroleum moves the relatively short distance of 20nm between Esso's Fawley Marine Terminal and the distribution depot in the Dorset port, Poole.

Why this traffic is worthy of note is that it is a manifestation of the cluster effect of barge companies, marine based customers and crewing expertise traditionally based in the port. The variety in trades allows operators maximum flexibility in vessel utilisation. For example, in the Solent, Williams' Shipping employs its tug, barge and crane fleet in vessel waste reception, project cargo transhipment and construction and infrastructure services. The 2850 dwt coastal tanker barge, *Jaynee W* (see plate 1) and other vessels belonging to the Whittaker Group, alternates trading between vessel bunkering services and short distance oil product movements to nearby coastal ports Shoreham, Portsmouth, Poole and Portland (illustrated in Figure 52). It is evident that all of these trades involve distances far less (all under 60nm) than that conventionally accepted as viable for shipping competitiveness.

The development of the windsail plant on the River Medina, Isle of Wight, has provided opportunities for barge transhipment from the Island to Southampton. The movement from the factory, 7kms up-river from the coastal town of Cowes, place considerable logistical demands on the factory owner, Vesta Blades UK. Two specialist barges, *Blade Runner 1* and *2* have been commissioned for the ferrying process to Southampton Docks for transhipment, as well the construction of a purpose built loading jetty on the River Medina. In July 2004, the operation handled the UK's biggest export of wind blades when 60 x 35 metre blades were exported to Napier, New Zealand via Southampton.[85] Similar moves towards sustainable energy creation around the British and Irish coasts have also been identified as potential demand generators for barging activity.[86]

373

Figure 52: Barging around Southampton

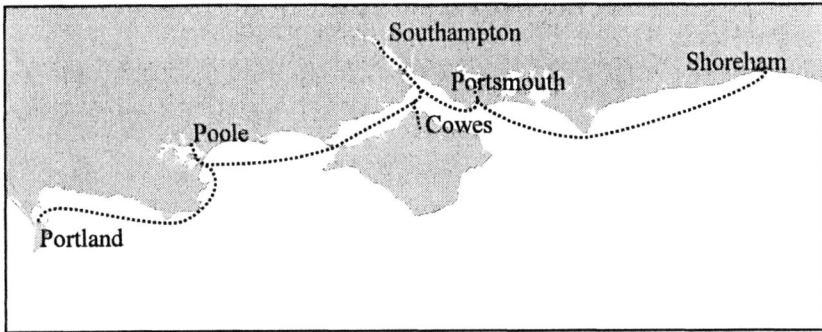

7.6.7 Case Study 7: Aggregates on the Trent

The potential for inland shipping is well illustrated by the flows of aggregates along the River Trent from rural Nottinghamshire to industrial Humberside and West Yorkshire locations. The Newark area sand quarries, Rampton and Besthorpe, owned by the world market leader, Lafarge Aggregates, provide regular work for up to eight barges, ranging between 200-500dwt. The geographic location of the Rampton Quarry – accessed by a narrow country lane – has led to planning restrictions on road haulage for the distribution of 170,000 tonnes per annum of washed sand and gravel.[87] The Besthorpe quarry with reserves of 4mt (in 2001) offers even greater potential for traffic expansion. Also, with planning restrictions on the use of road haulage, the quarry is dependent upon barge traffic. The issue of a Freight Facilities Grant (FFG) to Lafarge has helped to facilitate movements of up to 300,000 tonnes per year to their Whitwood Terminal, a 20-30 hours passage from Besthorpe Quarry, Newark. The winding 142km river and canal route (as opposed to 92km by road) takes the barges from the tidal Trent into the Humber, then the South Yorkshire Navigation at Goole, leading to the Aire and Calder Navigation and finally the River Aire at Castleford (see Figure 53). Fuel consumption for the round trip varies between

100-200 gallons, pending on tides. The FFG, somewhere in the region of £2m, has helped to improve terminal facilities, including access, plus a 300 tonnes per hour, 900 metre, loading conveyor which links the quarry with the river facility. In addition, the grant has supported the purchase of two barge conversions from tanker to dry cargo status to be owned and operated directly by Lafarge.

The success of the operation can be seen as the result of the positive collaboration between a number of stakeholders: Lafarge Aggregates, British Waterways and Associated British Ports (ABP), the Department of Transport, Government and the Regions and the commitment and skill of the Humber/Ouse/Trent barging community.

The large multinational Lafarge Group, with strengths in aggregates, cement, roofing and gypsum, has proved to be a major advocate of water transport. With a global turnover of €14.6bn in 2002 and 77,000 employees in 75 countries, Lafarge may not appear the obvious candidate to become one of the UK's leading proponents of inland water transport. However, Bertrand Collomb, chairman and chief executive of the group, has nailed the organisation's green flag to the mast and publicly espoused sustainable development. The use of rail and water transport is preferred as an alternative to road haulage. Lafarge's estimates are that 25,000 lorry journeys per year are taken off the UK's roads as a result of this strategy.

The green commitment has extended to Lafarge Aggregates owning and operating its own vessel, *Battlestone,* (see plate 2) as well as co-ordinating the activities of five other barge operators. The project of converting the 1968-built *Battlestone* from oil tanker to a two-hold dry bulk carrier was supported by a £2.36m Freight Facility Grant. This also helped to finance a new 800m long conveyor loading system at the Besthorpe Quarry in Nottinghamshire, plus a new discharge and 10,000 tonne storage and distribution depot on the River Calder at Whitwood, Castleford, Yorkshire. The enduring supply of barges in the Humber-Ouse-Trent region has been a key factor in achieving this significant modal switch from road to water. Considerable ingenuity has been evident in converting three tanker barges to dry bulk carriers, the recycling of vessels in itself providing a case study in sustainable economics. Despite their age, their robust specifications have enabled the vessels to endure the demands of river and canal work. The 35-year-old *Battlestone* is a credit to its (now defunct) shipbuilder, John Harker of Knottingley.

The barging community has had its share of setbacks in this region. De-industrialisation in the coalfields and steel plants has led to a demise of staple water traffic. In addition, those originating in the Humber region, such as petroleum flows to Nottingham, newsprint to York and grain to Lincoln, have been lost to road haulage. Typifying the longevity and commitment of the crews to the river, the Goole-based Branford family has provided seven generations of owner/operators. The 2003 appointment of 21-year-old Jonathan Branford as master of the barge, *Eskdale*, consolidated this tradition. Five operators, plus Lafarge, provide services. Despite the traditional competitive rivalry, there is also considerable camaraderie. The community is well represented by the eloquent David Lowe, who as managing director of Humber Barges has succeeded in raising the profile of inland shipping, including delivering supporting evidence to the Parliamentary Select Committee on Environment and Transport.[88]

It is apparent that patience is as much a prerequisite for a barge skipper, as waiting for tides is vital for movement in the upper reaches of the Trent. Advantages do accrue to the skilful skipper: working with the tides brings a 30% saving in fuel consumption with corresponding green savings in carbon and sulphur emissions. The economics of this freight flow are dominated somewhat by the usual cost problem that shipping faces — the cost of moving freight short distances to the vessel loading point. These costs can undermine the inherent scale economies of the bulk movement of 500 tonnes by barge. The evidence from this case study demonstrates the integration of planning policy, government support and commitment by business to the Green Highway alternative.

376

Figure 53: Aggregate Flows, Trent-Yorkshire Waterways

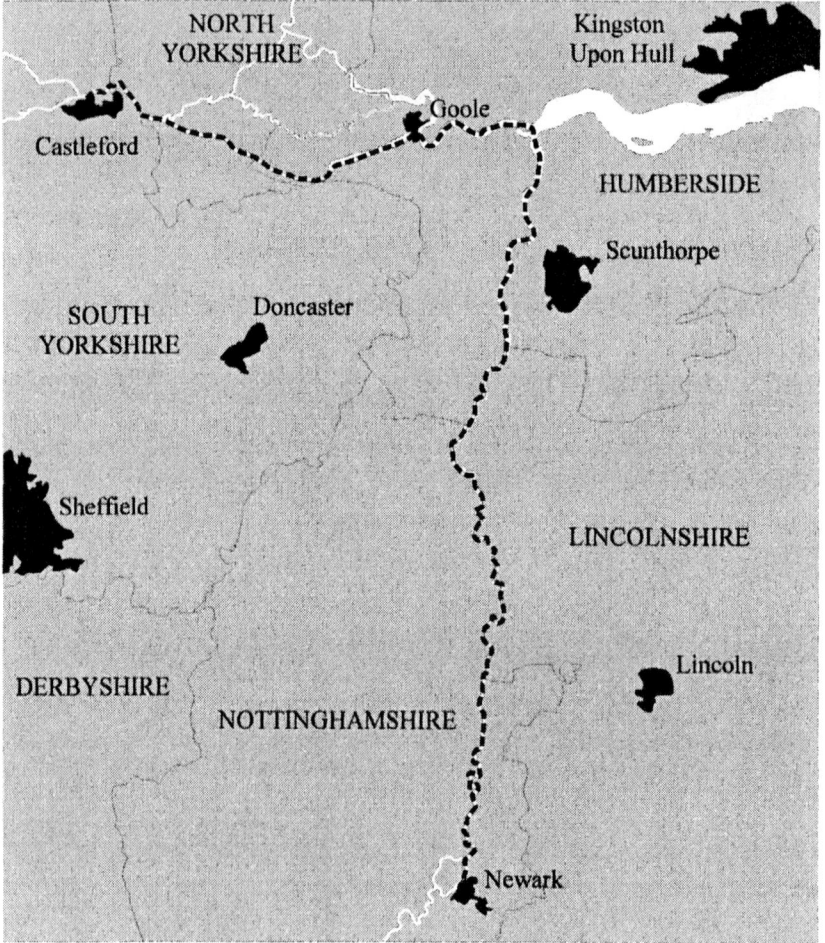

7.6.8 Case Study 8: Scottish Timber Trades

The West Highlands and Islands of Scotland have traditionally relied upon freight flows by sea, via the Clyde Puffer fleets. The geography of the trade is shaped by the many lochs, kyles and inter-island passages of the West Coast. The region supported a buoyant puffer trade up until the inter-war years. The familiar pattern of road haulage erosion of markets can be traced from this period. Furthermore, as RoRo technology improved in the post 1960s period, island ferry linkages induced increased road haulage activity, to the detriment of the puffers. The puffer and their crews were popularised by the novel and subsequent TV series, Para Handy Tales and have been seen as a romantic aspect of life on the Scottish West Coast. However, developments in road haulage technology and modest improvements in the region's road network have brought about a serious decline in the puffer fleet.

The commercial forestation of Scotland's Western Isles and Highlands has traditionally provided work for small coastal vessels. However, much of this trade was lost to a combination of road haulage and ferry boats by the early 1990s. One example of this trend has been the timber trade between the Isle of Islay and paper mills in both Troon and Workington. The loss of traffic suffered by the puffers/motor coasters resulted in heavy volumes of HGVs on the restricted roads of the West Highlands. Many of the region's roads are little more than improved farm tracks, with a bitumen and stonechips covering; as such they are completely unsuitable for 44 tonne gross trucks.[89] In addition, the geography of the region adds greatly to the road km incurred. The elongated route that the hauliers are forced to follow is via the Calmac ferry between Port Ellen and Kennacraig, then the long haul north (107km) along the shores of Loch Fyne, before eventually heading south at Tarbet. The respective road and water routes are illustrated in Figure 54. Comparative road and sea distances are given in Table 35.

378

Figure 54: Scottish Timber Flows

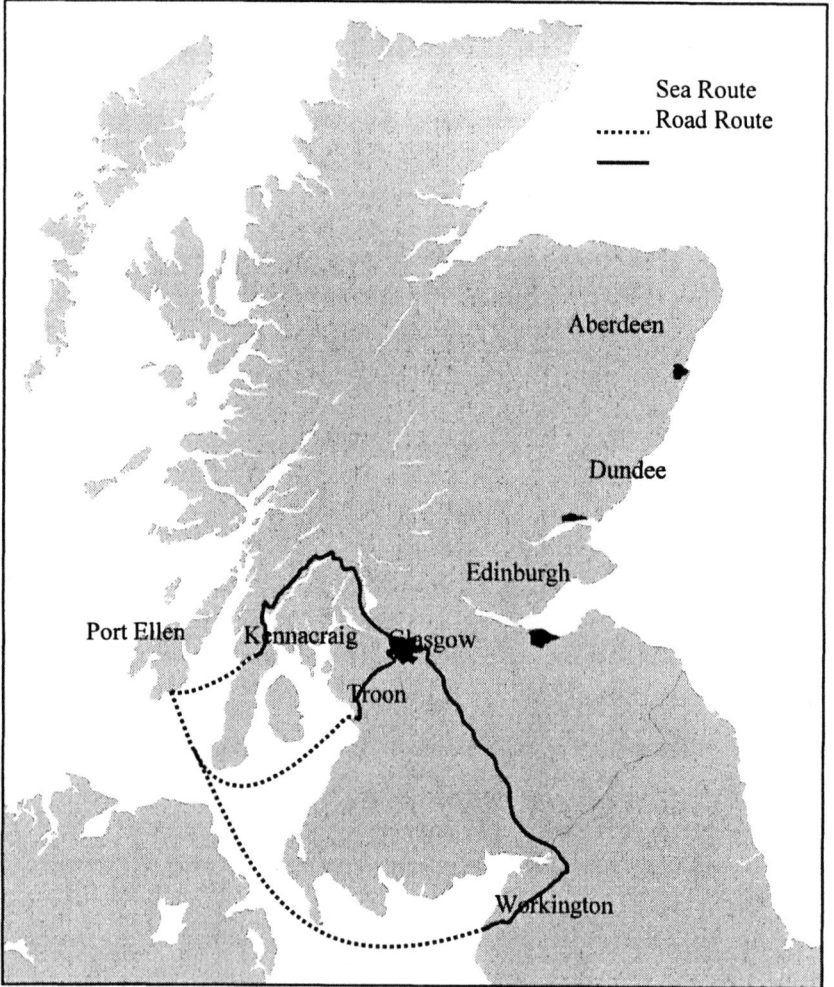

The huge disparity in distances can be seen, with road distances more than double direct sea routes. Despite this distance factor, traffic continued to be lost to shipping. Particularly problematic was the withdrawal of the Tariff Rebate System (TRS) by the Scottish Office in 1995. The TRS was introduced in 1979 as a means to support trade with the Western Isles, by providing for a subsidy of up to 40% of shipping costs. An immediate casualty of this decision was the collapse of the specialist timber shipping company, Glenlight Shipping.[90] Traditional dry-cargo shipping operators in the region's trades felt aggrieved that the ferry operators continued to be subsidised, allowing for discounted rates being offered to road hauliers.[91]

Table 35: Comparative West Highlands Distances, Road & Water.		
Route	Distances (Km)	
	Sea	Ferry/Road
Port Ellen-Troon	97	253
Port Ellen-Workington	177	419
Source: Author's calculations based on various distance tables.		

The problem caused by hundreds of weekly heavy truck journeys via this environmentally sensitive route has clearly provided opportunities for a revived Green Highway. A combination of a proactive management at ABP's West Highland ports, Ayr and Troon, the support of the trade's customers, along with an accommodating Scottish Executive has led to a significant proportion of the timber traffic returning to the sea route. ABP was awarded a FFG of £4.4m in 2000 in order to achieve a reduction of 2.24m lorry kms annually. Much of this traffic is moved under the aegis of the Timberlink project – a collaboration between ports, British Waterways hauliers, shipping companies, forestry industries, local government, the Forestry Commission and the Scottish

Executive. This environmentally driven initiative is aimed at reducing timber movements by road and increasing the use of sea transport. In 2004, the two ports handled nearly 257,000 tonnes of timber through this project.[92] The first Timberlink 1000 tonne shipment by sea between Islay and Troon was greeted by ABP's port manager as a reduction in 30,400 lorry kms and the customer, sawmill owners Adam Wilson & Sons Limited proved an enthusiastic recipient:

> We are keen to support this new development which gives us the opportunity to move large volumes of sawn logs over a short timescale, to meet the production demands of the sawmill at Troon and, at the same time, to reduce heavy-goods traffic on the roads from Argyll to Ayrshire.[93]

Integral to the logistics of the Timberlink project was the ABP charter of the Troon registered vessel, *Red Baroness*. The deployment of this vessel involves servicing a number of regional timber trades in addition to ABP traffics. With British Waterways port Ardrishaig loading over 60,000 tonnes of timber annually, the *Red Baroness* is kept fully employed. Scotland's annual timber output is set to grow from 5m to 10mt by 2015-20,[94] thus the potential for the Green Highway looks positive.

The Timberlink partnership demonstrates what can be achieved with integration. Following the demise of Glenlight Shipping it became obvious that market forces alone could not sustain shipping services. The positive dialogue between politics and business grounded in sustainable transport has found a Green Highways solution.

7.6.9 Case Study 9: Liverpool-Manchester Grain Flows

The rise in deep-sea vessel size has posed many problems for the Manchester Ship Canal (illustrated in Figure 55), post 1970s. A mixture of size restrictions – channel draft, air draft, lock gates – meant that the upper reaches of the waterway could not handle vessels in excess of 12,000dwt. Up until the 1970s ocean going vessels such as the 12,000dwt, *Manchester City*, had provided a North Atlantic liner link with Manchester. Growth in vessel sizes post 1970 led to the switch of North American grain imports to the Port of Liverpool. The development of Liverpool's Seaforth grain terminal in the mid-1970s meant that 70,000dwt panamax bulk carriers could be handled, thus contributing to a significant per tonne freight rates reduction in the trade. The logistics problem, however, was how to move the large grain volumes 75 kilometres inland to the flour and bread mills of Manchester. Initial attempts at a shuttle barge service were replaced by road tankers. The uncertainties over the future of the Manchester Ship Canal and the completion of the M62 motorway between the two cities proved conducive to this switch to road. The re-appearance of barge traffic in 1999 was the result of the entrepreneurial K.D. Marine (UK). With the assistance of a Freight Facilities Grant a 1000dwt seagoing barge was procured and named, *Gina D.* By the second year of operation, trade had built up to >100,000 tonnes per annum and a second barge of 450dwt was added to the fleet. The success of the revived service can be apportioned to a number of factors, principally:

- the enterprise and tenacity of the owners in pursuing the trade;
- the total supply chain package offered by K.D Marine (UK) which includes discharge and a short road transhipment distance of 250 metres;
- the support of the DETR in supplying a grant to support the capital outlay of the vessel and discharge equipment;
- the willingness of the millers, Rank-Hovis and Allied Mills, to reconsider the water option.

382

Figure 55: Liverpool-Manchester Grain Flows

The net result of the barge shuttle is that 266 round trip lorry movements per week are removed from the congested Liverpool-Manchester corridor. A unique feature and obvious selling point of this service is the diversification of traditional ship operators into supply chain management, encompassing chartering, storage, discharge and road delivery to the grain silo.

7.7 Chapter 7 Summary & Conclusion

This chapter has provided focus on the role and potential of the Green Highway in the British and Irish supply chain. The historic trends in industrial location and production have been identified. The spatial spread of industry, the switch to just-in-time output and increased adherence to inventory management have all favoured the use of haulage rather than rail or water. Reasons for the growth of road haulage can be aligned with these logistical trends. Despite its seemingly unassailable position, a number of factors are now conspiring to reduce the appeal of the road option. Congestion has had a negative impact on haulage efficiency. Rising diesel fuel prices, driver shortages and reductions in permitted driving hours have exacerbated these problems. As a result, transport users have proved more amenable to rail and water alternatives.

It has been made apparent that a major obstacle to be overcome if the Green Highway is to achieve freight transfer from road is that of the hinterland barrier. The cost penalties of transferring freight from ships to trucks for inland transit can effectively destroy the intrinsic transport cost advantages of shipping. It was shown that distance and volume factors were a determinant of shipping competitiveness. As a result, concentration on keeping handling and road-transfer costs to a minimum is vital, predominantly where short sea-legs are marginally competitive with road competition. The competitive position *vis-à-vis* railfreight was also considered. It was demonstrated that geographic restrictions were a main determinant of modal choice between rail and water. Also, evidence on examples of rail-water collaboration was provided, demonstrating the Green Highway's participation in the sustainable inter-modal supply chain.

Concentration on the supply of shipping has revealed a number of challenges. The issues of precarious shipping investment raises questions over the ability of the shipping industry to fulfil its potential, especially in market sectors restricted to smaller ships (below 2000dwt). The enduring investment problem results from the uncertain, erratic returns on shipping investment. For operators embarking upon new route start-up there is a long lead time before revenues can achieve economic viability in the liner and break-bulk trades. The emphasis on vessel costs and the distinct components of the charter market have revealed contrast in exposure to financial risk. Specifically, the short-run markets emphasise low entry barriers and acute cost competitiveness with other shipping companies. The implications are that higher quality (higher cost) operators will look to long-run, more secure, markets where reduced levels of competition are less likely to lead to economic vulnerability. Conversely, evidence of a dynamic, burgeoning European shortsea sector has been provided. Ultimately this bodes well for a revived wave of investment. Evidence drawn from the nine case studies provides for an identification of five key factors that shape the vitality and the viability of Green Highway logistics:

> (1) seamless integration of shipping into the supply chain;
> (2) commitment of Green Highway users to sustainable transport;
> (3) shipping enterprise and initiative;
> (4) adherence to long-run logistics strategy;
> (5) public support, such as FFG and Waterborne Freight Grant.

Looming large in the successful examples provided is the highly positive impact of modal and organisational integration of shipping into the supply chain. It is clearly obvious that the Green Highway works most effectively where a seamless flow of transport, cargo handling, storage and distribution can be achieved. This entails organisational "joined-up thinking" as much as physical integration. The vertical integration practised by the two selected aggregates specialists, Foster Yeoman and Lafarge, displays the benefits of linking shipping – both coastal and inland – with their high volume quarrying activities. The whole transport package is viewed not only as a seamless supply chain but also as a tangible example of sustainable transport. Such commitment becomes a pre-requisite to achieving a successful Green Highway venture into the supply chain. The Scottish timber case study recognised the commitment of both the service provider and customer to the sustainable transport concept.

The need for enterprise and initiative is vital to the vibrancy of the Green Highway. The Widnes haulier, O'Connor, has exploited a niche area of potential in matching inter-modal resources with trade flows. By linking sea-rail-road the haulier offers a truly inter-modal supply chain alternative at competitive rates. The entrepreneurial strength of KD Marine (UK) lies in their ability to vertically integrate their barge operations with cargo discharge and road distribution – therefore, all supply chain tasks and their associated costs are managed in-house.

It has also been made evident that the entrepreneurial stance of operators has led to shipping successfully competing over relatively short distances, far below the assumptions of the *Roads to Water* study.

Boston's inter-modal steel flow, Clydeport's feeder service and Lafarge's excursion into barge-owning all share commitment to the long-run investment strategy in transport. Clydeport can be singled out here as the one operator in the nine case studies presented, to have taken on the financial risk of the new service, unaided by public support. The long lead-time of such projects can present considerable obstacles to the new investor. It is apparent that strong corporate nerves are required for Green Highway projects that may take several years to achieve a positive return. The 2005 retrenchment by Superfast on the Rosyth-Zeebrugge service examples the difficulties faced by new entrant operators attempting to build up traffics. Finally, the public role in supporting eight of the nine routes discussed deserves some acknowledgement. The capital costs of new ventures can be prohibitive in that they outweigh the savings in transport tkm costs. The allocation of FFG can be seen, with hindsight, as integral to modal-shift.

Having now discussed the role and shown the potential for shipping in the supply chain, the following chapter will examine the environmental integrity of Green Highway operations.

CHAPTER 7: ENDNOTES

[1] Zachcial, M. (2001) "Short Sea Shipping and Intermodal Transport", in European Conference of Ministers of Transport (2001). *Short Sea Shipping in Europe*. Paris ECMT. p. 26.

[2] Armstrong, J. Cutler, J. Mustoe, G. (1998) "An Estimate of the Importance of the British Coastal Liner Trade in the Early Twentieth Century," *International Journal of Maritime History*, Vol.X, December. p.57.

[3] McKinnon,A. (1989) *Physical Distribution Systems*. London: Routledge. p. 241.

[4] Woods, D. (2002) *Operations Management: Producing Goods and Services*. Harlow: Pearson: p. 455.

[5] Paixão, A.C. and Marlow,P.B. (2005) "The Competitiveness of Shortsea Shipping in Multimodal Logistics Supply Chains: Service Attributes". *Maritime Policy & Management*. Vol.22. No.4. Oct-Dec 2005, pp363-382.

[6] Dupuit, J. "On the Measurement of the Utility of Public Works," reprinted in *International Economic Papers*. No. ", translated from the French by R.H. Barback (London: Macmillan, 1952),p. 100.

[7] "We need parity, not charity," *International Freight Weekly*. 12.2.01. p. 6.

[8] King, R. (2001) "Haulage – an industry in crisis? http://www.publicservice.co.uk/pdf/freight/autumn2001/p10.pdf accessed 3.6.06.

[9] Lyons,G. Chatterjee,k. (2002) *Transport Lessons from the Fuel Tax Protests of 2000*. Abingdon: Ashgate.

[10] The normal maximum driving period for heavy goods vehicles is defined as 2 x 4.5 hours driving stints. This must be punctuated by a 45 min break. Two 10 hour driving extensions are permitted per week but these must compensated on other driving days. 90 hours is the maximum driving permitted in any fortnight period. Source: DfT (2005) *Drivers' Hours and Tachograph Rules for Goods vehicles in the UK and Europe*. London: TSO.

[11] *Loc.cit.*

[12] *International Freight Weekly Op.cit.* p.6.

[13] Hailey, R. (2001) "OOCL in box first with Freightliner," *Lloyd's List*. 21.8.01. p. 1

[14] *Loc.cit.*

[15] *Loc.cit.*

[16] Casagrande, S. Fromme, H. (2000) "Customers will not pay a premium for green transport," *Lloyd's List*. 10.11.00.

[17] Packer, J. (1994) *Roads to Water: Overview of Coastal and Short-Sea Shipping*. London: HMSO.

[18] ECMT (2001) *Short Sea Shipping in Europe*. Paris: OECD.

[19] Hilling, D. Brown, M. (1998) in (ed) Hoyle, B. Knowles, R. *Modern Transport Geography* London; John Wiley. p.243.

[20] Zachcial, M. (2001) "*Short Sea Shipping and Intermodal Transport*," (in) ECMT Short Sea Shipping in Europe. OECD: Paris. p. 24.

[21] "Sea motorways: Full speed ahead," *Lloyd's Shipping Economist*. August 2002. p. 8.

[22] European Projecton Shortsea Shipping & Intermodality project (2003) Brussels: AMRIE. http://www.realise-sss.org.

[23] Swedish Transport Research Board (1993) *Coastal and Shortsea Shipping: Technical Feasibility Study*. Goteborg: Swedish Transport Research Board.

[24] Mulrenan,J. "Everard calls for UK ports fees cut." *Lloyd's List*. 12.4.95.

[25] Lapthorn,D. Letter to the Editor "Port cost discrimination must end," *Lloyd's List*. 7.1.04.

[26] GNER Corporate Affairs, *Inside Track: the Electronic Newspaper for Stakeholders*. May 2004.http://www.gner.co.uk/GNER/PressCentre/Inside+Track.htm

[27] SRA: West Coast Route Modernisation. http://www.sra.gov.uk/projects/wcrm accessed 18.4.06.

[28] Gourvish, T. (2004) *British Rail 1974-1997 From Integration to Privatisation*. Oxford: OUP. pp.365-91.
[29] "Rail takes the strain as imports increase," www.coaltransportinternational.com May-June 2005.
[30] http://www.sra.gov.uk/freight/strategy/freight_strategy_may_2001/freight_strategy.pdf.
[31] McNally,L "Rail Freight – Time for Action," *Mayo News* .2.2.05. http://www.westontrack.com/news109.htm Accessed 13.9.06.
[32] Molloy,C. "Ireland's ports in an integrated system", *Irish Independent*, 11.3.05.
[33] Wall, M. "Private firm to enter rail freight market" *The Irish Times*, 31.10.05.
[34] "Shipbuilding & Engineering: Barrow yard back in mercantile work: James Fisher products carrier signifies end to 20-year break in GEC Marine merchant ship production: New Tonnage." *Lloyd's List*. 3.12.97.
[35] "Flexible new tonnage for Crescent", *Fairplay* 5.4.01.
[36] *Loc.cit.*
[37] Interview with Mr. Max Heinimann, MD Union Transport, Bromley 19.5.05.
[38] "Carisbrooke gains AIM delisting clearance," *Lloyd's List*. 14.7.99. p. 2.
[39] IMO (1995) STCW 95 Section A VIII/2. London: IMO.
[40] *Loc.cit.*
[41] Porter,J. "LR warns of feedership dearth," *Lloyd's List*. 8.9.05.
[42] "Asperity a showcase for Singapore newbuilding," *Lloyd's List*. 30.4.97. p. 7.
[43] "Irish labour court backs ferry unions," *Fairplay International Shipping Weekly*, 16.11.05.
[44] "Stena quashes HSS speculation," *Fairplay International Shipping Weekly*, 21.2.06.
[45] Alderton, P. (1995) *Sea Transport Operation and Economics*. Hampton Court: Thomas Reed. p.167.
[46] Dystra, D. (2005) *Commercial Management in Shipping*. London: Nautical Institute. pp.62-69.
[47] Strange, J. (2000) *Dry Cargo Chartering*. London Guildhall University. Unpublished. p. 8.
[48] "Louis Dreyfus says smaller is better for new Airbus ro-ro transporters," *Lloyd's List*. 30.1.06.
[49] Wynn, J. (1995) *Wynns: The First Hundred Years*. Stafford: Forward House Publishing.
[50] Robert Wynn & Sons Ltd: Press release: The MPP Project: An Overview. www.robertwynnandsons.co.uk.
[51] Harman, L.P. (2002) *The Prior Family Business*. Fingringhoe: Distributed unpublished by Priors.
[52] http://www.jjprior.co.uk/ accessed 2.6.06.
[53] www.foster-yeoman.co.uk.
[54] Tinsley, D. (1991), *Op.cit.* p. 82.
[55] *Ibid.* p. 81.
[56] Conversation Mr. Michael Magnus, Shipping Operations Director, Foster Yeoman, Frome, Somerset.
[57] http://www.foster-yeoman.co.uk/index.cfm?fuseaction=web.ObjectId.1620 accessed 19.5.06.
[58] "Building boom paves way for two family companies to forge closer links," *Port of London*, May/June 2003, Vol.2. No.69.p.4.
[59] Klinger, P. "Foster Yeoman founding family agrees to £300m Swiss takeover," *The Times* 22.6.06.
[60] http://www.rfg.org.uk/library/?pid=3158&lsid=3290&edname=20997.htm&ped=20997 accessed 19.5.06.
[61] http://www.realise-sss.org/ accessed 19.5.06.
[62] http://www.oconnor.co.uk/ accessed 19.5.06.
[63] Stares, J. Hauliers derail UK port plan. *Lloyd's List*. 16.10.97.
[64] Rowley, C. (1983) *The Use of Roll-on Roll-off Vessels for Moving Domestic Freight between the Tees and the Thames* Newcastle: University of Newcastle.
[65] Baird, A. "The Japanese coastal ferry system" *Maritime Policy & Management*. vol.27. no.1 Jan-March 200. pp.3-16.

388

[66] http://www.scottish-enterprise.com/sedotcom_home/services-to-the-community/stc-keyprojects/edinburghandfife/ferries.htm accessed 20.5.06.
[67] Hailey, R. "Superfast ferry chiefs dismiss doubts over Scottish route," *Lloyd's List*. 14.4.04.
[68] Hailey, R. "Scottish hauliers committed to Superfast link," *Lloyd's List*. 19.8.02.
[69] *Loc cit.*
[70] Hailey, R. "Superfast ferry chiefs dismiss doubts over Scottish route," *Op.cit.*
[71] "Ferry subsidy failed to save nightly route," *The Scotsman*. 9.3.06.
[72] Lowry,N. "Superfast reduces Rosyth sailings to meet demand," *Lloyd's List*. 21.10.05.
[73] "Geest pullout boosts P&O ferries ro-ro link", *Lloyd's List*. 1.2.06.
[74] Somner, G. *DP&L: A History of the Dundee, Perth & London Shipping Company Ltd and Associated Shipping Companies*. Kendal: WSS. p.35
[75] Hailey, R. "Tunnel bottleneck gives whisky trade hangover," *Lloyd's List*. 29.11.01.
[76] "Feeders in bloom," *Fairplay* 25.4.02.
[77] "Peel ports launch feeder facility," *Fairplay*. 7.6.04.
[78] "Progress on plans to take ships into the heart of the city," *Lloyd's List* . 13.11.04.
[79] McNamara, T. (2005), British Waterborne Freight: The Waterborne Alternative to Road Transport in the UK. Southampton Institute/Solent University PhD Thesis.
[80] Packer, J (1994_ *Op.cit.*
[81] "Three-year LASH Agreement," *Port of London*. September/October 2003. Vol.2. No.71. pp. 4-.
[82] http://www.dft.gov.uk/stellent/groups/dft_freight/documents/page/dft_freight_038079.hcsp accessed 13.5.06.
[83] *Loc.cit.*
[84] "Henty oil in £1.5m expansion," *Lloyd's List*. 29.7.02.
[85] Wingrove, M. "Bladerunner leaves Britain," *Lloyd's List*. 5.7.04.
[86] Wingrove, M "Wind farms inflate demand for barges," *Lloyd's List* . 24.9.04.
[87] Lafarge Aggregates (2001) North Midlands Area Information Pack.
[88] Examination of Witnesses, 1.11.00. Select Committee on Environment, Transport and Regional Affairs. http://www.publications.parliament.uk/pa/cm200001/cmselect/cmenvtra/317/01102.htm. Accessed 21.8.06.
[89] Dixon, G. "Sea change for growing timber industry pays off," *Scotland on Sunday*. 15.9.02.
[90] Paterson, L.N. (1996) *The Light of the Glens: The Rise and Fall of the Puffer Trades*. Colonsay:House of Lochar.
[91] *Loc.cit.*
[92] "Distinguishing the wood from the trees is crucial for ABP," *Lloyd's List*. 12.5.05.
[93] "Timberlink gets under way," 6.4.00. http://www.abports.co.uk/news2000638.htm accessed 24.5.06.
[94] *Scotland on Sunday*. 15.9.02. *Op.cit.*

CHAPTER 8

The Green Credentials of Shipping?

So far it has been accepted that the intrinsic environmental appeal of the Green Highway has boosted the image of shipping in transport policy in recent decades. However, this must be measured against the negative public view of reckless shipping operations, causing accidents and pollution around European shores. This means that the assumption of green integrity cannot be taken as read. The environmental performance of shipping, therefore, requires further scrutiny.

The comparative social costs of shipping are firstly identified, particularly within the context of a green marketing of these attributes. Given that businesses are beginning to associate themselves with green issues, shipping has significant potential for winning new business. Against this apparent and intrinsic environmental advantage a number of critical areas are identified and discussed. The broad definition of environmental integrity adhered to here encompasses not only issues in air and sea pollution but also in the quality and safety of crew and port-worker employment. This chapter, therefore, will focus on:

- marketing the green image;
- exhaust emissions – the air pollution issue;
- vessel speed issues;
- waste dumping at sea – the sea pollution issue;
- quality issues in management and crewing;
- coastline regulation;
- port operations.

8.1 Green Image, Green Highway?

The performance of the Green Highway, in terms of quality shipping operations, is integral to its environmental integrity. If shipping has the ability to sustain a high level of operational quality there are opportunities for marketing its green credentials. Given the increasing importance of delivering environmentally sound performance, the Green Highway can become attractive to business.

Progressive shipping companies such as Naples' Grimaldi Line, have successfully developed the idea of shipping as the green alternative. A spin-off from increased environmental concern in recent decades has been the emergence of business marketing its environmental commitment. The US owned, global provider of health and hygiene services, Kimberly-Clark, has provided an example of a prestigious company that has shown willing to associate itself with the environmental benefits of the Green Highway. The parent company is responsible for such household brands as Andrex, Kleenex, Kotex and Huggies. It was announced in June 2006 that an estimated 41,000 tonnes of pulp is to be shipped annually, direct from Flushing in Holland, to the Port of Barrow in North West England. Previously, the product was shipped through Kimberly-Clark's terminal on the River Thames and then transported by 480 kilometres by road to its Barrow paper mill. The new operation will spare Britain's busy road networks from 1783 (560km distance) lorry journeys formerly needed to deliver the product to the factory every year. This results in a reduction of nearly 1m lorry kms every year from Britain's roads. Peter Taylor, Manager of Kimberly-Clark's Barrow-in-Furness Mill, commented: "Environmental considerations, combined with those of being a good neighbour within the local community, are at the heart of our business and this arrangement benefits all…"[1]

It has become evident that corporate attitudes, plus behaviour towards the environment, have responded to the need for change. Public concern has become increasingly vigilant on green issues. The widespread European consumer reaction to Shells' plans to sink the Brent Spar oil rig in the Atlantic announced the arrival of the green consumer. The Greenpeace campaign against Shell's plan to dump the massive (135m high) oil rig structure out at sea led to a widespread Northern European and Scandinavian boycott of Shell petroleum, costing the corporation several $m in lost sales.[2]

The debate on sustainable transport has focused on the question of externalities. Comparative analysis between transport modes seeks to identify the social (external) costs generated per mile or per tonne. The fuel performance of shipping *vis-à-vis* road haulage was identified in chapter 1 as a key determinant of its competitiveness. This in itself fits the sustainable criterion by recognising shipping's ability to conserve fuel oil. Likewise, carbon emissions per tkm were shown to be much lower than road, thus contributing to the strategy for reducing global warming. Additionally, noise, vibration and infra-structure damage are minimised if the shipping option is preferred to road.

Scientific data presented by Professor Theo Notteboom to the European Conference of Ministers of Transport (ECMT) in 1998 incorporated the findings of three transport research teams. The evidence clearly contrasted the difference in external costs between inland shipping and road haulage, with rail transport occupying a low-middle position. Figure 56 represents a sample of one of the three studies discussed by Professor Notteboom. A more extensive tabulation is presented in Appendix 2, illustrating that road haulage generates between 13 and 45 times higher social costs than inland shipping. Whilst Notteboom used inland shipping in comparison with rail and road external costs, evidence from a 1999 study by the Italian environmental pressure group, Amici Della Terra, points to inter-European shipping having similar advantages. The research was based upon freight shipments between Southampton and Livorno. Table 36 Utilises data from the fixed day, weekly, Euro-Med service, operated by Grimaldi Line. The *Grande Europa* class of vessel was used for the modelling and a cargo totalling 14,500 tonnes was assumed. These ships, with their capacity for 4600 cars, or a combination of cars, trucks and containers, offer the economies of scale for RoRo traffics.

Figure 56: Comparative External Costs, Inland Shipping, Rail, Road, in The Netherlands.

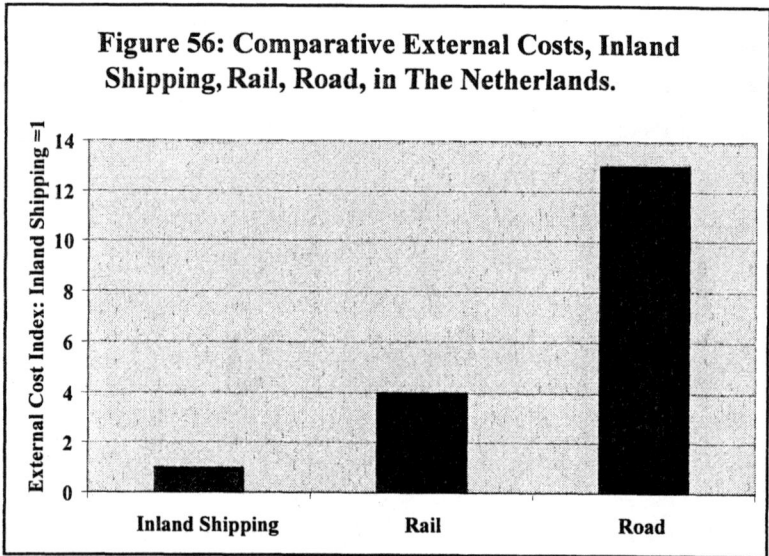

Source: Notteboom,T " Spatial and Functional Integration of Container Port Systems and Hinterland Networks in Europe," in Economic Research Centre, *Land Access to Sea Ports, Round Table 113*. Paris: ECMT/OECD. p.15

Despite the sealeg distance being more than double the overland distance the total external costs of the shipping option are estimated to be only around nearly 25 percent of those of road transport, a clear example of sustainable transport.

8.1.1 Ports in the Green Agenda?

One area where coastal shipping has achieved an enhanced profile is in the current and intense debate on new/expanding ports. It was argued in chapter 7 that the process of freight traffic concentration around port regions provides opportunities for the Green Highway. From the mid 1990s onwards it became evident that European port capacity would have to be expanded if demand in the first decades of the Millennium was to be met. In particular, the deepsea container trades would require increased capacity. This has induced a number of new port and existing port expansion strategies; and this in-turn has been met with considerable opposition from environmentalists seeking to preserve waterside environments. Port expansion schemes for Southampton, Felixstowe and Antwerp have faced considerable opposition from the green lobby. New ports, such as the proposed container terminal at Shellhaven (London Gateway) and Willhelshaven's Jade port have faced environmentalist scrutiny. Coastal and shortsea container shipping has become an integral part of the debate on environmental impact. A major concern with port developments is the impact of increased road haulage traffic generation.

Table 36: Comparative External Cost Modelling, Southampton–Livorno		
	Sea	Road
Trip Length(km)	3713	1731
No Equivalent Vehicles	I Ro-Ro Ship *Grande Europa* Class	1000 Trailers(300 car transporters and 700 heavy duty vehicles)
Tonnes Moved	14,500	14,500
Traffic (million tonnes x kilometres)	53.9	25.1
External Costs	€319,000	€1,246.000

Source: "Maritime Transport Scientifically Proven to be the Leading Transport Mode,"*Grimaldinaples News 8.* The Quarterly Publication of the Grimaldi Group, Issue 8 July-September 2000,p.13.

Nowhere was this concern more acute than in the 1994-2004 debate on the Southampton container port expansion scheme, Dibden Bay. Verging on the edge of the environmentally sensitive, New Forest, one of England's largest natural spaces it was no surprise when local residents and environmentalists became extremely active in opposing planning permission. The scenario of hundreds of extra container lorries traversing the Forest obviously weighed against the case of Associated British Ports(ABP) to build the port, which they held as imperative to the future success of Southampton in the major league of European container ports.

The UK planning permission criteria for port developments is focused on the national interest, with the attempt to weigh the environmental impact against the important regional and national economic impact of the scheme. The position of ABP's Environmental Manager was that new developments can help promote coastal and shortsea shipping and help reduce road haulage levels:

> ...government needs to be a lot clearer about over-riding public interest and that the maintenance of international trade is in general an overriding public interest...In fact maintenance of domestic trade by sea is perhaps an even greater overriding interest if it is going to reduce the amount of traffic on the road and the amount of pollution.[3]

Despite the emphasis on national importance placed on the scheme by ABP and its supporters, the environmental costs were seen as prohibitive. In April 2004 the Government refused planning permission.[4] A similar port expansion inquiry took place in 2004-6 on the application to develop new terminals at Harwich, Bathside Bay. As with the Southampton project, coastal shipping and rail linkages were championed as integral to the green integrity of the project.[5]

Railway linkages and feeder ship services have become paramount in the debate. Similarly, inland waterway barge services have become integral to expansion schemes in Rotterdam and Antwerp. Rotterdam's ambitious expansion plans feature a sustainable approach utilising, water, rail and pipeline linkages, minimising, where feasible, road transport.[6] Antwerp has an active promotional policy of sustainable transport, attaining a 59 percent share of hinterland traffics moved by barge and rail.[7] It has been made clear that there is a complementary relationship between the Green Highway and port expansion schemes. It has also become evident that port's are astutely marketing their commitment to sustainable operations.

8.2 Shipping, the Green Option?

It has been shown that the apparent environmental advantages of the Green Highway are derived from fuel efficiency, low tkm carbon emissions and its ability to reduce the burden of road pollution, accidents and congestion. It is clear that the Green Highway has the potential to fit with the desire of logistics to become more sustainable, to have a green integrity. Against these green strengths it cannot be denied that shipping does have performance weaknesses. These are manifest in air pollution, dumping wastes, navigational accidents and/or oil pollution incidents. It is, therefore, incumbent here to critically examine the relative merits of shipping's environmental performance in order to assess the possible contribution of the Green Highway to sustainable mobility.

8.3 The Air Pollution Issue

It is irrefutable that shipping exhaust emissions are in average terms much lower per tkm than road equivalents. If total emissions are measured (as opposed to average per tkm) however, a different picture emerges. In March 2007 *The Guardian* ran the headline:

> And you thought air travel was bad for the climate... Emissions from shipping are more than double those of aviation, report says.[8]

The article maintains that global shipping is responsible for some 4.5% of total CO_2 emissions, as opposed to aviation's 2%. UK Green Party MEP, Caroline Lucas, has added to the criticism that shipping has failed to improve its environmental performance and, "...has got away with doing nothing and maintained a clean image which it does not deserve."[9] The reverberations of the article where felt across Europe. In Italy, national truck owner's representative, Maurizio Longo, called for a re-assessment of the environmental status of haulage *vis-à-vis* shipping on the basis of an almost emissions parity between the road and water mode:

> Heavy goods vehicles in Italy, for instance, produce 162,000 tonnes of nitrogen oxide a year, while maritime traffic produces 113,000 tonnes...[10]

The tone of *The Guardian* article (plus similar criticisms) has led to a defensive stance by the shipping industry. The response of the UK Chamber of Shipping (was to remind the public that shipping not only carries 90% of world trade and, moreover, generated, "...less greenhouse gases per tonne mile than any other form of transportation..."[11] It is becoming obvious that emissions scrutiny will continue to intensify into the first decade of the Millennium. The polemical discussions surrounding exhaust emissions can be welcomed in that it can only serve to sharpen the resolve of the shipping industry to consistently improve its green performance.

European Commission (EC) concerns have focused on the impact of air pollution from ship exhausts, in particular where heavy concentrations of shipping occurs. Local communities in port areas and coastal residential spread are at the highest levels of threat. The Norwegian Marine Technology Research Institute A/S has found evidence of high concentrates of air pollution on major traffic flows – the Baltic, North Sea, English Channel, Black Sea.[12] The global convention on marine pollution, Marpol Annex VI, places a sulphur cap of 1.5 percent for ships passing through selected Sulphur Emission Control Areas (SECA), such as the English Channel, North Sea and Baltic territorial waters and, moreover, a cap of 0.2 percent (reducing to 0.1 percent in 2010) in EU port areas. From May 2006 it was incumbent on vessels >400gt to carry an International Air Pollution Prevention Certificate (IAPP) accompanied by an Engine International Air Pollution Prevention Certificate (EIAPP).[13]

The English Channel-North Sea (SECA) actually stretches from the Western Approaches to Mongstad in Norway and comes into force in Autumn 2007. The Baltic Sea SECA came into force in May 2006. It is seen as protective measure given the heavy volumes of maritime traffic in the region; particularly as the Scandinavian nations have been particularly vulnerable to acid rain pollution. The cross-industry Shipping Emission Abatement & Trading (SEAT) committee has identified the extent of the problem in Europe. At the May 2006 International Bunker Conference in Gothenburg SEAT Secretary General, Cor Nobel, outlined the challenge facing shipping given that 14 percent of global NOx and 6.5 percent of SOx came from marine related activities.[14] The Conference heard that emissions pollution from ships travelled between 400 and 1200km inland. The implications for Europe were made clear when it was added that some 70 percent of shipping activity took place within 400km of land! This evidence points to the negative side of the Green Highway. However, it is also evident that regulatory initiatives are improving the position.

Environmental gains in fuel burning are at the expense of higher voyage costs. Increased fuel costs have been a concern of shipowners as the purer the oil product, the higher its cost. The International Bunker Industry Association (IBIA), has expressed concern over the impact on voyage costs. In 2002, the IBIA outlined the example of a voyage from Gothenburg to Belfast which under proposed EC rules would require a continuous use of 0.2 sulphur fuel as it consisted of a 100 percent EC voyage. The IBIA estimated that vessels bunkering in European waters could face an additional $20 per tonne premium. [15]

Another problem facing the shipping industry has been accessing the limited availability of low-sulphur oil supplies. It is apparent that the industry is having difficulties in delivering the 1.5 percent sulphur target. A 2006 study by DNV Petroleum Services identified the shipping market's "lack of readiness in meeting the 1.5% sulphur requirement of SECA Regulations".[16] The report found rising sulphur levels in 8 out of 20 ports sampled. For large deepsea ships, the practice of burning high sulphur fuel outside of port regions has kept costs comparatively low. The switch to low sulphur diesel in port regions raises costs, but improves engine performance and reduces sulphur emissions in coastal and urban regions. Regarding Green Highway, vessels predominantly in the <5000dwt range tend to be solely diesel fuel burners. However, larger bulk carriers and shuttle tankers are likely to be burners of heavy, high sulphur, fuel oil and obviously contribute to SOx levels. There is an interim alternative for vessels unable to access the lower level sulphur content fuels. This is to employ a pollution preventing Exhaust Gas Cleaning "Sea Scrubber" system.[17]

Generally, it appears that a mixture of public scrutiny, legislation and pro-active shipping management will move the industry towards improved environmental performance in terms of air pollution. This will be at additional cost but leading owners are responding positively. The global shipowners forum, International Chamber of Shipping (ICS) has championed improvements in hull design and engine performance and acknowledged the trend towards larger ships has helped to reduce fuel consumption, thus emissions. [18]

8.3 1Vessel Speed, Environment and Safety

An additional dimension to the fuel consumption debate is the speed factor. In shortsea and coastal shipping, higher vessel speeds lead to increased competitiveness with rail and road alternatives, particularly in the high value freight sectors. However, this advantage is likely to be at the expense of fuel consumption. The dynamics of hull design and wave resistance mean that fuel consumption accelerates at a faster rate than the rate of speed increase. In shortsea container shipping vessel speeds have crept upwards from 14 to 18 knots in recent decades. This greatly increases vessel performance. The addition of two new 18 knot vessels, *Geestroom* and *Geestdijk*, to Geest Line's Tilbury–Rotterdam container service allows for a sea passage under 7 hours and facilitates round trip workings every 24 hours. The price to pay, however, is the extra fuel consumption, ergo fuel emissions. Figure 57 shows the estimated fuel consumption ranging from 5.3 at 12 knots to 36.0 tonnes per day (Tpd) at 18 knots for a 700teu vessel. High speed ferries have even higher consumption levels: 30 knot plus vessels would require over 200tpd Within the Green Highway debate the balance between speed and fuel consumption is dichotomous: increased speed = increased time competitiveness against road haulage, but this is at the expense of rising levels of fuel consumption! At the time of writing high fuel oil costs were making fast ship operations uneconomic. Even in the deepsea container trades fuel cost savings have been sought at the expense of sacrificing speeds. The October 2006 announcement that major lines in the Asia-Europe Grand Alliance, also CMA-CGM, were adding extra vessels to routes in order to maintain service levels at lower speeds shows the seriousness of fuel oil price increases. This would achieve a reduction in fuel expenses of 10%.[19] Also in this period, the high speed Stena Line, Harwich-Hook of Holland service was withdrawn as a result of high bunker costs. Table 37 displays the 254% rise in intermediate fuel oil (IFO) and 280 percent rise in marine diesel oil (MDO) between 2001 and 2006. The decision taken by Stena Line to re-focus on conventional ferries operating at lower speeds, illustrates the obstacles still facing the fast-ship project.[20]

Table 37 Rotterdam Bunker Fuel Prices Per Tonne 2001-06		
IFO	MDO	Date
$114	$175	19.10.01
$159	$228	29.10.03
$290	$490	19.10.06
Source: *Cockett Bunker Market Reports.*		

Figure 57: Speed Fuel Consumption, 700 TEU Container Vessel

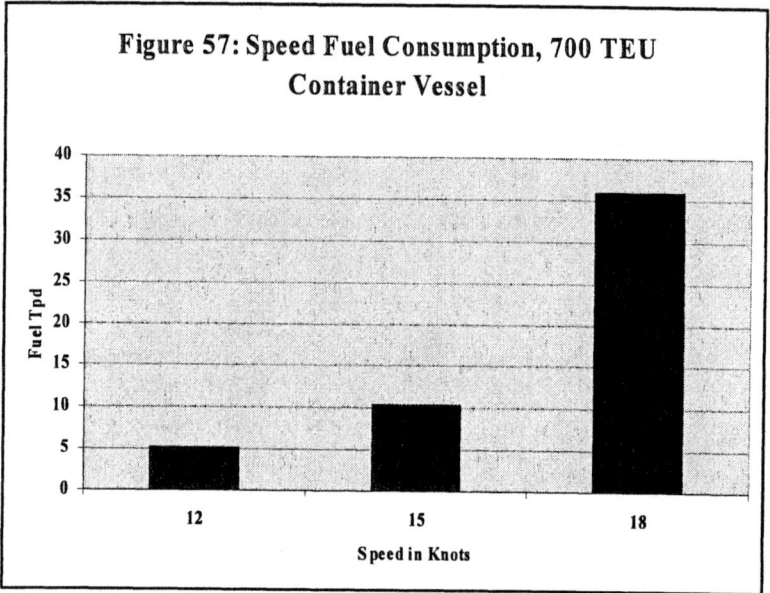

Source: Author's own calculations based upon Royal Institution of Naval Architect's Annual, *Significant Ships*.

The response from business has also been guarded. In 2005 Volkswagen's (VW) transport specialist, Johanes Fritzen, questioned the value of fast ships serving VW's Wolsburg supply chain:

> It is very expensive to increase the speed of ships because the accompanying fuel costs rise exponentially, both in terms of investment and the actual weight of the vessels. Unlike cars, the speed spectrum for ships is very limited. [21]

Moving up the speed chain, catamaran and trimaran hulls offer great attraction to the time conscious shipper. This has to be balanced against questions of safety and all weather reliability. The High Speed Craft Safety Code 1991 lays down the principles and regulations for the safety of High Speed Craft.[22] These can be seen as the response to the sharp learning curve that operators have been on since the widespread use of fast ferries in the last decade or so. Non-fatal accidents such as the overboard loss of a loaded 35 tonne articulated lorry and two minivans from the stern of the *HSS Stena Discovery* in 2000 serve as a reminder that basic crew operations such as lashing down heavy vehicles must be implemented.[23] More seriously, the loss of the Norwegian fast passenger ferry, *Sleipner* in 1999. In this case the shortcomings of the crew was evidently manifest as navigational error in adverse weather conditions. This shows the risk potential of fast ferries. With a passenger payload of 76, plus 9 crew, the 35 knot vessel struck rocks which the watchkeepers had spotted too late to make a successful avoidance manoeuvre. The vessel's bow broke off within 30 minutes of impact, leaving the hull to sink. Sixty nine passengers were picked up alive, 15 dead were retrieved and one passenger was reported missing. In the ensuing investigation the Norwegian authorities expressed the concern that the vessel's officers were unaware that they were operating in unsafe wave height conditions (2.3 metres):

> The navigators lacked satisfactory procedures for assessing wave height. Nor did the owner have procedures to ensure that the craft operated within the applicable operation restriction of 1.0m significant wave height.[24]

The fatal mistake of failing to keep a sharp look out when operating at high speeds, especially in adverse weather conditions was identified as a major cause of the disaster:

> At the decisive time, immediately prior to grounding, both navigators were busy adjusting his radar, which distracted their attention from navigation based on visual observation of lights and course run." [25]

It is evident that speed has a price to pay in terms of both increased fuel consumption and also in safety concerns. The "holy grail" of naval architecture is to develop a safe, reliable and fuel efficient high speed ship! Undoubtedly this will be achieved but the timescale can only be seen as long-term!

8.4 The Sea Pollution Issue

Major environmental advances have occurred in the international maritime regime in recent decades. These include, the prevention of waste dumping into the sea, the outlawing of oil tank slops dumping, double hull regulations for oil tankers, segregated ballast water systems and toxic anti-fouling hull protection chemicals. Cultural change in the disposal of waste has occurred in recent decades. The clean seas strategy of the International Maritime Organisation (IMO) has led to an enhanced ethical attitude towards waste. The problems of tank cleaning slops being discharged in the ocean was highlighted by the Norwegian explorer, Thor Heyerdahl, in 1948. On his *Kon-Tiki* raft expedition to the South Seas, the explorer was shocked to find a trail of large oil globules thousands of miles from land.[26] Nautical Institute Secretary, Julian Parker, succinctly summarised the previously acceptable "over the wall" culture" of rubbish dumping into the sea. This led to all the main trade routes identifiable by the trail of beer cans on the bottom of the ocean".[27] In short, ships' crews were treating the ocean as a garbage can! In European waters the problem of tank washing and its overside disposal was evident from coastline pollution. Main tanker routes generated oil trails with disastrous impact on the coastline environment. Up until the impact of environmental concern and sensitivity of the late 20th Century, much of the vessel's waste went "over the wall". This would include oily rags, empty oil drums, beer and food cans and food waste as well as oily wastes.

Public awareness of such abuse of the oceans has necessitated that shipping cleans up its act! Regulation has provided a punitive deterrent, ergo an inducement towards improved environmental behaviour. In addition, the step changes in operational integrity have been proactively encouraged by such strategies as the "Green Award".[28] A form of historical environmental redress was achieved in 2005 when the Japanese shipping major, NYK Line, was actually recognised by the Thor Heyerdahl Foundation for its "ceaseless" commitment to environmental performance.[29]

8.4.1 The Green Awards System

Leading ports and shipowners, particularly in the oil trades, have demonstrated their commitment to environmental integrity by participating in the Green Awards system. This voluntary system is focused on attention to quality issues in such environmental risk areas as port entrance and exit, cargo pumping, bunkering, waste removal. The Shetland oil port, Sullom Voe has been a leading UK advocate of the Green Awards System. In 2003, the port claimed that the award was a necessity as Sullom Voe dealt with some of the largest tankers in the world, "...in a pristine environment which supports major seafood industries but which is subject to severe weather from time-to-time."[30] Rotterdam is a major proponent of the award, too. Ship operators have an incentive to comply with the high environmental standards inherent in the award as rebates on port dues are awarded. The professional organisation of Master Mariner's, The Nautical Institute, has also supported the Green Award system.[31]

In drawing up the system a synergy became apparent between inland shipping and deepsea operations. This was referred to in chapter 1 (see above pp.30-1) as an example of the symbiotic relationship between large sea-going vessels and much smaller inland barges. The Green Award's Council was able to draw on the vast expertise in the inland barge operations of hazardous cargo movements on European waterways. Inland and coastal vessels have a much more intense loading/discharge programme than deepsea vessels. Nautical Institute Secretary, Julian Parker, has argued that, "...although the relevance to deepsea shipping may at first appear remote, the reality is that these river tankers are handling cargoes in critical areas on a ratio of about 20 voyages to one".[32] It

404

is the operational experience that such intense operations generate that make the inland sector such a valuable contributor to the safety of the Green Highway.

8.4.2 Waste from Ships: Changing Behaviour?

Concerns over the amount of carbon soaked and plastic based wastes finding their way into the ocean from ships led to a 1995 amendment of the International Convention for the Prevention of Pollution from Ships (Marpol 73/78).[33] This stipulates that all vessels over 400gt are required to have a garbage management plan and record book. A 2000 study into the efficiency of waste disposal at sea by Captain Patraiko of the Nautical Institute has found that a contrasting pattern exists in how the plans were initiated.[34] Clearly, the evidence of the study found that advances were being made in the education of crews and the development of a waste management culture. Examples of waste segregation were found in 70 percent of vessels surveyed. Also, the practice of incinerating wastes such as plastic and oil was well advanced.

A problem area identified was that of poor waste reception facilities in some ports. Examples of positive crew attitudes to waste recycling being undermined by inadequate port reception systems. These include simply amassing the carefully segregated waste into one single disposal container. Likewise, the efforts of the crew to achieve efficient waste disposal standards were undermined by poor information on port facilities and in some cases bureaucratic non-user friendly procedures. In coastal vessels, everything thrown into "the big green bin" was prevalent.[35] The lack of segregated waste containers somewhat negates the recycling principle. Overall, the evidence is of a slow, incremental, but positive change in waste disposal behaviour, with ships' crews and port management increasingly adopting an environmentally friendly response. The challenge of attaining a fully segregated waste strategy is obviously taking time to implement. The problem of oily waste disposal has always provided a challenge for operators seeking to comply with the MARPOL regulations. In European waters failure to comply, even accidentally, is met with stringent prosecution. Shipping market leaders have not proved exempt when faced with the increased vigilance and punitive stance of the coastal authorities. In 2005, the Maersk-Sealand chartered, 2328teu, container vessel, *Maersk Barcelona,* was impounded in the Brittany port of Brest. A $500,000 bond was placed on the vessel after coastguard air patrols detected a 61km oily waste slick in the vessel's wake.[36]

Increasingly the practice of waste dumping at sea is being monitored and offenders prosecuted. Likewise, accidental cargo spills are scrutinised and prosecuted. Figure 58 demonstrates the trend towards declining levels of accidental oil spill at sea. However, the disappointingly marginal improvement in the 1990s (compared with the 1980s) begs some explanation. The 1991 explosion on-board the ULCC, *ABT Summer,* led to a massive increase in the 1990s statistics - 260,000 tonnes of crude oil was spilled in the South Atlantic. Nearer to home, but significantly adding to the spill statistics, the groundings of the *Braer* (Shetland) and the *Sea Empress* (Milford Haven) accounted for a further 157,000 tonnes spilled in this decade. This shows how the statistics are sensitive to large tanker accidents.

Even the most careful of ship-operators have to face up to the enduring problem of "human error" and malpractice. In September 2002, F.T. Everard & Sons were fined £10,000 + £7,173 costs for a cargo spill accident in the Manchester Ship Canal. Following an on-board communications breakdown between the Chief Officer and an Able Seaman on the tanker, *Averity,* diesel was spilt into the loading dock.[37] In mitigation, the prosecuting Chester Magistrates averred that the firm had immediately admitted blame, had paid all clean up costs and implemented a spill prevention programme.[38] Other leading coastal tanker operators to be prosecuted in the UK, post-Millennium, include, Brostrums for a

406

bunker oil pollution incident in the Forth,[39] and the Danish operator Lauritzen for dumping garbage from the chemical tanker, *Lotta Kosan*, into the Solent.[40] These selected examples demonstrate the need for sustained vigilance in even the most highly regarded, environmentally focused companies.

Figure 58: Oil Spill Tonnages 1970-2005.

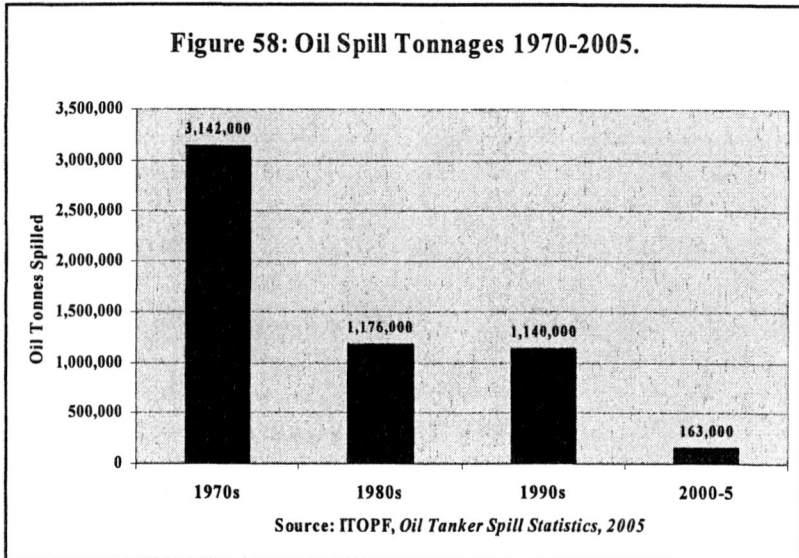

Source: ITOPF, *Oil Tanker Spill Statistics, 2005*

Generally, the pattern is for decline in the amount of pollution discharges reported in UK waters. A 2005 survey conducted by the Advisory Committee on Protection of the Sea (ACOPS),on behalf of the MCA, reported a consistent decline in discharges from ships. An annual average reduction of 15 percent for reported discharges by ships in UK waters, 2000-04 was recorded.[41] This is shown in Figure 59, which also provides a contrast to the increase in pollution from oil and gas installations. The picture, however, is not clear; there is some evidence that an aversion to the use of shoreside waste disposal systems is persisting, even increasing. In July 2005 *Lloyd's List* ran the sub-heading: "North Sea is still 'cheapest garbage can.'"[42] The Dutch environmental group, North Sea Foundation, has monitored waste dumping from ships, estimating that 20,000 tonnes is dumped into the North Sea per year; furthermore, the group has produced evidence to show that shipboard waste dumping increased in 2005 compared to 2004.[43]

Figure 59: UK Annual Reported Sea Pollution Discharges, 2000-4

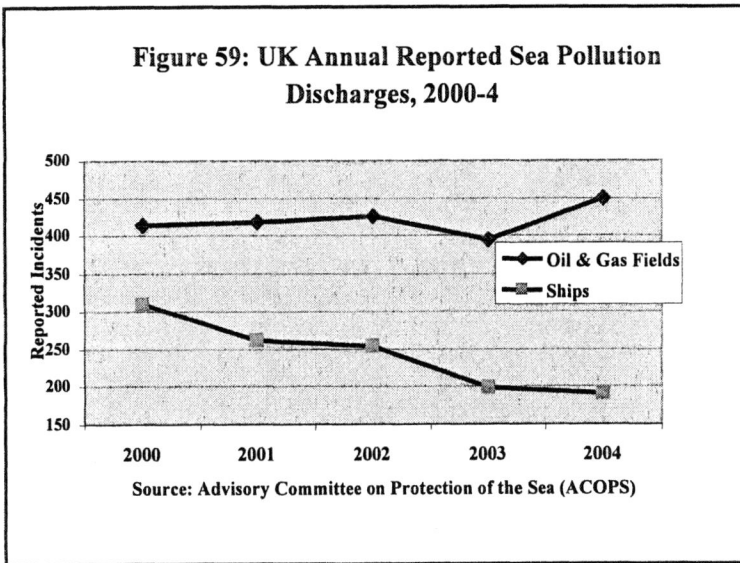

Source: Advisory Committee on Protection of the Sea (ACOPS)

These findings, plus the charges that the shoreside waste disposal was either too costly or too bureaucratic and inflexible, have provoked questions in the European Parliament.[44] The situation along the Irish coast is illustrated in Figure 60. The rise in reported pollution incidents can be aligned to the growth in the Irish economy and resulting increase in maritime traffics. Table 38 contains details of the sizes and causes of accidental spills. The statistics compiled by the Independent Tanker Owners Pollution Federation Ltd (ITOPF), illustrate that nearly 84 percent of spills in 2005 were of less than 7 tonnes. Also clearly shown are the risks associated with tanker operations, particularly loading and discharging. Whereas a large deepsea tanker may only achieve 8 or 9 loading/discharge cycles in a year, a small shortsea tanker may achieve 3 or 4 cargoes per week.

Figure 60: Irish Coastguard Pollution 1990-2004

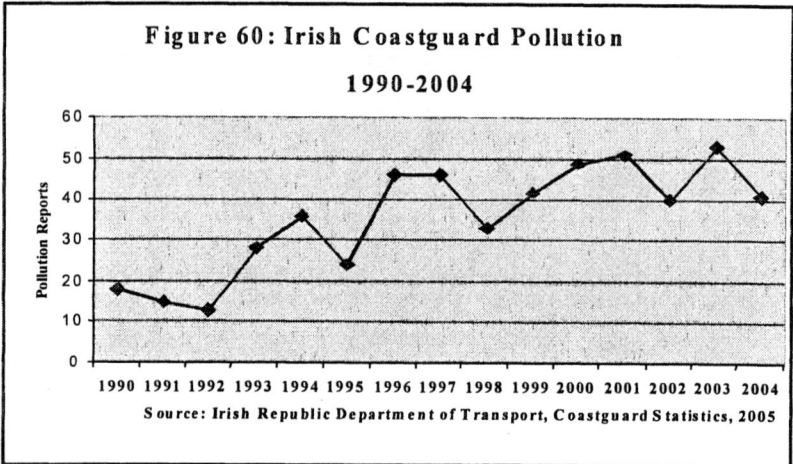

Source: Irish Republic Department of Transport, Coastguard Statistics, 2005

From Table 38 it can be seen that the majority (91%) of spills in operational areas such as loading/discharging are in the <7 tonnes category. Conversely, 84% of spills in the >700 tonnes category are a result of accidents, predominantly collisions and groundings. This endorses the vulnerability of coastlines adjacent to tanker terminals to large oil spills, such as the *Sea Empress* spill in Milford Haven in 1996. Table 39 shows the extent of small operational spills in the Bristol Channel region. The predominance of bunker spills is evident, particularly involving fishing boats. However, the Green Highway of oil tanker movements is placed under suspicion with the two largest Bristol Channel spills in 2004. The two spills of paraffin wax, 2.5 tonnes and 8 tonnes respectively, requiring shoreline clean ups, were attributed to "unidentified" vessels. These were undoubtedly tankers cleaning out tank slops before proceeding to load a new cargo. Tank cleaning procedures should allow for oil slops (wastes) being pumped ashore for treatment and recycling or environmentally acceptable disposal. This of course creates expense and possible vessel delay; the cost-cutting, time- saving alternative is to pump the waste into the sea. Such cynical, calculated, cost-cutting malpractices do great damage to the environmental integrity of the Green Highway.

Table 38: Reported Global Accidental Oil Spill Causes 1974-2005.			
	< 7 tonnes	7-700 Tonnes	> 700 Tonnes	Total
OPERATIONS				
Loading/discharging	2820	328	30	3178
Bunkering	548	26	0	574
Other operations	1178	56	1	1235
ACCIDENTS				
Collisions	171	294	97	562
Groundings	233	219	118	570
Hull failures	576	89	43	708
Fires & explosions	88	14	30	132
Other/Unknown	2180	146	24	2350
TOTAL	7794	1172	343	9309
Source: *ITOPF Oil Tanker Spill Statistics* http://www.itopf.com/stats05.pdf				

8.5 Safe Ships, Cleaner Seas?

A major commitment to achieving a "greener" response from shipping in British waters came with the reaction to the *Braer* oil spill disaster. The Shetland grounding and eventual loss of the tanker and its cargo of 84,700 tonnes of Norwegian crude oil in January 1993, prompted public concern over not only the quality of shipping but also the emergency preparedness of the UK for dealing with maritime accidents. The response of Government was to appoint Lord Donaldson to lead an Inquiry into the prevention of pollution from merchant ships: *Safer Ships, Cleaner Seas.*[45] The report acknowledged not only the global nature of shipping activity around the UK coast but also the negative impact of competitive forces on safety at sea, particularly in times of overcapacity of tonnage supply, when:

> This produces low or negative profit margins and a strong temptation to cut corners. In one way or another we have to make it unprofitable to cut corners[46].

Such pronouncements are highly pertinent to the Green Highway in that they demonstrate rigour and a political will towards achieving quality in shipping operations. The "Donaldson Report" provided a wide ranging study of the risks of pollution from ships and how this can be avoided. The Report explores the international law context and questions over flag state and port state control of shipping are asked. Also included are issues in vessel design, vessel crewing and types of pollution. Accident and near miss investigations are seen as integral to a safety culture that seeks to positively educate, not simply apportion blame. Probing the safety issues of vessel navigating, routing, identification and tracking were seen as vital to the safety regime. The establishment of Marine Environmental High Risk Areas (MEHRA'S) was seen a way of advising masters, owners and insurers, particularly Protection and Indemnity Clubs (P&I Clubs), of specific navigational risks and environmental sensitivity.[47] Another radical approach to accident prevention came with the recommendation that Emergency

Towing Vessels (ETV's) are stationed in high marine risk zones.[48] The delay in getting salvage tug assistance to the *Braer*, as well as to the *Sea Empress* in Milford Haven (1996), has led to the stationing of four MCA chartered tugs in the following areas.

- Northern Isles,
- The Minches;
- South Western Approaches;
- Dover Straits..

The value to the Green Highway of having the tugs on station was demonstrated in the winter of 1999-2000. The South Western Approaches tug attended 21 vessels, including three coasting vessels. A mechanical failure on the *Arklow Meadow*, required tug stanby, Crescent Tankships, *Blackfriars*, needed assistance after grounding and the ex Crescent dry cargo vessel, *Boisterence*, needed a tow into Plymouth after a complete engine failure.[49] In January 2007, the profile of the ETV's was further raised when a combination of French and British Government chartered tugs assisted in the emergency salvage operation of the 4200 TEU container vessel, *MSC Napoli* in the English Channel. The assistance of the tugs undoubtedly averted a major pollution incident as the vessel was loaded with 2400 containers plus over 3000 tonnes of heavy fuel oil.[50]

Finally, improvements in the delivery of Port State Control monitoring of shipping safety and the investigation of accidents and near misses were advocated by The "Donaldson Report," which can be seen as a response to the environmental risks of shipping on the UK coastline. By identifying the problems of sub-standard operations and laying the framework for emergency response when accidents occur, the Report has defined the benchmark for safe, environmental practice. Despite the rigour of the report, however, it would be remiss to ignore the extent of sub-standard practice that has the potential to subvert the implicit environmental integrity of the Green Highway.

8.6. Quality Issues in the Green Highway: The Sub-standards Issue.

Whilst all ship-operators need to pay particular attention to the navigational demands of the UK and Irish coastlines, it is evident that in some shipping sectors operational quality is questionable. This raises the question of standards and sub-standards. The benchmark of standards has been defined by six major conventions[51]:

    (1)   The International Convention on Load Lines;

    (2)   The International Convention for the Safety of
           Life at Sea (SOLAS);

    (3)   The International Convention on the Protection of
           Pollution from Ships (MARPOL), 1973;

    (4)   The International Convention on Standards of Training,
           Certification and Watchkeeping for Seafarers (STCW)
           1978;

    (5)   The International Convention on the International
           Regulations for Preventing Collisions at Sea
           (Collision Regulations) ,1972;

    (6)   International Labour Organisation (ILO)
           Merchant Shipping (Minimum Standards) Convention
           147, 1976.

Adherence to the Load Lines Convention seeks to prevent the overloading of ships, a practice detrimental to seaworthiness. The SOLAS Convention has its provenance in the need to provide life-saving equipment following the 1912 *Titanic* disaster. The express purpose of MARPOL is to prevent the accidental or intentional discharge of oil and/or other noxious cargoes and bunkers, as well as wastes from ships. The STCW Convention stipulates minimum safe standards in crewing numbers and levels of competence. The regulatory procedure for the safe navigation of passing ships is defined by the Convention on Preventing Collisions at Sea. Finally, ILO Convention 147 defines minimum safe standards for the safe and humane employment conditions of seafarers. Under the UK flag, adherence to these Conventions is legally enforced by a series of evolving Merchant Shipping Acts, stretching back to 1894. In addition, the Safety Official and Reporting of Accidents and Dangerous Occurrences (SORADO)[52] Regulations provide for a system of on-board safety standards by the vessel's Safety Officer and Safety Representatives.

Despite the historic incremental strengthening of marine safety regulation, the international safety regime was particularly shaken by the tragic loss of the *Herald of Free Enterprise* in 1987. Reaction led to the 1993 International Safety Management (ISM code). The Code has set out to provide a proactive Safety Management System linking shoreside management and on-board operations. European commitment to improved standards was outlined in six principles by Transport Commissioner, Neil Kinnock, in 1996:

(1) Promotion of IMO regulations on flag administrations responsible for ship registration and control;

(2) Definition of common registration principles within the EU;

(3) Adoption of a code of conduct on maritime trade;

(4) Encouragement of owners to achieve high standards of operational quality;

(5) Legislative and financial penalties imposed on shippers employing sub-standard vessels;

(5) Introduction of compulsory third party insurance for vessels trading in the EU.[53]

Given this panoply of safety regulation it is apparent that the framework for a Green Highway exists. The reality of shipping markets, however, leads to a dogged persistence in infringements. Sub-standard operations continue to undermine the integrity of the Green Highway.

8.6.1 Persisting Sub-standards?

The desire to establish shipping services at lowest cost can be seen as a result of both competition with road and intra shipping – between shipping rivals. In some instances this can prove to have a disastrous impact on quality. For example, the mid-1990s scandal of Adriatic Tankers featured the operation of chemical tankers on the North European and Mediterranean coasts in a poorly maintained, unsafe condition, not to mention the wholesale exploitation of developing nation crews.[54] This was despite many of the cargoes involved being of a volatile, environmentally sensitive nature, and the trading routes amongst the most confined and congested channels in the world.

The constant pressure on freight rates leads to shipping lines seeking low costs. This often means fewer crew members, leading to unreasonable, unsustainable, watch-keeping hours. In some instances less ethical owners employ sub-standard crews for extended duty tours. One example of the curtailment of normal leave patterns was evidenced by the author when interviewing a Filipino Chief Officer. Despite being employed in the intensive Northern Europe feeder trades, the Chief Officer was engaged for a full twelve month tour! This means a full year of 4-6 port call per week and the chances of more than 6 hours un-broken sleep, remote! By comparison, more reputable, safety conscious owners would limit intensive coastal tours-of-duty to 4-8 weeks!

Sub-standards were mostly confined to the deepsea sector up until the 1980s. Traditionally, shortsea and coastal shipping in Europe was carried out by locally owned and flagged ships. The extension of the flag of convenience arrangement from the deepsea to the shortsea sector was accompanied by, in many instances, a fall in standards. Additionally, the collapse of the Soviet bloc economies in the late 1980s saw large amounts of ageing tonnage and low cost crews entering into the European market. Particularly noticeable has been the incursions of the Russian river and lake barges into the trades. These vessels were originally intended for the calmer waters of the Volga and Lake Ladoga but can now be can now be seen precariously trading in the less clement waters of the North Sea, the Irish Sea and the Bay of Biscay. Whilst the Eastern bloc seamen had hitherto enjoyed a sound worldwide reputation for professionalism, the sub-standard conditions and ships they now find themselves serving in has diluted their seafaring status. Typical of the plight of these seamen in British waters was the case of the 2,317gt Maltese flagged coastal vessel, *Black Sea Star,* which ended up under arrest in the Port of Immingham in summer 2001. It became evident to Mission to Seamen Chaplain, Rev David Craig, that the Georgian crew were in a distressed condition; they had existed on a diet of potato soup for three weeks and some had not received any pay for over a year.[55]

The safety record of the Cambodian registry has also created consternation in European circles between 1995 and 2002 at least 25 Cambodian registered vessels were wrecked or stranded.[55] In some circles it is felt that sub-standard operators are attracted by easy internet access, as well as low registration fees, to the aggressively marketed registry. The ICS has criticised the poor regulation of the Cambodian registry, as well as other open registries and called for its ban. [56]

The reality of shipping supply and demand is that in many markets a large number of shipowners compete for the business of much fewer buyers of their services. The role of the buyer - the charterer - is crucial to improving the safe standards of ships in this oligopsonistic market, a market which bestows power on the buyer of shipping services. Leading UK shortsea operator, Michael Everard, has argued that "charterers should take responsibility for the ships they charter".[57]

The history of oil tankers has been punctuated by a number of serious, defining accidents. For the European populace the impact of tanker disasters in home waters has had a detrimental impact on the image of shipping operations.

The concern expressed following the 1967 *Torrey Canyon* grounding on Seven Stones reef was instrumental in promoting the English Channel Vessel Traffic Separation Scheme (TSS). The 1977 *Marion* incident in the mouth of the Tees provoked questions over navigational standards in UK waters. The Liberian registered tanker managed to foul the direct North Sea oil pipeline from the Ekofisk Field to Teeside. The accident investigation revealed that the vessel's master was using out-of-date navigational charts which did not contain details of the new pipeline.[58] Similarly the large scale pollution following the groundings of the *Exxon Valdez*, the *Braer* and the *Sea Empress,* intensified public concerns over shipping standards. The oil pollution shock of the 1999 *Erika* break up and sinking had implications for the industry stretching into the new Millennium.[59] Ostensibly, the tanker on passage between Dunkerque and Livorno with a cargo of heavy fuel oil, was a tangible example of the Green Highway at work. The 25,000 tonnes cargo represents the equivalent of more than 800 road tanker journeys across the Alps. However, the combination of gale force weather conditions and an ageing, metal corroded, vessel was to result in an environmental disaster for the French coastline and its ecology. For the chartering oil major, TotalFina, the result was not only the inevitability of a heavy fine, but also the loss of corporate reputation.[60] The ripple like effect of public concern in the immediate aftermath of the *Erika* break up led to a re-defining of tanker standards and included the "blacklisting" of sub-standard vessels by the EU.[61] The US coastguard had already targeted the oil majors, following the *Exxon Valdez* pollution disaster in 1989.[62]

In Europe the environmental sensitivity of large stretches of coastline has focused attention on qualitative factors, including the charterers vetting of ships. Safety standards such as ISO 9000 and the International Safety Management (ISM) Code have placed emphasis on the management systems of not only the operators but also the charterers. It is also evident that public opinion in Europe nations will no longer tolerate the environmental costs of sub-standard operations.

8.6.2 Fatigue and Alcohol

It has been estimated that around 80 percent of accidents at sea are caused by human error, with fatigue playing a major part in this failing.[63] International concern over the long hours worked at sea has led to the International Labour Organisation's convention: *C180 Seafarers' Hours of Work and the Manning of Ships Convention, 1996.*[64] The limits on hours of work/rest stipulated by the Convention are:

- 14 hours of work in any 24 hour period;
- 72 hours of work in any seven-day period;
  or
- 10 hours minimum of rest in any 24 hours;
- 77 hours minimum of rest in any seven-day period.[65]

Achieving compliance with this convention may not be feasible, given the demands placed on the "lean" crewing levels prevalent in shortsea shipping. In the instance of the loss of the *Cita* in 1997 the fatigue factor was a very real component of the vessel's grounding. Fatigue at sea has increasingly become manifest as a safety problem in recent decades and is now recognised as a factor in maritime accidents. The combination of minimal crewing levels and rapid port turnarounds can lead to an incremental build up of exhaustion and stress. In the coastal trades, the problem is exacerbated by the short passages and adverse weather conditions.[66]

The marginal nature of feeder trade economics was highlighted in chapter 7. In such markets attention will always be given to cost saving techniques. One way of reducing operational costs, introduced in the early 1990s, was the One Man Bridge Operation(OMBO). International Regulations stipulate that in the hours of darkness and also poor daytime visibility, two watchkeepers will carry out bridge duties. Primarily this is to limit the risk of watchkeepers losing concentration and/or falling asleep and to provide extra look out capabilities – a particularly welcome support in confined and congested waters. The OMBO system was devised as a labour saving device in that it facilitated one watchkeeper operation. Integral to the system is the anti-sleep alarm which ensures that the watchkeeper does not fall asleep. The need to respond to the alarm at frequent intervals, however, may be seen as an irksome task by the irritated officer in the middle of the night watch. Unfortunately this has led to irresponsible behaviour, with officers switching off the system. Invariably this leads to sleeping watchkeepers and ensuing near misses, collisions and groundings.

The apparent dichotomy between cost competition and the quality of operational standards was highlighted by the total loss of the *Cita*.[67] The fate of the feeder vessel was sealed when the Chief Officer switched off the system at around 01:00hrs on passage between Southampton and Belfast. The inevitable happened, the Chief Officer fell asleep, and the vessel grounded on St Mary's Isle (Scilly Isles) at full speed. In addition to the vessel being condemned as a constructive total loss along with her container cargo, localised pollution resulted from cargo spillage and the vessel's bunker fuels.[68] The incident revealed the gruelling schedule, detailed in Table 40, that such coastal feeder vessels need to adhere to.

Table 39: Feeder Service Schedule: Netherlands-UK-Eire		
Day	Depart	Arrive
Sunday pm	Rotterdam	
Monday Noon		Southampton
Monday pm	Southampton	
Wednesday Noon		Belfast
Wednesday pm	Belfast	
Thursday am		Dublin
Thursday pm	Dublin	
Saturday am		Southampton
Saturday pm	Southampton	
Sunday am		Rotterdam

Source: Marine Accident Investigation Branch (MAIB) Report 3/98 (1998), Report of the Inspectors' Inquiry into the Grounding of the Feeder Container Vessel, Cita, off Newfoundland Point, Isle of Scilly, 26.3.97. Southampton: MAIB.

A similar accident occurred in 2000 with the grounding of the shuttle feedership, *Coastal Bay*. The Antigua and Barbuda flagged vessel, chartered to - the Mersey Harbours subsidiary, Coastal Containers, operated an intensive Liverpool-Dublin service. The Marine Accident Investigation Branch (MAIB) inquiry into the vessel's full speed grounding in Anglesey Bay focused on the fatigue factor. Again it was a case of the Chief Officer being overcome by sleep and the inaction of the OMBO system. However, it was established that the vessel was operated by just two watch keeping officers, with the Master and the Chief Officer working a fatiguing rotating pattern of watch on, and watch off, system. *Lloyd's List's* reporting of the incident referred to the seven day overnight cycle for months on end:

> The mate was on a four month contract and had been operating for 84 days non-stop under a regime which never permitted either he or the master ever to enjoy a six hour period of real sleep.[69]

Blame was diverted from the watchkeepers. The MAIB targeted the vessel managers, Jungerhans & Co, imposing a $29,481 fine plus $8,844 costs.[70] In addition, the *Coastal Bay* incident, following closely after the *Cita* disaster, has focused regulatory attention on intensive feeder services. The MAIB recommended that a further watchkeeper be engaged in order to facilitate proper rest breaks in accordance with the stipulations of the STCW 95.

As the *Lloyd's List* editorial , "No mystery of the seas", pointed out, this was indeed an accident waiting to happen.[71] What the grounding again reveals is the marginal nature of the feeder trades with freight rates squeezed by intense competition from fellow shipping companies and the road haulage and rail freight sectors. It is obvious that charterers and ultimately their container industry principals, are searching out the lowest cost operators. In these conditions the low freight rates do not stretch to the "luxury" of employing an additional watchkeeper.

Fatigue in the shortsea and offshore supply boat sector has been a main target of Maritime labour unions, including the Officers' union, Nautilus and the ratings union, RMT. In 2000 Nautilus General Secretary Allan Graveson apportioned blame for a River Trent collision between two coastal vessels on under-manning, resulting in fatigue.[72] In the intensely congested and difficult coastline – not to mention the weather conditions of the shortsea British and Irish trades – a premium is placed upon high operational standards. In the confined waters of the English Channel vessels in the inward and outward traffic lanes have to contend with intense and high speed Cross Channel ferry services. Also, fishing flotillas working in and around the lanes. Erring rogue vessels, illegally crossing the shipping lanes add to the potential perils. In such conditions vessel on-board management are put to rigorous testing; when watchkeepers are fatigued the ensuing duress can prove critical. It has been estimated by Crescent Tankships that their fleet of 10 small product tankers in the Northern European trades make up to a total of 140 port calls per month.[73] Crescent have developed a strategy for risk limitation in areas of crew fatigue. During periods of bad weather the normal tour of three weeks at sea (followed by three weeks leave) is reduced to two weeks.[74] This is seen as a necessity given the twin pressures of intensive coastal and shortsea schedules - short voyages and daily port calls - is exacerbated by the poor weather conditions of the North European winter. For the Green Highway to sustain environmental integrity it is incumbent on the owners, operators and charterers of vessels to ensure crewing levels and standards of proficiency are a match for these demanding conditions.

8.6.3 Managing Safety?

The need to balance the efficient, economic, performance of vessels against cost and revenues is a critical element of the environmental integrity of the Green Highway. Ship safety expert, Professor Chengi Kuo[75] has identified four: separate criteria which present themselves as challenges to ship operators:

> (1) Competitiveness;
> (2) Specification;
> (3) Cost-effectiveness;
> (4) Safety.

The competitiveness criteria is obviously paramount to any business in a market economy. The crucial question is whether profit can be achieved whilst addressing the importance of the other three criteria. Specification covers the description of the product, process and service level. For example, the specification of the ship and how it fits the demands of a certain trade. Cost-effectiveness implies value for money in relation to delivering the task. Kuo has argued for the definition of safety to be recognised in its many forms. These stretch from engineering functions to operational procedures, human error considerations and decisions taken by managers and ship designers.[76]

The capsizing of the feeder vessel, *Dongedjk*, in 2001 illustrated the critical margin that coastal ships operate on. The vessel turned-over in calm weather as a result of being overloaded resulting an excessively low freeboard. The issue here has long historical antecedents, stretching back to the campaigns of British MP, Samuel Plimsoll, in the mid 1800s. Concerned at the high loss of seamen due to overloaded ships, the MP campaigned vigorously for a load-line system which would prevent unscrupulous shipowners from loading their vessels beyond the safety margin, with precariously low freeboards. [77] As ever, the problem was one of balancing profits with safety. The cost of adding additional freeboard to such small container ships as the *Dongedjk* would be in the region of €230,000.[78] Stoop, (et.al)[79] has observed the dichotomy in negotiations between masters and charterers in the sea-river trades: in order to maximise the vessel's payload the charterers,

> will invite the captains to accept an increased draught and tight sailing schedule. The captain will not be inclined to refuse. This may cause risk for the operational behaviour but at the same time is a challenge to the professional skills of the captains and pilots.[80]

Stoop's analysis of the safety record of sea-river ships operating in tightly constrained inland waters identifies the importance of quality management. Findings were that vessels sailing under flags of high standard registries, operated by high quality management, were rarely involved in accidents.[81] Unfortunately, a vast spectrum does exist in the management of quality in global shipping; the implications are particularly acute in the confined and congested waters of the coastal and shortsea trades, where the highest standards of seafaring professionalism are called for

The question over shipping's environmental performance is inextricably linked with quality. The manner in which the vessel is crewed, maintained and operated is a function of management. This has long been established by a leading

Admiralty case involving the management of coastal shipping operations. Case law was provided by the *Lady Gwendolen* incident in 1965.[82] The vessel was directly owned by the Dublin brewer, Arthur Guinness, and was engaged on the vibrant Dublin-Manchester stout-beer trade. In order to keep to the schedule the master, Captain Meredith, adopted the practice of navigating at full speed, relying on radar observation, even in the frequently foggy conditions of the Irish Sea and River Mersey. The unfortunate outcome of this practice in November 1961 was a collision resulting in the sinking of the coastal vessel, *Freshfield*, which was anchored fogbound in the approaches to Liverpool. Although the recklessness of the master was found to be a contributory factor in the accident, the owners, Arthur Guinness, were deemed negligent in not adequately monitoring the way the *Lady Gwendolen* was operated. Lord Justice Sellers summarised:

> A primary concern of a shipowner must be the safety of life at sea. That involves a seaworthy ship, properly manned but also requires safe navigation. Excessive speed in fog is a grave breach of duty, and shipowners should use all their influence to prevent it.[83]

Although there was no evidence to suggest that the master was under pressure from the owners to maintain schedules in poor weather conditions, the case does illustrate the balance between shipping efficiency and operational safety in the shortsea trades. The principle of vicarious liability was a major factor in the judgement. It was held that this principle rendered the employer responsible for the actions of its employees, ergo Arthur Guinness were liable for the navigational behaviour of Captain Meredith.

A more serious accident, one which brought severe condemnation of the shoreside management, was that of the *Herald of Free Enterprise* disaster in 1987.[84] The partial sinking of the ferry in Zeebrugge Harbour with the loss of 189 passenger and crew was to send shock-waves around the global maritime community. The disaster had a devastating impact on the UK seafaring

424

community. The vessel attempted to leave Zeebrugge without securing her bow doors. The resulting water ingress (from the bow wave), as the vessel picked up speed, quickly led to the vessel entering into an irretrievable listing-over situation. The vessel was operated by a hitherto reputable British company, sailing under the British flag with a full British crew. Such slip-shod practice was not supposed to happen under these circumstances! Following the lengthy investigation into the disaster management systems failures were identified as a principal cause. The dichotomy between commercial considerations and basic seafaring safety was highlighted by the report.[85] In evidence it became apparent that ferry vessel's leaving port on intensive Channel routes with their bow-doors was not an uncommon practice. Several Masters of the ferries had requested a double check system which assured them that the doors were secured before sailing. This request was denied by a disdainful management.[86]

8.7 Shuttle Tanker Operations

In the field of marine environment and safety, tanker vessels have the highest profiles. The high volumes of oil running down the UK coast, the "Route One" of the Green Highway were identified in chapter 1. In addition to navigational practice in tanker movements, critical areas of marine safety are: oil tank slop disposal, bilge waste pumping and oil spills following collisions and groundings. Tanker design has been held up to a great deal of scrutiny following well publicised disasters such as the *Exxon Valdez, Braer, Sea Empress* and *Erika*. As well as the devastating potential for large volume spills of crude and black oils, there is also the problem of the release of volatile organic compounds (VOC) into the atmosphere during loading operations. Naval architects, Armstrong Technology, have identified tanker risks, including a 0.2 percent cargo loss equalling 200 tonnes of crude in a typical 100,000dwt shuttle tanker loading operation.[87] The result of this emission is that lower order hydrocarbons (non methane VOCs) react in sunlight with nitrous oxides (NOx) and contribute to ground level ozone. Armstrong's have identified a number of critical areas where risk can be reduced in the tanker trades. Their safety case is built around the following key design features:

- Double hull construction in excess of Marpol rule 13f;
- All bunker and ready use fuel tanks protected by double hull;
- A volatile organic compounds (voc) recovery system;
- designed for ballast water exchange at sea;;
- reliability assessment of hull girder structure;
- designed structural connections to have a fatigue life with a minimum factor of safety equal to twice the operating life;
- diesel-electric propulsion which ensure machinery operates at it most efficient loading.[88]

Such initiatives towards a state-of-the-art risk-aversion in the tanker trades can only contribute to higher safety thresholds. The evidence on double hull shuttle tankers in the North Sea points to a big risk reduction compared to single hull tankers. A 1998 study[89] by US oil offshore oil specialist, Amerada Hess, in conjunction with Lloyd's Register, has concluded shuttle tankers were more at risk than deepsea trading tankers because of their frequent port calls and passages through confined waters, including the loading zones. Three particular areas of risk were identified – collision, contact (objects other than ships) and grounding. Risk is specifically acute when tankers are manoeuvring close to loading platforms in the North Sea.[90] The Amerada Hess study also found that double hull tankers would reduce spillage from the three risk areas identified by 75 percent.[91]

The demand of North Sea loading operations, frequently in adverse weather conditions, places great stress on skill and managerial systems. The study found that almost all reportable incidents were attributable to human error. Although the shuttle tankers are fitted with dynamic positioning devices this manoeuvring aid needs the utmost level of skill and concentration. A 1999 study by the International Marine Contractors Association (IMCA) concluded that better training is required in order that vessel operators understand the limitations of their vessels under the strained circumstances of platform manoeuvring. In adverse weather conditions the decision to disconnect connections and temporarily abandon loading needs to be made. Cost factors as well as safety considerations are involved here. The IMCA has argued that masters need the courage to take this costly decision to disconnect as soon as unacceptable positional instability occurs in heavy weather (when extreme conditions jeopardise safe loading operations and accelerate the risks of a serious oil spill). Furthermore, it is incumbent on management to support such safety oriented decisions.[92] Disconnecting a tanker from its loading arm can prove to be a costly and time consuming practice. The good practice of temporarily abandoning loading operations in rough weather conditions is clearly an area where risks are balanced against costs. The UK Offshore Operator's Association (UKOOA) provided clear guidelines for such loading decisions in 2001.[93]

Environmental concerns are to the forefront in the North Sea oil shuttle trades. Scandinavian tanker operators tend to be in the vanguard of safety innovation. The NKr 1.7b 1998 order of three 120,000 dwt twin screw tankers for the Norwegian Government's Statoil fleet featured attention to safety attributes. The 1999 new building, *Navion Britannia*, for the Norwegian state owned Statoil Group (now partly privatised) and its joint venture partner, Rasmussen, was the first of the trio of advanced, environmentally focused, 120,000dwt shuttle tankers. The trio were greeted as providers of "A new era in shuttles" by *Lloyd's Tanker Focus* in October 1998.[94] Built by the state owned Spanish yard, Astilleros Espanoles, Astilleros Sestao, for the crude oil trades of the Norwegian Field. These vessels operate effectively as coasting vessels and can be found trading at such British oil refinery ports as Corytown, Fawley, Tranmere and Milford Haven, as well as Cork's Whitegate Terminal. These include double hulls, tank design which provides increased control of the production and emission of volatile compounds and improved vessel manoeuvring aids.[95] The double hull facility strengthens the integrity of the cargo holds. This is of particular importance in vessel grounding accidents and was a key talking point in the *Sea Empress* Milford Haven environmental disaster. Loading tanks are arranged with three per section – with two longitudinal bulkheads instead of one – to reduce the release of volatile organic compounds which build up during the loading process. The high degree of manoeuvrability is of special value in the demanding North Sea waters, particularly in the oil rig zones. In addition to twin propellers the vessels are assisted by two bow thrusts and a stern thrust. The prime propulsion system is provided by two symmetrical but independent engine rooms, divided by a fire-resistant, watertight bulkhead. The advantages of this are that in the event of a breakdown in one of the engines, the master is still able to control the vessel on one engine. Manoeuvrability is a critical safety factor in the off-shore trades and this is aided by twin bow thrusters, a stern thruster, twin rudders and propellers. The vessels loading capability is greatly aided by a dynamic positioning system. The vessels 18 cargo tanks and fuel oil tanks are encompassed in a double hull arrangement which reduces the risk of oil leakage in the event of a collision or grounding. Tanker safety in the Russian oil trades was boosted in 2006 when the Swedish operator, Stena Bulk, commissioned the 117,000dwt, *Stena Arctica* under the high cost Swedish flag. Attention to high standards, including ice strengthened vessels, is seen as an imperative by Stena.[96]

Evidence from the North Sea off-shore sector in 2002 points to the increased willingness of seafarers to report near miss situations involving both oil-rig support vessels and tankers.[97] These vessels routinely practise close manoeuvring situations with oil rigs and loading installations. The reporting of near-misses is symptomatic of a healthy safety-management culture. Instead of trying to "hush up" such incidents in order to avoid blame repercussions, the organisation of safety management benefits from discerning what went wrong. In 2003 a boost to accident and near miss reporting was achieved by the introduction of the MAIB administered, Confidential Human-Factor Incident Reporting Programme (CHIRPS).[98] In the long term such trends are healthy as they allow for scrutiny of near-misses, providing for the dissemination of information for the educational guidance of seafarers in similar critical situations.

8.8 Port State Control

Moves towards an international benchmark in shipping safety standards is facilitated by the inspection system of port state control. This allows for state authorities to examine ships regardless of their flag state. Whilst the flag state is the country whose flag the vessel is flying, the port state is the country within which the port of call is located. This level of global regulation marks a departure from the laissez-faire tradition in shipping operations.

In the 1980's the countries of Europe, concerned about safety standards on ships trading in, and coming to, Europe, signed up to the Paris Memorandum, which set standards for the inspection of a percentage of these ships. Broadly speaking, each country agreed to have a consistent regime of inspecting ships, with trained a qualified personnel (Port State Control Inspectors – PSCI) and to inspect 25% of the ships calling into each port, on a targeted basis so that the worst ships or flag states received the most attention. The ships are inspected with reference to the international conventions and flag regulations in force, and if deficiencies are found there is a well ordered system for improvement. This can be either rectification of minor deficiencies before the ship sails, or a detention until serious deficiencies have been eradicated. A serious deficiency would be, for example, insufficient officers or lack of proper certification for officers or crew, defective fire fighting or life saving gear, out of date statutory certification, or engine room defects liable to lead to pollution. About 5–10% of all ships inspected are detained – typically for 1-2 days, although sometimes for much longer. All inspections, defects, detentions and ship and operators details are recorded on a database. Ships with defects or detentions attract a higher target factor and are therefore most likely to be inspected again.[99]

A sample of PSC ship inspections in the Port of Cork, provided in Table 41 reveals a variety of flags of ships with defects. It can be seen that developing nation, open registries are prevalent. A notable fact revealed by the PSC reports was the fragmented nature of flag, ownership. For example Cambodian registered vessels trading in North European waters are managed by Estonian operators. The North Korean flagged, Lebanese operated, general cargo vessel, *Lady Hesen*, achieved notoriety in 2004 when it was retained in detention in the Port of Cork for 392 days following a PSC inspection list of 71 safety deficiencies.[100] A sample of serious detentions (Table 42) in UK ports, February 2005, reveals a similar pattern of general cargo and bulk carriers and flags of convenience.

Table 40 Sample of PSC Deficiencies & Detentions, Port of Cork 2002-06.

Vessel	Type	Flag
Baltic Forest	General Cargo	Panama
Draco	Container	Denmark
Keeper	General Cargo	Belize
Lady Hesen	General Cargo	North Korea
Linda	General Cargo	Cambodia
Spear 1	Oil-Bulk-Ore	Panama
Superferry	RoRo	St.Vincent& Grenadines
Winger	General Cargo	Belize
Zaher	General Cargo	St. Vincent & Grenadines
Zaher III	General Cargo	Lebanon

Source: Paris MOU Port State Control

Table 41: Sample of Serious Detentions in UK Ports, Feb 2005			
Vessel	Type	Flag	Port
Aqua Pioneer	Bulk Carrier	Malta	Blyth
Balaba 1	Bulk Carrier	Turkey	South Shields
Gloria	General Cargo	Estonia	Silvertown
Hawk Bay	Reefer	Netherlands Antilles	Portsmouth
Midland 21	General Cargo	Malta	Birkenhead
Normandy	RoRo	Bahamas	Belfast
Ocean Comfort	Bulk Carrier	Panama	Redcar
Oliver Felix	Tug	Honduras	Lowestoft
Paris Texas	Bulk Carrier	Jamaica	Cardiff
Petra	General Cargo	Netherland Antilles	Grangemouth
Urana Naree	Bulk Carrier	Thailand	Immingham
Ziemia Geriezinska	Bulk Carrier	Liberia	South Shields
Source: Paris MOU Port State Control			

8.9 The Coastguard Role

The "motorway police" role on the Green Highway falls to the UK and Irish coastguard services, respectively. Essential to the safe functioning of shipping movements around the coastline is the effectiveness of the Coastguards. The Coastguard system has a long and often traumatic history.[101] Three themes emerge when looking at the historic and evolving role of the Coastguard:

    (1) The Historic Tradition of Public Service;
    (2) the changing demands on the Service;
    (3) the dedication of the Service.

The early history of the Coastguard Service was one of variety, flexibility and outstanding bravery. Gradually the broad, sometimes conflicting remit of the service has given way to a specialised, dedicated and professional organisation. In the 1600-1700s Coastguard Officers patrolled the coastline as a deterrent to endemic smuggling of brandy, tobacco, tea and silks. In 1743 it was estimated that 50 percent of the nation's tea was smuggled in! Despite today's romantic image of smuggling, the early Coastguard Officers had to contend with dangerous and desperate men. Close linkages with the Royal Navy allowed for the service to become a reserve for fighting men. The appointment of ex-navy boatmen in 1831 had an immediate impact on reducing smuggling activities.

8.9.1 The Changing Demands on the Service:

The Coastguard Service has consistently evolved in its public role over the last two Centuries. The need to prevent smuggling has been supplemented by coastal protection, the removal of mines in times of hostilities and life saving has become a major objective. The development of Life Saving Apparatus enabled the countless saving of sailors' lives from ships stranded off-shore. In addition, the protection of shipwrecks and their cargo became part of the Service's responsibilities, once the business of life saving was completed. Assisting the role of the Post Office and Lloyds, signalling and telegraphy communications were pioneered by the Coastguard in the early days of telegraphy and wireless media.[102]

The evolving workload of the Coastguard reflects the changing demands placed on the Service. In recent years, the Service has had to contend with rising traffic levels and increased vessel size. Pollution prevention and managing the Traffic Separation Scheme in the English Channel has become a major challenge. The development of oil and gas fields in UK coastal waters has brought additional safety demands. Contributing significantly to the 12,000 plus annual incidents handled by the Service, the increase in maritime leisure in recent decades has placed a big emphasis on Search and Rescue techniques. Supported by radar, satellite positioning, as well as helicopters, the service has shown a willingness to embrace new skills, new technologies. Co-ordination of the Service's Emergency Towing Vessels, Search and Rescue Helicopters, as well as Fixed Wing Aircraft and Lifeboats is integral to the Coastguard's duties. The Service has a well established tradition of playing a co-ordinating and educational role between maritime agencies and organisations.[103] The extent of marine activity in UK waters is borne out by the number of Search and Rescue (SAR) operations occurring annually. Table 43 shows over 16,000 incidents recorded incidents in 2005.

Table 42: Coastguard Search and Rescue Incidents, 2004-5		
	2004	2005
Total Incidents Reported	14,240	16,754
Assistance Rendered	8,056	7,252
Total People Rescued (Life at risk)	5,276	4,790
Total People Assisted (Life not at risk)	21,600	22,477
Fatalities	96	100
Source: MCA, Southampton.		

The dedication of Coastguard personnel is a major strength of the Service. In times of war the Service has played a important role in policing the coastline, and in co-ordinating the rescues of aircrews, ditched in the English Channel. In 1940 members of the coastguard bravely ferried the local Fire Service to the burning destroyer, *HMS Fame*. Ammunition was also removed from the ship and 104 crew were rescued from the threat of fire and explosion. Thus the Coastguard was able to returns its gratitude to the Royal Navy for its earlier support.[104] Today's professional Coastguards are highly concentrated in a small number of high-tech maritime co-ordination centres. They are supported by the Auxiliary members grouped around hazardous areas of the coastline. Specialism is also evident at the point of rescue with Auxiliary teams divided into Initial Response and Back up Teams. Trained and co-ordinated by the professional Coastguards, these volunteer Coastguard Rescue Teams now carry the proud tradition of life saving into a third century. The recognition of this fine tradition by the presentation of the Coastguard Colour by the Prince of Wales in 2005 serves as a tribute to all who have contributed to the Service.[105]

8.9.2 The Coastal Management System: Rogues and Zombies!

The work of the British and Irish Coastguard services is integral to assessment of the Green Highway's safety and environmental integrity. It is well known in the maritime circles industry that the free spirited, *laissez-faire,* history of shipping has proved sometimes problematic in terms of safety and an obstacle to the implementation of regulatory system of coastal management. British/French and Irish waters sustain some of the worlds highest traffic levels, the Dover Straits in particular. In 1999, 82,406 ship movements were reported by the Dover Coastguard, representing 1.8 billion dwt of shipping per year;[106]by 2006 this had increased by at least 35percent. with more than 400 merchant ship transits per day, totalling 2.4 billion dwt.[107] This places the Straits at the top of the global traffic density league, above the Singapore gateway bottleneck, Malacca Straits and the Black Sea passage way, Bosporous. Other areas of high UK traffic density are the Thames, Tees, Humber and Solent regions. With its mix of merchant ships, warships, ferries and high volumes of leisure craft, the Solent region consistently reports the highest level of incidents, including Search and Rescue (SAR) activity involving helicopters and fast rescue boats. The Minches and Pentland Firth passageways in Northern Scotland do not generate such heavy volumes but do pose considerable hazards. The combination of tanker traffics – serving the oil fields of the North Sea – extreme weather conditions, and the environmental vulnerability of the natural rocky coastlines, requires rigorous coastal management.

The upsurge in vessel traffic, in conjunction with increases in vessel size, began to manifest as causes of rising trends in serious English Channel collisions and groundings in the 1960s and 1970s. The following sequence of tragic events demonstrates not only the traffic intensity of the Dover Straits but also the need for effective traffic regulation.[108] Things came very much to a head in early1971 with the serious collision between the Panamanian flag tanker, *Texaco Caribbean,* and the Cypriot flag dry cargo vessel, *Paracas,* in the Dover Straits on January 11th. The tanker exploded, broke into two sections and eight crewmen were lost. The disaster was compounded the following day when the German vessel, *Brandenburg,* struck a section of the tanker at full speed and within 2 nautical miles capsized and sank, with the loss of 21 crewmen. The final part of this catastrophic sequence came on February 27th when the Norwegian tanker, *Hebris,* reported a vessel sinking ahead. This proved to be the Greek cargo vessel, *Niki,* which had run into one the sunken hulls; another 22 lives were lost as a result. The resulting loss of life (51 seafarers in total) wreck of ships and catastrophic oil pollution focused attention on the anarchic practice of navigation in such confined and congested waters.[109] Regulatory response followed in the form of the Vessel Traffic Regulation System which brought all vessels under the surveillance of the French and British Traffic centres, Cap Gris Nez and Dover Langdon Battery. Clearly defined Traffic Separation Schemes (TSS) had been first introduced in 1967, however "rogue" vessels straying outside of their allotted track still averaged 20-30 per day in 1972.[110] Gradually, however, intensified monitoring using radar and computer screen plotting of vessel headings has led to illegal incidents declining. By the 1990s "rogues" were down to around four per day.[111] High profile prosecution by the Dover Magistrates and their Normandy equivalents have helped to enforce TSS. One example of prosecution followed the traffic havoc caused by a Medway bound vessel, *Winter Star,* erratically departing its allotted track. It was reported that the officer of the watch, uncertain of his position, simply turned about in heavy traffic conditions in a bid to find the Thames Estuary! The master was fined £11,500.[112] Such maritime incidents can best be explained to the non-seafarer as the equivalent of wrong direction driving on the motorway!

Whilst it is clear that the problem of navigational errors and unsafe practices continue, the evidence also points to an improving pattern of behaviour.

Gradually, as a more genuine safety culture - enforced by intensified vessel tracking systems - takes hold, maritime safety is likely to improve.

8.10 Pilotage and Towage

An important element of the safety of the Green Highway is the professional services of the pilotage and towage providers. Pilotage falls into at least three categories: (1) the sea pilot; (2) the river pilot; (3) the dock pilot. Use of the sea pilot is most likely to be when large vessels transit the English Channel. Also, for large vessels crossing the congested waters of the North Sea. For example, a large container vessel on passage between Hamburg and Thamesport may benefit from the expertise of the sea pilot, particular if the Master has limited experience in these waters. It would be unusual for a small shortsea vessel on a regular North European trading pattern to take a seapilot. However when trading in hazardous harbour and inland locations a river pilot would probably be engaged. The exception here is that masters of regular trading vessels can apply for pilotage exemption.

An interesting adjunct of the pilotage laws is provided by the exemption clauses of the Rhine. The cost savings of pilotage exemption prompted one British flagged company to switch registries to Eire. Exemptions for the German sector of the Rhine were only granted to masters of German nationality. At the time (late 1980s) British nationality was a pre-requisite of becoming master on a British flagged vessel; no such proviso was imposed by the Eire flag. As a consequence the vessels were given German masters. In many ports the decision to take a pilot is left open. Masters facing stringent cost scrutiny may be persuaded to omit the pilot and berth their vessels themselves.[113]

The stability of the pilotage service was severely eroded by industrial action on the River Humber in 2002. The dispute between the Humber pilots and the pilotage management, ABP, led to bitter recriminations and concerns over safety. The dispute brought a new wave of untested pilots to the river and a number of grounding and collision incidents – the striking pilots claimed - occurred as a result. *Fairplay International Shipping Weekly* added its concerns in May 2002:

> Doubtless there are some very good mariners among the new boys, but there is no substitute for proper training by seniors. But decades of accumulated experience have been jettisoned on the Humber, opening the door to similar deeds across the UK and EU.[114]

Despite the concerns of *Fairplay* there has not been any replication of further managerial reforms leading to an assault on established pilotage contracts and conditions.

Harbour towage is mostly applicable to vessels of at least 4000 dwt and above. Regular shortsea vessels are normally below this size. Also, modern vessels are likely to be fitted with a range of manoeuvring aids such as bow thrust propellers. However, in bad weather conditions or in situations of engine or steering gear failure, collision, fire, groundings, tugs may be called for. In tanker terminals tugs have the extra responsibilities of fire watch and are provided with powerful water jet monitors for fire-fighting. In addition these vessels have chemical foam fire fighting and oil pollution clean up facilities.[115]

The aftermath of the *Exxon Valdez* environmental disaster brought about the imposition of tanker escort duties for tugs. It was made evident by the Alaskan disaster that large loaded tankers are at extreme risk in confined and congested waters. The tanker escort system necessitates the connection of a tug until open sea is reached. Along with the pilotage service, towage services have a long lineage and a strong community ethos. In ports such as London, Liverpool and Southampton the incumbent tugboat companies were established in the early years of steam technology (>1850s). Some incidents of de-regulation have occurred. The "tugwars" of Hamburg in the 1990s did appear as a precursor of market fragmentation.[116] In the UK, however, the new Millennium period has brought a process of market concentration with two major tug groupings, Switzer (a subsidiary of the Danish shipping giant, A.P.Moller) and Australia's Adsteam Towage. At the time of writing the proposed take-over of the latter by the former was under scrutiny by the UK government agency, Competition Commission.[117]

Coastguard management has been strengthened by the stationing of Emergency Towage Vessels (ETVs) at strategic points on the UK and Continental coastline. Following such environmentally disastrous tanker accidents as the *Braer* on Shetland and the *Sea Empress* in Milford Haven the provision of powerful tugboats with salvage and rescue facilities in high risk areas has been a priority of the British and French Governments. The loss of the *Braer* and her crude oil cargo in 1992 demonstrated the risk of Britain's perilous mix of rocky coastline, powerful tides and regular storm conditions.[118] The *Braer's* loss of power in gale force weather, South of Sumburgh Head, led to the vessel being driven side on by powerful waves produced by the marine junction between the Atlantic Ocean and the North Sea. Despite the heroic attempts by the tug, *Sirius Star* – attempting a rescue in a 70 knot gale and waves of 40 feet – the vessel was lost along with its crude oil cargo. The *Sirius Star* had been released from her designated oil-rig anchor-handling support work in order to steam to the stricken ship. Following this disaster, the question of designated available salvage tugs was forcefully raised.[119] The results of such concerns were the arrival of the ETV's.

The public investment in ETV's has proved beneficial in environmental terms. Cost-Benefit Analysis of the expenditure on tugboat charters has shown a positive rate of return when such elements of the marine environment are considered - fishing industry, coastal tourism, bird ecology. In a number of cases

438

the vessels have demonstrated their utility in salving and supporting ships in distress, ergo preventing pollution incidents.[120]

8.11 The Emergency Services

An essential back-up to the coastguard system is the emergency service provided by the Royal National Lifeboat Institute (RNLI). With 233 Lifeboat stations in UK and Ireland and 4800 crew members (mostly volunteers), the all weather service is a vital safety net for the Green Highway. The synergetic link between the Coastguard and the Lifeboat service was acknowledged by Parliamentary Under-Secretary, Glenda Jackson, in 1999:

> The Coastguard and RNLI do not react only to marine casualty situations but have an excellent relationship when working together towards promoting marine safety within the United Kingdom. This is achieved through such groups as the sea safety liaison committee, where the pooled knowledge of the two organisations gained through more than 350 years of experience between them of marine safety is being used to excellent effect.[121]

With a long history of bravery and devotion to life-saving the service has strong links with the coastal trades. As an example of the heroism practised by the service, the legend of the Cromer Coxswain Henry Blogg looms large. The Coxswain became a household name in his 53 year career up to 1947. It has been estimated that his actions saved 873 lives in 53 years of service, many of which were employed in the East Coast collier trades.[122] The link between the Lifeboat service and small coastal ships was illustrated tragically in December 1981, when the Penlee Lifeboat was lost in hurricane conditions whilst attempting to rescue the eight crew of the doomed sea-river ship, *Union Star*. In total 16 seafarers were lost in a tragedy that brought national mourning. A local Cornish appeal raised £3m for the dependents of the lost crews.[123] In addition to the dedication of the

Lifeboat crews, helicopters operated by the MCA as well as those of the Royal
Navy and Royal Air Force distinguish themselves in providing difficult rescue
missions. The sad loss of Coastguard Helicopter Winchman, Bill Deacon, in
November 1999 demonstrates the risks faced. The helicopter had been scrambled
to support the Lerwick lifeboat after the 4348dwt Bahamas registered, *Green Lily*,
had sent out a distress call following engine failure. The vessel had left the
Shetland port, Lerwick, in a Force 7 Gale, strengthening to Force 9-10, and had
immediately run into difficulties, failing to make headway in the high seas. The
Lifeboat had managed to rescue four crew members, the Winchman had
completed the process of rescuing the remaining six crew when he was hit by a
large wave and lost overboard.[124]

8.12 Port Deregulation & Safety Issues

An important adjunct to the probity of the Green Highway is the
operational practice of the ports. As discussed above in chapter 3 the deregulation
process has had a positive impact upon port performance. Generally, established
port operators have rigorous safety standards for permanent staff; however, the
deregulation process has enabled non-skilled, inexperienced labour into the ports.
Issues of safety have arisen where market considerations have taken precedence
over safety concerns. The abolition of the National Dock Labour Scheme
(NDLS) has been recognised as the catalyst for greatly enhanced labour flexibility
and productivity. The down-side of this process, however, has been the
increasing use of unskilled, casual labour in some ports. A number of concerns
have been expressed by waterfront unions, ranging from tugboat crews, pilots,
fork lift operators, hatch gangs. It is evident that considerable skill and
experience is still required on the waterfront if standards of safety, as well as
economic efficiency are to be maintained. The safety issue hit the headlines in
1998 when a 24 year old student, Simon Jones, was killed in the hold of a shortsea
vessel in the Sussex port of Shoreham.[125] In evidence it became clear that the

inexperienced Mr. Jones was placed at risk by the cargo handling company. In the second hour of his one day contract, unloading bagged stones in the hold of a shortsea vessel, Mr. Jones was killed by the jaws of a clam-shaped crane grab which closed over his head. At the High Court trial it was held that the employer was guilty of two Health and Safety breaches and was fined £50,000 and ordered to pay £20,000 costs. Judge David Stokes found that the accident was caused by the reckless practice of discharging bagged cargo (which required a dockworker to sling the bags within the confines of the vessel's hold) was an unsafe practice which the operator had consistently employed. Dismissing the excuses of the company as "lamentable", Judge Stokes charged that the company,

> ....between February 1997 and April 1998 failed to carry out any of the most important parts of its duty. The failure to do that was absolutely deplorable. If it had been done, the death of this young man might have been avoided.[126]

The inclusion of this sad accident demonstrates the grim reality of what can happen when basic safety principles are ignored in the supply chain. The issues of safety in the ports has been a controversial area of the EU Access to Ports Directive. EU policy on opening up ports to competition has raised the question of un-skilled and untrained labour entering into the ports. In July 2005 Southampton Itchen M.P, John Denham, raised the safety issues of the Directive, given the already high risk factors in port work. Mr. Denham reminded Parliament of the tragic case of Simon Jones and that a port worker was 3 times more likely to be killed at work than in the high risk construction industry.[127]

The prolonged dock strike in the Port of Liverpool, 1995-6 featured the use of untrained casual labour. It was reported on Labournet that shocked Customs Officers were concerned that the work gangs were operating in a patently untrained, un-protected, hazardous manner without proper supervision or any recourse to safety procedures. Specifically:

- hardly any workers wearing hard hats;
- no workers wearing safety boots (some in fact wore trainers);
- hardly any workers wearing reflective jackets;
- no evidence of 'manual handling' training having been applied;
- horseplay involving workers on a ladder entering the 'hold';
- one worker dangling into the 'hold' having his hand stamped on intentionally by a colleague;
- one worker using his hook to scale a ladder out of the ' hold';
- general lack of supervision;
- a crane working overhead for the duration.[128]

This inclusion of the issue of ports safety is justified by the concerns over a open-market in labour. Lower costs can undoubtedly be achieved by recourse to unskilled labour. The temptation here is to encourage this process as it could possible reduce port costs, thus Green Highway costs. However, as the salutary lesson from the Shoreham tragedy proves: this would be at the expense of life and limb. It can be seen, therefore, that issues of safety on the waterfront are integral to the integrity of the Green Highway; that standards in cargo-handling safety need to be maintained.

8.13 Chapter 8 : Summary and Conclusion

This chapter set out to examine the environmental credibility of the Green Highway. Green integrity has been considered within a wide context which includes the quality of shipping *vis-à-vis* environment but also the quality of employment in the Green Highway. It has been contended that environmental performance and safety performance are indivisible when appraising the Green Highway. It has been accepted that it is possible for shipping to claim environmental advantage, given its ability to cut congestion and pollution.

However, it is incumbent on the industry to achieve and sustain high standards in reducing air and sea pollution. It has been made apparent that there is potential for a "green face" of shipping marketing mission and some shippers and shipowners are already showing a willingness to associate themselves with the potential environmental gains. Regulation is moving the standards of air and sea pollution upwards and it is incumbent on ship owners and operators to comply. Generally, it is evident that oil pollution from ships is declining; however, despite improved legislation and the developing system for shoreside disposal, it is irrefutable that ships continue to dump waste in coastal waters. The attention given to the green issues of speed at sea focused on the balance between vessel performance and fuel consumption, as well as operational safety. It was made evident that design gains in fuel efficiency and improved navigational practice will be needed before high-speed ships can attain their full Green Highway potential.

It has also been necessary to consider the possible flaws in the green case for shipping. Quality issues have been identified in such critical area as crewing, training and vessel age and maintenance. Regulatory forces such as the PSC system have been identified as active in vessel inspection, in spotting defects and in some cases detaining vessels for poor safety standards. However, it was also made apparent that a constant supply of ageing, poorly maintained and/or crewed vessels, under a range of un-regulated flags has continued to join the supply chain of vessels on the Green Highway.

Attention has been drawn to the schism in standards to be found in shipping. Whilst leading companies invest in new tonnage, employ highly trained crews on sustainable contracts of employment, the opposite can also be found. In the predominantly low value, highly competitive sectors, it is evident that poorly maintained, ageing tonnage is employed with Third World crews on extended, unsustainably long tour-of-duty contracts. The enduring issues of fatigue and alcohol abuse can be seen as a symptom of the pressures placed on crews in the demanding trades of Northern Europe. In addition to the ethical issues of labour exploitation, it has been made apparent that sub-standard labour conditions generate a high propensity for accidents, ergo environmental disaster.

The infra-structure bedrock of safety support for the Green Highway lies in the Coastguard, lifeboat and armed forces emergency support. The quality of PSC inspection, coastguard management, including Traffic Separation Schemes (TSS), is integral to maintaining and improving the safety benchmark. Likewise, pilotage, towage and stevedoring has a major role in providing professional services. It has also been made evident that the quality of these essential services could be jeopardised by deregulation and cost-cutting. Overall, the pattern is one of incrementally improving environmental performance. However, it has also been made clear that there is little room for complacency. It is palpable the Green Highway does face considerable competitive pressures, that the temptation to "cut corners" in order to save costs will remain a force for many years to come.

444

CHAPTER 8: ENDNOTES

[1] ABP Press Release, "New Service at ABP Barrow will rid Britain's roads of over 600,000 lorry miles," 7.6.06. http://www.abports.co.uk/news20065182.htm accessed 16.6.06.

[2] BBC News: "Brent Spar gets chop". 25.11.98.
http://news.bbc.co.uk/1/hi/world/europe/221508.stm accessed 16.6.06.

[3] "Spurn Point, the entrance to the Humber Estuary: extra protection for the estuary is in the pipeline," Lloyd's List. 23.8.00. p.7.

[4] Jameson,A. "Fears for new ports after ABP blocked," The Sunday Times, 21.4.04.

[5] Press Release, Harwich International Container Terminal: "Hutchinson gets the go ahead for Bathside Bay Development. 29.3.06.

[6] http://www.portofrotterdam.com/en/port_authority/current_themes/portvision_2020/index.jsp Accessed 27.7.06.

[7] http://www.portofantwerp.be/html/00_home/main_set_TS.html Accessed 27.7.06.

[8] Vidal, J. "And you thought air travel was bad for the climate," The Guardian, 3.3.07

[9] Loc.cit.

[10] McLaughlin, J. " Italy demands reassessment of road vs rail green issues," Lloyd's List. 8.3.07

[11] McKay, M. Letter to Editor, "Overall impact of shipping reduces global warming," Lloyd's List. 8.3.07.

[12] International Chamber of Shipping (1999) , A Code of Practice, London: ICS. p.8.

[13] Lloyd's Register:
www.lr.org/Standards/Schemes/NOx+Emission+Certification+of+marine+diesel+engines.htm

[14] Nobel, C. "Low Sulphur the only option for shipowners,"
http://www.bi.no/ShippingakademietFiles/_nedlastingsfiler/27,%201230-1300,%20Nobel,%20Cor,%20SECA.pdf accessed 28.6.06.

[15] Fields, C. "IBIA backs BP trading system on emissions", Lloyd's List. 25.4.02. p.4.

[16] Smith,N Study shows shipping is failing to meet new sulphur emissions target Lloyd's List. 16.5.06.

[17] www.marintek.sintef.no/MarPower/State%20of%20the%20Art%20Report%20no%202.doc Accessed 27.7.06.

[18] International Chamber of Shipping (1999) Op.cit. p.8.

[19] Porter, J. "Asia-Europe lines cut speed to save fuel and soak up overcapacity." Lloyd's List. 20.10.06.

[20] Landon,F. "Stena brings to and end fast Harwich-Hook service. Lloyd's List. 5.10.06.

[21] Hailey, R. "Volkswagen blasts fast ships concept," Lloyd's List. 1.6.05

[22] Maritime Coastguard Agency (1999) The International Code of Safety for High Speed Craft. Southampton: MCA.

[23] "Three vehicles fall overboard from HS 1500," Fast Ferry International. March 2001. p.10.

[24] "navigational

[25] Ibid, p.31.

[26] Heyerdahl, T.(1963) The Kon-Tiki Expedition. Harmondsworth, Middlesex: Penguin.

[27] Parker, J. (2000) "environmentally friendly ship operations: risk and reward", Seaways: The International Journal of the Nautical Institute. June 2000. pp.11-13.

[24] http://www.greenaward.org.

[25] http://www.heyerdahlaward.com/default.asp?V_ITEM_ID=472 Accessed 14.9.06.

[26] Press Release May 2003: Port of Sullom Voe: Why Green Awards?
http://www.greenaward.org/ports/Port%20of%20Sullom%20Voe.pdf accessed 28.6.06.

[27] http://www.greenaward.org/defaulthome.htm Accessed 14.9.06.

[28] Parker, C.J. (2001) "Setting the Standard: The Nautical Institute and the Green Award", Seaways: The International Journal of the Nautical Institute, February 2001. pp.6-7.

[29] IMO: Protocol of 1978 Relating to the International Convention for the Prevention of Pollution From Ships, 1973. London: IMO.

[30] Patraiko, D(2000) "Managing shipboard waste: A Nautical Institute study", *Seaways: The International Journal of the Nautical Institute.* August 2000, pp.7-10.
[31] *Op.cit.*p.8.
[32] "Ukranian master to face spill charges,", *The Telegraph: the Journal of NUMAST.* Nov 2005. p.14.
[33] MCA Newsroom/Prosecutions 2002. http://www.mcga.gov.uk/c4mca/mcga-newsroom/mcga-dops_enforce_newsroom-prosecutions/mcga-dops_enforce_prosecutions_2002.htm?printout=1 accessed 17.6.06.
[34] *Loc.cit.*
[35] MCA Newsroom/Prosecutions "Brostrum Tankers AB fined for Pollution," http://www.mcga.gov.uk/c4mca/mcga-newsroom/mcga-dops_enforce_newsroom-prosecutions/dops_enforcement-2005.htm.
[36] MCA Newsroom/prosecutions "Shipowner and management company prosecuted for dumping garbage in the Solent," http://www.mcga.gov.uk/c4mca/mcga-newsroom/mcga-dops_enforce_newsroom-prosecutions/mcga-dops-enforce-prosecutions04.htm.
[37] ACOPS. (2005) *Annual Survey of Reported Discharges Attributed to Vessels and Offshore Oil & Gas Installations Operating in the United Kingdom Pollution Control Zone 2004.* London: MCA.
[38] Stares, J. "North Sea is still 'cheapest garbage can'", *Lloyd's List.* 14.7.06.
[39] *Loc.cit.*
[40] *Loc.cit.*
[41] CM 2560 (1994) Safer Ships, Cleaner Seas: Report of Lord Donaldson's Inquiry into the Prevention of Pollution from Merchant Shipping. London: HMSO.
[42] *Ibid.* p.XXV.
[43] *Ibid.* p.219.
[44] *Ibid.* pp, 289-319.
[45] http://www.mcga.gov.uk/c4mca/lrgtxt/mcga-17_annex_i_farm.pdf#search='Boisterence' accessed 2.7.06.
[46] BBC News 21.1.07, "Stricken cargo ship run aground," http://news.bbc.co.uk/1/hi/england/devon/6283455.stm.
[47] Ready, N.P. (1991) *Ship Registration.* London: LLP. pp.65-80.
[48] DfT Merchant Shipping Safety Officials and Reporting *Accidents and Dangerous Occurrences Regulations, SI 1982, No.876.* London:HMSO.
[49] Kinnock, N.(1996) "Developments in EU Maritime Policy," *Bimco Review 1996.* pp.61-65.
[50] Couper, A.D. et al (1999) *Voyages of Abuse: Seafarers, Human Rights and International Shipping.* London: Pluto Press. pp.66.70.
[51] "Immingham Centre Steps in to support crew who survived on potato soup". *Telegraph: The Journal of NUMAST.* Vol.34. No.10. October 2001. p.19.
[52] "Cambodia is the world's worst!" *Safety at Sea International,* June 2002. p.4.
[53] *Loc.cit.*
[54] Everard, M. (1995) "Rogue Ships a Shipowner's View". *Maritime Policy and Management.* Vol.22. No.3. pp.179-99.
[55] *Lloyd's Law Reports* 1984, 2nd Part.
[56] BBC News, 8.1.00. "French demand more spill damages." http://news.bbc.co.uk/1/hi/world/europe/595091.stm. Accessed 12.10.06.
[57] "Total to defend itself against Erika charges." *Lloyd's List.* 6.7.06.
[58] Hailey,R "Brussels set to name 'blacklisted' vessels." *Lloyd's List.* 2.12.02.
[59] Mulrenan,J. "Seatrade tanker industry convention: US promises action on poor operators," *Lloyd's List.* 29.9.03.
[60] Reyner,L. Baulk,S. (1998) *Fatigue in Ferry Crews: a Pilot Study.* Cardiff: SIRC, Cardiff University. p.9.

446

[61] International Labour Organisation (ILO) *C 180 Seafarers' Hours of Work and the Manning of Ships Convention, 1996.* Geneva: ILO.

[62] M-Notice (2002)*Min 117(M) Research Project 464 phase 1: Fatigue of Offshore Oil Support Shipping and the Offshore Oil Industry.*

[63] Marine Accident Investigation Branch (MAIB) Report 3/98 (1998), *Report of the Inspectors' Inquiry into the Grounding of the Feeder Container Vessel, Cita, off Newfoundland Point, Isle of Scilly, 26.3.97.* Southampton: MAIB.

[64] "Mate slept as Ship heads for Island," *Shipping Today and Yesterday,* Dec. 1998.

[65] "No mystery of the seas", *Lloyd's List.* 13.3.01. p.6.

[66] "Lean manned ships should be targeted", *Lloyd's List.* 13.3.01.p.17.

[67] "No mystery of the seas", op cit.

[68] "Seafarers call for action on fatigue risk," *Tinig ng Marino* July-Aug. 2000. www.ufs.ph accessed 21.6.07.

[69] "Fatigue control is key to safety". *Lloyd's List.* 28.6.01. p.17.

[70] *Loc.cit.*

[71] Kuo, C. (1998) *Managing Ship Safety* London: LLP.pp.1-5.

[72] *Ibid.* p.5.

[73] Peters, G.H. (1975) Plimsoll Line: *The Story of Samuel Plimsoll, Member of Parliament for Derby from 1868 to 1880.* Chichester: Barry Rose.

[74] "Solutions and Newbuildings: Vossnack's Reply", *Fairplay.* 7.2.02.

[75] Stoop,JA. Hengst,S. Dirkse,C. "Integrating Safety into the Shortsea Shipping System", in Peeters, D & Wergeland, T. *European Shortsea Shipping: Proceedings from the Third European Research Roundtable Conference on Shortsea Shipping.* Bergen, 20-21 June 1996. Delft: Delft University Press.. p.393.

[76] Stoop,JA. et.al. *Op.cit.* pp.398-9.

[77] Grimes,R. (1989) *Shipping Law.* London: Sweet and Maxwell. p.183.

[78] Cockcroft,A. (1990) *Collision Avoidance Rules.* London: Newnes. p.142.

[79] Great Britain Department of Transport.(1987) *Merchant Shipping Act 1894. Report of Court No 8074. M.V. Herald of Free Enterprise. Formal Investigation.* London: HMSO.

[80] *Loc.cit.*

[81] "Balancing safety and economy: A safety case approach to a green tanker," *Fairplay.* 3.8.00. p??

[82] *Loc.cit.*

[83] Reported in, "Double hulls are safer, says study." *Lloyd's Tanker Focus.* October 1998. p.21.

[84] "Shuttle tanker misses highlighted by new report," *Lloyd's List.* 1.3.99. p.1.

[85] Reported in, "Double hulls are safer, says study." *Lloyd's Tanker Focus.* October 1998. p.21.

[86] Reported in, "Shuttle tanker misses highlighted by new report," *Lloyd's List.* 1.3.99. p.1.

[87] UKOOA (2001) *FPSO Committee: Tandem Loading Guidelines, Vol. 1 &2.* Aberdeen: UKOOA.

[88] "A new era in shuttles", *Lloyd's Tanker Focus.* October 1998. pp.20-21.

[89] "Environmentally friendly shuttle tanker leads trio of twin screw ships", *Lloyd's List.*25.8.98. p.10.

[90] "Stena Bulk banks on quality card," *Tradewinds,* 28.10.05.

[91] "DP Incidents on the Wane", *Telegraph: The Journal of Numast,* Vol.35. No.3. March 2002. P.6.

[92] Corbett, A. "all clear for UK whistleblowers," *Tradewinds,* 31.1.03.

[93] Paris MOU on PSC: http://www.parismou.org/.

[94] *Loc.cit.*

[83] "History of the Coastguard," http://www.mcga.gov.uk/c4mca/mcga-hmcg_rescue/mcga-hmcg-history-of-coastguard.htm Accessed 19.8.06.

[96] *Loc.cit.*

[98] http://www.mcga.gov.uk/c4mca/mcga-dops_pr_newsroom-press-releases-release.htm?mcga_news_id=2996&month=7&year=2005 Accessed 19.8.06.

[99] Derived from information pack provided by H.M. Coastguards, Dover Langdon Battery, 2000.

[100] Author's own calculations.

[101] H.M. Coastguards Information Pack *Op.cit.*

[102] IMO, Ship Routing: http://www.imo.org/Safety/mainframe.asp?topic_id=770 accessed 18.10.06.

[103] Dover Battery, Channel Navigation Information Service. Visitor Information.

[104] *Loc.cit.*

[105] *Loc.cit*

[106] Stoop et.al. *Op.cit.*

[107] "Humber Humbug: UK Government sides against the pilots, " *Fairplay International Shipping Weekly,* 2.5.02.

[108] Gaston, J. (2002) *The Tug Book.* Yeovil: Stephens. pp.169-188.

[109] "Tug Wars! Coming Shortly to a Port Near You? Competitive Strategy in North European Towage and Salvage," with Rod Atkin, University of Greenwich, a paper given to the International Towage and Salvage Conference, Capetown,October/November 1998.

[110] Competition Commission, News Release. 31.8.06. Anticipated Acquisition by Svitzerwijsmuller A/S of Adsteam Marine Limited.

[111] CM 2560 (1994) *Safer Ships, Cleaner Seas. Op.cit.* Chap.20.

[112] Grey,M. "Braer Disaster 'Disaster could have been averted by tug.'"*Lloyd's List.* 7.1.93.

[113] MCA (2000) *A Review of the Emergency Towing Vessel(ETV) Provision Around the Coast of the United Kingdom.* Southampton: MCA.

[114] Parliamentary Minutes, 5.3.99.
http://www.publications.parliament.uk/pa/cm199899/cmhansrd/vo990305/debtext/90305-24.htm accessed 29.6.06.

[115] http://www.norfolkcoast.co.uk/pasttimes/pt_henryblogg.htm accessed 28.6.06.

[116] http://www.rnli.org.uk/rnli_near_you/southwest/stations/PenleeCornwall/history accessed 28.6.06.

[117] Marine Accident Report 5/99: "Report of the Inspector of Inquiry into the loss of the MV *Green Lily on the 19th November 1997 on the East Coast of Bressay, Shetland Islands.* Southampton: MAIB.

[118] Brooks, L. "Alarm as employer cleared in death case," *The Guardian.* 30.11.01. p.13.

[119] Parliamentary Minutes, 20.7.05.
http://www.publications.parliament.uk/pa/cm200506/cmhansrd/cm050720/halltext/50720h03.htm accessed 29.6.06

[120] Dropkin,G. "Casual Labour," http://www.labournet.net/docks2/9706/casual.htm accessed. 29.6.06.

CHAPTER 9

Summary and Conclusion

This work set out to explore the issues of and the potential for increased shipping participation in the domestic, coastal and shortsea trades of both Britain and Ireland. In one sense this was seen as a partial return towards the high market share of shipping activity attained up until the WW1 period. In addition to the potential for a revival of this historic shipping activity, it was also made evident that the early Millennium concerns over environmental issues were conducive to shipping as a sustainable transport mode. The green potential of shipping was stressed at the outset. Measured in terms of reduced congestion and noxious exhaust emissions, shipping was seen to have intrinsic environmental benefits *vis-à-vis* road haulage. The perception of a looming global warming crisis and, perhaps more tangibly, the inconvenience and inefficiency of traffic congestion, has induced the search for alternative modes of transport to road haulage. Shipping and rail-freight have been championed as sustainable transport modes.

The generic term, Green Highway, was developed in order to provide a catch-all descriptor of all water-borne freight traffic around the British and Irish coastlines, rivers and canals as well as connections to continental Europe. It was also made evident that within the wide boundaries of this term a number of distinct sub-sets of shipping existed. By identifying the principal shipping types this work sought to help clarify some of the public misconceptions that prevail. Despite the wide range of shipping organisation and activity it was made apparent that in the media perception these distinctions were somewhat blurred. Public concern in contemporary shipping activity appears mainly to be limited to headline news. This is when things go wrong - following a maritime disaster and/or traumatic oil pollution incident.

Another early observation made was the importance of North Sea oil movements to the market share. Given the imminent diminution of these oil reserves it is apparent that shipping's share of UK domestic traffics is set to decline dramatically if no new business is sought. This looming reality endorses the importance of a new impetus towards reviving the Green Highway and places emphasis on winning new traffics.

Comparison with continental Europe has been utilised in order to highlight not only the contrasts with the two island nations but also to reinforce the importance of the European connection. The intermingling of domestic shipping, inland and coastal with European shortsea has been deliberately employed in order to demonstrate the need to extend perceived boundaries of the Green Highway. This is necessary in order to reflect the political and economic trends towards European integration and, ergo, the business opportunities generated. It is felt that importing continental approaches towards operations, organisation, financing as well public perception can only serve to the benefit of the Green Highway in Britain and Ireland. The sharp contrast between the low levels of inland barge traffics in the UK - zero in Ireland – and burgeoning continental activity has been made. This contrast reveals the atrophy of the canal systems as freight arteries in the two island nations. With little modernisation taking place in the last century the canal system has failed to keep pace with the rate of change in industry and the emergence of a dynamic road haulage industry. As a result, canal gauges are now restrictive preventing the economies of scale normally enjoyed by shipping *vis-à-vis* road haulage. By way of comparison, consistent up-grading of continental systems has presented Belgium, French, Netherlands and German shippers with the opportunity to use a modern, increasingly competitive, water network. Despite the lag in standards a few areas of opportunity have been identified where inland waterways are capable of carrying barges large enough to compete: the rivers Ouse, Trent, Thames, Severn, Shannon, Weaver plus the Manchester Ship Canal.

Reasons for the neglect of British and Irish canals may be explained historically by a mix of geographic restraints and hitherto the paucity of political will towards freight on water. This is juxtaposed with the political preference for the road expansion option. The comparison with continental systems can be utilised in order to direct attention to the coastlines of the two island nations. This perspective was drawn from the insight of Ford and Bound's *Coastwise Shipping and the Small Ports*[i] in 1951 when they argued that Britain's coastline offered the same trading opportunities that continental inland systems did for their respective nations. Given the long coastlines available to shipping the opportunities for shipping activity become increasingly attractive for nations perturbed by the rapid increases in road freight - USA, Canada, Japan, Italy - as well as Britain and Ireland.

The historic context has helped to identify the distinct waves of transport activity in the UK economy, somewhat mirrored by the trends in Ireland. The early days of Industrial Revolution were characterised by, firstly, the canal age and secondly, the railway age. Spanning these two ages the emergence of steam powered coastal shipping was integral to both the surges in industrialisation and urbanisation. The growth of road haulage from the post WW1 period, more specifically in the post 1960s motorway age, was to signal a new force in the freight transport economy. Although it was recognised that shipping still moves around a quarter of UK domestic freight in tkms, if the North Sea oil traffics are subtracted this percentage share falls to below around 8%.

Given the dominant position that road haulage currently enjoys it would be unreasonable to anticipate a large scale modal shift. The intention pursued here has been to re-assess shipping incremental prospects rationally. It has been argued that in the rapid and comprehensive switch to road haulage some of the potential benefits of shipping have been ignored. The line of argument followed has been to promote the consideration of the Green Highway in discrete markets.

It follows that there has not been an overt attack on road haulage dominance; the approach here has been one of rationally selecting the mode of transport best suited to the freight and its route, but taking into consideration environmental as well as economic criteria.

Exploring the role and potential of the Green Highway firstly necessitated (chapter 2) some explanation for its decline, particularly contrasted with the emergence and dominance of road haulage. Of specific influence has been the impact of de-industrialisation with the disappearance of the coastal bulk raw material trades, most importantly the coal trades, registering a significantly detrimental effect on shipping tonnages. Changes in the relocation of industry away from the waterfront have served against the shipping supply-chain and proved conducive to a consistently improving road haulage performance – at least up-until the 1980s. Likewise the impact of the spread of just-in-time logistics has proved favourable growth opportunities for road haulage. In addition to these pressures on shipping, the trends towards the gentrification of the waterfront have denied access to docks and wharves. The development of the RoRo ferry has led to a loss of LoLo traffics in both the North and Irish Seas, also in the Scottish Western Isles. Moreover, the concentration of RoRo ferries on short crossing routes has minimised sea tkms whilst maximising road tkms. The loss of coastal liner services was identified, with the diversification of hitherto ship owners into lorry operators.

In chapter 3 the context for the potential Green Highway revival was outlined. It was contended that a number of conditions conducive to a shipping revival were beginning to manifest in the early Millennium. Part of the rationale for this work was the contrast in continental Europe's comprehensive use of domestic shipping and the much lower levels attained in both Britain and Ireland. The process of industrial integration provides opportunities for shortsea and inland shipping linkages; also, the spread of the European logistics practice naturally considers the shipping option – a contrast with road haulage myopia hitherto prevalent in British and Irish transport management. Highly complementary to European shortsea and inland shipping is the continued success of niche shipbuilding. Shipbuilders in Spain, Germany and the Netherlands have focused on shortsea whilst many of the deepsea shipbuilders have withdrawn from the market. The rise of the "Celtic Tiger" Irish economy is providing opportunities for shortsea shipping outside of the main RoRo corridors emanating from Belfast, Dublin and Cork. Regional ports such as Shannon, Waterford and Drogheda have shown signs of growth as a result. The latent potential of such West Coast ports as Galway lies in their ability to significantly reduce lorry miles on the rural roads of the West. Given the retrenchment freight strategy of Irish Railways, Ianród Éireann, the coastal option becomes increasingly valuable. Deregulation has promoted a more dynamic ports sector in the UK. This has provided for a more competitive approach and has also paved the way for port diversification into shipping line operations. It has been seen that Clydeport and Mersey Ports (now part of the same Peel Holdings conglomerate) as well as Forth Ports have launched successful shipping ventures.

Chapter 3 also identified an increase in political will towards shipping issues. In both Britain and Ireland concerns have registered politically over both the marine environment and the dependence of both island economies on non-national ships and crews. The developments in Tonnage Tax regimes and the setting up of the Maritime Development Office (MDO) in Ireland and the Maritime and Coastguard Agency (MCA) in the UK have been identified as pro-active organisations in regenerating national fleet activity. This approach has been strengthened by EU commitment to the concept of sustainable mobility – the championing of shipping as an alternative transport mode to road haulage.

In chapter 4 the emphasis was on the renaissance of shipping organisation under the UK flag. After several decades of what seemed an irreversible trend of decline the concerns of the maritime interest finally gained the ear of the respective governments. Tonnage Tax regimes have undoubtedly proved the catalyst for a revival of both national registries. In addition, the radical organisational reform of the UK Maritime and Coastguard Agency (MCA) has provided a more user-friendly access to the British registry.. The global attraction of both registries has provoked some criticisms in that ownership and crewing may be carried out by non-nationals. However, it is also evident that the re-affirmation of interest in shipping by leading companies, such as BP and James Fisher, bodes well for the profile and operational standards of the Green Highway. Also, new entrant companies such as Scotline have brought entrepreneurial impetus to the supply chain.

The profile of coastal Green Highway freight in chapter 5 has identified the scale and scope of traffics. The analysis of shipping movements around the UK and Irish coasts was aided by the 2002 survey. Un-surprisingly, the predominance of North Sea oil was made evident. Less immediately obvious is the complex pattern of oil product trading. It is evident that the mix of diversity in products, competitive rivalry and constant need to maintain adequate stocks of oil products causes a criss-crossing of flows. Also recognisable in the analysis is the tendency for shortsea and coastal traffics to seek back-haul cargoes, particularly in the dry-bulk trades. Loaded west-bound cargoes are often balanced by stone and aggregates cargoes from Belfast and North Wales. Steel cargoes into South Coast ports are balanced by grain or china clay cargoes from Poole, Teignmouth, Par and Bideford. The importance of such return traffics in attaining economic survival in the dry-bulk trades has to be stressed. The reality of these trades is that there is at least 3:1 imbalance between west-bound cargoes from continental Europe and east-bound freight ex Britain and/or Ireland. The survey identified a number of short distance freight flows, traversing distances well below the conventionally accepted threshold for shipping's tkm competitiveness.

In chapter 6 the profiled character of principal British, Irish and Continental, Scandinavian fleets, plus Russia's North-West Shipping Line, was provided. It was clear that a long historic tradition is still very much alive and kicking in the shortsea trades. The historic trail of the East Coast collier trades is now followed by the North Sea oil shuttle trades. The evolution of traditional collier operator, Stephenson Clarke, into a leading European wide trading bulk fleet points to the persistence of the shipping tradition in UK waters. Likewise the journey of the Thames sailing barge owners, Everard and Crescent into modern tanker fleet operations is testament to the tenacity of the coaster tradition. A clear process of capital deepening was identified as three of the UK's shortsea fleet – Crescent, Everard, Fisher - made an almost simultaneous decision (2002) to withdraw from dry-cargo shipping, concentrating on oil product tankers. The December 2006 take-over of F.T. Everard by James Fisher can be acknowledged as part of a consolidation process that secures employment for high cost, high quality, operations in the petroleum products trades.

The strategic behaviour of the three leading UK's firms in divesting their dry-bulk fleets demonstrates the difficulties faced by operators in this sector. The harsh experience suffered by Lapthorn Shipping clearly illustrates that in this sector a bustling fleet is no guarantor of profitability. The emergence of low cost Russian ships in the dry-bulk trades can only increase the emphasis on the critical levels of competitiveness in such low value freight flows as grain, stone and scrap.

Chapter 7 placed the Green Highway into the context of the logistics supply chain. The need for shipping to slot seamlessly into the supply chain was discussed, paying particular attention to such important modal determinants as cost, timings, reliability, inventory levels. The high cost of cargo handling/cargo transfer between the ship and lorry modes was identified as a potential barrier to the Green Highway. Similarly, the set up costs of new shipping services plus the slow build up of traffics was recognised as a further obstacle. More favourably, the problems of congestion, high fuel costs and driver shortages were identified as factors at work reducing the competitive edge of road haulage. Of the nine case studies selected, eight were acknowledged as successful new ventures. The one question mark was over the Rosyth-Zeebrugge RoRo ferry which has suffered from a service rationalisation by the operator, Superfast. Writing this conclusion in Summer 2007 it was clear that "the jury was still out" on this service, a service which had shown much promise in its first few years. The remaining eight freight flows were seen as viable if not growing. Examples of rail-sea integration were provided. Integration of shipping into the supply chain was clearly seen as positive factor in developing new traffics. The support of FFG was also prevalent as a catalyst for start up; however this example of state support should not be seen as negating the healthy levels of shipping enterprise found in the new ventures.

Finally, chapter 8 critically posed the question on the Green Highway's environmental integrity. The intention here was to objectively examine shipping's claim to be the green choice! Whilst it was recognised that improvements were taking place in reducing the dumping of waste materials at sea, it was also made evident that the industry still has a way to go before it can fully claim veracity. The accepted view of shipping enjoying much lower carbon emissions per tkm was provided. However, it was also made apparent that shipping's impact on the global warming process is becoming increasingly recognised. Against the criticisms that shipping had a high total sulphur emission performance, evidence of improved fuel burning technology was discussed, as was the latent imposition of Sulphur Emission Control Areas in the Baltic and North Sea-English Channel regions.

The enduring problem of sub-standard operations was not ignored, particularly in the low value, marginally profitable, dry-bulk and container feeder trades. The question of sub-standard vessels and over stretched crews – leading to fatigue and increased accident propensity – was considered. The link between vessel management and environmental risk was illuminated. It was argued that the environmental scrutiny of shipping was indivisible from the safe and humane standards of employment on-board as well as in the ports. The issue of de-regulation in the Pilotage service was identified as a possible threat to the quality of the Green Highway. It was felt necessary to outline the back-up emergency services of such well established institutions as the Coastguard, the Lifeboat service and the military helicopter services. These services were recognised as vital to the safe conduct of shipping along the operationally demanding British and Irish coastlines. As such they form an integral component of the Green Highway supply chain.

In order to make some final conclusion points on the future prospects of the Green Highway, the following synopsis of balanced critical analysis is offered. It has been re-iterated throughout this work that a critical approach was needed, that the challenges ahead demanded an objective assessment. The challenges are categorised into the following: competitive, logistical, European integration, environmental and investment.

The competitive challenge is undoubtedly led by the dynamics of road haulage; this will continue to be a major competitive obstacle to freight transfer, roads to water. Costs, speed and volume are all factors here. Whilst it has been made apparent that the sea-leg costs are favourable, it is also evident that port and collection and final delivery costs (by road) can prove prohibitive. It is therefore paramount that attention is given to the obstacle provided by these additional but unavoidable costs. The case for an integrated pricing strategy looms large here. Clearly a segregated approach to sea-costs, port costs and inland collection/delivery cost is a recipe for cost escalation. The looming imposition of road charging for haulage throughout Europe (as pioneered by the LKW-Maut system in Germany) will undoubtedly favour alternative modes to road. Speed will continue to be an obstacle, given the inherent advantages that road haulage has over shipping. However, it is also apparent that vessel speeds are increasing – at least in the container trades – and that road haulage delivery times are lengthening due to road congestion. The opportunity for shipping to focus more on container feeder movements and FMCG traffics results from the narrowing of the speed gap. The ability of road haulage to operate service to low volume (inc JIT) freight flows is obviously a barrier to freight transfer. The need to consolidate and store volumes in order to facilitate viable vessel loadings begs serious attention. Where a balance between cost and service frequency can be found then the steady increases in vessel speeds can enhance competitiveness. The continued growth of the global container trades, plus the step increase in deepsea vessel sizes provides increased volume opportunities for shortsea and coastal feeder services.

The logistics challenge stems from the need for shipping to fit seamlessly into the supply chain. Again the importance of integration is endorsed. The successful shipping operation is the one that proves complementary to the functioning of this supply chain. Where shipping can be vertically integrated with production, storage and distribution processes, opportunities for new traffics can prove attractive. The entrance of port operators into the shipping component of the supply chain can only serve this integration process.

The European dimension works on a number of levels. Firstly, the political climate of the EU is favourable to the promotion of shipping. Opportunities certainly exist within intra-European trade-flows. The high proportion of traffic volumes moving inland along North European rivers and canals serves as a benchmark. The coastlines of Britain and Ireland could prove similar Green Highway opportunities. The growth of inland ports such as Duisburg, Paris and Liege can prove attractive for sea-river services from Britain and Ireland. Furthermore, there are prospects for European shortsea traffics to disperse from the short crossing RoRo routes to increased sea-leg services to Britain and Ireland. Continental expertise in financing, designing, building and operating vessels provides a positive influence and creates opportunities for joint-ventures. The continental transport mind-set encourages a high profile role for inland shipping; the Green Highway has the opportunity to transplant this approach nearer to home!

The environmental challenge will test the green integrity of the Green Highway. Whilst it is evident that shipping has advantages in fuel consumption and exhaust emission terms there is little room for complacency. Developments in fuel efficiency and clean engine technology will encompass road and rail modes just as they will shipping. The move toward low sulphur fuels will certainly improve shipping's green performance. Developments in vessel design and in seafarer standards can only improve safety and environmental protection. However, it also evident that sub-standard operations are likely to resist the pressures to eliminate them, particularly in the low value bulk sectors. Continued vigilance is needed. There is an endemic danger that quality operators will be driven from the market. It is becoming apparent that business is enthusiastic about being associated with sustainable transport; it is also palpable that the integrity of the Green Highway only stretches as far as the next newspaper headline on marine pollution!

The need to generate investment is a very real challenge facing the Green Highway. The endurance of shipping enterprise has been acknowledged; but also, the marginal nature of many of the trades, particularly in the low value bulk sector. Moves towards market concentration in the container and oil product sectors point out the difficulties the smaller operators face. It is also evident that there is little enthusiasm for financing ships under 2000dwt, unless specifically for the inland trades. Pan-European collaborations in financing with such schemes as the German KG system, also with Netherlands shipyards provide access to finance capital. The UK and Irish Tonnage Tax regimes have also proved conducive to investment in new tonnage. The importance of FFG funding has become manifest, proving fundamental to new market entrants. It is vital that the Green Highway remains open to quality new-entrant enterprise.

The context for a Green Highway revival is positive, given increased political and business attention to environmental matters. The up-grading of national shipping registries and coastline custodianship in the British and Irish political agenda can only be seen as conducive. As business becomes more focused on sustainable issues the opportunity for shipping increases. By raising its performance, as well as its image profile, as a worthy member of the modern logistics family, the shipping operators of the Green Highway can meet the demands of the environmentally discerning customer. As a concluding comment, it is hoped that this work has helped to raise awareness of the shipping alternative. It has been made clear that opportunities exist for a selective transfer of freight from road to water. Likewise, the safe and environmentally acceptable targets that must be achieved have been alluded to. It is urged that the time is now right for the Green Highway to deliver!

CHAPTER 9: ENDNOTES

[i] Ford, P. Bound,J.A. (1951) *Coastwise Shipping and the Small Ports.* Oxford: Blackwell.

Plate 1: Sea-Rail Integration. Coal Traffic, Manchester Ship Canal.
Photo Permission by: Keith Rowlinson

Plate 2: **The Marine Motorway? Grimaldi Line's European RoRo Service. The 4300 car capacity,** *Grand Benelux* **discharges Ford Transits.** *Photo Permission by: Grimaldi Line.*

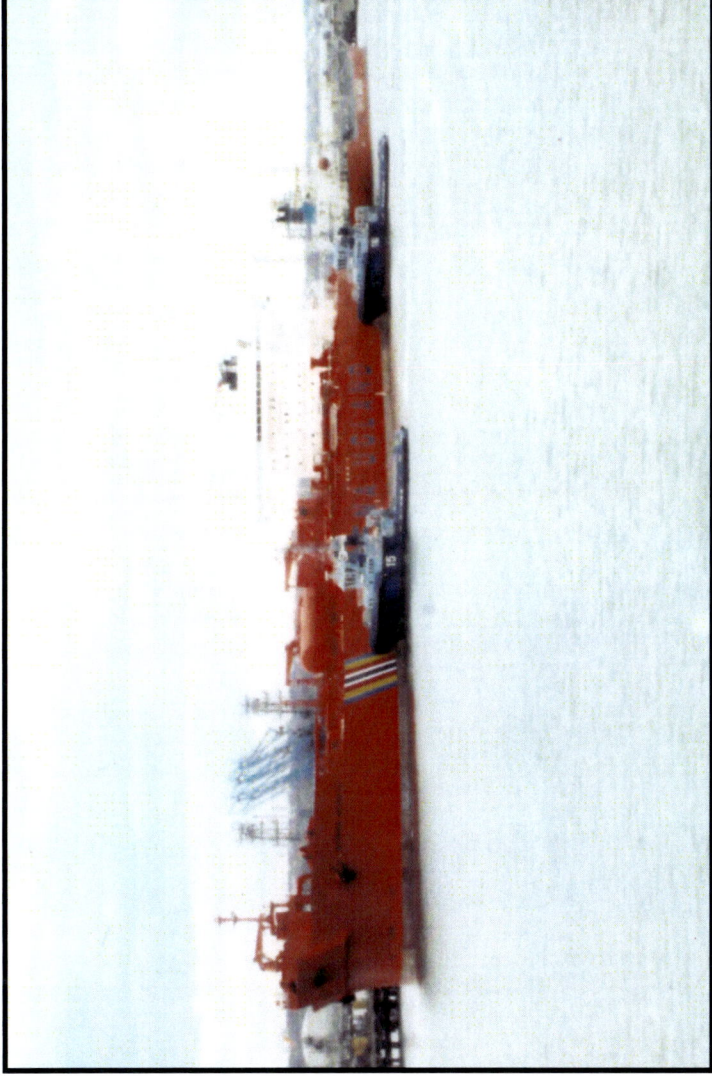

Plate 3: A Coaster? The 127,535dwt, North Sea Shuttle Tanker, *Stena Alexita* (Norwegian Flag), arrives in Southampton Water (Esso Fawley). *Photo Permission by: Russ Wilmott.*

Plate 4: A Regular Trader on the UK Coast, the 2004dwt, (Singapore Flag), LPG Tanker, *Sigas Lydia* **arrives at Fawley.**
Photo Permission by: Mike Hammond.

Plate 5: Scapa Flow Ship-To-Ship Transfer Russian Oil to 300,000dwt, VLCC, Iran Delvar.
Photo Permission by: Dr. Alfred Baird, Napier University.

Plate 6: Lapthorn Shipping's 1300dwt, *Hoo Maple*, Demonstrates Self-Discharge Flexibility in London Docklands.
Photo Permission by: Richard Buffey, Buffey & Buffey.

Plate 7: Union Transport and Lapthorn Dry Cargo Vessels serve the East Anglian Agricultural Trade, Sutton Bridge, Cambridgeshire. *Photo Permission by: Author.*

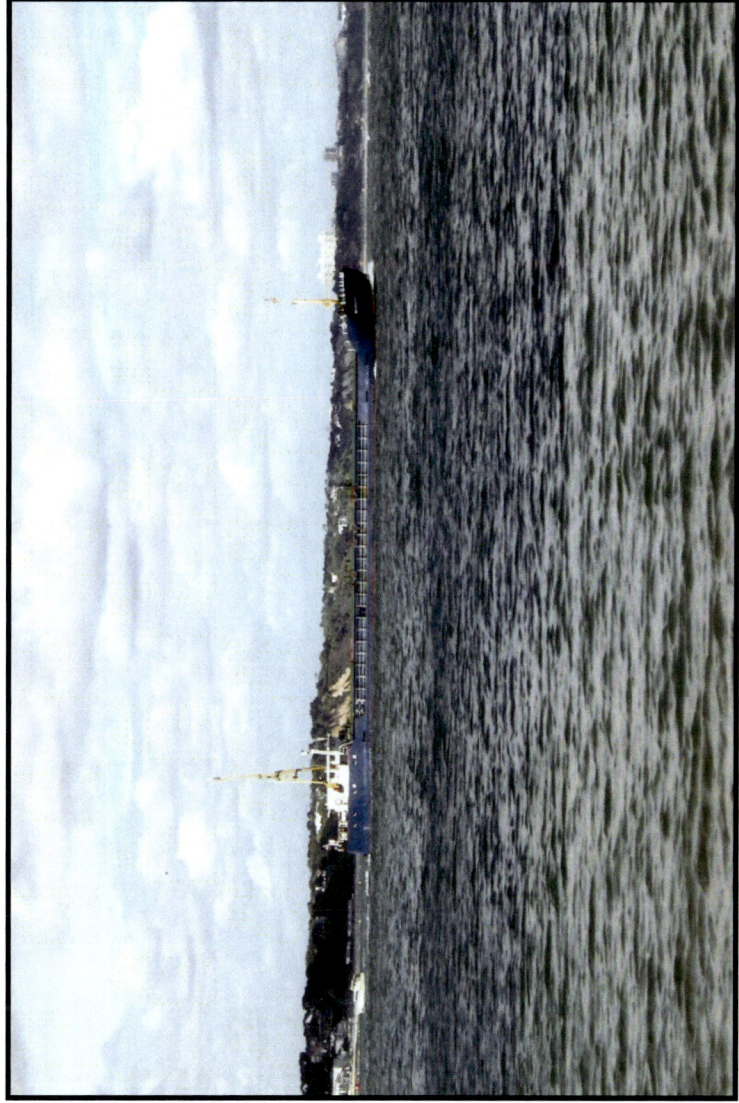

Plate 8: The Blue Highway! Alderney Shipping's, 1020dwt, *Mungo*, Leaves the Environmentally Sensitive Poole Harbour. *Photo Permission by: Grant Ausden.*

Plate 9: Lafarge Aggregates, 500dwt, Motor Barge, *Battlestone*, reaches the Castleford Terminal, 142km up-stream from the Trent-side Quarry at Besthorp. *Photo Permission by: Roger Dodman, Lafarge Aggregates.*

Plate 10: In the Garden of England! Union Transport's Low Air Draft Vessel, *Union Sun,* **in the River Medway, Kent.** *Photo Permission by: Richard Gough, Union Transport.*

Plate 11: K.D. Marine's (UK), 965dwt, Vessel, *Gina D*, Awaits Grain Discharge in the heart of Manchester Docklands.
Photo Permission by: Author.

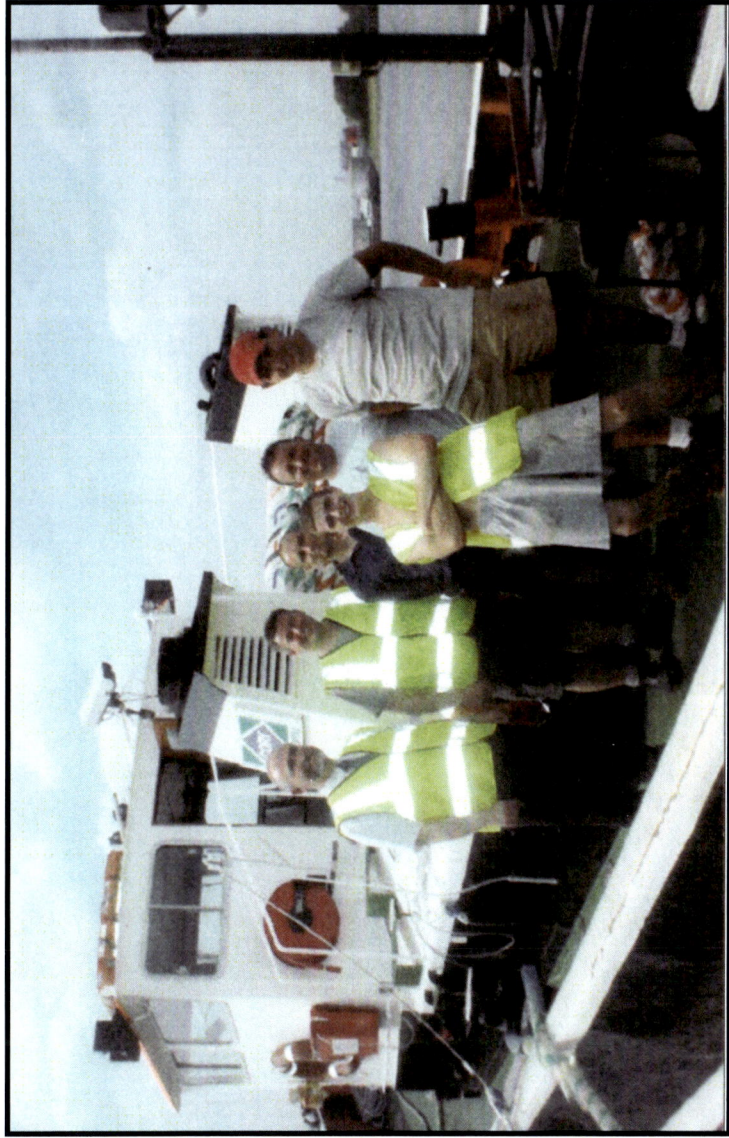

Plate 12: Thames Lineage - Representing a Long Family Line of Watermen aboard Cory Environmental's Tug, *Merit.*
Photo Permission by: Karim Yoshida.

Plate 13: Urban Highway – Cory Environmental's Barge Train Replaces > 100 Heavy Lorry Round-Trip Journeys in Central London. *Photo Permission by: Author.*

Plate 14: Cory Environmental's Barge Train Slides Under Tower Bridge. *Photo Permission by: Ozlem Kir.*

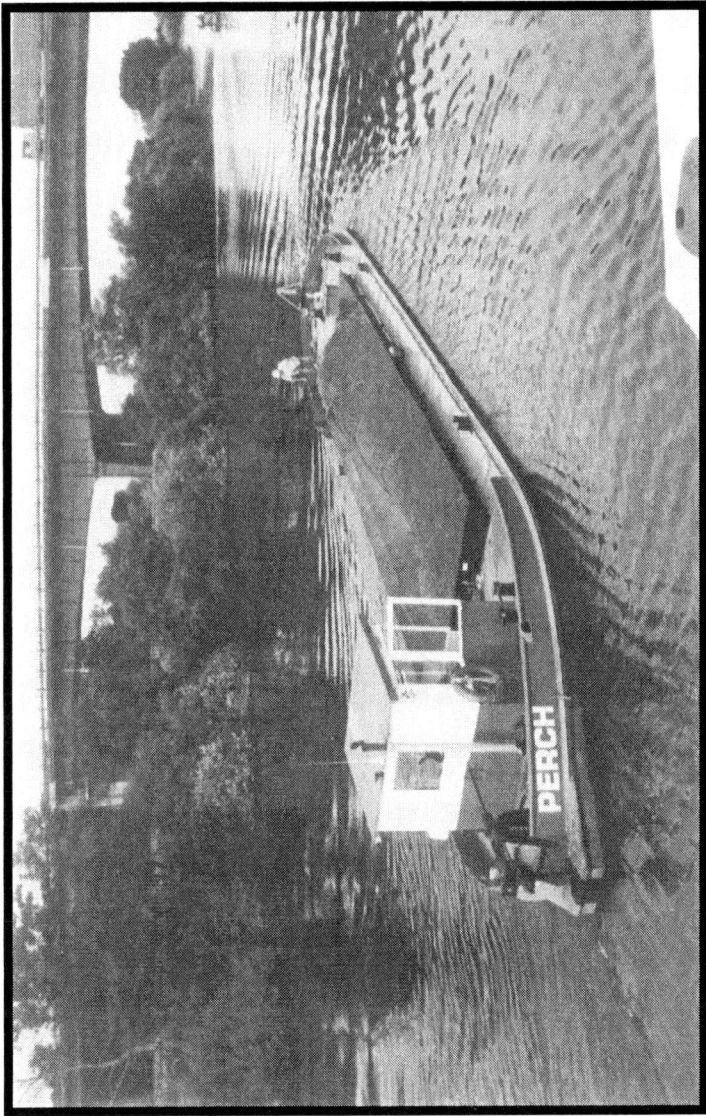

Plate 15: Aggregate Movements on the River Severn. The 180dwt Barge, *Perch*.
Photo Permission by: David Hilling.

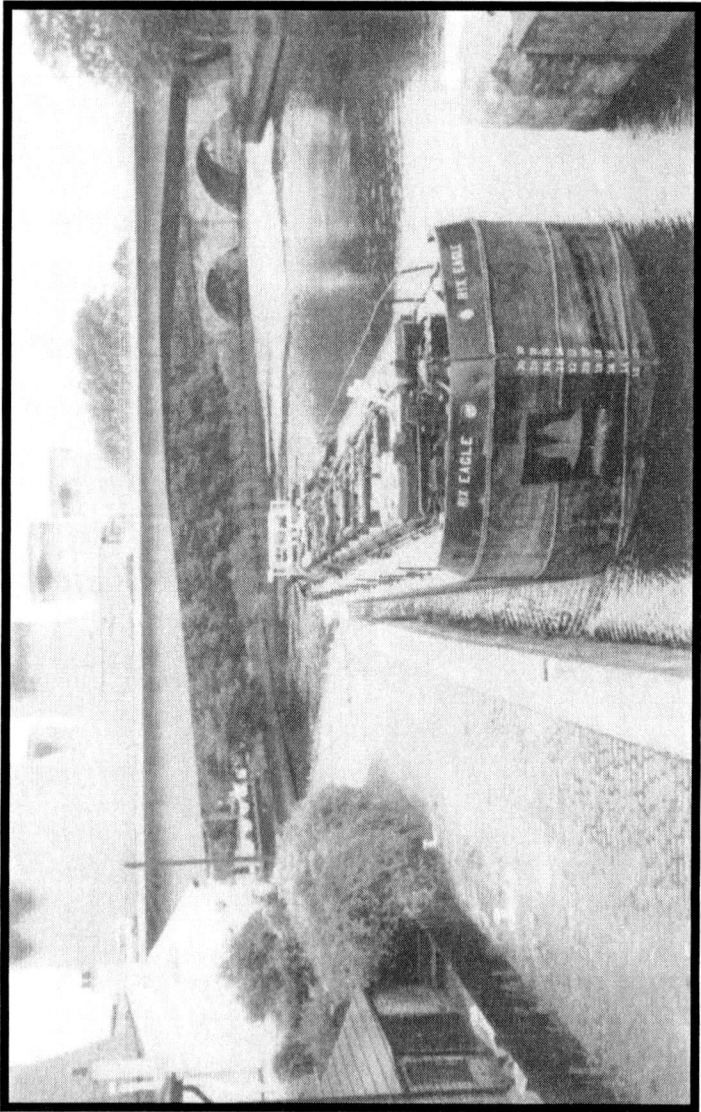

Plate 16: The 500 dwt Petroleum Barge, *Rix Eagle* in the Aire & Calder Navigation, Ferrybridge Yorkshire. *Photo Permission by: Fred Andrews.*

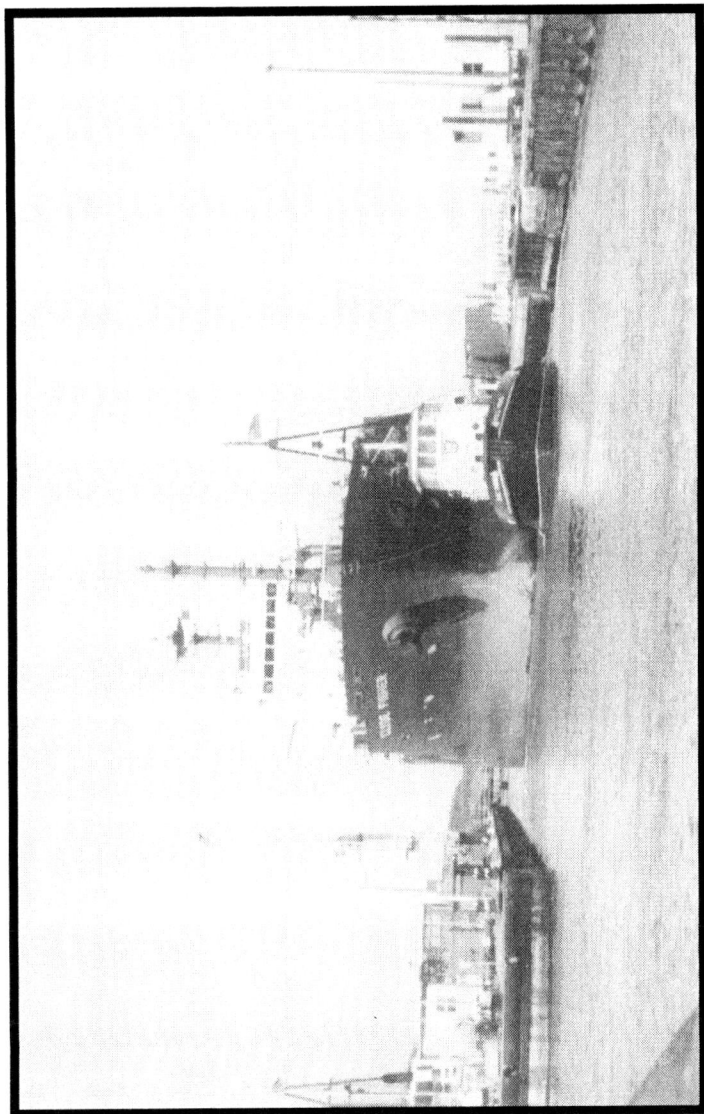

Plate 17: The 12,984 dwt Petroleum Products Tanker, *Clyde Fisher*, enters the Manchester Ship Canal. *Photo Permission by: Keith Rowlinson.*

Plate 18: European Shortsea Traders 40nm from the Open Sea at
Grove Wharf, River Trent. *Photo Permission by: Roger Dodman, Lafarge Aggregates.*

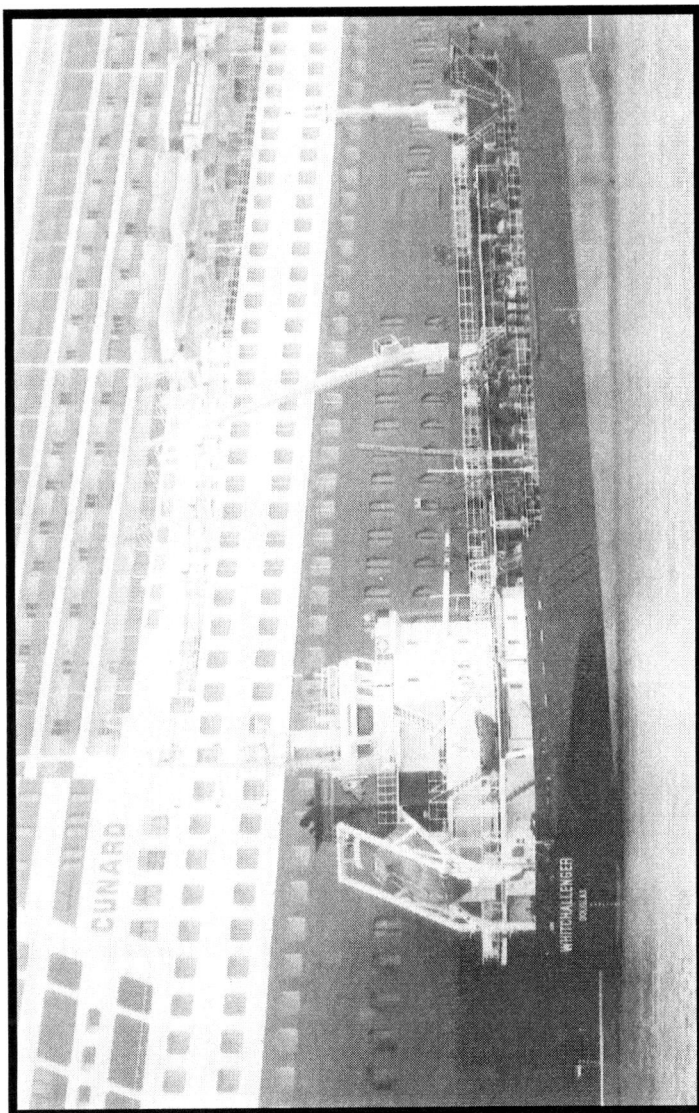

Plate 19: Southampton Based *Whitchallenger* Delivers > 3000 Tonnes of Fuel Oil to *Queen Mary 2.* *Photo Permission by: Russ Wilmott.*

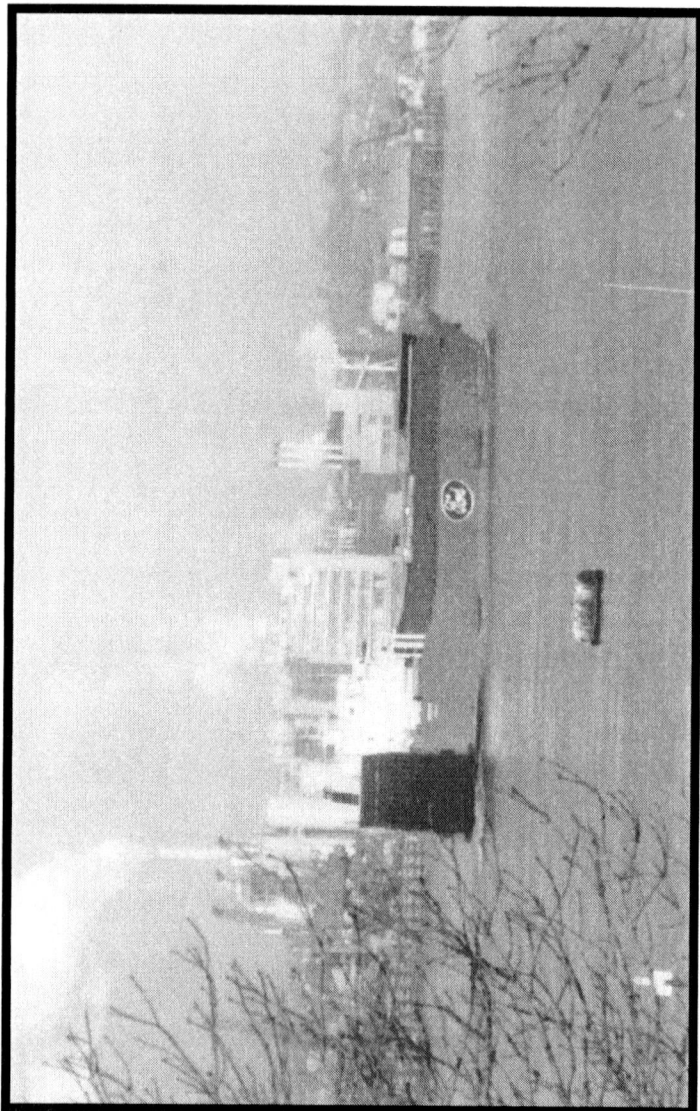

Plate 20: Vertical Integration. A Dedicated Carrier for Ford Europe serving the Dagenham-Zeebrugge Route. *Photo Permission by: Keith Rowlinson.*

Plate 21: The 300dwt, *James Prior*, Provides Central London Linkages for Essex Quarry owners, J.J. Prior. *Photo Permission by: Keith Rowlinson.*

Plate 22: >7000teu *Clementine Maersk* docks in Southampton generating demand for Container Feeder Services. *Photo Permission by: David Glen.*

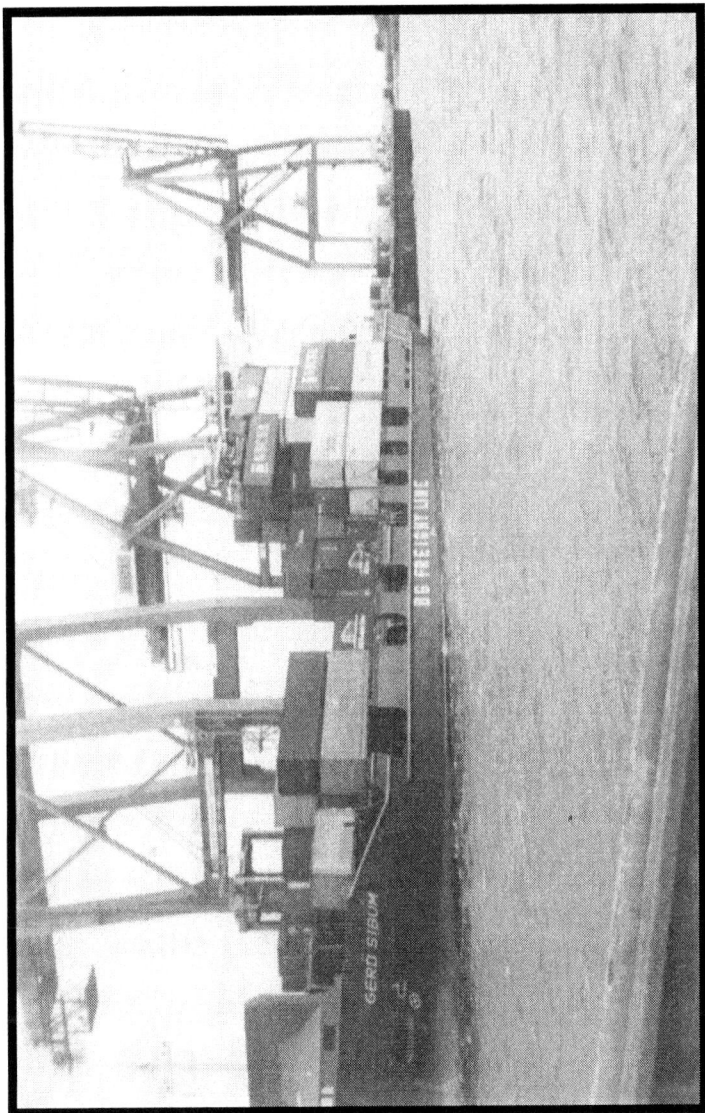

Plate 23: The 5272 dwt *Gerd Silbum* Provides Container Feeder Linkage at Southampton. *Photo Permission by: Author.*

Plate 24: Canal Revival? Commercial Traffic Returns on British Waterway's Grand Union Canal, Greater London. *Photo Permission by: David Hilling.*

Plate 25: Inland-Shortsea Linkages at the Inland Port of Goole.
Photo Permission by: David Hilling.

Plate 26: Trent Aggregates, the Motor Barge, *Maureen Ann W*, Prepares for the down-river voyage. *Photo Permission by: Author.*

Plate 27: Emerald Highway! Europe Line's, *Europe Orion*, Shuttles from Rotterdam to Drogheda.
Photo Permission by: Hek Van der Heijden.

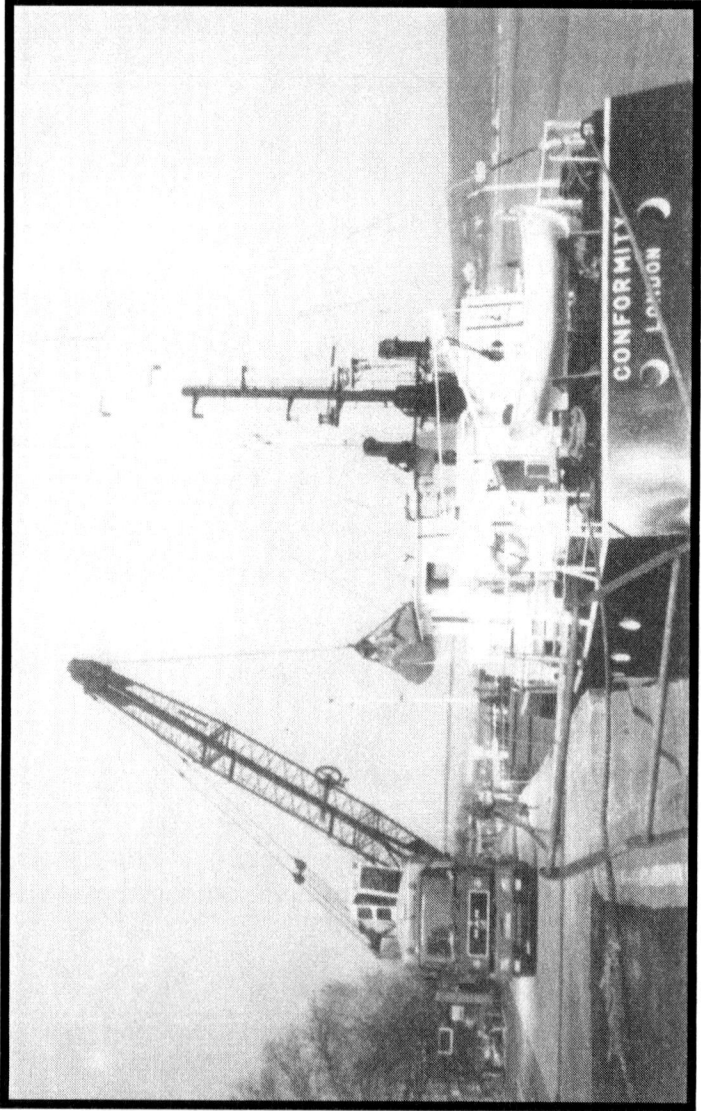

Plate 28: Sea-Road Integration. Agricultural Product Discharging at the North Devon Port, Bideford. *Photo Permission by: Fred Andrews.*

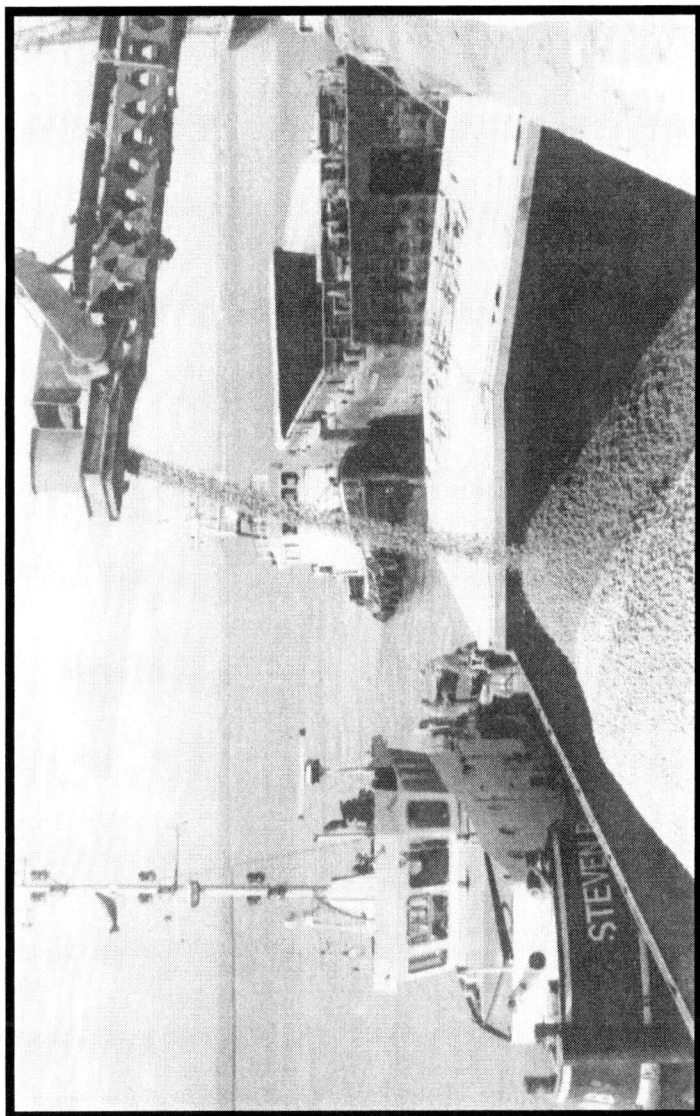

Plate 29: Coastal-Inland Integration, Foster-Yeoman Bulk Carrier and Bennett Tug & Barge, Stone Transhipment, Isle of Grain. *Photo Permission by: A.C. Bennett Tug & Barge Operators.*

Plate 30: Wine Flow! Mersey-Manchester Ship Canal barge combination servicing Tesco wine imports (transhipped Liverpool).
Photo Permission by: Tesco plc.

APPENDIX 1:

UK & Ireland Coastal Shipping Movements
Feb 2002 (includes North Sea UK & Norwegian Crude Oil Flows).

Ship	Flag	Type	DWT	From	To	Cargo
Aasfjord	NIS	Gen Cargo	3960	Grimsby	London	Timber (part cargo)*
Aasvik	NIS	Gen Cargo	4319	Foynes Belfast Port Talbot	Belfast Cardiff Glasgow	N/A Stone N/A
Aberdeen	BHS	Tanker	87,055	Captain Field Captain Field	Fawley Pembroke	Crude Oil Crude Oil
Agility	GBR	Tanker	3144	Immingham	Inverness	Oil Products
Agna	KHM	Gen Cargo	2536	Bright lingsea,	Ridham Dock,	Timber (part cargo)
Ajos G	DEU	Gen Cargo	3000	Halmstad/ Belfast Invergordon	Wicklow Ellesmere Port	Timber (part cargo) Stone
Alacrity	GBR	Tanker	3145	Pembroke Poole Pembroke Workington	Poole Pembroke Workington Stanlow,	Oil Products To load Oil Products To load
Alessia	CH	Gen Cargo	5647	Belfast	Avonmouth	Stone
Alissa	NLD	Gen Cargo	1490	Wick Kirkwall	Dundee Wick	Stone
Alk	ATG	Gen Cargo	2623	Belfast	Rochester	Stone
Allurity	GBR	Tanker	3027	Galway	Stanlow	To load Oil Products

Name	Flag	Type	Tonnage	From	To	Cargo
Alvita	BHS	Gen Cargo	2899	Bantry Bay	Newport	Stone
Anchorman	LBR	Tanker	6417	Grange mouth / Harwich	Saltend / Saltend	To load Oil Products
Anglia	ATG	Container	3765 218 Teu	Grange mouth/Newcastle	Felixstowe/ Thamesport	Containers
Anke Angela	GIB	Gen Cargo	1910 80 Teu	Llanddulas	Rye, Sussex	Stone
Anna C	GBR	Gen Cargo	5010	Teignmouth	Fowey/Par	To load China Clay for Alexandria
Anna Knutsen	NOR	Tanker	129,154	Statfjord Field	Milford Haven	Crude Oil
Anna Theresa	CYP	Tanker	3403	Poole / Stanlow, MSC	Stanlow, MSC / Dublin	To load Chemicals / Chemicals
Annlen G	ATG	Gen Cargo	3004 118 Teu	Aalborg/Shoreham	Medway	Timber
Annuity	GBR	Tanker	3294	Immingham	Sunderland	Petroleum
Aquatique	NLD	Gen Cargo	3200	Montrose	Erith	Dry Cargo

Ardent	GBR	Gen Cargo	1180	Tees	Dublin	Potash
Arklow Mill	IRL	Gen Cargo	2166	New Ross	Fowey/Par	To load China Clay for Antwerp
Arklow Star	NLD	Gen Cargo	3193	Llanddulas	Newhaven	Stone
Arklow Surf	IRL	Gen Cargo	3171	Workington	Limerick	Steel
Arno	ITA	RoRo	10,581	Salerno/Southampton	Sheerness	Multi-port New Cars
Atlantic Wind	CYP	Tanker	13,845	Milford Haven	Grangemouth	Chemicals
Auldyn River	IOM	Gen Cargo	650	Glasson Dock/Lancaster	Douglas, IOM x 12	Liner Service
Silver River	IOM	Gen Cargo	373			
Autoline	NIS	RoRo	1550	Grimsby	Southampton[1]	Multi-port New Cars

[1] Onward to Zeebrugge

Autoroute	NIS	RoRo	1894	Emden/Sheerness	Southampton	Multi-port New Cars
Autosky	NIS	RoRo	6670	Avonmouth	Dublin	Multi-port New Cars
Autosun	NIS	RoRo	6670	Avonmouth Emden/Sheerness	Dublin Southampton[2]	Multi-port New Cars
Averity	BHS	Tanker	1770	Pembroke	Workington	Oil Products
Baltic Magda	NLD	Gen Cargo	3284	New Ross	Fowey/Par	To load China Clay for Sundsvall
Baltiyskiy 103[3]	RUS	Gen Cargo	2600	Grimsby	Ridham Dock	P/C Timber
Ben Ellan	IOM	Gen Cargo	824	Liverpool	Peel	Gen Cargo
Ben Nevis	IOM	Gen Cargo	772	Western Isles	Workington	Timber
Ben Varrey	IOM	Gen Cargo	1544	Workington Liverpool	Arklow Belfast	Steelx2 Gen Cargo
Berit L	ATG	Gen Cargo	1529	Wick	Warren Point	Stone

						To Load
Blackfriars	GBR	Tanker	1570	Drogheda	Whitegate	
Blackheath	GBR	Tanker	1250	Grangemouth	Scapa Flow	Bunker Fuel
Blackrock	GBR	Tanker	2675	Fawley	New Ross	Oil Products
				Cambletown,	Belfast	Oil Products
Border Battler	GBR	Tanker	2257	Grangemouth	Lerwick/Kirkwall	Petroleum
Border Jouster	GBR	Tanker	2734	Grangemouth	Inverness	Fuel Oil
Borelly	GBR	Gen Cargo	905	Tees	Southampton	Potash
Bowcliffe	GBR	Gen Cargo	2220	Belfast	Brightligsea	Stone
Brabourne	GBR	Tanker	2675	Workington	To load Eastham, MSC	Oil Products
Braveheart	LBR	Tanker	94,998	Tees	Whitegate	Crude Oil
				Whitegate	Scapa Flow	To load Crude Oil for Rotterdam

469

Breaksea	GBR	Tanker	1570	Drogheda	Whitegate	Petroleum
Briarthorn	GBR	Gen Cargo	2435	Cambletown, Belfast	Ellesmere Port, Belfast	Petroleum, Stone
Bro Atland	SWE	Tanker	16,326	Braefoot Bay	Fawley	Oil Products
Bro Axel	SWE	Tanker	16,839	Pembroke, Pembroke	Avonmouth, Plymouth, Dublin	Oil Products, Oil Products, Oil Productsx2
Bro Joinville	SWE	Tanker	12,981	Pembroke	Waterford	Fuel Oil
Bro Nadja	SWE	Tanker	5752	Immingham, Fawley	Runcorn, Stanlow	Petro/Chemicals
Bro Star	SWE	Tanker	11,860	Pembroke	Ince, MSC	Fuel Oil
Bro Trader	SWE	Tanker	14,402	Milford Haven, Milford Haven, Pembroke	Purfleet, Dublin, Dublin	Oil Products

470

				Grange mouth	Coryton	Fuel Oil
Bro Transporter	SWE	Tanker	14,316			
Bro Traveller	SWE	Tanker	14,371	Finnart	Plymouth	Oil Products
Burhou I	GBR	Gen Cargo	953	Finnart, S / Weymouth	Belfast / Jersey/Guernsey	Gen Cargo
Cardissa	IOM	Tanker	22,291	North Sea / Fawley Southampton / Milford Haven	Fawley, Southampton / Milford Haven / Tranmere Liverpool	Crude Oil / Oil Products / Oil Products
Cargo Enterprise	LBR	Bulk Carrier	44,600	Belfast	Falmouth	For Bunkers
Catherine Knutsen	NOR	Tanker	141,720	Sture	Tranmere	Crude Oil
Celtic Forester	GBR	Gen cargo	2887	Tees	Humber	Dry Cargo
Celtic King	GBR	Container	6250 467teu	Tilbury/Thamesport	Dublin/Belfast	Containers X4

Cem Carrier	VCT	Gen Cargo	3001	Leith	Belfast	Cement
Cementina	HON	Gen Cargo	1205	Barry	Channel Isles	Cement
Cemile	NOR	Gen Cargo	4270	Swansea	Briton Ferry	To load for Rotterdam
Chartsman	LBR	Tanker	6397	Tees Fawley, Pembroke	London Pembroke Whitegate,	Oil Products
Christine O	DEU	Container	2262 145teu	Avonmouth	Waterford	Containers
Clarity	BRB	Gen Cargo	1448	Belfast Belfast	London Ipswich	Stone Stone
Clonlee	IRL	Gen Cargo	1622	Briton Ferry	Sharpness	To load for Ipswich
Coastal Wave	DEU	Container	1880 124teu	Cardiff	Dublin	Containers

Conformity	GBR	Gen Cargo	1450	Tees	Teignmouth	Potash
Corvette	ATG	Container	4654	Dublin	Cork	To load Container Feeder
Crescent Highway	GBR	Tanker	3122	Fawley,	Belfast/Dublin	Bitumin x2
Crescent Seine	ATG	Gen Cargo	2688	Lancaster Glasgow	Dublin Plymouth	Dry Cargo
Danchem East	DIS	Chemical Tanker	2774	Grangemouth	Hull	Chemicals
Don Quijote	SWE	RoRo	14,927	Japan/Avonmouth	Dublin	New Cars
Donaustern	IOM	Tanker	17,078	Fawley, Pembroke	Pembroke Waterford	Oil Products Oil Products
Donnington	IOM	Gen Cargo	12,134	Auginish	Blyth	Alumina
Douwe S	NLD	Gen Cargo	1771	Poole	Fowey/Par	To load China Clay for Dordrecht

Name	Flag	Type	Tonnage	Port	Port	Notes
Dowlais	GBR	Gen cargo	1394	Dean Quarry	Dagenham	Stone
Duobulk	NIS	Dry Cargo	2670	Aberdeen	Tees	To Load
Durrington	IOM	Dry Cargo	11,990	Aughinish	Blyth	Aluminax2
Dutch Mate	NLD	Tanker	6250	Immingham	Tees	To load Petro Chemicals for Wilhelmshaven
Eastgate	GIB	Tanker	3415	Whitegate	Avonmouth	Oil Products
				Pembroke	Shoreham	Oil Products
				Eastham, MSC	Ipswich	Oil Products
Eliane Trader	MLT	Gen Cargo	1623	Belfast	Coleraine	Loading for Pasajales
Elisabeth Knutsen	NOR	Tanker	124,788	Aasgard Field	Milford Haven	Crude Oil
Emily C	BRB	Gen Cargo	1650	Newport	Mostyn	To load Steel for Spain/Italy
Emmasingel	NLD	Gen Cargo	3100	Bantry Bay	Brighlingsea	Stone

Fast Slm	NLD		1590	Perth	Flixborough	To load for Flushing
Fastwil	NLD	Gen Cargo	2285	Belfast	Dagenham	Stone
Forth Fisher	GBR	Tanker	3628	Whitegate	Galway	Petroleum
				Stanlow	Dublin	Petroleum
Forth Fisher	GBR	Tanker	4973	Pembroke	Galway x2	Oil Products
Futura	FIN	Tanker	96,058	Alba Field	Pembroke	Crude Oil
Galway Fisher	GBR	Tanker	4968	Whitegate	Eastham	Oil Products
Giannuti	MLT	Tanker	31,489	Tees	Pembroke	Oil Products
Glennstar	TON	Tanker	1516	London	Liverpool[4]	Chemicals
Goodwood	SGP	Tanker	1400	Immingham	Tees	LPG
Grtea Kosan	DIS	Tanker	4811	Scapa Flow	Belfast	LPG

				Grangemouth/Newcastle	Felixstowe/ Thamesport	
Hajo	ATG	Container	4646 356teu	Grangemouth/Newcastle	Felixstowe/Thamesport	Containers
Hakufu	PAN	Bulk Carrier	26,600	Foynes	Falmouth	For Drydock
Hamilton	PAN	LPG Tanker	4298	Cork	Belfast	LPG
Happy Bee	IOM	Tanker	7,246	Pembroke	Grangemouth	LPG
Happy Girl	NIS	Tanker	4248	Fawley	Briton Ferry	Chemicals
Happy Lady	NIS	Tanker	7598	Coryton	Tees Coryton	
Heereweg	NLD	Container	2800	Grangemouth Felixstowe/Thamesport	Newcastle/Grangemouth	Containers
Heideberg	DEU	Gen Cargo	2892	Llanddulas	Dagenham	Stone
Helse	ATG	Gen Cargo	1900 75teu	Inverkeithing	Dagenham	Stone
Hester	NLD	Gen Cargo	1766	Falmouth	Swansea	To load for Ymuiden

476

Hildegaard	BHS	Tanker	99,122	Tees	Tranmere	Crude Oil
Hoo Dolphin	GBR	Gen Cargo	2225	Par	Erith	China Clay x2
Hoo Falcon	GBR	Gen Cargo	2225	Dean Quarry	Dagenham	Stone
Hoo Kestrel	GBR	Gen Cargo	2225	Teignmouth	Dean Quarry	To load stone
Hoo Laurel	GBR	Gen Cargo	2225	Teignmouth / Dean Quarry	Dean Quarry	To load Stone
Hoo Moss	GBR	Gen Cargo	1360	Dean Quarry	Rye, Sussex / Dagenham	Stone / Stone
Hoo Pride	GBR	Gen Cargo	1394	Neap House / Ipswich / Boston	Immingham / Boston / Inverkeithing	To Load for Calais / To Load / Barley
Hoo Swan	GBR	Gen Cargo	1412	Par	Erith	China Clay
Hoo Swift	GBR	Gen Cargo	1399	Inver keithing	Kings Lynn	To load Barley

Name	Flag	Type	No.			
Hoo Tern	GBR	Gen Cargo	1394	Plymouth	Dean Quarry	To load Stone for Dagenham
Iberian Coast	BHS	Gen Cargo	1391	Dean Quarry Drogheda	Dagenham Fowey/Par	Stone To load China Clay for Leixoes
Irishgate	GIB	Tanker	3284	Immingham	Aberdeen/Inverness	Oil Products
				Grange mouth	Inverness	Oil Products
Isis	IOM	Gen Cargo	953	Weymouth	Jersey/Guernsey	Gen Cargo
Isnes	CYP	Gen Cargo	6570	Immingham	Holyhead	Bauxite
Jackie Moon	ATG	Gen Cargo	2015	Southampton	Teignmouth	To load China Clay for La. Pallice
Jacobus Broere	NLD	Chem Tanker	5038	Liverpool	Runcorn	To load Chemicals
Jerome H	ATG	Gen Cargo	1525	Tees	Immingham	To load Potash for Corunna

Jill C	GBR	Gen Cargo	10,500	Llanddulas	Dagenham	Stone
Katja	BHS	Tanker	97,220	Sullom Voe	Tranmere	Crude Oil
Krems	CYP	Gen Cargo	3697	Wicklow	Fowey/Par	To load China Clay for Falkenberg
Kvitnes	ATG	Bulk Carrier	28,000	Glensanda	Leith	Stone
Lara	VCT	Gen Cargo	2650	Rosyth	London	Part Cargo Timber ex Baltic
Laura Kosan	DIS	Tanker	2223	Runcorn	Barry x7	Chemicals
Libra	NLD	Gen Cargo	2220	Methil	Southampton	Dry Cargo
Lieke Theresa	IOM	Tanker	3900	Pembroke	Plymouthx2	
				Pembroke	Poolex3	Petro Chemicals
				Pembroke	Falmouth	

Name	Flag	Type	Number	Port	Port	Cargo
Linda Kosan	DIS	Tanker	2004	Tees Fawley	Grangemouth Douglas, IOM	LPG
Lindholm	NIS	Gen Cargo	1265	Hartlepool	Cork	Dry Cargo
Linnea	NIS	Tanker	11,520	Milford Haven Pembroke Pembroke	Avonmouth Cardiff Dublin	Oil Products Oil Products x2 Oil Products
Lotta Kosan	IOM	Tanker	2004	Pembroke	Drogheda	Petroleum x2
Lough Fisher	GIB	Tanker	8496	Milford Haven Finnart	Belfast Belfast	Oil Products
Louise Trader	MLT	Gen Cargo	2319	Truro	Liverpool	Clay
Lydia Kosan	DIS	Tanker	2004	Drogheda	Fawley	To load Petroleum for Channel Isles
Maccado	NIS	Gen Cargo	9650	Birkenhead	Greenock[5]	Dry Cargo

Ship	Flag	Type	Tonnage	From	To	Cargo
Magnitude	NIS	Tanker	96,136	Tees	Pembroke	Crude Oil
Mare	NLD	Gen Cargo	2953	Ipswich	Orkney	Grain
Mersey Fisher	GBR	Tanker	4765	Eastham	Whitegate	Oil Products
Merwezoon	NLD	Gen Cargo	5004	Ipswich	Newport	To load for Safi
Mignon	SWE	RoRo	14,925	Dublin	Avonmouth	Cars ex Japan
Mike	ATG	Gen Cargo	2372	Southampton	Cork	Grain
Milford Fisher	GIB	Tanker	4973	Pembroke / Immingham	Falmouth / Plymouth	Petroleum
Millennium	NIS	Gen Cargo	7808	Bantry Bay / Bantry Bay	Victoria Deep, London / Victoria Deep, London	Stone / Stone
Molda	NIS	Tanker	96,437	Hound Point / Hamble	Coryton / Coryton	Crude Oil

Vessel	Flag	Type				
Muhlenberg	DEU	Gen Cargo		Glensanda	Great Yarmouth	Stone
Multitank Bahia	LIB	Tanker	2890	Salt End, Hull	Swansea	Petro Chemicals
Multitank Batavia	LBR	Tanker	5870	Tees	Ince	Petro Chemicals
Mungo	BHS	Gen Cargo	5846	Tees	Poole	Potash
			1020	Fingringhoe	Guernsey	Sand
				Guernsey	Poole	Gen Cargo
				Poole	Guernsey	Gen Cargo
				Guernsey	Plymouth	Gen Cargo
				Plymouth	Guernsey	Gen Cargo
				Guernsey	Boston	Gen Cargo
				Boston	Poole	To Load Gen Cargo
Muriel	BHS	Gen Cargo	1821	Cardiff	Warrenpoint	Dry Cargo

Name	Flag	Type	Tonnage	Location	Port	Cargo
Mutitank Bahia	LBR	Tanker	5846	Salt End	Swansea	To load for Barcelona
Nadezha	RUS	Gen Cargo	3080	Southampton	Dundee	Grain
Nadja	KHM	Gen Cargo	2957	Grimsby	Rosyth	Part Cargo Timber ex Riga
Navigator	ATG	Gen Cargo	2668	Flixborough	Tees	To Load Potash for Frederecia
Navigia	ATG	Container	2560	Aberdeen	Lerwick	Containers
Navion Brittania	NOR	Tanker	124,821	Draugen Field	Southampton Fawley Terminal	Crude Oil
				Norne Field	Immingham	Crude Oil
Navion Europa	NOR	Tanker	130,596	Heidrun Field	Humber Tetney Terminal	Crude Oil
Navion Hispania	NOR	Tanker	126,749	Norne Field	Immingham	Crude Oil
Navion Oceania	NOR	Tanker	126,760	Norne Field	Scapa Flow	Crude Oil

Ship	Flag	Type	Tonnage			Cargo
Navion Scandia	NOR	Tanker	126,741	Njord Field / Njord Field	Coryton Thames Tranmere Liverpool	Crude Oil
Nemo	EST	Gen Cargo	2350	Warren point[6]	Wicklow	Part Cargo Timber ex Baltic
Nikolaas P	CYP	Gen Cargo	37,450	Burntisland	Liverpool	To Load Scrap
Nord Star	GBR	Gen Cargo	727	Seaham	Stromness	Dry Cargo
Nordic Torinita	CYP	Tanker	106,852	Triton Field	Fawley,	Crude Oil
Nordsee	ATG	Container	2954	Southampton	Liverpool/Greenock x4	Containers
Norrisia	GBR	Tanker	127,540	Tees	Kittiwake Field	To Load Crude Oil
Northern Lindnes	MAL	Gen cargo	3680	Blyth	Montrose	
Northgate	GIB	Tanker	3290	Grangemouth / Immingham	Inverness / Lerwick	Oil Products / Oil Products

Northsea Trader	NLD	Containers	6928	Rotterdam/Southampton	Dublin	Container Feeder
Oarsman	GIB	Tanker	2547	Pembroke	Shoreham	Oil Products
Overseas Fran	MLT	Tanker	112,118	Hound Point	Fawley	Crude Oil
Pedoulas	PAN	Tanker	96,177	Hound Point	Pembroke	Crude Oil
Petrotroll	NIS	Tanker	67,000	Foinaven Field	Scapa Flow	Crude Oil
Petrotrym	NIS	Tanker	80,745	Foinaven Field	Scapa Flow	Crude Oil
Pointe du Croisic	ATF	Tanker	7721	Immingham	Leith	Oil Products
Prospero	SWE	Tanker	16,740	Fawley	Pembroke	Kerosene
				Pembroke	Dublin	Kerosene
				Finnart	Plymouth	Kerosene
				Pembroke	Belfast	Kerosene

Pyla	LUX	Tanker	6712	Whitegate,	Eastham, MSC	Oil Products
Rebecca	MHL	Tanker	94,872	Tees	Fawley	Crude Oil
Rebecca Hammann	DEU	Gen Cargo	2420	Grange mouth	Hull/Mantyluoto	Dry Cargo
Rhein	BHS	Bulk Carrier	38,596	Paranagua/Sheerness	Rosyth	Dry Cargo
River Dart	GBR	Gen Cargo	825	Flixborough	Cork	Steel
Robert	ATG	Cont ainer Feeder	4188	Southam pton	Dublin	Containers
Ronez	GBR	Gen Cargo	1117	Barry	Channel Isles	Cement x2
Rossini	CYP	Tanker	3090	Tees	Fawley	Oil Products
Roustel	BHS	Gen Cargo	1240	Lowestoft	Port Ellen	Grain
Rudderman	LBR	Tanker	6419	Gunness Wharf	Derry	Dry Cargo
				Pembroke	Cardiff	Oil Products

Samin Trader	MLT	Gen Cargo	1703	Mostyn,	Belfast	Steel
Sardinia	ATG	Gen Cargo	4433	Derry	Newport	To load Steel for Bilbao
Sc Baltic	BHS	Gen Cargo	3994	Grimsby	Tates Wharf, London	Dry Cargo
Scot Mariner	GBR	Gen Cargo	3300	Avonmouth	Cork	Paper
Scotia	ATG	Gen cargo	3214	Belfast	Teignmouth	Stone
				Belfast	Poole	Stone
Scotia	NLD	Gen Cargo	3214	Dundee	Liverpool	Stone
				Llanddulas	Dagenham	Stone
Sea Eagle	BRB	Gen Cargo	2535	Llanddulas	Dagenham	Stonex2
Sea Falcon	BHS	Gen Cargo	2273	Avonmouth	Briton Ferry	To load for N.Spain
Sea Merchant	CYP	Tanker	28,610	Grange mouth	Belfast	Oil Products
Sea Osprey	BRB	Gen Cargo	2192	Kalmar/Rochester	Shoreham	Timber

Sea Trust	PAN	Tanker	2067	Erith	Hull	Veg Oil
Seebrise	ATG	Gen Cargo	1530	Tallinn/Swansea	Wicklow	Timber ex Baltic
Severn Fisher	GIB	Tanker	11,250	Pembroke / Pembroke	Belfast / Avonmouth x3	Oil Products
Shetland Trader	GBR	Gen Cargo	1315	Kirkwall	Liverpool	Stone
Shetland Trader	GBR	Gen Cargo	1315	Lerwick / Boston / Lerwick	Blyth / Invergordon / Mulberry Wharf, London	Stone / Barley / Stone
Shizhnya	RUS	Gen Cargo	3997	Riga/Killingholme	Brightlingsea	Timber
Sigas Centurion	SGP	Gas Tanker	1872	Tees / Tees	Fawley / Coryton	Gas / Gas

Sigas Champion	SGP	Gas Tanker	2347	Milford Haven Coryton	Drogheda Swansea	Gas
Sigas Commander	SGP	Gas Tanker	2335	Pembroke	Stornoway	Gas
Solent Fisher	GBR	Tanker	4970	Milford Haven	Belfast x 5	Oil Products
				Milford Haven	Dublin	Oil Products
				Milford Haven	Bristol x 2	Oil Products
				Milford Haven	Galway	
Solvita	VCT	Gen Cargo	2703	Riga/Kings Lynn	Medway	Timber ex Baltic
Sormorskiy 3058	RUS	Gen Cargo	3853	Cork	Fowey	To load China Clay for Mussalo
Spruce	LBR	Lash	7258	Medway	Immingham	Lash feeder service to Rotterdam
St Elmo	MLT	RoRo	10,678	Salerno/Southampton	Sheerness	New Cars

489

Ship	Flag	Type	GT		Tilbury	To Load
Star Canopus[7]	GRC	Gen Cargo	24,943	Newport	Tilbury	Grain
Steersman	LBR	Tanker	6404	Pembroke	Belfast	Oil Products
Sten Tor	NIS	Tanker	13,864	Stanlow	Purfleet	Oil Products
Stena Akoria	BHS	Tanker	107,223	Pembroke	Stanlow, MSC	Oil Products
				Ross Field	Immingham	Crude Oil
Stina	NIS	Gen Cargo	1380	Lochaline	Dublin	Sand
				Lochaline	Runcorn	Sand
				Lochaline	Derry	Sand
STK-102	RUS	Gen Cargo	1002	Riga/Goole	Rosyth	Timber ex Baltic
Stolt Guillemot	CYM	Tanker	4698	Fawley	Birkenhead	Chemicals
Stolt Kittiwake	CYM	Chem Tanker	4710	Birkenhead	Canvey Island	Chemicals
Stolt Petrel	CYM	Tanker	4500	Fawley	Eastham	Chemicals

				Southampton	Tilbury	Containers
Sadwind	ATG	Gen Cargo	1624	Southampton	Tilbury	Containers
Sun Sophia	BHS	Reefer	5109	Plymouth	Killybegs	To load Fish for Alexandria
Swift	ATG	Container	2973	Grangemouth/Newcastle	Felixstowe/Thamesport	
Tai Shan	NIS	RoRo	15,577	Japan/Dublin	Avonmouth	New Cars
Tees Fisher	GBR	Tanker	3120	Stanlow	Derry	Oil Products
Thames Fisher	GBR	Tanker	4765	Grangemouth	Saltend	Oil Products
Tinka	ATG	Container	3205	Southampton	Greenock x 4	Containers
Tinnes/Telnes	PAN	Bulk Carrier	10,110	Hunterston,	Kilroot,	Transhipped Coal x 12
Torrent	GBR	Gen Cargo	1733	Tees / Tees	Kings Lynn / Sharpness	Potash / Potash
Trader	ATG	Gen Cargo	2290	Belfast	Grove Wharf	Stone

Trapper	SWE	Tanker	14,329	Milford Haven	Dublin	Oil Products
Union Jupiter	BRB	Gen Cargo	3274	Birkenhead / Teignmouth	Teignmouth / Fowey	To load China Clay / To load China Clay for Casablanca
Union Elizabeth	NLD	Gen Cargo	2665	Poole	Fowey	To load China Clay for Lixhe
Urkerland	NLD	Gen Cargo	1260	Kings Lynn / Kings Lynn	Aberdeen / Inverness	Grain / Grain
Ursula C	CYP	Gen Cargo	4164	Belfast	Wicklow	Timber ex Baltic
Valdai	RUS	Gen Cargo	5100	Riga/Rosyth	Tilbury	Timber ex Baltic
Valiant	LBR	Tanker	96,136	Tees	Pembroke	Crude Oil
Velox	NLD	Gen Cargo	2033	Inverness	Warren Point	Dry Cargo

Ship	Flag	Type	Tonnage	Port	Fawley	Chemicals
Verdi	ATG	Chem Tanker	3079	Tees	Fawley	Chemicals
Victress	BRB	Gen Cargo	1622	Tees / Boston / Invergordon	Aberdeen / Invergordon / Derry	Potash / Barley / Dry Cargo
Vinga Helena	SWE	Tanker	6400	Pembroke / Partington	Stanlow / Immingham	Chemicals / Chemicals
Western Trader	ATG	Container	4744	Felixstowe/Thamesport	Newcastle/Grangemouth	Containers x2
Westgate	GIB	Tanker	3368	Immingham / Immingham	Inverness / Plymouth	Oil products / Oil Products
Whitcrest	GBR	Tanker	3429	Cardiff	Tees	To load
Whittle	GBR	Tanker	2083	Pembroke / Pembroke	New Ross / Dublin	Oil Products / Oil Products
Windia	SWE	Gen Cargo	2226	Methil	Boston	Dry Cargo
Yeoman Bank	LBR	Bulk Carrier	43,728	Bantry Bay	Liverpool	Stone
Yeoman Bridge	BHS	Bulk Carrier	96,772	Glensanda	Isle of Grain X2	Stone

Appendix 1 sources: derived from, "Shipping Movements", *Lloyd's List*, "Tanker Fixtures", *Lloyd's Shipping Economist*, "Vessel Reports", *Coastal Shipping*, Mayes, G.(2001) *Short Sea Shipping, 2001/2*, McCall, B&D (2001) *German Short Sea Shipping, Lloyd's Seasearcher*. The intention is not to provide a definitive statistical monitoring but rather a indicative sample. In total, an estimated 3.7mt of cargo was identified. However, this included 1.0mt of Norwegian crude oil. Of the estimated 2.7mt of UK domestic traffics noted - approximating to around 35% of the monthly totals – almost 1.4mt are provided by UK crude oil movements.

*Flag Abbreviations

ATF: French Antarctic Territory
ATG: Antigua & Barbuda
BHS: Bahamas
BRB: Barbados
CH: Switzerland
CYM: Cayman Islands
CYP: Cyprus
DEU: Germany
DIS: Danish International Registry
EST: Estonia
FIN: Finland
GBR: Great Britain
GIB: Gibraltar
GRC: Greece
HON: Honduras
IOM: Isle of Man
IRL: Ireland
ITA: Italy
KHM: Cambodia
LIB: Liberia
LUX: Luxembourg
MLT: Malta
NLD: Netherlands
NIS: Norwegian International Registry

NOR: Norway
PAN: Panama
RUS: Russia
SGP: Singapore
SWE: Sweden
TON: Tonga
VCT: St.Vincent/Grenadines

APPENDIX 2:

Comparative European External Costs, Road, Rail Inland Shipping (per 100tkm; Inland Shipping Index =1).

Study/Paper	Country	Inland Shipping	Rail Freight	Road Haulage
Planco (1990)	Germany	DM: 0.35 Index: 1	DM: 1.15 Index: 3	DM: 5.01 Index: 15
VanGinkel et.al. (1995)	The Netherlands	ECU: 0.07 Index: 1	ECU: 0.3 Index: 4	ECU: 1.0 Index: 13
	Belgium	ECU:0.09 Index: 1	ECU: 0.15 Index: 1.6	ECU: 2.2 Index:: 25
	Germany	ECU: 0.04 Index: 1	ECU: 0.5 Index: 12	ECU: 1.3 Index: 32
Roos.et.al. (1995)	The Netherlands	GId:0.04 Index: 1	GId: 0.2 - 0.4 Index: 2 - 4	GId: 2.5 - 4.5 Index: 25 - 45

Source: Notteboom,T " Spatial and Functional Integration of Container Port Systems and Hinterland Networks in Europe," in Economic Research Centre, Land Access to Sea Ports, Round Table 113. Paris: ECMT/OECD. p.15

APPENDIX 3:

Sample of Vessels Loading
in the port of Bideford, 2005

Vessel	Flag	Crew
Lagoda 19	Russian	Russian
Celtic Pride	Bahamas	Polish
RMS Walsam	Antigua & Barbuda	German/Russian/Polish
Fir	Netherlands	Russian/Cape Verde/ Moroccan
Lagoda 12	Russian	Russian
Celticahav	Bermuda	Russian
Union Neptune	Barbados	Polish

Source: http: //www.bidefordbuzz.org.uk/shipping/index/html

GLOSSARY

Air-Draft = vessel height above the waterline;

Backhaul = attained cargo for return leg of a voyage for the purpose of minimizing empty running.

Bunkers = Fuel for consumption by ship's engine;

Bunkering Barge = barge for delivering fuel oil.

Charter Party = a contractual agreement between a ship owner and a cargo owner.

Collier = designated coastal coal carrier vessel.

Contract of Affreightment = a contractual agreement between a ship owner and a cargo owner to move a specified tonnage amount over a specified period.

Dead Weight Tonnage = a measurement of the vessel's cargo carrying capacity (minus fuel oil, fresh water, stores)

Draft = vessel depth below waterline;

Feeder = Small vessel providing links to deepsea hub ports - predominantly containerised trades.

Gross Tonnage = measurement of vessel's enclosed spaces - 1 tonne = 100 cubic feet of space.

LASH = integrated sea-river service featuring large floating containers carried aboard ocean going vessel

Liner Service = timetabled fixed itinerary service in unitised and breakbulk freight

Nautical Mile = 1.1508 land miles/1.852 kilometres

Knot = Vessels' speed in nautical miles per hour

T onnes Lifted = tonnage loaded

T onnes Moved = tonne x kilometres

BIBLIOGRAPHY

Books

Aldcroft, D.H.(1975) *British Transport Since 1914.* Newton Abbot: David & Charles.

Alderton, P. (1995) *Sea Transport Operation and Economics* Hampton Court: Thomas Reed.

Armstrong, J. ed (1996) *Coastal and Shortsea Shipping.* Aldershot: Scolar Press. ---,Aldridge, J. Boyes, G. Mustoe, G. Storey, R. (2003). *Companion to British Road Haulage History.* London: Science Museum.

Bagwell, P.S. (1974) *The Transport Revolution from 1770.* London: Batsford.

Brooks, M. (2000) *Sea Change in Liner Shipping: Regulation and Managerial Decision-Making in a Global Industry.* Oxford: Pergamon Press.

Charlesworth, G. (1984) *A History of British Motorways.* London: Thomas Telford.

Cheetham, C. Heinimann, M.(1993) *Modern Sea River Traders.* Teignmouth: Cheetham.

Cockcroft, A. (1990) *Collision Avoidance Rules.* London: Newnes.

Collard, I. (2000) *Coastal Shipping: The Twilight Years.* Stroud, Gloucester: Tempus.

Couper, A.D. et al (1999) *Voyages of Abuse: Seafarers, Human Rights and International Shipping.* London: Pluto Press.

Cuthbert, A.D. (1956) *Clyde Shipping Company Limited.* Glasgow: University Press, Glasgow.

Davies, H. (2001) *The Eddie Stobart Story.* London: Harper Collins.

Dickens, C. (1965) *Great Expectations.* Harmondsworth: Penguin.

Doganis, R. S. Metaxas, B.(1976) *The Impact of Flags of Convenience.* London: Polytechnic of Central London.

Dystra, D. (2005) *Commercial Management in Shipping*. London: Nautical Institute.

Fenton, R. (1997) *Mersey Rovers: The Coastal and Tramp Shipowners of Liverpool and the Mersey*. Gravesend: WSS.

Ford, P. Bound, J.A. (1951) *Coastwise Shipping and the Small Ports*. Oxford: Blackwell.

Forsythe, R.N. (2002) *Irish Sea Shipping Publicised*. Stroud: Tempus.

Francis, D. (2004) *Out of Rochester: Memoirs of a Thames and Medway Barge Skipper*. Unpublished.

Garrett, K. S. (1991) *Everards of Greenhithe* Kendal: World Ship Society.

—— (2001) *R. Lapthorn and Company: A Ships in Focus Fleet History*. Preston: Ships in Focus.

Gourvish, T. (2004) *British Rail 1974-1997 From Integration to Privatisation*. Oxford: OUP.

Grammenos, T.H. (2002) (ed) *The Handbook of Maritime Economics and Business*. London: LLP.

Grimes, R. (1989) *Shipping Law*. London: Sweet and Maxwell.

Hadfield, C. (1971) *The Canal Age*. London: Pan Books.---. (revised by Boughey, J.) (1998) *Hadfield's British Canal's* 8th edition. Stroud: Budding Books.

Hall, P. Breheny, M. McQuaid, R.W. Hart,D. (1987) *Western Sunrise –the genesis and growth of Britain's major high-tech corridor*. London: Allen & Unwin.

Harman, L.P. (2002) *The Prior Family Business*. Fingringhoe: Distributed unpublished by Priors.

Harper, L. Birch, C. (1995) *On the Move: The Road Haulage Association, 1945-1994*. London: Baron Birch.

Harvey, W. J. (2004) *Arklow Shipping: A Group Fleet History*. Bristol: McCall.

Heyerdahl, T.(1963) *The Kon-Tiki Expedition*. Harmondsworth, Middlesex: Penguin.

Huckett, A. (2002) *Rowbotham.* Gravesend: WSS.

Jamieson, A.G. ((2003*) Ebb Tide in the British Maritime Industries: Change and Adaptation, 1918-1990.* Exeter: University of Exeter.

Keenan, K. E. (1997) *The Fires of London: A History of the Thames lighterage operations of William Cory & Son Ltd.* Waldron, East Susex: Keenan.

Kreukels, T. Wever, E. (eds) *North Sea Ports in Transition: Changing Tides.* Assen: Van Gorcum.

Kuo, C. (1998) *Managing Ship Safety* London: LLP.

Lane, T. (1986) *The Grey Dawn Breaking: British Seafaring in the Late Twentieth Century.* Manchester: MUP.

Lyons,G. Chatterjee,K. (2002) *Transport Lessons from the Fuel Tax Protests of 2000.* Abingdon: Ashgate.

McKinnon, A. (1989) *Physical Distribution Systems* London: Routledge.

Marsh, A. Ryan, V. (1989) *The Seamen: A History of the National Union of Seamen.* Oxford: Malthouse.

Matson, L. *et.al* (2006) *CPRE Beyond Transport Infrastructure: Lessons for the Future from Recent Road Projects.* London: CPRE.

Masefield, J. (1924) *Salt Water Ballads* (10th ed)*.* London: Elkin Mathews.

Mayes, G. (2001) *Shortsea Shipping 2001/2.* Preston: Ships in Focus Publications.

Middlemiss, N.L. (1998*) Coast Lines.* Gateshead: Shields Publications.

Mustoe, G. (1997) *Fisher Renwick: A Transport Saga, 1874-1972,* Nynehead: Roundoak.

Nicholson, T. (1990) *Taking the Strain; The Alexandra Towing Company and the British Tugboat Business, 1833-1987.* London: Alexandra Towing Company.

Paterson,L.N. (1996) *The Light of the Glens: The Rise and Fall of the Puffer Trades.* Colonsay:House of Lochar.

Peters, G.H. (1975) Plimsoll Line: *The Story of Samuel Plimsoll, Member of Parliament for Derby from 1868 to 1880.* Chichester: Barry Rose.

504

Ready, N.P. (1991) *Ship Registration.* London: LLP.

Roberts, R. (1984) *Coasting Bargemaster*. Lavenham, Suffolk: Lavenham Press.

Ross, F.L. (1998) *Linking Europe: Transport Policies and Politics in the European Union.* Westport: Praeger.

Somner, G (1999) *D.P.L: A History of the Dundee, Perth and London Shipping Company Ltd and Associated Shipping Companies.* Kendal: WSS.

Spong, H. S. (1983) *Irish Shipping Ltd. 1941-1982.* Kendal: WSS.

Starkey, F. (1998) *Schooner Port: Two Centuries of Upper Mersey Sail.* Bebbington,: Wirral: Garth Boulevard.

Sturmey, S. G. (1962) *British Shipping and World Competition*; Oxford: Athlone Press.

Tinsley, D. (1991) *Short-Sea Shipping: A Review of the North European Coastal Bulk Trades.* London: Lloyd's of London Press.

Tusiani, M.D. (1996) *The Petroleum Shipping Industry: A Non-Technical Overview*, Vol.1. Tulsa, OA: PennWell.

Watson, N. (2000) *Around the Coast and Across the Seas: The Story of James Fisher and Sons*. Leyburn, N.Yorks: St.Matthews Press.

Wheatley, K. (1990) *National Maritime Guide to Maritime Britain.* Exeter: Webb & Bower.

Whitelegg, J. (1993) *Transport for a Sustainable Future: The Case for Europe.* Chichester: Wiley and Sons.

Wiljnost,I.N. Peeters,D.C. (1995) *European Shortsea Shipping: Proceedings from the Second European Research Roundtable Conference on Shortsea Shipping.* Delft/London: Delft University Press/Lloyd's of London Press.

Woods, D. (2002) *Operations Management: Producing Goods and Services.* Pearson: Harlow.

Wood, P. J. (2000) *Tanker Chartering.* London: Witherby.

Wynn, J. (1995) *Wynns: The First Hundred Years.* Stafford: Forward House Publishing.

Official Reports:

ACOPS. (2005) *Annual Survey of Reported Discharges Attributed to Vessels and Offshore Oil & Gas Installations Operating in the United Kingdom Pollution Control Zone 2004*. London: MCA.

Bosch: *Global Responsibility Environmental Report, 2003-4*. www.bosch-umwelt.de. Accessed 14.9.05.

CEC (1993). "The Future Development of the Common Transport Policy. A Global Approach to the Construction of a Community Framework for Sustainable Mobility." *Bulletin of the European Communities, Supplement 3/93*. Luxembourg: OOPEC.

CM 2560 (1994) *Safer Ships, Cleaner Seas: Report of Lord Donaldson's Inquiry into the Prevention of Pollution from Merchant Shipping*. London: HMSO.

Department of Transport (1972) *Roads in England 1971*. London: HMSO.

--- (1988) *Short Sea Bulk Shipping: An Analysis of UK Performance*. London: Department of Transport.

--- (2005) *Waterborne Freight in the United Kingdom 2004*. London: DfT.

Department of Environment, Transport and the Regions (1998) *Inland Waterway Freight Grants*. London: DETR.

Drewry, H. P. (1997) *Shortsea Container Markets: the Feeder and Regional Trade Dynamo*. London: Drewry.

European Conference of Ministers of Transport Report (2001): *Short Sea Shipping in Europe*. Paris. ECMT.

European Commission White Paper (2001) *European Transport Policy for 2010: Time to Decide*. Luxembourg. EC.

The Freight Study Group. (2002) *Freight on Water: A New Perspective*. London: DEFRA.

Glen, D Dowden, J. Wilson, R. (2005) *UK Seafarer Analysis: Report for the Department of Transport*. London: DfT.

Great Britain Department of Transport.(1987) *Merchant Shipping Act 1894. Report of Court No 8074. M.V. Herald of Free Enterprise. Formal Investigation.* London: HMSO.

HM Inland Revenue (2000) *Tonnage Tax in the UK: A Brief Guide.* London: Inland Revenue Tonnage Tax Unit.

H.M. Revenue and Customs(2000) *Inland Revenue Tonnage Tax Manual TTM01001. Origin and brief chronology of tonnage tax.* www.hmrc.gov.uk/manuals

H.M. Treasury. (1999) *Independent Enquiry into a Tonnage Tax: A Report by Lord Alexander Weedon, QC.* London: HMSO.

IMDO: *TENS and the Irish Motorways of the Sea.* www.imdo.ie/tens Accessed 15.8.05.

International Chamber of Shipping (1999) , *A Code of Practice,* London: ICS.

International Labour Organisation (ILO) *C 180 Seafarers' Hours of Work and the Manning of Ships Convention, 1996.* Geneva: ILO.

INTERTANKO, (2001) "Safety, quality issues top agenda," *The Tanker Newsletter* Issue 5. May 2001.

The Inland Waterways Association, Inland Shipping Group (1996) *UK Freight Waterways: A Blueprint for the Future.* London: IWA.

M-Notice (2002)*Min 117(M) Research Project 464 phase 1: Fatigue of Offshore Oil Support Shipping and the Offshore Oil Industry.*

Marine Accident Investigation Branch (MAIB) Report 3/98 (1998), *Report of the Inspectors' Inquiry into the Grounding of the Feeder Container Vessel, Cita, off Newfoundland Point, Isle of Scilly, 26.3.97.* Southampton: MAIB.

--- Report 5/99: *Report of the Inspector of Inquiry into the loss of the MV Green Lily on the 19th November 1997 on the East Coast of Bressay, Shetland Islands.* Southampton: MAIB.

--- 1993) *Report of the Chief Inspector of Marine Accidents into the engine failure and subsequent grounding of the motor tanker, Braer, at Garths Ness, Shetland on January 5th, 1993,* Southampton: MAIB.

MCA (2000) *A Review of the Emergency Towing Vessel(ETV) Provision Around the Coast of the United Kingdom.* Southampton: MCA.

MCA Newsroom/Prosecutions "Brostrum Tankers AB fined for Pollution," http://www.mcga.gov.uk/c4mca/mcga-newsroom/mcga-dops_enforce_newsroom-prosecutions/dops_enforcement-2005.htm

NUMAST (1990) *Information Bulletin, Seafarers Hour's: Time to Act.* London: NUMAST.

Packer, J. (1994) *Roads to Water: Overview of Coastal and Short-Sea Shipping.* London: HMSO.

Port of Antwerp Annual Report, 2002.

Reyner, L. Baulk, S. (1998) *Fatigue in Ferry Crews: a Pilot Study.* Cardiff: SIRC, Cardiff University.

RMT (2000)Submission to the ITF on the Isle of Man Flag. www.rmt.org.uk

Rowley, C. (1983) *The Use of Roll-on Roll-off Vessels for Moving Domestic Freight between the Tees and the Thames* Newcastle: University of Newcastle.

Royal Commission in Environmental Pollution Eighteenth Report, (2004) *Transport and the Environment.* London: HMSO.

Select Committee on the Environment, Transport and Regional Affairs. (2004) Appendices to Minutes of Evidence. Supplementary Memorandum by NUMAST (FUS1A) *The Future of the UK Shipping Industry.*

Swedish Transport Research Board (1993) *Coastal and Shortsea Shipping: Technical Feasibility Study.* Goteborg: Swedish Transport Research Board.

UKOOA (2001) *FPSO Committee: Tandem Loading Guidelines, Vol. 1 &2.* Aberdeen: UKOOA.

Volvo Annual Reports: http://www.volvo.com/logistics/global/en-gb accessed 6.11.06.

Journals/Newspapers:

Accountancy Age

The Baltic

BlackJack:The Quarterly Magazine of the Southampton Branch of the World Ship Society

BIMCO Review

Coastal Shipping

Containerisation International

Dredging & Port Construction

Economic History Review

Fairplay International Shipping Weekly

Fast Ferry International

Focus (ILT)

Freight Magazine (FTA)

Geography

The Guardian

The Irish Times

Journal of Commerce

Journal of Transport Geography

International Freight Weekly

International Journal of Maritime History

International Freighting Weekly

International Journal of Physical Distribution & Logistics

International Journal of Tug & Salvage.

Liverpool Echo

Lloyd's Law Reports

Lloyd's List

Lloyd's Shipping Economist

Lloyd's Ship Manager

Lloyd's Tanker Focus

Logistics Today

Marine Information Association News

Marine Policy,

Maritime Journal of Ireland

Maritime Policy & Management

Naval Architect

New York Times

The Observer

Port of London News

Pravda

Public Service Review

Safety at Sea International

Sea Breezes

Seaways

Scotland on Sunday.

The Scotsman

Shipping Today and Yesterday

Southern Daily Echo

Tanker Times

The Telegraph

The Telegraph (NUMAST)

The Times

Tradewinds

Transport Policy

Transport Reviews

World Cargo News

World Transport Policy & Practice

Yorkshire Post

Statistical/Technical Sources:

BPF/DoT *Port Statistics* (Annual).

CSO, Dublin: *Statistics of Port Traffic* (Annual) www.cso.ie.

DfT Merchant Shipping Safety Officials and Reporting *Accidents and Dangerous Occurrences Regulations, SI 1982, No.876.* London:HMSO.

--- (Annual) *Statistics Bulletin: Waterborne Freight in the United Kingdom* . London: DfT.

510

Detlefsen, V. G. U. (2004) *Detlefsens Illustries Schiffsregister, 2004-5.*

European Commission Directortate-General for Energy and Transport, (Annual*)* *EU Energy and Transport in Figures: Statistical Pocketbook*. EC: Luxembourg.
IMDO (Monthly) *The Irish Maritime Economist.*

Lloyd's Register.

Lloyd's Register of Shipping List of Shipowners. (Annual).

RINA, *Significant Ships (Annual).*

Conferences:

Ahern, D. (2002.) "Out of Sight, Out of Mind: Shipping Challenges for Ireland".
Seminar, Dublin Castle, 7.11.02.

Baird, A. (2001). "A new economic evaluation of the hubport versus multiport strategy," A Paper given to the International Association of Maritime Economists Annual Conference 2001, Hong Kong Polytechnic University, 18-20.7.01.

Atkin, R. & Rowlinson, M (1998) "Tug Wars! Coming Shortly to a Port Near You? Competitive Strategy in North European Towage and Salvage," a paper given to the International Towage and Salvage Conference, Capetown.

"Britain's Water Highways (1999): A New Agenda for Freight". Birmingham, 19.10.99.

Stoop,J. A. Hengst, S. Dirkse, C. (1996)"Integrating Safety into the Shortsea Shipping System", in Peeters, D & Wergeland, T. *European Shortsea Shipping: Proceedings from the Third European Research Roundtable Conference on Shortsea Shipping.* Bergen, 20-21 June 1996. Delft: Delft University Press. p.393

Government Minutes:

Bell Lines debacle: serious repercussions for the South East," Adjournment Debate. Tithe Oireachtais. www.gov.ie/debate 9.7.97.

British Motor Shipowners' Association, Memorandum to House of Commons Transport Committee, Session 1987-88, *Decline in the UK Registered Merchant Fleet*, Vol.2 pp.172-5.

Parliamentary Debate on UK Ports: http://www.parliament.the-stationery-office.co.uk/pa/cm199697/cmhansrd/vo961205/debtext/61205-09.htm.

Parliamentary Questions on Coastguard Service. Glenda Jackson, Under Secretary of State for Environment, Transport & the Regions. *Hansard*, Col 1413. 5.3.99.

Select Committee on Environment, Transport and Regional Affairs.(2001) http://www.publications.parliament.uk/pa/cm200001/cmselect/cmenvtra/317/0110 2.htm.

Press Releases:

Competition Commission, News Release. 31.8.06. Anticipated Acquisition by Svitzerwijsmuller A/S of Adsteam Marine Limited.

Harwich International Container Terminal: "Hutchinson gets the go ahead for Bathside Bay Development. 29.3.06.

IMDO Press Release: "Statement from the IMDO" 2.12.03. www.imdo.ie Accessed 15.8.05.

Lafarge Aggregates (2001) North Midlands Area Information Pack.

MCA Newsroom/prosecutions (8.9.03)"Shipowner and management company prosecuted for dumping garbage in the Solent," http://www.mcga.gov.uk

--- Newsroom/Prosecutions (17.3.04)"Brostrum Tankers AB fined for Pollution," http://www.mcga.gov.uk.

Select Committee on the Environment, Transport and Regional Affairs (2004). Appendices to Minutes of Evidence. Supplementary Memorandum by NUMAST

(FUS1A) The Future of the UK Shipping Industry.

Scottish Enterprise, "Superfast Ferries" www.scottish-enterprise.com Accessed 26.11.05.

Sea and Water Press releases: "Bosch moves white goods by water,." www.seaandwater.org/news 12.7.05.

"Better by Rhone than Road," www.seaandwater.org.news 6.10.05.

"Transport Minister launches new barging scheme," Buckinghamshire County Council Press Release, 1.7.03.

WWF Press Statement (2000) "Oil tanker accidents off the UK coastline increasing", London: WWF. 15.2.00.

Worsford,F. (2000) Memorandum to the Select Committee on Environment, Transport and Regional Affairs, *Inquiry into Inland Waterways*, 18.9.00.

Web Sites:

Associated British Ports (ABP): http://www.abports.co.uk.

Autoroutes et Tunnel du Mont Blanc: www.atmb.net.Inland.

BBC News: http://news.bbc.co.uk.

BI Norwegian School of Management: www.bi.no.

Birdlife International: www.birdlife.net/news.

Borchard Lines: www.borlines.com/history.

Carisbrooke Shipping: www.carisbrookeshipping.net.

Clydeport: www.clydeport.co.uk.

Coal transport International: www.coaltransportinternational.com.

Coastal Bulk Shipping: www.coastalbulkshipping.co.uk.

Crescent Tankships: www.clipper-wonsild.com.

Department for Environment, Food and Rural Affairs (DEFRA): www.defra.gov.uk.

Department for Transport (DfT): www.dft.gov.uk.

Deutsche Post: www.dpn.de.

Discovering Distilleries: www.discovering-distilleries.com.

EU Marco Polo Project: http://europa.eu.int/comm/transport/marcopolo.

European Bank: www.ebrd.com.

European Intermodal Association: www.eia-ngo.com.

European Project on Shortsea Shipping & Intermodality project (2003) Brussels: AMRIE. http://www.realise-sss.org.

European River Sea Transport Union e.V: www.erstu.com.

Expansion Management: www.expansionmanagement.com.

Foster Yeoman: http://www.foster-yeoman.co.uk.

Friends of the Earth: www.foe.co.uk.

FT Everard & Sons Ltd: www.ft-everard.co.uk.

GB Railfreight: www.gbrailfreight.com/news.

Gloucester Docks: www.gloucesterdocks.me.uk/vessels.

GNER Corporate Affairs, *Inside Track: the Electronic Newspaper for Stakeholders* http://www.gner.co.uk/GNER/PressCentre/Inside+Track.htm

Green Award: http://www.greenaward.org.

Henry Blogg GC, BEM,Lifeboat Coxswain, Cromer: www.norfolkcoast.com.

HM Coastguard: www.mca.gov.uk.htm.

Inland Waterways Association: www.waterways.org.uk.

Interactive Services: www.isl.ie.

International Maritime Organisation(IMO): www.imo.org.

Irish Business & Finance Portal: www.finfacts.com.

Labournet: www.labour.net.

Lapthorn Shipping: www.lapthorn.co.uk.

Lifeboat Service: www.rnli.org.uk.

MultiMedia History: www.mmhistory.org.uk/cce/Elaine/Vandervord.

North-Western Shipping Company. hptp://www.ceebd.co.uk/ceebd/nwshipco.

Norwegian Marine Technology Research Institute: www.marintek.sintef.no.

Norwegian Shipowners' Association: www.rederi.no/file.asp.

O'Connor Group (Widnes) http://www.oconnor.co.uk.

Port of Antwerp: www.portofantwerp.be.

Port of Duisburg: www.duisport.de.

Port of Liege: www.liege.port-autonome.be.

Port of London,: "Cory Environmental – London's green electricity boost." 15.6.06.
Port of Paris: www.paris-ports.fr.

Port of Rotterdam: http://www.portofrotterdam.com.

Port of Waterford: www.portofwaterford.com.

Port State Control: http://www.parismou.org.

Ports of Felixstowe & Thamesport: www.hutchinson-whampoa.com.

Prior Aggregates (Fingringhoe): http://www.jjprior.co.uk.

Public Service Review: www.publicservice.co.uk.

Railfreight Group: www.rfg.org.news.

Railway & Maritime Transport Workers' Union: www.rmt.org.uk.

RMS Europe: www.rms-europe.co.uk.

Road Haulage Association: www.rha.net/public/news

Robert Wynn & Sons: http://www.robertwynnandsons.co.uk.

Scottish Enterprise: http://www.scottish-enterprise.com.

Seawheel: www.seawheel.com.

Shortsea Ireland: www.shortsea.ie.

Strategic Rail Authority: www.sra.gov.uk.

Thames Sailing Barge organisation: www.thamesbarge.org.uk.

The Slate Industry of North & Mid-Wales: www.penmorfa.com.

The Thor Heyerdahl International Maritime Environmental Award: www.heyerdahlaward.com.

Union Transport: www.uniontransport.co.uk.

Up the Cut: www.upthecut.co.uk.

West of Ireland Rail Forum: www.westontrack.com.

World Cargo News on-Line: www.worldcargonews.com.

Zeevart (Rotterdam) www.zeevaart.web-log.nl.

Research Degrees:

McNamara, T. PhD (2005) *The Waterborne Freight Alternative to Road Transport in the UK and its Role in Sustainable Mobility.* Southampton Institute/Solent University.

Rowlinson, M. P. PhD (1995) *The Decline of UK Merchant Shipping 1975-90: Beyond the Market View.* City of London Polytechnic/London Guildhall University.

INDEX

526

Merv Rowlinson

Dr. Merv Rowlinson received his Ph.D. from London Guildhall University in Maritime Business. He is a Principal Lecturer at London Metropolitan University in Shipping and Transport. Dr. Rowlinson has served in the Merchant Navy and the railway industry. His particular research interests are shortsea shipping and its potential for delivering sustainable transport.